P9-DHS-864

BIBLIOGRAPHIC GUIDE TO STUDIES ON THE STATUS OF WOMEN

Development and Population Trends

BIBLIOGRAPHIC GUIDE TO STUDIES ON THE STATUS OF WOMEN

Development and Population Trends

Unesco

Bowker / UNIPUB / Unesco

United Nations Educational, Scientific and Cultural Organization,
7 place de Fontenoy, 75700 Paris, France
Bowker Publishing Company
Erasmus House, High Street, Epping, Essex, CM16 4BU, England
UNIPUB, 345 Park Avenue South, New York, N.Y. 10010, U.S.A.

First edition 1983

The designations employed in this volume do not imply the expression of any opinion whatsoever on the part of Unesco concerning the legal status or political system of any country or territory or concerning the delimitations of its frontiers.

The opinions expressed are those of the authors and do not necessarily reflect the views of Unesco.

British Library cataloguing in publication data
Bibliographic guide to studies on the status of women.

1. Women's studies—Bibliography
I. Unesco
016.305'4 Z7961

ISBN Bowker 0–85935–067–3
ISBN Unipub 0–89059–028–1
ISBN Unesco 92–3–102122–2

Printed in Great Britain by The Eastern Press Ltd., London and Reading

Contents

Preface

A considerable amount of research on the status of women is being carried out in many parts of the world. After the declaration of 1975 as the International Women's Year, interest in the study of women in national development planning and programmes became even greater. This was reflected in an increase of bibliographical works, guides to the literature and compilation of resources. The reader may well ask: 'Why another bibliography?' Apart from the necessity of updating materials in a fast-moving field, Unesco is able to offer a bibliography which is different both in scope and in method. In terms of scope, it is uniquely wide, since it covers three general regions which are seldom found in a single volume: the Western industrialized countries, the Socialist countries and Third World countries. In terms of method, it is the product of a particular kind of team effort. Each regional annotated bibliography was compiled by women social scientists working, teaching, and doing research in their areas: Mere Kisekka (Africa), Soha Abdel Kader (Arab States), Kimi Hara (Asia), Barbara Tryfan (Eastern Europe), Maria del Carmen Feijoo (Latin America), and Janet Holland (Western Europe and North America). This meant that the annotated bibliography could also cover untranslated works written in local languages, theses, unpublished documents and up-to-date information on institutions undertaking research and major events (meetings, etc.) related to the field of women's studies. Janet Holland wrote a general introduction, edited the volume and developed an indexing system which makes the bibliography easy to use.

Each major regional section is divided into five thematic sub-sections. The first provides not only an overview of the major theoretical and practical concerns for each region, but also lists already existing regional bibliographies. It is followed by sections on women's work and labour force participation, family and household, education, demographic features. The coverage, although systematic, cannot, of course, claim to be completely comprehensive, but had to be selective in such a way as to provide a primarily comparative focus.

It is expected that the bibliography will serve as a useful tool for scholars, planners, policy makers and all interested organizations.

This bibliography does not pretend to be exhaustive and Unesco would welcome further contributions of titles with a view to an updated version. These should follow the presentation used in this work and comments and suggestions may be addressed to:

Serim Timur
Population Division
Sector of Social Sciences and their Applications
Unesco
Paris

General Introduction

General Introduction

As this collection of bibliographies attests, there is a considerable amount of research on the status of women taking place in many countries of the world. Different problems arise, stimulating research at different times and in different countries, although perhaps three general regions in each of which the emphasis overall is relatively similar can be identified: The Western Industrialized countries, the Socialist countries and Third World countries. The differences in the condition of women which emerge from this array of material and data can help in an understanding of the way in which certain aspects of women's status and position in society are culturally defined. Despite the immense variation throughout the world, even within individual societies, in the conditions of life and the status of women, there are similarities across these differences of class, culture and state. The most fundamental and stable fact of women's lives throughout the world is their responsibility for the home, the family, and domestic labour.

To whatever extent women are integrated into production and the labour force, at whatever levels (in Sweden in 1978, 72 per cent of women worked; in the USSR in 1970, 93 per cent of women between the ages of 30 and 39 years worked) they still bear the responsibility for this basic element of human existence.[1] An ancillary feature of this responsibility is that it is hidden, not considered real work, since it does not impinge on economic production in any obvious ways. Certain feminist theorists have attempted to bring domestic labour into the open, to gain recognition for the work that women do in the home either by incorporating it into production or by postulating a production unit parallel to economic production, where labour is exchanged for wages. The first gave rise to the domestic labour debate[2] which, centred on Marxist concepts of productive labour and surplus value, attempted to demonstrate or refute the fact that work in the home produced surplus value. The debate raged in the literature on women of the Western Industrialized world, particularly the United States and the United Kingdom, and whatever the merits of the specific arguments advanced, or however economistic the basic conceptualization was, it did succeed in making labour in the home visible, in putting this aspect of women's work onto the agenda. A similar contribution was made by the second position quoted above; the argument that there is a mode of production which is parallel to that based on the division of labour and the principle of class. This second mode of production is based on the productive unit of the family and organized by the principle of patriarchy, or male power over women and younger men.[3] The interrelationship between these two areas – home/family and work, public and private spheres – is a crucial area for development of feminist theory and for a genuine understanding of the way in which societies exist and are reproduced, and must be the arena for future theoretical work.

This might seem a far cry from the concerns of women in developing countries whose problems are immediate and acute. On a theoretical and methodological point, Dube (1980)[4] argues quite forcefully that indiscriminate application to Third World women of models and concepts developed to explain the position of women in Western societies could miss what might be a radically different explanation for the phenomenon in question, related to the historical and cultural specificity of the particular group of women under study:

'Superficially similar situations may have radically different explanations and cannot be treated as identical. For example, the low levels of literacy and education amongst females, the acceptance of lower wages by women and the consequent preference of employers for female labour, and the overburdening with work of many women appear to be common features of the condition of women in many Asian countries. But the forces that bring these features into being are not the same in each country. It follows that any remedial measures that are planned would have to take note of these differences.' (Dube 1980 p. 30.)

It is extremely important to note the specificity of the situations in which women find themselves and the particular cultural, historical, social and economic factors which contribute to what emerges from the material gathered into this collection. The generally inferior status of women with respect to men, and the point about policy implications is well taken. It is also clear, however, that general models can provide a broad theoretical framework within which the specific nature of any particular case can be viewed and related to other particular instances. In the case of an adequate theory to explain the interrelationship of the private and public spheres of social life through the roles played by women in each of them as suggested above, there is clear applicability to a major area of research on women in the Third World. The recently recognized damaging impact of economic development on women and the crucial nature of the work they performed and still perform, prior to and outside the existence and development of the 'modern sector' are clearly related issues.[5] The relationship between private and public spheres of women's activities are elements reappearing in studies on women in cultures and societies throughout the world. The conceptual framework within which these concerns are currently articulated is quite different, the former frequently based on arguments about peripheral capitalist economies and economic imperialism,[6] and the latter related to cultural and religious considerations.[7] The development of a general framework on the basis outlined above could, however, provide an extremely valuable theoretical approach for looking at women's status and place in society. This theoretical framework could also provide a means of understanding the persistence of 'the women's question' in countries with clearly expressed policies, and to a certain extent practices, directed towards equality of women and men, for example the socialist countries of Eastern Europe and the Scandinavian countries.[8] Bujra (1978)[9] argues that the concept of domestic labour (socially reproductive labour expended in the context of the domestic unit) can form a bridge between the biological facts of women's existence and the infinitely varied forms of her social existence. She suggests that rather than an analysis of women's status in various societies, attention should be placed on understanding the articulation of domestic labour with differing modes of production, and the groupings which are built up on the basis of interlocking productive and reproductive processes, for example forms of the family.[10]

In this introduction I shall review briefly the status of women in each of the geographical regions covered by the bibliographies contained in this collection, as indicated by the types of research concerns which have come to the fore.[11] A review of this nature cannot help but be cursory, but I hope to give here some indication of the major aspects of women's experience, the sources of information on women, and the themes which have been most apparent in research on women for these areas. The geographical regions will be reviewed in the same order as they appear in the bibliography, and are: Africa, the Arab Region, Asia, Eastern Europe, Latin America and Western Europe and the United States.

*AFRICA**

Research on women in Africa has historically been undertaken by individuals and agencies foreign to that continent, but is now being incorporated into studies generated at regional and local levels and by indigenous researchers, and has focused on labour force participation, women and development, education and demographic features.

Labour force participation and women's role in economic development

Although women are scarcely represented in industrial work, and then chiefly in work which is labour intensive or needs precision and patience – such as industrial fishing[12] and textiles,[13] they in fact participate to a high degree in productive work. Most of this work takes place in the informal sector, and is either of a self-employed nature in sales or food processing, or work in the family or household unit, largely in agriculture. Some countries, particularly in East, Central and Southern Africa are characterized by a female farming system.[14] (In Botswana and Tanzania 52 per cent of those employed in agriculture are women.) In others, women are found chiefly in petty trading. (In Ghana 88 per cent of sales workers are women; in Nigeria 60 per cent and Sierra Leone 42 per cent.) Most studies indicate that these women traders,[15] operating largely as retailers, whilst men control the more lucrative wholesale subsector, earn little and like other workers in the informal sector (domestic service, prostitution etc.), suffer from 'invisible underemployment' characterized by abnormally small productivity or earnings, labour intensity, small scale operation, and unregulated and competitive markets.[16]

The picture of female employment in the formal sector is distorted by a racial factor in those countries with sizeable numbers of privileged white, Asian or coloured minorities. For example, in Kenya women constitute 86 per cent of employees in the secretarial, stenographic and typing services[17] and in South Africa women constitute 42 per cent of employees in administrative, managerial and clerical posts. In Botswana 39 per cent of professional and technical posts are taken by women, in Mauritius 37 per cent and in South Africa 46 per cent, a situation very different from other African countries where even low level skilled jobs in clerical and professional areas are not feminized. A similar racial bias is reflected in the high level of participation of women (black) in services – Botswana 57 per cent, South Africa 67 per cent and Mauritius 52 per cent.

The focus for research on women and development has been on the negative impact on the status and position of women of modernization processes such as the commercialization of land, monetization of agriculture and land reform. Starting in the colonial era with the introduction of perennial cash crops, women became the chief cultivators of food crops and unpaid family workers

* Drawn from a report by Mere Kisekka.

on men's farms. Systematically new technology in farming, farm inputs and credit extension have increased demand for women's labour whilst creating wide income and productivity differentials between the sexes. A few examples will serve as illustrations. In a cultivation scheme for rice in Sierra Leone, it was observed[18] that while the tractors did 'male' jobs like cutting, burning and hoeing the ground, the vast additional acreage to be planted increased labour for women in weeding, harvesting and threshing the rice. Similarly in the fishing industry, modernization leads to the introduction of petrol engines which do the male work of paddling a boat, and refrigerated storage which benefit male wholesalers but not female retailers and petty traders. In the Gambia, women's working week in agriculture rose from 19 to 20 hours when improved methods were introduced while men's working week fell from 11 to 9 hours.[19] In Kenya, maize grinding, formerly a female task, is now done by men for money.[20]

Loss of subsidiary sources of income is the typical story on improved irrigated land and resettlement projects. On these schemes it is rare to allocate women independent plots or suitable land on which they can grow crops for consumption and their remuneration for joint labour on these projects is usually given to the husband, causing women to lose their independent source of income and see diminishing returns for their labour. For the family, especially children, these projects result in a decline of nutrition standards, as men tend to invest their extra income in purchasing radios, watches and alcohol rather than in the necessities of life.[21]

Modern trends in land reform, towards the equitable redistribution of land to individual families, privatization or collectivization of land have certainly liberated men and women from clan dictatorship in decision making, from discriminatory inheritance, insecurity, and tax or other legal complications. Nevertheless, at the same time, such land reforms have created other unequal relationships and dependency for women, by bestowing land titles on men. It is argued that only legal co-ownership of land together with husbands or the granting of land on an individual basis without regard to sex, can protect women from the exigencies of divorce, death and separation. Even in Ethiopia the revolutionary land reform of 1974 discriminated against women by the unilateral assumption of the man as head of the family, ignoring the reality of polygamy and forcing men to register only one wife in a family unit.[22] In Tanzania on the staff-managed and heavily capitalized government settlements, the *ujamaa* collective villages, in the early 1960s Brain (1976)[23] observed that women were in a condition of virtual serfdom as they had no rights to land, were expected to work in the fields for eight hours like men and yet received none of the proceeds of the harvest, which went to the men.

New technologies and other enabling institutions have not been extended to women. Governments and agricultural extension services have invested money and effort almost exclusively in technologies, credit facilities and improved methods for cash crops or capital intensive large scale farming,[24] all under the control of men. Suggestions for improvement in the situation of women, frequently based on the development of intermediate technology, which would draw them out of unremunerated or low paid work into economic co-operatives or group ventures such as commercial farms, shops, public transportation, or village based food processing in dairy products, bottling, smoking and drying fish, and canning,[25] can only be effective if governments give priority to decentralization of industries to rural areas, develop the rural infrastructure and pursue compensatory policies designed to integrate women in development.

Education

In Africa the pattern of educational attainment reveals an imbalance of sex and sex typing similar to that in the colonial Western capitalist countries, with the additional facet of lack of access to any education at all for some women. Census figures for Kenya (1969) show that 54 per cent of illiterates were women and women formed only 39 per cent of those with one to eight years of education. In the Gambia between 1965 and 1975 girls' enrolment in primary schools did not rise above 25 per cent of the total enrolment, and 1969 census figures for Zambia indicate that of those between ages 15 and 18, 27 per cent of boys and only 16 per cent of girls had completed primary school.[26] In Nigeria in 1970 girls formed 37 per cent of the total student body in primary schools and 34 per cent of that in secondary schools. Unesco projections for the decade 1975–85 are bleak for Africa, indicating that during that period girls in West and Middle Africa will continue to suffer some of the lowest enrolment rates found in the entire world at all levels of education.

Even countries with comparatively equitable educational records at the lower levels, show high disparities at technical, vocational and university education levels. In the 1960s, the proportion of university enrolment which was constituted by women was 15 per cent in Tanzania, 21–25 per cent in Uganda, 15 per cent in Ghana (1970/71), and for the period 1968–76 ranged between 13 and 16 per cent of the total student body in Nigeria. Taking the example of Nigeria, with respect to areas of specialization, enrolment was highest in education (26 per cent) arts (19 per cent), and medical and nursing courses (17 per cent). A large proportion of women in education are taking home economics courses, and the high number enrolled in certificate and diploma courses are in sex-typed courses. Whilst the relatively high representation of females in law (17 per cent) and pure science (15 per cent) deviate pleasingly from the normal expectation, one must also note the low proportions of women in fields in which men traditionally predominate. Only 9 per cent of those enrolled in agriculture[27] and veterinary medicine were women.[28] Again in Nigeria, according to UNECA (1973)[29] in Kaduna Polytechnic by December 1972 the number of females in the various courses in commerce and social services was 16 per cent of the total. This lack of training has even pushed women out of 'women's' jobs such as laundering, catering, food processing and consumer economics, in the modern sector.

There is a growing realization that such disparities in education arise from both socialization practices and explicit discrimination, and it is argued that governments can help to rectify the situation by legislating for positive discrimination in favour of women – in Tanzania for example, it is now a legal requirement that 50 per cent of the enrolment in all secondary schools should be female.

Non-formal education for women has traditionally concentrated on literacy training and other non-economic activities such as improved methods of cooking, and housekeeping. The current emphasis is to train women to acquire the skills necessary for income generation, which, as Dixon[30] points out, implies raising the productivity of the labour in which rural women currently engage, transforming subsistence activities into income-generating activities, and creating opportunities for women outside agriculture. In this connection it is suggested that women should train in animal husbandry, horticulture and consumer economics.

Demographic features

Until recently migration from rural to urban areas has been male-dominated. In Southern and Central African countries, men migrated to the gold mines and industries of South Africa in the face of explicit laws banning permanent African settlements and unemployed accompanying wives. But even in other African countries with no legal ban on wives the same sex imbalance has been observed among migrants who come either seasonally or on a long term basis while intending or actually returning to their home villages periodically and/or for retirement. This pattern of migration has contributed to an increasing matrifocality, a point highlighted in a recent report[31] which charts male migration from Lesotho, Mozambique, Malawi, Botswana and Swaziland to South Africa, and from rural to urban settlements in Kenya. This pattern is reproduced in Ghana.[32]

The high population growth (2.5 to 3 per cent) which is prevalent in Africa has exacerbated this pattern of migration, and as a result women's responsibilities have been tripled. In some cases, they are now the sole or major providers of the family's material needs, including children's school fees, due to the frequent reduction or disappearence of support from migrant husbands. In other cases, the absence of adult males in the homes has led to under-utilization of land when women cannot afford the time or energy to devote to men's agricultural labour of clearing the bush, and breaking the ground. In the south-eastern part of Ghana, Bukh[33] has for example reported that in one-third of households headed by women there were no adult males over the age of 15 years, and that men's migration has resulted in the abandoning of yam as a food crop and the substitution of the less laborious but much less nutritious cassava crop.

Female migration to urban areas has been largely motivated by a desire to join a migrant husband, or a need to escape rural drudgery and undesirable marital situations. Educated unaccompanied women and prostitutes seem to form quite a large proportion of people leaving politically or economically crisis-ridden countries for other African countries.

Female migrants and household heads are amongst the most economically depressed segments of the urban population. They predominate in low-level industrial jobs, in the informal sector, in prostitution and other exploitative situations. Palmer's (1979)[34] review of an ILO report on Nairobi, Kenya, focused on the problems of urban unemployment and poverty, showing that 31 per cent of the female labour force in Nairobi earned less than 200 shillings a month (a critical level) compared with 14 per cent of males; over half of female headed households did not have any visible income while 41 per cent earned less than the critical level a month. The corresponding figures for male heads of household were 14 and 15 per cent respectively.

The relationship between women's fertility and other variables such as education, urban residence and labour force participation are extensively debated in the literature. These factors interrelate in a complex fashion and a range of other socio-economic and cultural variables play a part in the specific pattern which emerges in any given context, as we see in the examples to follow, and in the discussions in other areas in the Third World. In Western Nigeria, for example, Lucas found that the fertility of educated wives was just as high and sometimes even higher than that of uneducated wives, showing that there were fewer infant mortalities amongst educated wives and that they refrained from traditional customs and engaged either in limited breastfeeding or bottle feeding which resulted in short pregnancy intervals. Improved medical facilities in the urban areas have led to a reduction in the incidence of pregnancy wastage and infertility. Lucas shows that the mean age at first marriage is roughly the same in towns as in villages and that clear rural-urban differences emerge only with respect to the incidence of polygamy and literacy, and that the incidence of divorce is highest among those whose first marriage was at under 20 years of age, a customary contracted rather than legal marriage, among the uneducated and most especially those in polygamous unions. These results are echoed in hundreds of studies in Nigeria and other parts of Africa.

Research carried out in the 1970s indicates that a high value is still placed on large family size and even among the educated elite the ideal family size ranges from between four to six children. Family planning clinics show that the majority of clients are concerned with problems of infertility, sub-fertility and spacing as opposed to family limitation.[35] Other studies indicate that even in rural areas there is a widespread recognition of problems related to large family size, but that despite this there is no evidence to show that the acceptability of a small family size is gaining ground.

Finally, some controversial findings related to fertility and women's status were reported by Buchwald and Palmer (1978).[36] They found that, in some situations, women entered employment only when they had small families, while in other cases they were driven into the wage market by the need to feed large families. They also found that young urban migrant women had lower fertility than young urban natives.

*THE ARAB REGION**

The two major sources of information on the status of Arab women, related to socio-economic development and population trends, are demographic studies, based on census data, vital statistics and sample surveys, and social science research. The former, focusing only incidentally on women, despite the professed concern of many governments in the region that women should be integrated into development, deal directly with differential fertility and, to a much smaller extent, with labour force participation and internal and external migration. The latter usually focus on the ideological, cultural and value systems which determine the status of women in the Arab region, identifying Islam as the single most important factor in contributing to the 'traditional' position of women.

Labour force participation and women's role in economic development

For the past two decades, serious development efforts have been made by the

* From a report by Soha Abdel Kader.

governments of the countries of the region to improve the standard of living of the people. One common and distinctive feature of their development strategies has been an over-emphasis both on production, that is, the achievement of high rates of growth in output, and on the development of urban areas at the expense of rural areas.[37]

In 1950 the economically active population in agriculture constituted 68 per cent of the total labour force in the countries of the region. Today, in the predominantly oil producing as well as predominantly agricultural countries the percentage of the economically active labour force in agriculture constitutes only 25–30 per cent of the total population and about 40–50 per cent of those who are economically active.

The inevitable result of such strategies has been increased rural-urban migration, and this upsurge has resulted in high levels of unemployment, underemployment and disguised unemployment in both rural and urban areas. The absence of resources and lack of expansion of education and training, which has retarded industrial and technological advances, have contributed to this situation. The problem is most acute for young people since rapid growth has increased the proportion of young to total population in most countries of the region. The relatively early age of entry into the labour force, and the low level of education and skills, coupled with a low rate of job creation, have resulted in high rates of unemployment and consequently high dependency ratios. Rates of unemployment are higher in rural than in urban areas, because of the breakdown of the 'traditional' sector unaccompanied by an expansion of the modern sector. Unemployment by educational level repeats the patterns of many developing countries, low employment for illiterates gradually increasing with educational level, and reaching high proportions among the 'educated'. Except in the very skilled and educated class, these rates of unemployment and dependency are very high indeed and constitute a serious social problem in many Arab countries.

Changing the status of women in general and Arab women in particular, could be seen as an appropriate goal for ideological reasons. The literature on population trends and development in the region supports the argument that changing the status of Arab women in terms of improved education and increased participation in the labour force would contribute considerably to national development. This is particularly true for countries where rapid population growth poses a serious obstacle to more rapid rates of socio-economic development (those with low GNP, for example Egypt, Sudan, Jordan, Syria, Yemen, Democratic Yemen and Bahrain). In these countries, changing the educational and economic status of women could ease the way to development in two major ways: first by decreasing fertility rates, since most available studies on differential fertility indicate an inverse relationship between fertility rates and the educational and occupational status of mothers.[38] And second, by increasing the utilization of human resources and hence reducing dependency rates, since women constitute a very large proportion of the economically inactive labour force and of the categories which constitute dependency rates.

In 1972, the Cairo Demographic Centre issued Monograph Series No. 3 entitled *Demographic Aspects of Manpower in Arab Countries*. The Monograph includes studies of 'manpower' in Libyan Arab Jamahiriya, Egypt, Sudan, Jordan, Syrian Arab Republic, Iraq and Kuwait. In discussing the results of these studies Vavra (1972)[39] points out that it is difficult to summarize the main features of female economic activity in the arab region as female labour force participation rates differ so much.[40] In addition, it is with respect to female labour force participation rates that most deficiencies in the statistical data are encountered – the estimations of these rates suffer most from the variations in concepts and methods of enumeration used in labour force census data and labour sample surveys in the region. Such variations are related to

(1) The difficulty in defining the 'labour force' in simple terms, as the boundary between economic and non-economic activity is blurred. A substantial part of economic activities in countries of the Arab region is carried out by family enterprises in which both housewives and school children participate. Differences in definition of 'dual' activities vary from country to country and from census to census and in different regions of a country.
(2) The times at which censuses are taken vary considerably.
(3) Differences in criteria of defining unemployed and economically inactive persons resulting mostly from inaccuracies in reporting age, and economic activity.

Most adult women who are not economically active outside the home are engaged in productive activities within the home (rendering services and producing goods of high economic value) yet they fall under the general heading of 'unpaid family workers'. Their inclusion or non-inclusion in rural or urban labour forces produces great variations in the estimation of the economically active female labour force.

Generally speaking, the findings of the studies included in the monograph *Demographic Aspects of Manpower in Arab Countries* indicate:

(1) Very low labour force participation rates for women in the Arab region.
(2) Lower female labour force participation rates in rural than urban areas.
(3) Lower female participation rates for young married as compared with single, divorced, widows, and older women. Marital status was found to be a very significant factor in determining the participation of women in the labour force.
(4) The rate of female labour force participation increases with education, being lowest amongst illiterates and highest for those with a university degree.
(5) In terms of occupation, females occupy a higher proportion of the professional, clerical and service occupations than men.
(6) In terms of economic activity, women's participation rates were lowest in construction and industry and highest in services.
(7) In terms of status, female labour as a percentage is lower in groups of employers and self-employed than in the employee group.
(8) Unemployment rates for women are highest in the youngest age group 15–19, single, decline in the 25–34 years and married group, and increase amongst older, divorced or widowed women.

Local customs and traditions which delineate and define the roles of women in the Arab region have been considered by many researchers as major obstacles in the face of the more active participation of women in the labour force and in activities outside the home, since the latter have until recently been considered strictly male domains.

'Many factors determine the extent of female participation in economic activities and attitudes and customs with respect to appropriate roles for women in economic and social life vary tremendously in different societies. There are differences in the ages at which women marry and in their responsibilities for the care of young children which have a bearing on their availability for employment outside the home' (p. 315) (Vavra 1972).[41]

Education

The literacy rate for women in Islamic societies ranges between 6 and 15 per cent,[42] and the median number of years of educational attainment for women of 25+ in all Moslem countries ranges from 0.5 to 0.98 of a year[43] (figures for 1972). The percentage of girls in the total group in secondary level education varies from 13 per cent in Libyan Arab Jamahiriya to 24 per cent in Syrian Arab Republic, and in higher education the range is from 9 per cent in Libyan Arab Jamahiriya to 39 per cent in Iraq. Despite this very bleak overall picture and the great variability within the region, both in terms of the policy stance towards education for women and women's actual educational acquisition, there are in some cases signs of improvement. For example, in Egypt female enrolment in university increased from 8 per cent in the period 1952–72, and in the Lebanon there are government schools in most towns and villages and a large number of vocational schools. An educated and professional elite of women in medicine, law, higher education and the arts has emerged. In Iraq, women contribute 30 per cent of doctors and pharmacists, 33 per cent of teachers and university lecturers, and 33 per cent of staff of government departments[44] and in Kuwait education is compulsory for all and 60 per cent of the students at Kuwait University are women.[45] It is clear however that for the bulk of women in this region, education is non-existent.

Demographic features

There is considerable variability in the quantity and quality of data available in the region from which demographic features of fertility patterns and migration can be assessed. Egypt is best served in this respect with census figures going back to 1882, the latest being in 1976. In addition, vital registration statistics and sample surveys in labour force participation, family budget and other topics are abundant, gathered under the auspices of the Central Agency for Public Mobilisation and Statistics. Lebanon, however, has not held a census since 1932 due to the sensitivity concerning the size of the Christian and Moslem populations, and since the Lebanese economy is largely orientated to economic interests outside of the country, those in control have not required demographic data for economic planning and national development. There was a 1970 Lebanese Labour Survey and a 1971 KAP survey sponsored by the Lebanese Family Planning Association, but vital registration for Lebanon is incomplete.

Census data are available for Iraq, Jordan, Syrian Arab Republic, Bahrain and Kuwait, but apart from Kuwait, vital registration statistics for these countries are relatively poor. Democratic Yemen has census data only for Aden and this was conducted when the country was occupied by the British. For the Gulf States, Saudi Arabia, Qatar, Oman, the Emirates and Libyan Arab Jamahiriya, there are no census data and vital registration is very incomplete;

the same is true for Sudan and Yemen where the demographic situation remains virtually unknown.

Differential fertility studies are particularly abundant in Egypt, the country of the region with the most serious population problem and with a national population policy and a National Family Planning Association in addition to a Population and Family Planning Board.

The most significant finding of these studies is that there is evidence of an inverse relationship between educational and occupational status of the wife and fertility. Socio-economic class was also found to be inversely related to fertility (Abu-Lughod, 1966; Khalifa, 1973).[46] The literature does not indicate a clear pattern of rural urban differentiation in Egypt.

Based on the 1970 census, differential studies in Syrian Arab Republic indicate slight rural-urban differences in fertility rates, but a very marked difference in regard to the average number of children born alive per woman for all groups when level of education was taken into account (Unesco, 1974; Kjurciev, A. et al., 1976).[47]

Two studies on differential fertility in Sudan indicate rural-urban differentials and differentials by socio-economic class and standard of living; a third indicates that nomads have a lower fertility rate than rain cultivators. (Nour Eldin, S. A., 1971; El Tay, O. A., 1972; Henin, R. A., 1969.)[48]

A household survey in Libyan Arab Jamahiriya in the cities of Tripoli and Benghazi found fertility tended to be lower in higher income groups. (Nour Eldin, S. S., 1971.)

Another source of information on the status of women and population trends are KAP surveys. The availability of these studies in the region is again positively correlated with availability of demographic data, in addition to the presence or absence of family planning associations and/or national population policies and Egypt figures prominently once again in this respect.

As indicated in this brief review, the major problems with both fertility and KAP studies are that they are repetitive and descriptive, as Cho[49] (1970, p. 296) points out 'studies of differential fertility have been almost completely descriptive and have shunned the task of developing a general theory concerning the subject'.

In the same way that studies on labour force participation in the Arab region focus only incidentally on women, studies on migration both internal and external focus only incidentally on sex.

The Cairo Demographic Centre in 1973 issued Monograph Series No. 4. on *Urbanization and Migration in Some Arab and African Countries*.[50] This Monograph includes studies on internal migration patterns in Libyan Arab Jamahiriya, Sudan, Egypt, Jordan, Syrian Arab Republic, Iraq and Kuwait. All studies with the exception of the study on Jordan include sex as a variable in looking at the demographic characteristics of in-migrants and out-migrants, but it is interesting to note that despite the inclusion of sex as a variable in the tables used, the analytical, descriptive report rarely makes any reference to women. Analysing these tables one could say that male migrants slightly outnumber female migrants. In terms of rural to urban migration there is a lower percentage of female out-migrants than male out-migrants, a lower percent of net migration for females than for males and a lower percentage and rate of return migrants among females than among males.

A recent report[51] suggests that for Egypt the early pattern of male dominance amongst migrants of productive age is changing towards a more balanced sex ratio, and it is possible that this pattern may also apply to other countries of the region.

In terms of external migration, there are a number of studies dealing with the topic, once again, particularly in Egypt. Two volumes of annotated bibliographies published by the Family Planning and Population Board[52] include a number of citations on the topic where 'sex' is again incidentally considered a variable in determining the direction, magnitude and size of external migration. However, informal observation and one study of migrants in Kuwait[53] reveals that many Egyptian women, particularly school-teachers, are emigrating alone to countries of the Gulf area. For many of these women, the economic incentive is probably very strong; but in a field study on the brain drain in Egypt based on interviews with women who have migrated to Europe, and the United States, the prevalent strong cultural norms proscribing the status of women are recurrently mentioned as incentives for women to migrate to countries where they can have more personal freedom.[54]

One last word on studies of the family emanating from social science research: Some have argued that certain aspects of the Arab family have a direct bearing on the lives and status of Arab women and these tend to stress the unequal relationship between the sexes.

Studies on the status of women in the Arab family have dealt with topics such as women and chastity and men's honour and the measures taken to preserve the balance between these two interrelated variables, which include circumcision, early sex-role socialization and early betrothal and marriage. Other aspects of the Arab family that have been studied extensively are *family typologies*; in this respect the traditional Arab family is seen as 'extended, patriarchal, patrilineal, and patrifocal'. Cross-cousin marriage, endogamy, bride price, polygamy, high rates of divorce have also attracted the attention of scholars, particularly Western scholars or Arab scholars trained in Western universities. All the above factors have led to the belief that in the Arab family there is a public domain and a private domain, the former that of men and the latter that of women, the public/private dichotomy as a way of characterizing male/female relations is a *leitmotif* of the literature on Middle Eastern women.[55]

*ASIA**

In surveying Asia we are looking at an area which covers almost one-third of the world's land area and contains more than half of the world's population, a continent of immense diversity and vast contrasts, with all of the world's major religions, cultures, social and political systems represented. Amongst Asian women there are differences based on these fundamental divisions of socio-political system, ethnicity, religion, culture, class and urbanization, but as we have seen in other broad geographical regions, there are also similarities.

There is a considerable amount of research on women in Asia, varying in approach from country to country, and conducted within the framework of a range of institutions, including government agencies, international bodies, universities, and women's organizations. Much of the material is descriptive, frequently emerging from the disciplines of anthropology, (initially focused on kinship and family systems), demography, economics and law. In the past, such

* Drawn in part from a report by Kimi Hara.

studies might have included women incidentally, but increasingly, the study of the status and situation of women is being recognized as a significant area of research in the social sciences.[56] An example of stimulus for research on women, in this case in India, was the finding of a Committee on the Status of Women in India, set up by the Union Government in 1972, that the situation of women was deteriorating.[57]. The Indian Council of Social Science Research set up a women's programme and a research Unit on Women's Studies at SNDT University.[58] Two points can be raised in this connection (1) that the status and position of women appears to have continued to deteriorate in India[59]; and (2) that much of the research stimulated was funded by the Indian Government or international agencies, from which sources it might be difficult to obtain support for research which would reach to the root of the problem, and point to the necessity for fundamental changes in policy and practice.[60]

A brief review of the position of women in a number of Asian countries with respect to labour force participation, involvement in economic development, education and demographic features will suffice here to indicate both similarities and differences in the position and status of women in the countries of this region.

Labour force participation and women's role in economic development

As with other indicators of women's status in this region, the proportion of women in the labour market varies from country to country. In South Asia women's participation in the labour market is marginal. According to the 1971 census the female work participation rate in India was 12 per cent and for the decade 1961–71, while the population increased by about 25 per cent (20 per cent in the working age group) the proportion of male workers increased by 15 per cent and that of women workers declined by 42 per cent.[61] In Bangladesh, in 1961, women represented 15 per cent of the civilian labour force and this proportion fell to 4 per cent by 1974.[62] In Pakistan, women form 8 per cent of the labour force (1977–78 figures).[63]

In these countries women have been displaced in the process of economic development and modernization from their traditional work in agriculture and cottage industry, and forced into marginal occupations, based on low technology and labour intensive techniques of production, where labour is largely unorganized – a pattern we have seen in the countries of Africa (see pp. 3–5, above).

Where women do work in agriculture, their work is often unpaid and unrecognized, either by their families or in government and international statistics.

Two studies in Pakistan indicate that women from different backgrounds are in different stages of emancipation from tradition. The first looking at women workers in a match factory[64] found them totally lacking in confidence, overcome by feelings of helplessness and unable to recognize their own contribution to the industry. The other, of women administrators, found that whilst recognizing discrimination against them, they were on the periphery of gaining acceptance and recognition, were able to manage their dual work load, and reported a favourable impact on the personalities of their children from the fact of their working outside the home.[65]

In the less poor countries of South East and East Asia women have a higher rate of participation in the civilian labour force – in the Philippines 33 per cent of women are in the labour market; in the Republic of Korea 39 per cent and in Japan over 50 per cent. But women in these countries are still employed at the lower levels of the occupational hierarchy, and face the additional hazard of fluctuation in employment opportunities with economic recession and boom. In China, (where the labour force participation rate is 36 per cent) this is further complicated by changes in the ideological positioning of women in the home or in the work force over time. In Japan, rapid economic development and growth has drawn women into the labour market, increasing both the number of women working and the range of occupations in which they are found, but, as a result of the factors suggested above and lack of access to vocational training, there is a very wide gap between men and women in terms of wages and promotion.

An OECD report (1973)[66] indicates that women receive different treatment from men in the labour market. A further study suggests that economic growth can lead to greater subjugation of women if policy-makers are not prepared to counter these developments with positive action,[67] particularly with respect to two basic facets of the Japanese labour market, which virtually eliminate married women from successfully pursuing a career; the seniority wage system and lifetime employment.

This pattern is repeated in the Philippines where women earn 44 per cent less than men of comparable educational level and only 0.6 per cent of them ever become administrators, executives or managers.

Much of the research on women in the Philippines is concerned with the problem of integrating women into the economic development of the area, and the impact of a range of factors, for example, education, social class background, family responsibilities and size, on their labour force participation. These factors also interact – a paper by Miralao (1980)[68] indicates that women's employment is negatively associated with number of children in high income households, and positively among women in low income households.

In general, however, women are either regarded primarily as housewives and mothers, or if they are engaged in the labour market are also expected to fulfil the functions of childcare and domestic labour in these countries.[69]

Education

Literacy rates for women in the countries of Asia range from 12 per cent in Pakistan to 98 per cent in Japan. At the other end of the educational scale in universities the percentage of women varies from 12 per cent of the student body in Bangladesh to 55 per cent in the Philippines.[70] Improving educational access for women is a theme in several of these countries, for example, Sri Lanka, Indonesia, and, as we have seen, in the Philippines equality of educational enrolment with men has been achieved, although women generally need a higher level of education than men to get good jobs.[71] In some countries, however, traditional and cultural values militate against improvement in educational access for girls. In India, for example, discrepancies in male and female rates of access to education and training exist at all levels – school, university, technical and non technical – and there is a high tendency to keep girls away from school, since women are regarded as non-productive members of the household, primarily responsible for domestic chores – rendering the content of education irrelevant to them. Other factors also contribute to this general lack of concern for the education of girls – the use of child labour, the fear that education might undermine the traditional and cultural values, which contribute to the formation of a women's acceptance of her role in the family and household. In Bangladesh, the only socially acceptable role for a women is that of wife and mother and she is trained for this from her earliest years – in rural areas especially, very few girls go to school, and those who do, do not remain there for long. The majority of girls in Bangladesh do not attend schools beyond the primary level and can expect to have a marriage arranged for them at a very early age (14–15 years). Even in countries which have a formal commitment to equal education for all citizens, for example, Indonesia and Republic of Korea, compulsory education is not enforced, and limited resources (both nationally and within families) lead to priority being given to the education of boys.

Under the Education Law of 1947 in Japan every child is entitled to advance through the education system to college depending on their level of ability, but since the female proportion of the university student body is 20 per cent (1973 figures), and if we include both university and junior college students it rises only to 30 per cent, women are not experiencing equal access to higher education. It is also the case in Japan that once graduated a woman will find considerable difficulty in finding employment commensurate with her level of education and qualification.

Once again, in educational provision for women in this area, although there is very considerable variation in the quantity and quality of education achieved by women, both within and between the countries considered here, there is a common theme of women lagging behind men. This lack of skill and training has obvious implications for women's labour force participation, experience of and integration (or lack of integration) into the process of economic development, and for their status in these varied countries.

Demographic features

Population predictions indicate that nearly 60 per cent of the increase in total world population to the year 2000 will be in Asia; today half of the population is women, and 80–90 per cent of them live in rural areas, the majority of them in situations of dire poverty as small farmers, share croppers, servants, tenants and landless labourers. Many of the countries in the area have problems of rapid population growth and increasing migration from rural to urban areas and have felt or are experiencing an alarming gap between economic growth and the growth of population. Research, which has family planning as part of its focus, and large scale demographic studies can frequently, therefore, find support from government and international agencies.[72]

A number of countries report a decline in fertility, although many factors are considered to have contributed to this state of affairs. For example, in Sri Lanka a rising age of marriage for women coming from problems of providing a dowry, unemployment, more education and changing attitudes towards marriage on the part of girls themselves are some of the factors.[73] In the Philippines, the population growth rate has declined from 3.0 per cent in 1960–70 to 2.78 per cent in 1970–75.[74]

Individual demographic indicators show considerable variability across the countries of the region, for example, infant mortality rates vary from 9 per 1,000 in Japan, to 140 per 1,000 in Bangladesh, but these indicators must be questioned more closely to gain a clear picture of what is happening in any country. One must differentiate between male and female infant mortality rates – for example, if we compare female infant mortality rates in India and Indonesia, Indonesia has a higher figure; however male infant mortality is higher than female in Indonesia, and this too must be taken into account in the comparison.[75] The same care must be taken with average life expectancy figures.

The relationship between fertility, education, the status of women, socio-economic class, labour force participation, and participation in the development process, is a focus for research in all Third World countries, and provides crucial information for the formulation of policy and programmes in these areas. A few examples will illustrate contributions to this type of study in Asia. White (1976) (a)[76] argues that, since the basic unit of demographic and economic labour is the family, to understand the economic rationality of demographic behaviour, we must look at the economic environment of individual couples rather than large scale aggregate statistics. In this connection, he saw children (in Java) as having two levels of economic value for parents – immediate, in terms of their labour contribution at an early age, and potential, in terms of support as adults. In Java, in fact, girls stay close to the parental home after marriage and contribute substantial work in the parental home prior to marriage and these factors might explain why the Javanese, in contrast to parents in most other Asian families do not express any significant preference for sons as opposed to daughters.[77]

A study of female employment and fertility in Thailand[78] indicated that in both rural and urban areas work for pay before and after marriage were more crucial independent variables affecting fertility, than current work status. In Java, once again, Hull and Hull (1977)[79] found a positive relation between economic class and fertility, indicating that in Javanese society the fertility of the poor is lower than the rich, and contributing factors are infertility, divorce, accidental abortion, breastfeeding and abstention from sexual relations after childbirth.[80]

*EASTERN EUROPE**

The literature on the status and experience of women in the Eastern European countries reflects the changing focus on the 'the question of women' over time and its interrelation with broader economic, social, demographic and policy factors. Before the First World War, publications, stemming from the Women's Movements in Russia stressed the struggle for equal social and political rights for women. In 1917, in the USSR, legal and civil codes, which extended full citizenship to women and pronounced them equal in economic, political and family life were promulgated. The rest of the Eastern European countries followed suit after 1945.[81] The formal commitment to equality in these countries is in no doubt. The degree of success in achieving these aims is the subject of some controversy. Soviet official sources, for example, as well as some Western accounts, point to a long list of achievements and considerable change in the status and position of women, especially in comparison with Western societies. They point to the full political and legal equality of women; the extensive role they play in the labour force and in the professions; their educational achievements; and the protective legislation and social services

* Drawn in part from a report by B. Tryfan.

which support women in their dual roles as workers and mothers.[82] Other authors, both in the West and in the Eastern European countries, point out that despite the incorporation of women into the labour force and public affairs, they do not hold positions of responsibility and status. As in the West the higher one goes in the pyramid of any organization the fewer women are to be found. Moreover new economic and political roles for women have been superimposed on the traditional responsibilities which they have had for the family and domestic labour, and the impact of this dual burden is detrimental to women's health, welfare and opportunities for self-realization.[83] As has been pointed out in more general terms by Jowitt (1974)[84] the regimes in Eastern Europe 'simultaneously achieve basic, far-reaching, and decisive changes in certain areas, allow for the maintenance of pre-revolutionary behavioural and attitudinal postures in others, and unintentionally strengthen many traditional postures in what for the regime are often priority areas'.

The changes of focus in the literature on women in these countries can be briefly outlined as follows: in the 1950s and 1960s, studies looked at women's work and possibilities for promotion and the implications of this for their personal development and family life and the most frequent topics were women's occupational preferences, their qualifications or lack of them, their housing needs and household organization, time budget material, wages, and attitudes of women and their husbands to women working. In the last decade, attention has turned to women in the professions, the feminization of certain professions (for instance pharmacy, medicine, scientific and educational workers) and to the links between employment and the material conditions of the family, in the studies of social security provisions, childcare, employee and material rights. A further recent theme has been the problems of rural women, their work in agriculture, participation in social life, family duties and activity in socio-political organizations.

The underlying and interacting demographic and economic facts of life in this area over the period since the Second World War have been declining birth rates (after a brief, immediately post-war rise) and increasing demand for labour in the push towards economic development and the expansion of industry. These have called on women both to enter the labour force in increasing numbers and to respond to pronatalist policies in the face of a projected future decline in the size of the workforce. The birth rate dropped between 25 per cent (in Bulgaria) and 45 per cent (in Poland and Romania) in the period 1956 to 1966. The net reproduction rate fell below 1.0 in Hungary in 1960, Bulgaria and Romania in 1961 and Czechoslovakia in 1967, meaning that these countries were no longer reproducing their population.[85]

Occupational hazards to women's health and reproductive capacity were rediscovered, and protective legislation revived which prevented women from holding non-traditionally female jobs; gynaecologists in Hungary and Czechoslovakia in particular began to publish evidence that abortion impaired women's ability to conceive and carry to term future wanted pregnancies.

The faith in collective child care was being undermined by the belated arrival in Eastern Europe of arguments on 'maternal deprivation'.[86] Arguments were raised against it by child psychologists and pediatricians, pointing to inadequacies in day care facilities and possible negative effects on the children. Economists argued that the cost of such provision was too high. The impetus grew behind a high priority being placed on the role of mother. All countries increased family allowances and other financial benefits to families, and Hungary (1967) and Czechoslovakia (1971) brought in a child care allowance enabling a mother to be paid to stay at home with her baby until it is several years old. This necessity for meeting current and future labour force requirements, which falls entirely on women, is an unresolved problem for the countries in this area.[87]

Labour force participation and women's role in economic development

The proportion of the labour force who are women in this region is between 45 and 50 per cent, virtually saturation point, given that the sex imbalance in the population created by internal and external conflicts in the area over the past 60 years is now disappearing. Czechoslovakia, for example, is characterized by nearly universal female participation. The question which arises is – Does the sex stereotyping of work exist in the countries of Eastern Europe in the same way as we have seen that sex segregated labour markets are found in the United States and Western Europe?

If we take Czechoslovakia, for example, women are more evenly distributed over the occupational structure than they are in the West, and their penetration into professional areas considered typically male in the West is often high. (40 per cent of physicians in Czechoslovakia are women; the figures for some other countries are United States 7 per cent, Canada 10 per cent, United Kingdom, France, Italy and Federal Republic of Germany range between 13 and 21 per cent, USSR 74 per cent.)

Sex typing does occur within professions – despite the fact that female medical students achieve higher theoretical standards than male, in practice it is the male doctor who is considered more talented and skillful and patients tend to trust male doctors more than females.[88]

Women constitute 45 per cent of the manual labour force, but they predominate in food, textiles, ready-made clothes, tanning and fur industries.

So it can be said for Czechoslovakia that, as in the West, sex continues to be an important criterion for the social division of labour, and that 60–80 per cent of all Czechoslovak women are employed in traditionally 'feminine' sectors of the economy; teaching, health service and social welfare, trade and public catering and the industries listed above. This pattern is similar to that found in the West; an additional area of feminization in Czechoslovakia, unlike the West, is ports and communications.[89]

If we look now at the USSR, we find that 45 per cent of the industrial labour force is women, and that there are areas in which women predominate and those which are largely male. Some examples of industries which are 70–98 per cent female are: textiles, garments, leather goods, the food industry, 'orderlies, nurses, nursemaids' and 'communal, household and everyday service personnel'. Males predominate (70–95 per cent) as woodworkers, construction workers, and machine construction and metal workers.[90]

Women in the Soviet Union had more diverse work during and after the Second World War, but as the sex ratio has become more balanced, prosperity has grown and the service sector has expanded, cultural and educational biases in women's work have returned.

In the professions in the Soviet Union, women are to be found highly represented in professions where their share is smaller in and the United States – 82 per cent of Soviet economists and planners are women, 77 per cent of dentists, 57 per cent of designers and draughtsmen (*sic*) 40 per cent of engineers, 43 per cent of teachers in higher education and 40 per cent of scientific research personnel. The years 1959 to 1970 saw a slight decline in the proportion of women who were physicians (79 to 74 per cent) and dentists (83 to 77 per cent) apparently as a result of conscious efforts to increase the number of men in these areas, due to fears of feminization, assignment problems, and women's lower working load.[91]

If we now look at the vertical distribution of women in professions and semi-professions, we find that despite the fact that the Soviet women has a much higher chance of entering and succeeding in a professional career than her Western counterpart, the proportion of women decreases with each successive increase in rank in each economic branch, occupational group or profession. The prospects for advancement to the top of the occupation or profession are much lower for women than for men, and even in areas where women predominate, such as education and health, men dominate the upper ranks.[92] The same is true in agriculture, where 56 per cent of workers engaged in physical occupations are female, whereas they are scarcely represented among collective farm chairmen and other top management, and industrial administration, where only 9 per cent of enterprise directors are women.[93]

Wage differentials seem to persist in the countries of Eastern Europe, despite legal requirements of equal pay for equal work. As in the West, labour market segmentation and feminization of certain areas, leading to lower overall wage levels, contribute to this situation. It has been estimated that the Soviet women's wage is 75 to 80 per cent of men's compared with figures of 40 to 60 per cent in the West.[94] In Czechoslovakia, where figures are published on male and female wage levels, income differences persist when all factors thought to account for the difference – level of skill, educational attainment, type of work performed and hours of work – are held constant.[95]

Education and training

Soviet educational policies have promoted women's advancement and greater equality between the sexes. All children, except the physically handicapped, are required to complete eight years of education (starting at seven years old) with a common curriculum in which maths and science occupy a prominent place. Women have been encouraged to take advanced training, and on average today young soviet women reach a higher level of education than men, and there is as we have seen, a high level of representation of women in science and technology, the professions and semi-professions as a result.[96] Studies of schoolchildren also show that girls achieve higher levels of academic performance in school than boys.[97]

Certain factors affect the educational chances of girls; social origins in terms of level of education and income of the family of origin influence the performance and aspiration of girls, and girls from materially advantaged backgrounds also receive more support from their families in pursuing their education.[98] Although the education of girls in rural areas is improving, they are still generally at a disadvantage compared with their urban counterparts.[99]

Once again in general in this region we could say that despite a considerably better situation for women in training and education than that experienced by women in the West, the deeply entrenched sexual divisions of society nonetheless have some impact on male and female evaluations of occupations which then reflects on their distribution in education, training and the occupational sphere. In Czechoslovakia, for example, not only has the proportion of girls amongst apprentices declined[100] but girls applied for training (in order of popularity) in jewellery making, glass-painting, photography, dressmaking, window-arrangement, hairdressing, pastry-making and switch-board operating; boys wanted to be housepainters, electronic mechanics, automobile mechanics and butchers. Both boys and girls were interested in being cooks and waiters/waitresses.

Home and family

The fundamental problem which still remains in the countries of Eastern Europe, despite great advances in labour force participation and educational attainment for women, is that of domestic labour, including reproduction and child care – in its broadest sense, the reproduction of the labour force. We have seen here, as in all the countries of the world, where women have entered the labour force, they still retain responsibility for domestic labour. Heitlinger (1979)[101] suggests that in the USSR 'women's heavy burden of housework and family responsibility, together with men's unwillingness to undertake an equal share, provide a large part of the explanation of why women have failed to achieve the equal status the leaders of the revolution believed it would bring' (p. 94). She also points out that on average men tend to have twice as much leisure as women, and consequently time to take part in sport, further education, and involvement in community affairs. Despite the fact that the original intention of socialist regimes was to reduce the importance and role of the family as a prerequisite for the emancipation and equality of women, the family is still a fundamental and significant unit in socialist life, buttressed by state policy and programmes. Indeed many of the articles in the bibliography on this region directed towards the family and the relationships within it, indicate fears of instability and family disintegration, demonstrating its prime function as an agency of socialization and reproduction of the values and aims of the society in the consciousness and practices of the individual members.[102]

Rural women receive considerable attention in the literature. In the last two decades, accelerated industrialization and increased migration of men to other sectors of the economy have led to the feminization of agricultural work in a number of East European countries. Proportions of the agricultural labour force which are women, are, for example, 72 per cent in Romania, 55 per cent in Bulgaria, and 53 per cent in Yugoslavia. In Czechoslovakia at 48 per cent, USSR 45 per cent and Poland 46 per cent it is still very high. Except for Poland and Yugoslavia there has been almost complete collectivization of agriculture. In all of these countries, considerable differences have existed in the past between the situations of the urban and rural population. Much effort has been put into improving rural conditions and giving the male population opportunities for advancement in terms of training and education, as well as improved material conditions of life and consumer services. But a large gap still remains, particularly for rural women. Dunn (1978)[103] suggests that for the USSR 'there is evidence to suggest that they are not participating fully in one of the major efforts to provide full employment and a better standard of living for the rural population'. A major factor, once again, is women's responsibility for domestic labour, and particularly for child care.

*LATIN AMERICA**

Interest in studies of women and their status and position has been growing steadily in Latin America since the early 1970s, although it is still the case that most academic centres do not formally recognize such studies and in most countries research is carried out on an individual basis. A major impetus for such study came from international conferences organized by national or international agencies, and from meetings of the Latin American Studies Association, which brought people working on the problems of women in Latin America in contact with feminist scholarship emanating from the USA.

These meetings have produced a series of papers which are basic to the development of studies on the status of women in Latin America, some of which are included in the annotated bibliography on this area.[104]

A number of centres in several countries are now involved in research on women, as a major focus of their work, funded from government or private sources; examples are Centro Brasileiro de Analisis et Planejamiento, São Paulo (CEBRAP), Centro de Estudios de Poblacion, Buenos Aires, Argentina (CENEP) and Asociacion Colombiana para el Estudio de Publacion, Bogota, Columbia (ACEP).[105]

Labour force participation and women's role in economic development

Despite the contact with feminist scholarship, for a number of reasons, studies on women in Latin America, are not undertaken from a feminist perspective[106]; their writers even expressly reject being considered so, and the focus on women did not grow out of an active women's liberation movement, as has been the case in the United States, United Kingdom and much of Western Europe. In Latin America the focus derived from work in the field of development[107] and whilst some studies were undertaken within a strictly Marxist framework, most have been heavily influenced by the work of Cardoso and Faletto.[108] These writers argued that in Latin America a form of structurally dependent capitalism had developed, with its own cultural specifity and types of social structures and their particular internal and external contradictions. Most of the Latin American social scientists working on women have as their main objective the analysis of a capitalist mode of production in a dependent form, with women embedded in the socio-economic conditions of a peripheral, developing economy. Much of the work then is related to: women's labour force participation; the impact of the processes of development on them; their 'invisible' labour in the home, in subsistence agriculture and in the informal sector; and the relation between work and household.[109] There is a strong argument that women's participation in the economic sphere is grossly underestimated, and many agree with the approach in the work of Jelin (1977)[110] who argues that a new classification of work and non-work is needed and considers that the household should be adopted as the unit of analysis. (Figures given for female participation rates in Latin America range from 11 per cent in Venezuela to 26 per cent in Uruguay.[111])

Recent discussions on the meaning of domestic work in different modes of production have demonstrated that the 'non-work' socially attributed to the role of the housewife, conceals the performance of a series of essential tasks connected with the daily and generational reproduction of the members of the

* Drawn from a report by Maria del Carmen Feijoo.

family. Attention has also been drawn to the fact that the performance of these tasks, essential for the other members of the household, severely restricts the availability of women to participate in the labour market. Latin American authors have indicated that the exclusion not only of domestic work but also of domestic production of goods from 'social production' results in very poor descriptions of the functioning of the economic structure and of the role played by women in economies as heterogeneous as those in Latin America. This domestic production of goods, for self-consumption or for sale, carried out by women, must be seen in relation to activities performed in the developed, technically advanced, capitalized and modern sectors of the productive structure.

Studies within this framework stress the fact that the productive and reproductive behaviour of the family is not a mere mechanical response to the expansion or contraction of the economic system, and more complex processes are involved than the accommodation of family size and function to the process of transmission from a traditional to a modern stage of development, the classical movement from extended to nuclear family kinship groups. From this perspective, it is possible to understand the survival of extended families in urban areas. The definition of the family in this type of work expands the more usual reference to kinship ties; the family becomes a unit linked by ties of kinship and/or affinity, where productive and reproductive activities take place in a co-residential group. Migrants to urban areas frequently move into this type of household unit, and it also provides a structure in which female workers can more adequately meet the responsibility of child care, especially in the case of female headed households.[112]

A number of authors criticize the application of the U curve model of female participation in economic development to Latin America. This model postulates a relationship between female participation in the labour force and stages of economic development in which female participation is high in the early phase, characterized by domestic unpaid production, diminishes in the intermediate phases, and is high again in later stages, involving extra-domestic paid work.[113] The major revision of this approach which is called for, is that the curve of female participation should be seen as an aggregation of a number of distinct curves and that disaggregation of the data and qualification in terms of age cohorts, occupation and sector of the economy will provide a more fruitful approach. This should be supplemented by case study material, which would supply historical and cultural specificity.

The unfavourable impact of development on women[114] is a pattern we have seen in other developing countries. Women's traditional work and roles are lost as industrialization expands or new technology is acquired, and they become concentrated in services, domestic service, seasonal agricultural work or home industries – the informal sector. Women who do find themselves in the more formal part of the labour market, experience the problems of the double burden of domestic labour and wage labour.[115] A paper by Ribiero and Barbieri (1978)[116] analyzes the situation arising from the triple condition of worker, wife and mother and the difficulties which female labour poses for managers in Chile. Mothers and housewives receive no support from factory or state, since both consider the family a 'private area', despite the fact that such female labour is essential, both from the point of view of the productive system and for the women themselves.

Two new trends of research are concerned with this problem. One highlights the economic participation of women who are totally responsible for a household, female heads of household. These women have no choice: The survival of their household group depends on their participation in the labour market.[117] The other and very recent perspective is concerned with the problems which urban lower-class women have to face, either in paid or domestic work, in the framework of the spectacular growth of some Latin American cities. In these cities, the growth of services seldom matches the growth of population, and this fact is particularly burdensome for the women, who have to face daily scarcity and lack of essential services such as water, electricity, schools, means of transportation and medical provision.

Very little written on women in Latin America pays attention to women of the middle and upper classes, given the overall framework within which these studies are conducted. There are exceptions, for example, Lomnitz and Perez (1977)[118] study of 400 members of an upper class family clan, which looks at five generations of a family descended from a small merchant in the state of Puebla, one of whose sons migrated to Mexico City at the end of the 19th century and became a pioneer of Mexican industry. Lira (1978)[119] looks at the sociological and demographic characteristics of families in Chile, including middle- and upper-class urban families.

Education

Women's labour force participation is related to many factors, amongst them fertility and education. The educational experience of women in Latin America is quite variable, both between and within countries (in terms of social class location). In Uruguay and Argentina for example, the female literacy rate is 90 per cent, 53 per cent of secondary level enrolment is female, and women form 41 per cent of the university students. In general, there seems to be a relatively high level of female enrolment in secondary education, ranging from 37 per cent in Bolivia to over 50 per cent in a number of countries, including Chile, Panama, and as mentioned above Argentina and Uruguay. (Average for area is 47 per cent.)[120]

The decade 1960–70 was called the 'decade of women's invasion of secondary education' and was marked by an annual increase of 12 per cent of enrolment of women in intermediate level schools. By 1970, females also made up 48 per cent of primary school enrolment.[121] This should be seen in the light of the fact that for seven of the Latin American countries the median years of educational attainment for women over 25 is less than one year. The literacy rate for women is lowest in Guatemala at 32 per cent and they also have one of the lowest proportions of women university students compared to the total group of students, at 16.7 per cent. As a result of the specific concerns of research in general in Latin America and in particular research on women, there is not a large amount of work on women's educational experience. Education is incorporated as a variable which influences fertility and labour force participation.[123]

Demographic aspects

Fertility patterns in Latin America are usually incorporated into studies of female labour force participation in the context of a capitalist peripheral economy, as we have mentioned is also the case with considerations of women's education. A considerable amount of demographic information is available from censuses in the region, and a study by Recchine de Lattes and Wainerman (1979)[124] reviews the information from all censuses in Latin America and the Caribbean in 1970, evaluating the deficiencies in this data, and making recommendations for improvement. A collection of papers edited by Burch, Lira and Lopes (1976)[125] gives a general picture of the state of demographic research on the family and problems and difficulties associated both with the data and with conceptual and methodological aspects of the work involved.

Studies of migration, much of which are made up of the movement of daughters of rural peasant families into urban areas, stress the importance of relating those movements to the economic changes in the particular areas concerned in relation to two mediating structures; that of the social class, and the household. Arizpe (1979)[126] sees migration as a compensatory mechanism, directed against pressures which are transforming rural economies, and lead to the proletarianization of their members. These families manage to survive, despite the destruction of their domestic economies, the fragmentation of their plots and increasing impairment of their conditions of life, by a strategy of stage-migration. Permanent and consecutive migration of children enables the peasant family to gather resources to cultivate the land and reproduce itself. This also has an impact on the reproductive function of women in the peasant household because of the need to increase the number of income-earners.[127] These migrants to the cities are the women we have been considering above, in other aspects of their condition – many go into the informal labour market (Marias, domestic workers), they might live in extended co-residential groups, or they may be female household heads.

As can be seen from the above brief review of studies on women in Latin America, most authors are concerned with issues well established in the Latin American social sciences, either exploring social inequalities for which they find an explanation in the prevailing socio-political system, or resolving and developing theoretical and methodological issues. There is a considerable amount of information on women in Latin America, but little research goes on outside this framework, and there is for example, very little interest in issues which exercise Western studies of women, such as sex roles, images of women, and women's autonomy over their own bodies.

UNITED KINGDOM, UNITED STATES AND WESTERN EUROPE

Since the early 1970s there has been a tremendous growth in research on the status of women, and all aspects of their life experience, particularly in the United States and United Kingdom, but also in the countries of Western Europe. The major stimulus has been the Women's Movement, which emanating from the United States in the late 1960s, has spread to most, if not all, of the countries covered here, most of which have a vigorous and active women's movement.[128]

In the past, movements for female emancipation in these countries had women's franchise as a prime goal and achieved this aim at widely different times (Finland 1906, Denmark 1915, Austria, Federal Republic of Germany 1918, United States 1920, Sweden 1921, France 1944, Switzerland 1971). Amongst the aims of the current movement are those of bringing women into focus, exposing the processes and practices through which female subordination in all areas of life is maintained, and changing and improving the status and situation of women. The specific approaches and theoretical explanations for the phenomenon of female subordination and the consequent programmes for action, demonstrate considerable variation.

Research on women in these countries is undertaken under the aegis of a range of different organizations; government agencies, political organizations of various types, academic institutions, feminist organizations, and of course by individual researchers. The purposes for which information on women is sought may vary: For example government agencies are oriented towards policy implications, or 'manpower' considerations; political organizations require information to support their programmes for action. International agencies are frequently concerned to show how the actual practice in various countries with respect to the status and experience of women, belies the formal claims for equality of the government concerned.[129]

The overall aim of research from a feminist perspective can be seen as 'the expansion of empirical knowledge, the critique of existing theory, and the reconceptualization of core concepts'.[130] To this end, feminist scholarship, for example in the discipline of history, has sought to recover women's history, to overcome the prejudice resulting from a male orientation to historical research which focuses on major movements, catastrophic events, and the contributions of men, and to reassert both the part played by women in history, and the history of its suppression.[131] In anthropology, as we shall see in considering work in Africa (see page 41 and Hafkin and Bay, Entry 5),[132] the aim has been to explore the androcentrism of earlier studies in which women were regarded as marginal adjuncts to men, and to *focus* on women and their experience, on their role in history and in economic development or change in different societies.

In sociology, feminist research attacks the invisibility of women in earlier work and their relegation to the status of 'problems' like juvenile delinquency and other forms of 'deviation'.[133] In general then, in the social sciences, feminist research aims to displace the male perspective and replace it with one in which women are moved from the periphery of social life to the centre of focus. An additional aspect, which has been emphasized in some research on women, is the importance of subjective experience and the valuable insights which it can give. This is related to a questioning of the objectivity and neutrality of research from a male perspective, which sees males as the norm and women as an anomaly.

The work outlined above produces a considerable amount of empirical data on women, and amongst the areas to which attention has been directed are: women's labour force participation, their distribution in the occupational hierarchy and sectors of the economy[134]; women's work in the home, and its relation to their role in the labour market[135]; child care and reproduction[136]; the role of the state in the status and position of women[137]; women's education[138]; women's sexuality[139]; sexual harassment[140]; violence against women[141]; sex role socialization[142]; the impact of the media on women[143]; women's political activity[144]; women and language.

With the expansion of empirical evidence about the situation of women has come an expansion of theoretical formulations and explanations for women's subordination to men.[145] In some cases existing theories from the 'malestream',[146] notably those of Freud and Marx, have been appropriated; in others these theories have been explicitly attacked and replaced by alternative formulations. Feminist objections to Freud's psychoanalytic theory have argued that it provides ideological reinforcement for women's oppression by describing the characteristics of femininity in terms of immutable structures of the psyche. It is suggested that the theory itself is the product of a particular cultural and historical situation, incorporating historically and socially specific notions of male superiority whilst claiming to be an ahistorical and universalistic theory of psychic development.[147] Mitchell,[148] however, wants to use Freud's concepts for an analysis for the functioning of the ideologies of sex and gender and argues that the social nature of sexual definition is inherent in his theoretical formulations.[149]

Socialist feminists see the root of female oppression in the working of the capitalist system, and use Marx's theory as a starting point for an explanation.[150] The positions taken in utilizing a Marxist framework can range from that of a primary concern with Marxist analysis and the application of this analysis to women without questioning the categories and concepts employed, to a position which sees fundamental problems with Marx's theoretical formulations and their application to women. The latter group consider that Marx's theory is in need of modification if it is to articulate the interaction between class and gender, and they frequently use the concept of patriarchy as a starting point for their reformulation.[151]

Another area of Marxist feminist theorising on women, which utilizes the concept of patriarchy, draws attention to the articulation between relations of production and relations of reproduction.[152] There are two orientations here: the first defines the relations of production in materialist terms and sees them as deriving from patriarchial control over women's labour in the family and procreative capacity[153]: the second sees patriarchial control as resulting from ideological and political interpretations of biological differentiation, and the social relations of production as ideological or cultural relations.[154] A criticism which has been raised in this type of theorizing (usually from a Marxist perspective) in which the emphasis is on women's reproductive capacity, is that it leads to an analysis in which society is conceptualized, as consisting of two separate structures, production and reproduction, and the precise relationship between the two is not confronted.[155]

A further concept taken from Marx and applied to women is that of the reserve army of labour. Beechey (1977, 1978)[156] argues that married women may have become a reserve army of labour for capital for low paid unskilled and semi-skilled work in particular areas of modern industry because they offer certain advantages: (a) they can be paid at a price below the value of labour power; and (b) they provide a flexible working population, which can be brought into production or dispensed with as the conditions of production change. Married women can be treated in this way because they are dependent on the husband's wages for part of the cost of producing and reproducing their own labour power.[157]

A considerable discussion grew up in the literature around the possibility of applying Marx's categories and concepts which were developed to explain the workings of the capitalist economic system and the free exchange of labour in the market, to domestic labour.[158] The orthodox viewpoint rejected the possibility of applying such concepts as surplus value and productive labour to domestic labour.[159] The unorthodox argued that such an application was legitimate, thereby incorporating women as housewives into a social group with whom the revolutionary class could form an alliance.[160] This discussion which was couched in economistic terms and ultimately became a sterile debate did, however, point to the importance of an understanding of the contradictions inherent in the demands made on women as workers in the labour market and as domestic labourers. The discussion indicated that an adequate analysis of women's situation must take account not only of the material base in exploitation at work and in the home, but also the ideological processes which help to create and maintain that situation.

One feminist theorist who has moved away from Marx, whilst retaining a materialist analysis of women's oppression is Delphy (1977, 1980),[161] who sees the family as the site of economic exploitation of women, where their productive and reproductive labour is appropriated by men. Delphy sees two modes of production in contemporary society, that defined by capitalist property relations and exploitation – the industrial mode of production; and that defined by patriarchal/familial relations and the exploitation of women by men – the family mode of production. In contrast to an emphasis on class relations in society amongst socialist feminists, whatever particular interrelationship with gender is proposed, radical feminists emphasize patriarchal relations as fundamental in determining and maintaining women's subordinate position, and postulate women as a sex/class. In consequence they emphasize the family and its functions and specific aspects of women's oppression concerned with motherhood, childbirth, and abortion.[162] Revolutionary feminists take this argument one stage further and maintain that gender differences can be explained in terms of biological differences between the sexes, and that male control over female reproductive capacity is the crucial factor in women's oppression.[163] Biological reductionism is the major shortcoming of the latter approach.

Parallel with the growth of research on women, in both empirical and theoretical aspects, there has been a growth in women's studies, most spectacularly in the United States, where 'In 1980, courses are too numerous to count and programmes, which now number hundreds, are available at all levels including PhD.'[164] Women's studies developed initially in disciplines in which women are numerous, modern languages (which includes English) and sociology and other social sciences, and the courses were designed for female students to supplement their regular studies. But the aims expanded and now encompass quantitative and qualitative changes in specific educational contents, in the whole curriculum of primary, secondary and higher education and in the structures of educational institutions. The feminist perspective which characterizes women's studies in the United States has a wide ideological spectrum, ranging from the demand for equal rights for women within the existing system, to radical, socialist, and androgynous feminist critiques of the system.[165]

In France, despite both the high esteem in which intellectuals are held, the stimulating intellectual environment and the existence of very high quality research and publication on women, there is little governmental or university support for feminist endeavours and women's studies. Various courses do run however, as the result of the energy of individual women. Attention can be drawn to some courses in Paris, for example, those run by M. Perrot working in history, A. Michel in the sociology of women, and H. Cixous of the *psychologie et politique* school, blending literature, psychoanalysis and linguistics into a new framework based on the feminine subconscious and sexuality and women's passage from repression to expression.[166]

In England, women's studies courses originated in the early 1970s and have been particularly prolific in adult education. In 1980, there were at least 40 courses at more than 20 universities, and many courses in other institutions including adult education and schools. The discipline which predominates in women's studies courses in the United Kingdom is sociology. In the Netherlands[167] and Scandinavia there are a number of courses and considerable research, and some courses are run in the Federal Republic of Germany, Spain and Italy. In Italy these are largely based in women's centres rather than in the universities.

Some information on the status of women emerging from empirical research

The percentage of women who work shows some variation in the countries reviewed here, but all have had an increase in the labour force participation of women, particularly of married women over the past 20 years. In Sweden,[168] for example, in 1978, 72 per cent of women worked (69 per cent of those who had children under seven) an increase of 17 per cent on the figure for 1968, and in 1980 women formed 45 per cent of the labour force.

In the United States, in 1977, women formed 40 per cent of the work force. The figures are similar for the United Kingdom, Federal Republic of Germany and France.

In the Netherlands where the proportion of women going out to work has traditionally been lower than in other industrialized countries, there has also been a marked increase. In 1960, 23 per cent of women aged over 15 went out to work; in 1980 the figure was 30 per cent, and women formed 29 per cent of the labour force.[169] Much of the increase in labour force participation has also been in part-time work, an area normally associated with insecurity and lack of protective legislation and rights. Manley and Sawbridge (1980)[170] argue that the part-timer component of the female labour force has been particularly high in the United Kingdom compared with the other European countries of comparable size, and/or economic development, and that a prime factor in the explanation for this phenomenon (on the supply side) is actual or perceived need on the part of the women.[171] The distribution of women in the labour force within and across sectors of the economies considered here demonstrates a depressing similarity, with women clustering in service industries, and the public sector, (particularly health and medical services and teaching at primary level). In Sweden, of the 300 occupations listed in the population and housing census in 1975, 30 contained 75 per cent of the female work force. Women also cluster in the bottom ranks of the occupations in which they are found.[172]

A study of the 1974–75 recession and its impact on the employment of women[173] concluded that: 'In overall terms the study shows women workers were affected differently than male workers. Women because of their disproportionate concentration in the service sector were insulated from the harshest effects of the recession which had its greatest impact in the industrial sector. However, those women who did hold industrial jobs experienced greater employment losses than men' (p. 202 – Amsden, A., Entry 406).

As far as income is concerned, average earnings of women are always lower than those of men. These discrepancies are usually explained in terms of employment in different occupations, and on different tasks, different educational attainment and probably age differences. But in all of these countries, when these and other factors are held constant, there is always an irreducible element of female/male pay differential which, as the National Committee for Equality between men and women in Sweden points out[174] 'does not seem to have any objective basis whatever' (p. 53). Trade union movements have been slow in (a) organizing women, and (b) looking after their interests, even when they form the bulk of the union membership.[175]

Education

In looking at educational positions in the United States and Western Europe, we are dealing with different problems from those which are relevant in Third World countries – literacy, access to and duration of education. Most of the countries in these regions have extensive periods of compulsory education and girls have equal access and more or less equal representation in primary and secondary levels of education.[176] Byrne[177] suggests that there is an emerging pattern in France, Federal Republic of Germany, Italy, Ireland and the United Kingdom, where two or more of a set of indices of potential inequality are aggregated, which creates a cumulative cycle of under-achievement. These factors are (1) sex; (2) lower social class; (3) lower range of intelligence; (4) residence in certain regions with a history of under-achievement and (5) residence in rural areas. Byrne considers that this cycle of under-achievement can only be overcome by positive, affirmative, interventionist programmes aimed at increasing resources, counteracting social and cultural barriers, and adding to skill and experience.

Even without the compounding of these factors, in most of the countries in this area, it is recognized that girls do not actually receive the same education as boys.[178] When policy action has removed all other sources of difference, for example in Sweden, 'at the second and tertiary level, girls tend more than boys to take shorter courses. But the biggest difference of all is that boys and girls select different curricula or educational programmes' (p. 23, *Step by Step*).[179] One explanation for the sex-typed traditional educational and vocational 'choices' made by girls is that the processes of socialization into male and female roles which begin in the home and family, continue in the school. A number of writers argue that schools reinforce sexual divisions through their organizational arrangements, curricula, timetables, teaching materials and textbooks, teacher expectations, and the ideological messages which they transmit to the pupils. Some suggest that this is in fact a major function of the educational system. McDonald (1980) for example, looks at the ways in which 'schooling produces both classed and sexed subjects, who are to take their place in a social division of labour structured by the dual, yet often contradictory forms of class and gender relations'.[180]

The pattern of sex typed programmes and courses continues at the tertiary level for the varying proportions of women who manage to achieve this standard of education.[181] The extent to which women receive technical training or gain apprenticeships is also considerably lower than that of men.

If we look at the field of education as an employer, we find that although the large majority of teachers at primary level are female in most of these countries, they, and their sisters teaching at the secondary level, are discriminated against in terms of promotion.[182] This pattern continues at the higher levels of the academic profession.

Family and home

The family has become, as the discussion of theoretical approaches outlined above indicates, an important focus for research on women. It is a crucial socializing institution, and for many seen as the major site of women's oppression. One aspect of this research has been to look at the role of the state in changing or maintaining women's position in the family.[183] In the United Kingdom for example, David (1980)[184] argues that the family and education system are used by the state in concert to maintain and reproduce the social and economic *status quo* and the sexual division of labour. Wilson (1977)[185] investigates the development of welfare state intervention in the United Kingdom from the 19th century to the present day, arguing that an understanding of the definition of women enshrined in welfare policies and provision is essential to an understanding of the welfare state. Women are defined in terms of their role in the home of servicing the worker and bringing up children. This definition, and its accompanying ideological support which locates women firmly in the family as the economic dependant of her husband, the breadwinner,[186] was enshrined in the Beveridge Report (1942),[187] the basis for welfare provision in the United Kingdom. 'During marriage most women will not be gainfully employed'; 'the great majority of women must be regarded as occupied on work which is vital though unpaid'; 'In the next 30 years housewives as mothers have vital work to do in ensuring the adequate continuance of the British race.'

Family policy in Scandanavia formerly implicitly regarding women as they are seen in the United Kingdom model, was influenced by the needs of changing national economies, and the importance of bringing women into the work-force, and welfare provisions were directed towards this end.[188]

Although all of the countries in Europe have a formal commitment to equality between the sexes, the degree of persistence with which they pursue that objective varies, and the situation of women with it. The highest commitment and the most consistent effort seems to be undertaken in the Scandinavian countries, especially Sweden, which is often held up as a model in terms of social policy affecting women by those criticizing ineffectual or inadequate measures taken in other countries. In Sweden, with social policies and programmes which are the envy of women in other countries, the intransigence of the problem of inequality between the sexes is demonstrated. Various studies attest to the fact that the Swedish labour market is segregated by sex, that women are to be found concentrated in occupations and work areas which are characterized by low status, low pay, small opportunities for further education and poor chances for promotion, that they earn less, that half of them work only part-time giving them weaker status in the work place, and that a large part of the blame for this state of affairs can be laid at the door of the sexual division of labour in the home, and lack of child care facilities.[189] Further disabilities experienced by the female work force can be associated with types of educational experience and qualification inappropriate for technical, skilled and higher level professional work.

Despite the familiarity of this catalogue, as we have seen, it is a general description of women's status and position, which could be accurately applied to any of the countries in the area under review, the social policies and programmes in the Scandinavian countries have probably enhanced the prospects for increasing equality between the sexes.

THE BIBLIOGRAPHIES

Each of the bibliographies was compiled by a different author (with a few minor additions by the editor) and is prefaced by a very brief introduction describing the specific bibliography, and making a general statement about research in the area. The major categories into which each of the bibiographies is divided, where relevant, are:

I. *General*, which includes bibliographies, conceptual and methodological work, general studies on women and their status or aspects of it, including psychological and related formulations.

II. *Women's work and labour force participation*, which includes women and development, studies on women's professional and managerial work, specific studies on women in the agricultural or rural sector related to their work rather than to the impact on the family or household unit (which appears in the following section) and individual country studies on women's work in the labour force.

III. *Family and household*, which includes general studies of the family and women's position in it, references to domestic labour, studies of the rural or agricultural family, divorce, maternity, and work on women family heads.

IV. *Education*, studies directed towards all levels of education, including training and apprenticeships.

V. *Demographic features*, including demographic aspects of the family, migration, and broad population concerns.

VI. *Other*, which covers research on culture, the law, health and social policy.

When a particular bibliography has no entries in a category, the category is omitted. The sub-categories vary for each bibliography, depending on the particular focus of concern in that region, and the interpretation of the compiler of the brief. Within these sub-categories the entries appear in alphabetical order. The section on the United Kingdom, the United States and Western Europe is divided in addition into four sections prior to this general categorization. These are: Cross-Cultural, United Kingdom, the United States, and Western Europe.

This major categorization provides an overall entry into the bibliographies, but many studies cover more than one aspect, and indeed the divisions between major categories are somewhat blurred as each area of concern in women's issues flows readily into another. The subject index provides a way of finding individual items which deal with specific topics. Entries which deal with individual countries are listed for each country, followed by a much more detailed categorization of topic areas, with the entries relevant to these topics. A perusal of these listings enables the reader to identify individual entries relating to specific countries on particular topics. This listing is followed by an author index. At the end of each regional bibliography a short list of journals, or journal issues, which may be of interest, is given. In some cases relevant organizations engaging in research on women are also listed.

NOTES

1. See Gronseth, E., Worksharing: A Norwegian example, in: Rapoport, R. and Rapoport, R. N., *Working Couples*, London, Routledge and Kegan Paul, 1978, p. 108–121.
2. See discussion in section on Western Europe and United States, pp. 26–27. See also Malos, E.,

The politics of housework, 1980 (Entry 494), for a collection of studies in this debate; and Molyneux, M., Beyond the domestic labour debate, 1979, (Entry 435) for a definitive statement of the end.

3. Delphy, C., *The main enemy: a materialist analysis of women's oppression*, WRRC, Explorations in Feminism, No. 3, 1977; and A materialist feminism is possible, *Feminist Review*, No. 4, 1980, p. 79–105. For a critique of Delphy, see Molyneux, M., op. cit. Further discussions of patriarchy are to be found in Beechey, V., On patriarchy, *Feminist Review*, No. 3, 1979, p. 66–82, and Dale, R., Esland, G., Fergusson, R., and MacDonald, M., *Education and the state*, Vol. 2: *Politics patriarchy and practice*, Barcombe, The Falmer Press/The Open University Press, 1981.

4. Dube, L., *Studies on women in South East Asia: A status report*, 1980 (Entry 94).

5. Boserup, E., *Women's role in economic development*, London, George Allen and Unwin, 1970.

6. Recchini de Lattes, 1977, and 1979 (Entries 280 and 271).

7. Van Dusen, R. A., The study of women in the Middle East: Some thoughts, *Middle East Studies Association Bulletin*, Vol. 10, No. 2, 1976.

8. See Heitlinger, A., *Women and state socialism: Sex inequality in the Soviet Union and Czechoslovakia*, 1979 (Entry 167), p. 241; discussion in the Eastern European countries section of this introduction; Lapidus, G. Warshofsky, *Women and work in the Soviet Union*, London, M. E. Sharpe, 1981; Murray, N., Socialism and feminism: Women in the Cuban revolution, published in two parts in *Feminist Review*, No. 2, 1979, p. 57–71 and No. 3, 1979, p. 99–108; and the introduction by Dahlberg, G. and Mattsson, K., to Holland, J., *Women's occupational choice: The impact of sexual divisions in Society*, Reports on Education and Psychology Nr. 3, Stockholm Institute of Education, Department of Educational Research, 1980.

9. Bujra, J. M., in: Caplan P. and Bujra, J. M., *Women United, women divided*, 1978 (Entry 399).

10. See also Lesser Blumberg, R., A paradigm for predicting the position of women: Policy implications and problems, in: Lipman-Blumen, J. and Bernard, J., *Sex roles and social policy: A complex social science equation*, 1979 (Entry 391), p. 113–142. This author tries to develop a paradigm starting from the basic postulate that in conceptualizing the position of women in any society the standard to be applied is the level of men in the same society (more specifically, men in the same class or group in that society) and not women in other societies.

11. The discussion of the individual geographical regions here owes a debt to the compilers of each of the bibliographies who also provided a report on their area from which much of the following material is drawn.

12. Akerele, O., *Women and the fishing industries in Liberia*, Economic Commission for Africa/African Training Research Center for Women, Addis Ababa, 1979.

13. UNECA/ATRCW, *Women textile workers in Ethiopia*, Addis Ababa, 1979.

14. Boserup, E., op. cit.

15. Trager, L., Market women in the urban economy: The role of Yoruba intermediaries in a medium-sized city, *African Urban Notes*, No. 2, 1976/77, p. 1–9.

16. Palmer, I., New Official ideas on women and development, 1979 (Entry 15).

17. Gutto, S. B. O., *The status of women in Kenya: A study of paternalism, inequality and underprivilege*, Institute for Development Studies, University of Nairobi, 1976, Discussion Paper No. 235. (Entry 21).

18. MacCormack, C. P., Control of land labor and capital in rural Southern Sierra Leone, 1976, Entry 27.

19. Boserup, E., op. cit.

20. Monsted, M., The changing division of labor within rural families in Kenya, 1977, Entry 28.

21. Hanger, J. and Morris, J., Women and the household economy, in: Chamber, R. and Morris, J. (eds.), *Mwea: An irrigated rice settlement in Kenya*, Munich, Welforum Verlag, 1973.

22. Tadesse, Z., *The conditions of women in Ethiopia*, Report to the Swedish International Development Agency, 1976.

23. Brain, J. L., Less than second-class: Women in rural settlement schemes in Tanzania, in: Hafkin, N. J. and Bay, E. G., *Women in Africa*, 1976 (Entry 5).

24. Spring, A. and Hansen, A., *Women's agricultural work in rural Zambia: From valuation to subordination.* Paper presented to the African studies Association Annual Meeting, Los Angeles, October 1979.

25. Dixon, R. B., *Jobs for women in rural industry and services*, Washington, D.C., Women in Development Office, July 1979.

26. Mwanamwambwa, C. and Tadesse, Z., *The situation of children in Zambia*, Swedish International Development Agency, 1979.

27. In the Western State, Nigeria, at the Institute of Agricultural Research and Training in 1970–72 there were only 15 females out of 265 students and at the School of Agriculture, Samaru, Zaria, in the period 1965–66, 1970–71, only 91 out of 673 students were females.

28. The figures are from Kisekka, M. N., *The identification and use of indicators in socio-economic*

development in the context of Nigeria and Uganda. Paper presented to a Unesco Meeting of Experts on the Indicators of Women's Participation in Socio-Economic Development, Paris, 1980.

29. UNECE/ATRCW, *Nigeria Country Report*, Addis Ababa, 1973.

30. Dixon, R. B., 1979, op. cit.

31. Youssef, N. et al., *Women in migration: A Third World focus*, Washington, D.C., Women in Development Office, 1979.

32. See Caldwell, J. C., *Population growth and family change in Africa: The new urban elite in Ghana*, Canberra, Australian National University Press, 1968, 222 p.

33. Bukh, J., *Women in food production, food handling and nutrition.* Paper presented to the Association of African Women for Research and Development (AAWORD) Workshop, Dakar, December 1977.

34. Palmer, I., op. cit.

35. Okojie, X., Hospital based family planning in rural Africa: some lessons from the midwestern state of Nigeria, *Transactions of the Royal Society of Tropical Medicine and Hygiene*, No. 69, 1975, p. 189–197.

36. Buchwald, U. and Palmer, I., *Monitoring of changes in the conditions of women: A critical review of possible approaches*, Geneva, United Nations Research Institute for Social Development, 1978. See also, Ware, H., *The relevance of changes in women's roles to fertility behaviour: The African evidence.* Paper presented at the Annual Meeting of the Population Association of Africa, Seattle, Washington, 1975. The author questions whether raising the status of women reduces their fertility.

37. Nour Eldin, S., Population trends and problems, in relation to agricultural development and food supplies in the Near East, in: *Demographic aspects of socio-economic development in some Arab and African countries*, Cairo Demographic Centre, Monograph Series No. 5, 1974, p. 79–115.

38. A more complicated pattern of interrelationship is suggested by the African literature. See pp. 6–7 above.

39. Vavra, Z., Demographic patterns of labor force in Arab countries: An overview, in: *Demographic Aspects of manpower in Arab countries*, Cairo Demographic Centre, Monograph Series No. 3, 1972, p. 315–541.

40. For example, women as a percentage of total labour force constitute 48 per cent in Egypt, 34 per cent in Iraq, 17 per cent in Lebanon, 11 per cent in Syrian Arab Republic, 5 per cent in Libyan Arab Jamahiriya and 1 per cent in Saudi Arabia. (Source: *Arab Women*, Report No. 27 (revised edition), Minority Rights Group, September 1979, Entry 59).

41. Vavra, Z, 1972, op. cit.

42. Youssef, N. H. and Hartley, S. F., Demographic indicators of the status of women in various societies, in: Lipman-Blumen, J. and Bernard, J., op. cit. (Entry 391).

43. Youssef, N. H. and Hartley, S. F., op. cit., p. 110.

44. 1974 figures published in the Iraqi Women's Association Journal.

45. It should be pointed out here that a large number of Kuwaiti men choose to go abroad to university.

46. Abu-Lughod, J., The emergence of differential fertility in urban Egypt, *Milbank Memorial Fund Quarterly*, Vol. 43, No. 2, 1965, p. 235–253. Khalifa, A. and Khalifa, A. M., *Status of women in relation to fertility and family planning in Egypt*, Cairo, National Centre for Social and Criminological Research, 1973.

47. Unesco, Regional Centre for Education in the Arab States, *Population dynamics and educational development in Syria, Exhibit 1: Population dynamics*, Beirut, Unesco, 1974. Kjurciev, A. et al., *Population dynamics and education in the development process of the Arab countries*. Paper read at the Seminar of Experts on Population, Education and Development in the Arab Countries, ASFEC, Sir El Layyon, Egypt, 1976.

48. Nour Eldin, S., Analysis of data of fertility mortality and economic activity of urban population in Libyan Arab Jamahiriya based on a household sample survey, *Egyptian Population and Family Planning Review*, Vol. 4, No. 1, 1971; El Tay, O. A., *Country statement — Sudan*, Addis Ababa, Economic Commission for Africa, working group on fertility levels and differentials in Africa and prospects for the future, 1972; Henin, R. A., Nomadic fertility as compared with that of rain cultivators in Sudan, *International Population Conference*, Vol. I, London, International Union for Scientific Study of Population, 1969.

49. Cho, L. et al., *Differential fertility in the United States*, Chicago, Community and Family Study Center, University of Chicago Press, 1970.

50. See Entry 77.

51. Ibrahim, S., *Internal migration in Egypt: A critical review.* Presented to the Population and Family Planning Board, 1980.

52. See Entry 31.

53. Seetharam, et al., Migration and population growth in Kuwait, 1957–70, in: *Urbanization and*

migration in some Arab and African countries, Cairo Demographic Centre Monograph Series No. 4, 1973 (Entry 77), pp. 383–403; and in the same volume, Urbanization and migration in Arab countries: An overview, pp. 473–505.

54. Saleh, S., Professional women and national development: Women's response to migration, Open University Seminar Series on *Women, Work and Social Change*, AUC, Cairo, 1977.

55. Van Dusen, R. A., 1976, op. cit.

56. Dube, L., 1980, op. cit. (Entry 94).

57. India, Ministry of Education and Social Welfare, *Towards Equality*. Report of the Committee on the Status of Women in India, New Delhi, 1974, 480 p.

58. See Entry 87 for a bibliography they have produced.

59. See Jain, D., Singh, N. and Chand, M., India, in: *Women in Asia*, London, Minority Rights Group, 1980, p. 24 (Report No. 45) and Mazumdar, V., Fertility policy in India, in: Lipmen-Blumen, J. and Bernard, J., *Sex Roles and Social policy*, 1979, Entry 391.

60. Shah, M., *Research and teaching on women's studies in the Asian region*, Paris, Unesco, mimeo, 1980.

61. Indian Council of Social Science Research, *Critical issues on the status of women*, Table Va, p. 25. See also *The Indian women: A statistical profile*, Ministry of Education and Social Welfare, Department of Social Welfare, 1975.

62. Bangladesh Bureau of Statistics, Ministry of Planning, *Statistical Pocket Book of Bangladesh*, 1978, pp. 320–21. See also for Bangladesh, Women for Women (ed.), *The situation of women in Bangladesh*, Dacca, 1979; Islam, M., *Bibliography on Bangladesh women with annotation*, Dacca, Women for Women, 1979.

63. Government of Pakistan, *The Fifth Five Year Plan 1978–1983*.

64. Hafeez, S., *Women in industry: A study of women employed in a match factory in Pakistan*, The Ford Foundation, 1978.

65. Hafeez, S., *Women in administrative posts: A summary of a study*, The Ford Foundation, Pakistan, 1978. This contrasts with the findings in studies of middle class women in India, see Entry 106.

66. OECD, *Manpower policy in Japan*, 1973 (Entry 158). See also Entry 92.

67. Hara, K., *Economic growth and women's role in Japan*. Paper presented at session on sex roles in society, IX World Congress of Sociology, 1978.

68. Miralao, V. A., *Female employment and fertility in the Philippines*, 1980, Entry 126.

69. For further information: On the Philippines see Castillo, G. T. *The Filipino woman as manpower: The image and the empirical reality*, University of the Philippines at Los Banos College, Laguna, 1976; Mangahas, N. and Jayme-Ho, T., *Income and labor force participation rates of women in the Philippines*, Institute of Economic Development Research, University of the Philippines, 1976. On Korea: Lee. H.-C. and Kim, J.-S., *The Status of Korean women*, Seoul, Ewha Woman's University Press, 1976; Yoon, S.-Y. S., *The emergence of the Fourth World: Korean women in development*, Korea Journal, 1977 (available in English).

70. 1969 figures. 'Tertiary education in the Philippines is comprised more of women than of men, which could be attributed to the compulsory elementary education and democratization of education for both sexes during the American regime, which added impetus to female students in pursuing tertiary education': Paul P. Zwaenepoel, *Tertiary education in the Philippines 1611–1972: A systems analysis*, Manila, Alemar-Phoenix Publishing House Inc. 1975, p. 113. Nursing, teacher education and home economics are included in the classification of tertiary education in the Philippines. The colleges under the Bureau of Public Schools, which offer mostly teacher education courses had 82 per cent female and 18 per cent male students (1969–70). Women are slightly less than half of the student body in state universities. In the private sector universities the composition of the student body in various areas of study was as follows: chemistry 77 per cent female and medical science 81 per cent; commerce and business administration 98 per cent. Males feature in agriculture at 89 per cent, engineering and technology 95 per cent; law and foreign service 88 per cent and nautical 99 per cent.

71. Eviota, E. U., Philippines, in: Minority Rights Group, *Women in Asia*, 1980, op. cit., p. 14.

72. Some examples are: Debavalya, N., *Female employment and fertility. Cross-sectional and longitudinal relationships from a national sample of married Thai women*, Institute of Population Studies, Chulalongkorn University, Bangkok, 1978; Philippines National Demographic Surveys of 1968 and 1973; Federation of Family Planning Associations, Malaysia, *Women today in Peninsular Malaysia*, Kuala Lumpur, 1975.

73. Economic and Social Commission for Asia and the Pacific, Country Monograph Series No. 4, Bangkok, 1976, p. 141.

74. National Commission on the role of Filipino women for the World Conference of the United Nations Decade for Women, Copenhagen, 1980, *Women in the Philippines: A country report*, p. 51.

75. See Dube, L., 1980, op. cit., p. 32.

76. White, B., The economic importance of children in a Javanese village, in: Banks, D. J., *Changing identities in modern Southeast Asia*, Mouton, The Hague, 1976.
77. Nag, M., White, B. and Peet, R. C., An anthropological approach to the study of the economic value of children in Java and Nepal, *Current Anthropology*, Vol. 19, No. 2, 1978.
78. Debavalya, N., 1978, op. cit.
79. Hull, T. H. and Hull, V. J., The relation of economic class and fertility: An analysis of some Indonesian data, *Population Studies*, Vol. 31, No. 1, 1977.
80. For a bibliography on women and development see Buvinic, M., *Women and world development: An annotated bibliography*, 1976, 162 p. (Entry 262).
81. Compare the struggle to get the Equal Rights Amendment to the Constitution ratified in the United States.
82. See for example Nikolaeva-Tereshkova, V., Zhenskii vopros v sovremennoi obschchestvennoi zhisnc (The women's question in contemporary social life), *Pravda*, March 4, 1975, p. 2–3, and for a Western account Mandel, W., *Soviet Women*, New York, 1975.
83. See for example Lapidus, G. W., 1981, op. cit.; Iuk, Z. M., Trud zhenshchiny i sem'ia (The labour of women and the family) Minsk, 1975.
84. Jowitt, K., An organizational approach to the study of political culture in Marxist-Leninist systems, *American Political Science Review*, September 1974, p. 1176.
85. David, H. P., *Family planning and abortion in the socialist countries of Eastern Europe*, New York, The Population Council, 1970, gives details of abortion legislation in these countries up to 1969. Tietze, C. and Murstein, M. C., *Induced abortions: 1975 factbook*, Reports of Population/Family Planning, No. 14, New York, The Population Council, 1975. These authors argue, as do others, that liberalized abortion laws played a part in the birth-rate decline.
86. Bowlby, J., *Childcare and the growth of love*, Harmondsworth, Penguin Books, 1965.
87. See Heitlinger, A., 1979, op. cit., p. 197 ff. (Entry 167) for details of pronatalist population policies in the Eastern European countries. Heitlinger concludes that whilst 'the state socialist maternity laws and benefits are very impressive when compared with those of most capitalist countries, they fall short of providing any satisfactory solution to the problem of integrating women's productive and reproductive roles' (p. 199).
88. Bártová, E., Nekolik informací o postavení zen v socialistickych zemich, *Sociologicky Casopis*, Vol. 12, No. 1, 1976.
89. See Heitlinger, A., 1979, op. cit., p. 148, 149.
90. The figures are for 1970. See Sacks, M. P., Women in the industrial labor force, in: Atkinson, D., Dallin, A., and Lapidus, G. W., *Women in Russia*, Hassocks, UK, The Harvester Press, 1978, p. 202 (Entry 162).
91. See Rosch, G., Situation, evolution et perspectives effectoire de medecin en France et dans les pay d'Europe et aux Etats Unis, *Association Medicale Mondiale*, March 24, 1969, p. 9.
92. See Dodge, N. T., Women in the professions, in: Atkinson et al., 1978, op. cit., p. 214.
93. In the United Kingdom in 1979, 2 per cent of the Institute of Directors were women.
94. Holt, A., *Women in the Soviet Union: Recent change, present policies and their implications*. Paper presented at Women in Eastern Europe Conference, Birmingham, October 1976.
95. See Heitlinger, 1979, op. cit., p. 156.
96. For a history of education in Poland see Mrozowska, K., 1971, Entry 243; and Tatara-Hoszowska, 1970, Entry 244.
97. Vasil'eva, E. K., *The young people of Leningrad: School and work options and attitudes*, White Plains, New York, 1976.
98. See Dobson, R., Social status and inequality of access to higher education in the Soviet Union, in: Karabel, J. and Halsey, A. H., *Power and Ideology in Education*, New York, Oxford University Press, 1977, p. 254–275.
99. Ikonnikova, S. N., Molodezh': Sotsiologischeskii i sotsial' no-psikhologischeskii analiz (Youth: a sociological and social psychological analysis), Leningrad, 1974.
100. Kadlekova, Z., Zena soucasnosti, *Sociàlni politika*, No. 2, March 1974.
101. Heitlinger, 1979, op. cit., Chapter 9, gives a detailed discussion of housework in the Soviet Union.
102. See Jurkiewicz, N. G., *Soviet family functions and stability questions*, 1970 (Entry 234); Lobodzinska, B., *Family and professional women's roles in the World*, 1972 (Entry 236) and Yankova, Z. A. (ed.), *Problems of sociological studies on the family*, 1976 (Entry 240).
103. Dunn, E., Russian rural women, in: Atkinson, D. et al., 1978, op. cit., pp. 167–188.
104. See pp. 180–181 for a list of crucial international meetings in Latin America and publications which have emerged from them.
105. See also Leon de Leal, M., Personas interesadas en la problematica Femenina, *Latin American Research Review*, Vol. 14, No. 1, 1979, p. 134–144. Most work on women undertaken in Argentina, Brazil, Colombia and Mexico. See also two bibliographies by Knaster, M., 1975, and

1977 (Entry 266) the first for North American scholarship on Latin American women, and the second for more extensive coverage.

106. Navarro, M., Research on Latin American women, *Signs: Journal of women in Culture and Society*, Vol. 5, No. 1, 1979, pp. 111–120. This article has proved a useful source of support for some of the arguments presented here.

107. Boserup, E., 1970, op. cit.

108. First published in Spanish in 1969, English version: Cardoso, F. H. and Faletto, E., *Dependency and development in Latin America* (translation M. Mattingley Urquidi), Berkeley University of California Press, 1979. The major criticisms of the type of developmental theory which had been used to analyse economic processes in the Latin American countries prior to the advent of the 'depencia' was that concepts such as labour force, informal and formal labour market, even occupation, have been defined on the basis of an advanced capitalist mode of production and are therefore inappropriate for the analysis of the complexity of the Latin American peripheral economies, with their own historical developmental processes.

109. In general, social research in Latin America has paid special attention to the labour force and to fertility patterns, as a result of the pressures of an increasing population and the consequent need for more health and educational provision, but less attention to education and migration. This work may not be particularly focused on women, but does provide information on them. See Barbieri, T., *La recherche sur la femme en Amerique Latine: bilan et perspectives*, Paris, Unesco, 1980.

110. See Jelin, E., The Bahania in the labour force, and Migration and Labor Force Participation in Latin American women: The domestic servants in the city, in: Wellesley Editorial Committee (eds.), *Women and national development: The complexities of change*, Chicago, University of Chicago Press 1977; and La mujer y el mercado de trabajo urbano, CEDES, *Estudios CEDES*, Vol. 1, No. 6, 1978 (Entry 276).

111. Youssef, N. H. and Hartley, S. F., 1979, op. cit.

112. See Franco, R., Llona, A. and Arriagada, I., Women in a situation of extreme poverty, 1978, Entry 286; and Rodrigues, J. M., The working woman: a study of female textile workers, 1979, Entry 294.

113. See Recchini de Lattes, Z. and Wainerman, C. H., Female employment and economic development: some evidence, 1977, Entry 280, for a review of work based on the U curve approach, and a critique.

114. See Tinker, I., The adverse impact of development on women, in: Tinker, I. and Bramsen, M. B., *Women and world development*, Washington, D.C., Overseas Development Council, 1976. See also for example in Latin America, Rubbo, A., The spread of capitalism in rural Colombia: Effects on poor women, in: Reiter, R. (ed.), *Towards an anthropology of women*, 1975, Entry 375; and Lisansky, J., Women in the Brazilian Frontier, 1979, Entry 325.

115. Safa, H. I., Class consciousness among working class women in Latin America, Puerto Rico, 1976 (Entry 306).

116. Ribeiro, L. and Barbieri, T., de La mujer Obrera Chilena: una aproximacion a su estudia, 1978 (Entry 293).

117. See Entries 334 to 337.

118. Lomnitz, L. and Lizaur, M. P., Kinship structure and the role of women in the upper class of Mexico, 1979, Entry 329.

119. Lira, L., Sociological and demographic aspects of the family in Chile, 1978, Entry 349.

120. Youssef, N. H. and Hartley, S. F., 1979, op. cit.

121. Orrego de Figueroa, T., A critical analysis of Latin American programs to integrate women in development, in: Tinker, I. and Bramsen, M. B., 1976, op. cit.

122. El Salvador, Guatemala, Honduras, Mexico, Bolivia, Peru, and Venezuela.

123. See for example Silva, J. A., Participation of women in the labour force, 1976, Entry 297; Angulo, A. and de Rodriguez, C. L., Female participation in economic activity in Colombia, 1978, Entry 308; and Elizaga, J. C., Participation of women in the labour force in Latin America: Fertility and other determinants, 1977, Entry 302.

124. See Entry 271, see also Entry 292.

125. See Entry 343. This book includes an annotated bibliography on the family.

126. Arizpe, L., Female participation in agriculture and the selectivity of migrants, 1979, Entry 341.

127. See Young, K., Modes of appropriation and the sexual division of labour: a case study from Oaxaca, Mexico, 1978, Entry 326.

128. Adams, C. T. and Winston, K. T., *Mothers at work: Public policies in the US, Sweden and China*, 1980 (Entry 386), argue that in Sweden despite 'the high visibility of women's issues in the media and in public debate, a women's liberation movement as such is barely visible' (p. 135) and suggest that the explanation is that Swedish feminism is embedded in virtually all the country's major social, political and economic organizations. The current women's movement in Greece emerged

only after 1974 and the fall of the junta. (Engberg, S., Women's liberation movements in Greece, 1980 Entry 538. See also Moskou-Sakorafou, S., The feminist movement in Greece, *History* (Athens), No. 30, 1970, p. 48.) Sinkkonen, S. and Haavio-Mannila, E., The impact of the women's movement and legislative activity of women MPs on social development, in: Rendel, M., 1981 (Entry 403), argue that there have been three waves of feminism in Finland, the first starting in 1884, the second in 1966 with the goal of changing the gender-based functional division of labour in society by equalizing sex roles, and the third in the mid-1970s, when the ideas of radical and marxist feminists reached Finland.

129. See OECD, *Equal Opportunities for women*, Paris, 1979.

130. Boals, K., Political science, *Signs* (1), 1975, p. 161.

131. Daniels, A. K., *A survey of research concerns on women*, Association of American Colleges, 1975, p. 5.

132. Hafkin, N. and Bay, E. G., 1976, Entry 5.

133. Oakley, A., *The sociology of housework*, London, Martin Robinson, 1974, Chapter 1.

134. Blaxall, M. and Reagan B. (eds.), *Women and the Workplace*, Chicago, University of Chicago Press, 1976; Manley, P. and Sawbridge, D., Women at Work, *Lloyds Bank Review*, January 1980, p. 29–40 (Entries 481 and 383).

135. Molyneux, M., Beyond the domestic labour debate, *New Left Review*, 1979, Entry 435.

136. Chodorow, N., *The reproduction of mothering: psychoanalysis and the sociology of Gender*, Berkeley, University of California Press, 1978.

137. Wilson, E., *Women and the Welfare State*, 1977, London, Tavistock Publications; Lipman-Blumen, J., Bernard, J., 1979, Entry 391.

138. Byrne, E., *Women and Education*, Tavistock Publications, London, 1978; Deem, R. (ed.), *Schooling for women's work*, 1980, Entry 440; Lobban, G., The influences of the school on sex-role stereotyping, in: Chetwynd, J., and Hartnett, O. (eds.), *The sex role system*, Routledge and Kegan Paul, London, 1978; Albjerg Graham, P., Expansion and exclusion: A history of women in American higher education, *Signs*, No. 3, 1978, p. 759–773; Deble, I., *The school education of girls: An international comparative study on school wastage among boys and girls at the first and second levels of education*, Paris, Unesco, 1980; and Stanworth, M., *Gender and schooling: A study of sexual divisions in the classroom*, London, WRRC 1981, Explorations in Feminism No. 7.

139. Stimpson, C. R. and Person, E. S. (eds.), *Women: Sex and sexuality*, 1980, Entry 520.

140. MacKinnon, C. A., *Sexual harassment of working women*, 1978, Entry 514.

141. Kemmer, E. J., *Rape and Rape related issues: An annotated bibliography*, New York, Garland Publishing, 1977, 190 pp.

142. Chetwynd, J. and Hartnett, O., 1978, op. cit.; Broverman, I. K. et al., Sex role stereotypes: a current appraisal, *Journal of Social Issues*, Vol. 28, No. 2, 1972, pp. 59–78.

143. Friedman, L., *Sex role stereotyping in the mass media: An annotated bibliography*, New York, Garland Publishing, 1977, 350 pp.

144. Mossuz-Lavau, J., *Les femmes francaises en 1978: Insertion sociale, insertion politique*, Paris, Rapport pour le Cordes 1980; Evans, J., Women and politics: A re-appraisal, *Political Studies*, Vol. 23, No. 2, 1980, p. 210–221.

145. In the following discussion illustrative references are largely drawn from the American and British literature, but could be matched with material from other Western European countries.

146. Introduction in O'Brien, M., *The politics of reproduction*, 1981, Entry 371.

147. Millett, K., *Sexual politics*, New York, Doubleday, 1970. Burniston, S., Mort, F., Weedon, C., Psychoanalysis and the cultural acquisition of sexuality and subjectivity, in: Centre for Contemporary Cultural Studies, *Women take issue*, London, Hutchinson, 1978.

148. Mitchell, J., *Psychoanalysis and feminism*, London, Allen Lane, 1974.

149. See also Chodorow, 1978, op. cit., for another psychoanalytically based conceptualization, with a strong socially constituted element in the explanation. The journal m/f (*sic*) (London) is a forum for feminist work arguing for the compatibility of psychoanalysis and materialism, and contains general theoretical discussions of capitalism and patriarchal psychic structures, studies on the application of psychoanalysis to cultural analysis and reworking of Freud's cases.

150. See Barrett, M., *Women's oppression today: Problems in marxist feminist analysis*, London, Verso, 1980, 269 pp., for a lucid and illuminating discussion and review of socialist feminist theories and analyses of women's subordination and oppression, tested against the evidence of women's situation in advanced capitalism typified by contemporary Britain.

151. Beechey, V., On patriarchy, *Feminist Review*, No. 3, 1979, p. 66–82; Hartmann, H., Capitalism, patriarchy and job segregation by sex, in: Eisenstein, Z. R. (ed.), *Capitalist patriarchy and the case for socialist feminism*, 1979, Entry 469.

152. In this connection see also Meillassoux, C., *Femmes, Greniers et Capitaux*, Paris, Maspero, 1975; Rubin, G., The traffic in women: notes on the 'political economy' of sex, in: Reiter, R. (ed.), op. cit., 1975, Entry 375; Edholm, F. et al., 1977, Entry 364; Mackintosh, M., Reproduction and

patriarchy: A critique of Claude Meillassoux *Femmes, greniers et capitaux*, *Capital and Class*, No. 2, 1977, p. 119–127; McDonough, R. and Harrison, R., Patriarchy and relations of production, in: Kuhn, A. and Wolpe, A. M. (eds.), *Feminism and Materialism*, 1978, Entry 411.

153. McDonough and Harrison, 1978, op. cit.

154. Eisenstein, Z. R., 1979, Entry 469.

155. Beechey, V., 1979, op. cit., p. 77.

156. Beechey, V., Some notes on female wage labour in capitalist production, *Capital and Class*, No. 3, 1977, p. 45–66; and Women and production: a critical analysis of some sociological theories of women's work, in: Kuhn, A. and Wolpe, A. M., *Feminism and Materialism*, 1978, Entry 411.

157. Bland, L., Brunsdon, C., Hobson, D. and Winship, J., Women 'inside and outside' the relations of production, in: Women's Study Group, Centre for Contemporary Cultural Studies, *Women take issue*, Hutchinson, London, 1978, provide an elaboration of the argument that women are a reserve army of labour and Breugel, I., Women as a reserve army of labour: a note on recent British experience, 1979, Entry 423, and Ferber, M. A. and Lowry, H. M., Women: the new reserve army of the unemployed, in: Blaxall, M. and Reagan, B. (eds.), 1976, op. cit. provide supportive data for the argument in the United Kingdom and the United States, respectively.

158. As mentioned briefly above, p. 1.

159. Harrison, J., The political economy of housework, *Bulletin of the Conference of Socialist Economists*, No. 4, 1973, pp. 35–51; Coulson, M., Magas, B. Wainwright, H. The housewife and her labour under capitalism – a critique, *New Left Review*, 89, 1975, pp. 59–71; Smith, P., Domestic labour and Marx's theory of value, in: Kuhn, A. and Wolpe, A. M., 1978, Entry 411.

160. Dalla Costa, M. and James, S., *The power of women and the subversion of the community*, Bristol, Falling Wall Press, 1972. Seccombe, W., The housewife and her labour under capitalism, *New Left Review*, 83, 1974, p. 3–24; Middleton, C., Sexual inequality and stratification theory, in: Parkin, F. (ed.), *The social analysis of class structure*, London, Tavistock Publications, 1974.

161. See footnote 3, above, for references.

162. Millett, K., 1970, op. cit.

163. Firestone, S., *The dialectic of sex: the case of feminist revolution*, New York, Morrow, 1970.

164. Rendel, M., *Report on programmes of research and of teaching related to women.* Paper presented to World Conference for United Nations Decade for Women, Copenhagen, 1980; Paris, Unesco, 1980.

165. Schöp-Schilling, H. B., Women's studies, women's research and women's research centres: Recent developments in the USA and Federal Republic of Germany, *Women's Studies International Quarterly*, Vol. 12, No. 1, 1979, p. 103–116. See also *Women's Studies*, No. 2, 1974, and *Women: A journal of liberation*, Spring 1975, for a sense of the debate on androgyny.

166. Stoddart, J., Feminism in Paris, *Canadian Newsletter of Research on Women* (Toronto), Vol. VII, No. 1, 1978, p. 62–67.

167. Huisman, J., Women's studies in the Netherlands, *Higher Education and Research in the Netherlands*, Vol. 22, Nos. 3/4, 1978, p. 3–14.

168. Wistrand, B., *Swedish women on the move*, Stockholm, The Swedish Institute, 1981, 112 pp.

169. Ministry of Social Affairs and Employment, *The Netherlands: Women in the labour market*, Amsterdam, February 1979.

170. Manley, P. and Sawbridge, D., 1980, op. cit., Entry 383.

171. Hamill, L., *Wives as sole and joint breadwinners*, London, Government Economic Service Working Paper, No. 13, Nov. 1978. Hamill found that, in 1974, for 4 per cent of families, the wife's earnings prevented the family falling below Supplementary Benefit level – a measure of absolute poverty. See also Land, H., Women: supporters or supported, in: Barker, D. L. and Allen, S., *Sexual Divisions and society: Process and change*, 1976, Entry 407.

172. See Sloane, P. J. and Chiplin, B., *Women and low pay*, London, Macmillan, 1980. For the other end of the scale, Epstein, C. F. and Coser, R. L. (eds.), *Access to power: Cross national studies of women and elites*, 1981, Entry 400, provide a collection of studies of women and their access to elite, decision-making careers in public and economic sectors, and in the professions in the United States, United Kingdom, France, Federal Republic of Germany, Austria, Norway, Finland, Yugoslavia and Poland. See also Fogarty, M., Allen, I. and Walter, P., *Women in top jobs, 1968–1979*, London, Heinemann Educational Books, 1981. See Barron, R. D. and Norris, G. M., Sexual divisions and the dual labour market, in: Barker, D. L. and Allen, S. (eds.), *Dependence and exploitation in work and marriage*, 1976, Entry 407, for a discussion of the dual labour market and Beechey, V., in Kuhn, A. and Wolpe, A. M., Entry 411, and op. cit. for a critique of this approach. Amsden, A., *The economics of women and work*, 1980, Entry 406, contains readings by economists on job segregation by sex and women's lower pay.

173. OECD, The 1974–1975 recession and the employment of women, 1976, Entry 385. Also in Amsden, A., ibid. See also Neimi, B., Geographic immobility and labour force mobility: A study of female labour force unemployment, in: Lloyd, C. (ed.), *Sex discrimination and the division of labour*,

New York, Columbia University Press, 1975, p. 86, for data showing that in the United States women have higher rates of unemployment than men, and that the situation has worsened over time.

174. *Step by Step*, 1979, Entry 540.

175. See for example Boston, S., *Women workers and the Trade Unions,* 1980, Entry 422; Kyle, G. *Gastarbeterska i manssamhallet, studier om industriarbetande kvinnors villkor i sverige*, 1979, Entry 558; and Hartmann, H., in: Eisenstein, Z. R., 1979, Entry 469.

176. In Switzerland, however, girls constitute only 38 per cent of the upper classes of secondary schools (*Modern Switzerland*, Palo Alto, The Society for Promotion of Science and Scholarship, 1978, p. 362). In Austria, twice as many males as females finish some type of secondary school. (*The Status of women in Austria*, Austrian Federal Ministry of Social Affairs, Vienna, 1976.)

177. Byrne, E., 1978, op. cit., p. 20.

178. See for example for the United States Pottker, J. and Fishel, A. (eds.), *Sex bias in the schools: The research evidence*, Cranbury N.J., Fairleigh Dickinson University Press 1976.

179. *Step by Step*, 1979, op. cit. (Entry 540).

180. MacDonald, M., Socio-cultural reproduction and women's education, in: Deem, R. *Schooling for women's work*, 1980, Entry 440, p. 13. See also Delamont, S., *Sex roles and the school*, London, Methuen, 1980; David, M. E., *The state the family and education*, 1980, Entry 431; and Wolpe, A. M., *Some processes in Sexist education*, London, Women's Research and Resources Centre Publications (WRRC), 1977 (Explorations in Feminism No. 1).

181. See for example for France, Bisseret, N., *Education, class language and ideology*, London, Routledge and Kegan Paul, 1979, p. 34 and for the United Kingdom, Byrne, E., op. cit., Chapter 6.

182. See for United Kingdom for example the NUT/EOC Report *Promotion and the woman teacher*, 1980, Entry 443.

183. See Kamerman, S. B. and Kahn, A. J. (eds.), *Family policy: Government and families in fourteen countries*, 1978, Entry 389; David, M., op. cit. (Entry 431); Lipman-Blumen, J. and Bernard, J., op. cit., 1979, Entry 391.

184. David, M., 1980, op. cit. Entry 431.

185. Wilson, E., *Women and the Welfare State*, 1977, Entry 438.

186. Trade union demands for 'a family wage' echo this conceptualization of women. See Campbell, B., United we fall, *Red Rag* (London), September 1980, p. 18–22. See Land, H. (a), Social security: A system for maintaining women's dependence on men, British Association, Sociology Section N, August 1975; (b) Women: supporters or supported, op. cit. (Entry 407) and (c) Who cares for the family?, in: Dale, R., Esland, G., Fergusson, R. and MacDonald M., op. cit. (footnote 3); for (a) social policies reinforcing women's dependence, (b) data on women's actual role in supporting their families, and (c) implicit assumptions in social policy about the sexual division of labour and women's caring role in the family.

187. Beveridge, Sir W., *Social insurance and allied services*, London, HMSO, 1942, reprinted in 1974.

188. See Baude, A., Public policy and changing family patterns in Sweden 1930–1977, in Lipman-Blumen, J. and Bernard, J., op. cit., and Holter, H. and Ve Henriksen, H., Social policy and the family in Norway, in the same volume.

189. See for example, *Step by Step*, 1979, op. cit., Entry 540; Liljeström, R., Roles in Transition, 1978, Entry 559.

Research on the Status of Women, Development and Population Trends in Africa:
An Annotated Bibliography
by Mere Kisekka

Research on the Status of Women, Development and Population Trends in Africa: An Annotated Bibliography by Mere Kisekka

A. INTRODUCTION

Research in Africa and on Africans has historically been undertaken by non-Africans, and this is also true of research on African women. The growing amount of material on women and development, specifically in Africa, is largely contributed by scholars from outside the continent.[1] In recent years, however, there have been major advances and shifts in studies on the status of women carried out by African women social scientists. A small but significant volume of studies on women in Africa have focused on substantive criticism of the dominant methodologies currently in use.[2] The topics covered in such research are inclined to be action orientated and are predominantly concerned with: women's employment in private and public sectors; their self-employment as traders; or their educational opportunities and legal rights. As in the case in Latin America, international conferences, particularly since International Women's Year, have provided the impetus for questioning existing research on women in the Third World, clarifying objectives for future directions in research, and encouraging support and acceptance for such research within Third World countries. The Association of African Women for Research and Development, founded in 1977, with the aim of reducing the isolation of African women researchers and providing opportunities for collaboration and mutual support, is an example of one product of such efforts.

The current bibliography is a brief and selective collection of works from all of the above sources and falls into six major categories, with subdivisions according to the focus of interest in the studies included. These categories are:

I General, including bibliographies and a study on politics;
II Women's work and labour force participation, including studies on women and development and on individual countries;
III Family and household, including general studies, rural studies, and those on women family heads;
IV Education;
V Demographic features.
VI Other

NOTES

1. Saulniers, S. and Rakowski, C., *Women in the Development Process: A Select Bibliography on Women in Sub-Saharan Africa and Latin America*, Austin, University of Texas, 1977.

2. Tadesse, Z., *Research Trends on Women in Sub-Sahara Africa*, Paris, Unesco (SS-80/CONF. 626/1) (Entry 10).

B. THE BIBLIOGRAPHY ON AFRICA

I. General

BIBLIOGRAPHY

1. Hafkin, N. J. (Compiler). *Women and Development in Africa: An Annotated Bibliography*. Addis Ababa, UNECA African Training and Research Centre for Women, 1977. 177 p. (Bibliographic Series No. 1.)

An extensive guide to materials on the topic produced or held in the documents section of the African Training and Research Centre for Women. Includes population studies and women in rural development. Entries are annotated in English.

POLITICS

2. Allen, J. V. Political and Apolitical Styles of Modern African Women. In: Jaquette, J. S. (ed.). *Women in Politics*. New York, Wiley and Sons, 1974.

The central argument in the paper is that, whereas in traditional society African women exercised some autonomy in farming or trading and also power in a dual sex political system, modern urban social and economic life have eroded their position. The battle between the sexes which existed in secret societies, has now been intensified by the centralized political institutions, sex-biased educational system, the marginalization of women's agricultural roles and their increased work load. Allen examines three categories of African women to highlight their potential for radicalization and mobilization and confrontation with men. The first category consists of *femmes libres* who are in fact not free. These are migrants to cities trapped in the informal sector as traders and prostitutes. The public stigmatizes them as exploiters and pleasure seekers and perpetuates the myth that they are free and independent. Unless organized in some form of collective action, they cannot challenge the exploitative male *status quo*. The *memsahib* group consists of a small cadre of westernized and educated women. Their associations reflect cultural activities of the West, welfare services to children's institutions, fashion, jewellery and entertainment. The newly burgeoning urban women's groups, who are speaking on a platform of women's rights, are emphasizing demands for greater access to all levels of education, to jobs and political office, and reform in marriage and property laws, which will not immediately benefit the more than 80 per cent of rural, illiterate women. The last category consists of women *militantes*. These women have been influenced by their countries' challenge to western-controlled development and commitment to women's emancipation. In Guinea for example, Sekou Toure's ruling party is said to have made progressive marriage and divorce laws and required a certain proportion of female representation at local, sectional, regional and national levels. Women party members have then been able to challenge traditions that restrict women. In Tanzania, the government has provided a conducive atmosphere for women's rights by reducing the aggrandizement of the elite and polarization of the urban/rural and elite/peasantry dichotomies. These progressive measures, as seen in *Ujamaa* and reform in marriage, divorce and inheritance, are, however, usually sabotaged by male political and social dominance. From these examples the author concludes that women's status can only be raised by the conscious organized efforts of women and of male leadership in nationalist parties, movements, and liberation wars.

OTHER

3. Axinn, G. N. and Axinn, N. W. An African Village in Transition: Research into Behavior Patterns. *Journal of Modern African Studies*, Vol. 7, No. 3, 1969, p. 527–537.

   The research focused on hourly, daily and yearly behaviour patterns of rural people living in Nsukka division during 1966. Sex differences in involvement in agricultural activities, recreation such as sleeping, drinking and listening to the radio and the seasonal variations in these activities are detailed. In one location, men tend to rest or sleep for two or more half hours per day more than women, while in all of the villages, women devote more time to eating and drinking than men. Women also spend less time reading or listening to the radio than men. As far as work was concerned, for the total year, men averaged 7.87 half hours per day, whereas women averaged 10.09 half hours of work per day. Age differences in these activities are also shown in relation to each sex.

4. Chinnery-Hesse, M. Women and Decision Making – Some Comments on the Theme with Special Reference to the Ghanaian Situation. *Labour and Society*, Vol. 1, No. 2, 1976, p. 33–36.

   The author discusses the division of labour based on sex, which emerged historically from the conditions of everyday life. The conditions which gave rise to this division no longer exist, but the sex roles persist. In Ghana, tasks, traditionally done by women, include tilling the ground and the transportation of farm produce as headloads – the rigidity of this division of labour is further buttressed by taboos, which discourage change.

5. Hafkin, N. J. and Bay, E. G. *Women in Africa: Studies in Social and Economic Change*. Stanford, Stanford University Press, 1976. 306 p.

   A selection of readings focusing on women and change in Africa in two senses: (1) the women are discussed from a new viewpoint, as actors not objects, in contrast to the methodologically and ideologically problematic approaches resulting from male perspectives in studies on African women. (These studies may have been undertaken by male or female scholars, but viewed women only in terms of their relationships to men.) (2) From this new perspective, women are seen as agents of change within African societies. The papers include 'The Dual Sex Political System in Operation: Igbo Women and Community Politics in Midwestern Nigeria' by K. Okonjo; 'Aba Riots or Igbo Women's War: Ideology, Stratification and the Invisibility of Women' by J. Van Allen; 'Luo Women and Economic Change During the Colonial Period' by M. J. Hay, looking at the problems of women in the rural areas of Western

Kenya due to changes imposed by the colonial economy; 'Ga Women and Socio-economic Change in Accra, Ghana' by C. Robertson, looking at the changing socio-economic status of a non-elite group of women during this century 'The Limitations of Group Action amongst Entrepreneurs: The Market Women of Abidjan, Ivory Coast' by B. C. Lewis; 'Rebels or Status-Seekers? Women as Spirit Mediums in East Africa' by I. Berger, which indicates that regardless of religions or social structure, a small number of women everywhere emerged in institutionalized positions of religious leadership, but this rise above customary status for a few individuals did not challenge the dominant ideology or structure of subordination with respect to women in general; 'From Lelemama to Lobbying: Women's Associations in Mombassa, Kenya' by M. Strobel; 'Protestant Women's Associations in Freetown, Sierra Leone' by F. Chioma Steady; 'Women and Economic Change in Africa' by L. Mullins, which looks at some of the effects of class stratification accelerated by colonialism on the status of women in African Societies using a materialist perspective; 'Less than Second Class Citizens: Women in Rural Settlement Schemes in Tanzania' by J. L. Brain, arguing that women were far worse off on the settlement schemes than in their traditional societies.

6. Oppong, C., Okali, C. and Houghton, B. Women and Power: Retrograde Steps in Ghana. *The African Studies Review*, Vol. 18, No. 3, Dec. 1975, p. 71–84.

   The paper looks at women's position in agriculture, particularly cocoa production, and their access to land and labour, where they are disadvantaged compared with their male counterparts. The effects of spatial mobility on women's resources and domestic position are also considered (1) in their roles as farmers, contrasting two cocoa communities; and (2) women as mobile professionals and as the wives of mobile professionals. A striking contrast is found between women in the first migrant cocoa community who are relatively independent of their husbands, and women in the other groups, who find themselves to a greater or lesser degree depending on their husbands for the continuity of their present way of life. The authors conclude that if current patterns of restricted access to higher education and farm land continue for women and migration away from kin becomes more widespread, women will find themselves increasingly at a disadvantage in situations in which resources mean influence and opportunity.

7. Peil, M. Female Roles in West African Towns. In: Goody, J. (ed.) *Changing Social Structure in Ghana*. London, IAT, 1975.

   Basing her paper on literature on West African urban life, various national censuses and sample censuses and interviews collected between 1968 and 1972 in two Ghanaian and four Nigerian cities (Kaduna, Lagos, Abeokuta and Aba), the author focuses on the interaction between economic and other roles in the lives of urban women. Detailed analyses and discussion are made of: economic opportunities and participation in the labour force; ethnographic background; social life, family and marriage relationships. The author concludes that 'participation in the labour force is a more important factor in a woman's marital life than in her social adjustment'. For example, the Ibo women who have recently become traders, are said to feel guilty about neglecting their husbands and children; this is not the case for Yoruba women, amongst whom the practice is traditional. Although urban women often demand and achieve higher status, this is not at the expense of their husbands' status and authority in the home. The women who prefer greater autonomy often divorce or contract polygynous marriages. Elite women tend to share their husbands' status rather than taking their status from their own achievements, and even though they prefer companionate marriages, they often find themselves in authoritarian ones. The author suggests that increased trading activity is more often the result than a cause of the loosening of the conjugal tie and hence associated with divorced or widowed women or women who are older or in polygynous marriages. The social life of most women urban residents is similar to that of rural women, except that there is increased free time because of urban amenities.

8. Perry. E. H. O. *The Influence of Environment in Medicine*. Report on the Annual Conference of the Physicians of Nigeria held at Ahmadu Bello University, Zaria, February 28–March 2, 1974.

   The symposium was addressed by speakers from various disciplines, including geography, human and veterinary medicines. Directly relevant to women were papers on the effects of drought on availability of crops, and outbreaks of gastro-intestinal infections, including cholera. The hazards of eating cassava, particularly its effects on the nervous system, vision and hearing were highlighted. Cardiac failure after childbirth was identified as another seasonal disease which has higher rates among Zaria women than those in other societies. This was linked to the mother's practice of eating *Kanwa* (potash) after childbirth and of lying on a heated mud bed for 40–120 days. The seasonal increase of cardiac failures during the hottest time of the year and at the beginning of the rainy season was traced to the increased ambient temperature associated with the practice of lying on hot mud beds.

9. Staudt, K. A. Rural Women Leaders: Late Colonial and Contemporary Contexts. *Rural Africana*, No. 3, Winter 1978–79, p. 5–22.

   The research for this paper was done in Idakho in Kakamega district in Western Kenya during the period December 1974 to June 1975. The author conducted over 50 interviews in order to reconstruct historically women's mobilization in colonial days. She also utilized archives and district files. Her main thesis is that solidarity among women in contemporary days is being undermined by class differentiation and creating loyalties apart from those of sex loyalty. During the late colonial years, women formed a multipurpose organization – *Umoja*. Through *Umoja*, women leaders were absorbed into the male council system – they had special lectures and distributed seeds. But with the marginalization of local chiefs that has followed national politics, *Umoja* lost its political influence; *Umoja* leaders, who lacked education, could no longer manage group activity with its increased complexity and monetization. Instead of the broadbased, structurally centralized community politics typified by *Umoja* and customary male elders, there are now formalized national structures, with women's groups linked to them. The majority of women are now organized in small-scale, mutual aid groups, saving money and exchanging labour. Staudt found that over 90 per cent of women in a sample of more than 200 households belonged to one or more of such groups. The wealthier women in the community have now assumed political leadership. These women are usually highly educated in comparison with the rest of the community. Many are teachers with regular salaries or enterprising traders and managers of sophisticated farm operations on large pieces of land. These women are found on school boards, various development committees, and county councils. They make electoral campaigns and solicit money or donations for women's centres and nurseries. While they are the sporadic political formalizers, the terms on which they integrate women into politics are criticized as being less congruent with women's activities than was true in the past.

10. Tadesse, Z. *Research trends on women in Sub-Saharan Africa*. Paper presented at the Meeting of Experts on Research and Teaching Related to Women: Evaluation and Prospects, Paris, Unesco, May 1980. (SS-80/Conf. 626/3.)

    A review and critique of research on women in Africa, noting that until 1970 most of this work was done by anthropologists concerned with kinship, marriage, inheritance and types of production. These studies were descriptive with little analytical focus, lacking in policy orientation, and androcentric. Research by non-Africans does not find its way back to Africa, and local research is largely action orientated. The author draws attention to the importance of work which points up the differential effects of development on men and women, and to the fact that the incorporation of women as subsistence labourers is inherent in the process of capital accumulation.

11. UNECA. *Origin and Growth of the African Training and Research Centre for women of ECA*. Addis Ababa, UNECA, September 1977. 60 p. (E/CN.14/ATRCW/77/BD 7.)

    The African Training and Research Centre for Women grew out of the expanding work of the Economic Commission for Africa Women's Programme, which was established in 1972, and was itself officially titled in 1975. The objectives are to assist and encourage member states of ECA to raise the living standards of families and communities especially in rural areas, through the improvement of skills and opportunities for women so that they can participate more effectively in the development of their country. They carry out relevant research, provide in-service training, organize the African women's development Task Force, and serve as an information and resource centre. This report lists selected publications of the Centre. See also Hafkin, N. J., 1977 (Entry 1).

II. Women's work and labour force participation

WOMEN AND DEVELOPMENT

12. Benson, S. and Duffield, M. Women's Work and Economic Change: The Hausa in Sudan and in Nigeria. *Institute of Development Studies Bulletin* (Lagos), Vol. 10, No. 9, 1979, p. 13–19.

    A presentation of comparative material on the changing nature of women's economic roles amongst Hausa residents in Gwagwara within the Kano metropolitan area and descendants of Hausa migrants residing in Maiurno in Sudan. In both cases, the author discusses the undermining of the female economy in such occupations as spinning and weaving by the colonial social order and peripheral capitalism. The women of Gwagwara, however, have successfully moved to new occupations such as embroidery of men's caps and sale of cooked food and snacks to the burgeoning urban population in Kano. In contrast, women in Maiurno are now becoming economically dependent on their husbands because of the greater expansion of capitalist relations of production in agriculture and commerce.

13. Michelwait, D. R., Riegelman, M. A. and Sweet, C. F. *Women in Rural Development: A Survey of the roles of Women in Ghana, Lesotho, Kenya, Nigeria, Bolivia, Paraguay and Peru*. Boulder, Westview Press in cooperation with Development Alternatives, 1976, 224 p.

    A composite report on the current and potential roles of Latin American and African rural women based on field research in seven countries. The survey presents preliminary conclusions concerning project research required if local level rural development efforts are to succeed in drawing on the skills and work patterns of women, as well as men, in mobilizing human and natural resources for progress. The findings and conclusions are based on field study of existing rural projects and a preliminary survey of constraints and opportunities for women in the economies of Ghana, Kenya, Lesotho, Nigeria, Bolivia, Paraguay and Peru. The research focused on rural women's active decision-making and participation in agricultural production, the usual source of discretionary income in rural areas. Some attention is also paid to traditional women's concerns such as family care, family planning and education of children – concerns which have previously been the main object of developers' efforts with respect to rural women.

14. Monsted, M. *Women's Groups in Rural Kenya and their role in Development.* Copenhagen, Center for Development Research, June 1978.

    The author analyses the role of women's groups pre- and post independence in Kenya. In the 1950s women worked in the *Ma endeleo ya Wanawake*, led by the wives of white settlers and colonial administrators. Women's groups were really important, however, in the period 1970–74, when the government implemented an integrated rural development plan and gave support and finance to them. By 1978, there were more than 5,000 women's groups and of these the majority were in home economics. Some districts, such as Kiambu and Muranga, are marked by exceptionally high mobilization and 30 to 40 per cent of the adult women join groups. But in most of the districts women's groups involve less than 10 per cent of women. The lowest mobilization rates were found in the pastoral dominated drylands and Moslem areas, where, in some cases, less than 1 per cent joined in groups – in all groups, the landless labourers, poorest families and single women are under-represented. Women's group activities overlap with those of *Harambee*, a mobilization movement of rural peasants to improve their own infrastructure, which gained momentum in 1967. Women are also reported to have contributed as much as 50 per cent in some of the Harambee projects involving raising money and providing communal labour for the building of schools, churches, bridges, and cattle dips. Monsted stresses the point that there is no competition between women's group activities and those of women in general, but that the church was strongly opposed to any mobilization of women, which was not based on church groups, and the government emphasized family planning, which women themselves did not see as a priority. The few women's activities that went beyond the narrow confines of handicrafts and home economics involved agricultural, water and health projects, and women were found to emphasize water access before any other planned projects, such as the building of maternity wards, buying land or raising poultry. Their agricultural activities included poultry projects, farming on rented land and working as hired labourers. Other economic ventures consisted of running shops, beer halls, restaurants, hotels and maize mills; these were, however, run by very few women's groups. Monsted commends the emphasis on self-reliance, mutual assistance and joint development projects, and sees this as important for income generation and as a basis for a formalized system through which to steer government extension service and grants. She advocates a move to more economic projects, and away from handicrafts, with their insurmountable marketing problems.

15. Palmer, I. New Official Ideas on Women and Development. *Institute for Development Studies*, Vol. 10, No. 3, 1979, p. 42–53.

A review of the implications for women of ILO country mission reports and urban studies and their recommendations. For African countries, Palmer based her review on the following ILO studies: (1) Employment, Income and Equality: A Strategy for Increasing Productive Employment in Kenya (1972); (2) Employment and Unemployment in Ethiopia (1973); (3) Employment in Africa, Some Critical Issues (1973); (4) Abidjan: Urban Development and Employment in the Ivory Coast (1976). The Kenya report showed that the proportion of females seeking work in Nairobi is higher than that for males in all age groups except the 20–24 age group. Palmer criticizes the ILO for not emphasizing that inadequate employment is largely the lot of women and for neglecting the category of unpaid family labour. A second criticism relates to the definition of the working poor as those earning less than 200 shillings a month, when there is no indication as to whether this is in fact the poverty line for an individual or a growing family. Such an analysis,

Palmer suggests, implies that turning inadequate employment into adequate employment for men is a substitute for finding jobs for women; but this cannot reduce the largely unrecorded unemployment of women. The optimism about the informal sector as a future source of growth and vitality and of a new strategy of development in the report was considered unacceptable, since an increase in size of the informal sector would result in greater crowding and more intensive under-employment, and the nature of women's work in the informal sector does not lead to any potential improvement in their situation. Palmer particularly recommends upgrading female households, since the report found that over half of the households headed by women appeared to have no visible income or less than the critical level of 200 shillings a month. On the question of migration Palmer points out that the ILO reports rightly discerned the sex differentials in motivation, whereas men migrate with the hope of improving their wages or productivity, for women migration represents a totally new mode of economic productivity, namely control over the returns from their labour, hence they are ready to move into the informal sector simply as a survival strategy. Women's motives for migration include economic motives and the desire to escape from rural patriarchy. Palmer outlines the ILO recommendations for overcoming rural unemployment: intensive production methods on small farms for both crops and livestock raising; better seeds and chemical inputs, but not necessarily mechanization. The later programmes do not improve women's status. The ILO should raise the question of land reforms in order to give land to women; and in their vision for new jobs coming out of rural diversification, the ILO should caution against the trend of such work being handed to men and instead urge remunerated work for women. The ILO recommendation of establishing employment exchanges is acclaimed as a first step in monitoring conditions of work, providing information about available jobs and comparative wages, and therefore a possible step in unionizing women. In discussing the ILO's Basic Needs Approach, Palmer advances the same criticism of lack of reference to equal inheritance rights, resource requirements of mother-headed families, redistribution of land and other forms of wealth. She stresses the point that there is a case for giving priority to changing women's present inadequate employment even at the cost of retaining some male unemployment. As for the New International Economic Order which aims at solving the growing dualism between poor and rich countries, Palmer argues that whether or not women will benefit depends on pricing, marketing and investment decisions internal to the national economies of the developing countries.

16. Standing, G. and Sheehan, G. Economic Activity of Women in Nigeria In: Standing, G. and Sheehan, G. (eds.). *Labour Force Participation in* On the basis of a five-month study in 1978, the author investigates the

A study carried out in 1973 and 1974 to find out whether women have been pushed out of the labour force by the formalization of economic activity. The survey consisted of 2,700 women aged 20 and over from four cultural-social environments in Lagos, Enugu, Ibadan and Zaria. Amongst the findings are: that the presence of children appears to increase participation in rural Nigeria; education had a strongly positive effect; and that Yoruba women and women not receiving financial support had higher participation rates. The authors concluded that there was little tendency for urbanization to lead to a marginalization of women, and that increasing levels of female education represent a major means by which high rates of female labour force participation would be maintained in the course of the urbanization of Nigeria.

17. Tinker, I. *New Technologies for food chain activities: the Imperative of Equity for Women.* Washington D.C., Women in Development Office, 1979.

The paper analyses biases in economic development theory which perpetuate the dichotomy between modern and traditional sectors, economic activities done for money and those done as volunteers or citizens, productive work and welfare activities. The biases also centre on stereotypes of appropriate roles for men and women and neglect the informal sector. Lastly, economic theory has completely ignored women's contributions to family survival as food producers and heads of households. Consequently technologies for agricultural production have been concentrated on cash crops and on selected basic grains. Domestic water supply is not perceived in monetary value and planners, wishing to show an increase in GNP encourage only projects for irrigation water. In the same way, government policies favour large industry through subsidies and taxes. Tinker enumerates a number of measures aimed at reducing women's labour and increasing productivity. These include the development of intermediate technology; improved methods of storage for grains and smoking fish; for water and energy, she advocates reforestation, solar water heating and solar sprayers; and for women in single owner-operator businesses, she suggests co-operative organizations, in order to improve investment return, make credit easier and allow intermediate modernization of their businesses.

INDIVIDUAL COUNTRIES

18. Akerele, O. *Women and the fishing industries in Liberia.* Addis Ababa, Economic Commission for Africa/African Training and Research Center for Women, 1979.

On the basis of a five-month study in 1978, the author investigates the importance of women's role in industrial fishing, measuring the degree of their integration and participation in the growth and development of the industry in comparison with their earnings. Artisanal fishing is done in canoes and dominated by Fanti from Ghana, three-quarters of whom are men and the rest women. These fisherwomen are said to make 100 per cent profit in their business of selling, smoking or drying fish, and to constitute the most financially successful of all the market women. But Liberian women feature in industrial fishing, which consists of buying the fish catch from fish companies. Akerele delineates three historical stages in the fishing industry: (1) starting in 1953 with the establishment of mechanized fishing, when everybody, consumers and suppliers alike, bought the fish directly at the gates of the company; (2) 1960–62, when a 'mammie' system was introduced and women traders bought the fish from the company and retailed it in the market; (3) when the fish company introduced refrigerated trucks and a depot system, the women were dropped as the company's agents, to be replaced by Lebanese merchants who became the wholesalers throughout Liberia, receiving a commission from the company ranging from between $50 and $75 per ton. Three out of the six fish depots investigated paid commission to the women 'fishmammies' averaging between $7 and $10. Akerele shows that whereas the fishmammies are effectively the real salesman, rather than the Lebanese agents, they make marginal earnings ranging from between $50 and $87 a month. She suggests several changes which would improve the situation for women: effective government-supported institutions such as entrepreneurial development units and credit facilities; head 'fishmammies' should be put on a basic monthly salary to assure them of some income and get them out of their perpetual 'debt trap'; 'fishmammies' should form co-operatives to insure easy accessibility to loans. Women are also involved in industrial fishing in production and processing, where they do semi-skilled work – at one shrimp export company 60 per cent of the workers were women. They are also employed as seasonal unskilled workers.

19. Bujra, M. J. Women Entrepreneurs of early Nairobi. *Canadian Journal of African Studies.* Vol. 9, No. 2, 1975, p. 212–234.

The paper is based on a study in Pumwani, Nairobi's oldest existing African location. It was conducted in 1971 on a sample of 100 per cent resident landlords. Out of 317 houses, 42 per cent were owned by women resident landlords. The majority of women landlords had been prostitutes and it is the purpose of the paper to retrace the history and function of prostitution within the colonial context. Among the factors given which contributed to the rise of prostitution in Nairobi, some were linked to the colonial urban employment structure and some to the marital problems of women in their villages of origin. There was a sex imbalance in Nairobi, since Asians had a monopoly of petty trading and jobs available in the service sector were given to men. Prostitution in Nairobi was not organized and so was not subject to exploitation by brothel owners or pimps. The majority of prostitutes were Kikuyu, but others came from other tribes. Since the earliest men settlers in Nairobi were coastal Moslems, the majority of prostitutes converted to Islam. Various reasons for this conversion are considered: economic motivation, in order to gain patronage amongst the richer and more successful men; Islam offered women a new social cohesion not based on rural or ethnic modes of life and prostitutes discarded their tribal names gaining security in the Islamic community, where personal crises such death and burial were taken care of by the community; Islam also offered a way of disentangling themselves from parental and kinship obligations, since they could marry any Moslem outside their tribe; finally, Islam was more tolerant of prostitution and illegitimacy than Christianity. Prostitutes used their money to build or buy houses and those who did not have children adopted some, whilst others resorted to 'women marriage' to provide themselves with heirs to inherit their property. Bujra concludes that prostitution enabled women to gain an unusual measure of economic equality with men and create a socially viable urban community composed of diverse ethnic elements.

20. Economic Commission for Africa/African Training and Research Center for Women. Women Textile workers in Ethiopia. *Research Series* 79/03, Addis Ababa, 1979.

The study was conducted in April 1979 and points out that in the traditional sector of the textile industry most handweavers and tailors are men; whereas in the modern sector in thirteen of the major establishments more than 50 per cent of textile workers are women. One hundred and seventy-two women were interviewed in two pre-co-operatives employing nine to twenty workers, in four privately-owned and five state-owned enterprises employing 100 to 350 workers. Fifty-nine per cent of the women were unmarried or separated, and 49 per cent had young children. It was found that there were discriminatory practices in employment and undesirable working conditions for women. Women were paid less than men for equal work, specifically hand-weaving; (the smallest salary differential was 10 per cent and the highest 40 per cent); women were placed in the lowest paying jobs which were more labour intensive and needed less skill – men operated the sewing machines while women did the sewing and finishing, and men used hand-weaving machines whilst women used primitive tools to do the spinning and bobbing of the yarn. Various other negative aspects of the work are discussed, such as transport problems, shift working and short breaks. There were no daycare facilities although most women with children expressed a willingness to pay 5 per cent of their salaries to have them established in residential settings. At least 90 per cent of the women belonged to labour unions and had positive attitudes towards them. The study points out a number of changes in attitudes and laws which have occurred since the 1974 socialist revolution. For example, whereas earlier studies had found that employers complained about female absenteeism and the obligation to pay maternity leave, this was not the case in the current study. In fact, in five of the state-owned and privately-owned factories the social benefits given exceeded those stipulated by the labour law. In an earlier study, it was found that 33 per cent of the husbands and 34 per cent of parents disapproved of women working outside the home. In this study the corresponding proportions of such disapproval were 6 per cent of husbands and 15 per cent of parents.

21. Gutto, S. B. O. *The status of Women in Kenya: a study of paternalism, inequality and underprivilege.* University of Nairobi, Institute for Development Studies, 1976. (Discussion Paper No. 235.)

This is an excellent study which covers legal, educational and occupational barriers as they pertain to women. Gutto studied the major constraints against female entrepreneurship and proprietary control. Basing the analysis on the two largest money-lending institutions in the country, the Housing Finance Company of Kenya (HFCK) and the

Industrial and Commercial Development Corporation (ICDC) Gutto was able to demonstrate the vicious circle of women's problems – their legal inferiority, lack of education and wage labour were the major stumbling blocks in their urban proprietary control. In ICDC, which specializes in loans to small-scale and industrial scale business undertakings, the female share of applicants and acceptors in 1974 amounted to only 3 to 5 per cent. In HFCK in the period from November 1965 to March 1976 out of a total 4,115 loan allocations, women, singly or in partnership with men or each other, obtained only 15 per cent while men similarly categorized secured 94 per cent. Gutto draws attention to company practices which allow men to exploit women's legal inferiority. For example, the company allows married couples to register their salaries singly or jointly in order to meet the required basic minimum salary. Because of this men 'persuade' their wives into such a merger, then registering themselves as sole owners. The registration of the property can only be cancelled if the wife withdraws her consent before the contract is finalized, otherwise, thereafter she cannot withdraw her consent or demand that she be made a co-owner. In addition, once a wife gives her consent she becomes a guarantor, so that if the husband defaults on repayment of the loan, the HFCK has the power to revert to her in order to recover it. A further paternalistic practice is the company's requirement that female applicants who are married and are legally cohabiting with their husbands must seek their husband's permission before being allocated any loans or mortgage facilities, this is the case even when a woman has the necessary deposit or does in fact earn above the minimum salary. Gutto also draws attention to other types of inequities for employed women, for example their being restricted from contributing to social security funds. It was not until January 1975 that women were allowed to contribute to the Provident Fund which provides age benefits at 60 years, invalidity and survivors' benefits, and the Widows and Young Children's Pensions Act is still restricted to men for the benefit of their widows and children. Married women can contribute only after passing through a rigorous selection procedure, which involves petition to the president. In addition, widows cannot enjoy the benefits of the Fund if they cohabit with a male. Such restrictions are in total disregard of the common socio-cultural situation – in fact men rarely support children from a former marriage and there are increasing numbers of unmarried working mothers who need such funds for the benefit of their children. Finally, Gutto proposes specific reforms – the repeal of obsolete laws whose continuation in their existing form is injurious to society, and the reactivation of enforcement machinery for anti-discriminative laws already encoded; the outright repeal of laws identified as affording differential treatment to the sexes on the pretext that they protect the 'weaker' sex whereas, as the study reveals, they give force of law to paternalistic machination designed to lower the status of women and train them for exploitation; the establishment of legal duties for males and females, sharing equally the responsibilities arising from joint actions such as producing illegitimate children; legislative intervention in areas where social practice shows inequality of treatment between the sexes, as in the fields of education, employment, wages and loans; and the provision of a simply understood and mobilized enforcement machinery, with strict provisions, backed by the coercive powers of the state.

22. Lewis, B. C. The limitations of group action among entrepreneurs; The market women of Abidjan, Ivory Coast. In: Hafkin, N.J. and Bay, E. G. (eds.) *Women in Africa*. Stanford, Stanford University Press, 1978.

In this study, Lewis discusses the associational goals and financial problems of market women, pointing out that women's indigenous credit associations aim at providing a regular and systematic means of accumulating capital and defending their interests in conflicts with administrative authorities. The organizations serve as 'insurance, credit, savings and loan' and typically involve 15 to 20 people. The rotating credit association, also called *esusu* or *susu*, involves a group of people who make regular contributions to a fund which becomes the property of each contributor in rotation. It is equivalent to compulsory saving, which involves no fee or extra cost, although the order in which members receive the funds is a source of unequal advantage. Lewis stresses that those earliest in the cycle of distribution receive, in effect, an interest-free loan that they repay over time. This is financed by those at the end of the cycle for whom the system works in a manner little better than storing their savings under a mattress. These temporary advantages and disadvantages in the order of receiving money are the major cause of dissatisfaction with this system and of members dropping out, although they still participate outside the market in credit associations structurally identical to those shunned in the market. The 'ambulatory banker' system on the other hand, requires each participant to make a daily deposit of a fixed amount of money which she receives at the month's end, minus one-thirtieth (the banker's fee). Despite the loss of a small sum, women are reported to prefer this rather impersonal system where other savers are not known. The risks involved surround the chance of a banker absconding with money, and this realization leads the traders to bank with several bankers in order to insulate themselves against loss of money. The bankers are invariably men. Lewis observes that the ambulatory banking system is advantageous to only a few prosperous women who habitually deal in hundreds of dollars worth of stock with property and other commercial assets, who can receive regular advances from the bankers due to their large savings, and have an effective working capital of thousands of dollars.

OTHER

23. Awosika, K. Women's education and participation in the labour force: the case of Nigeria. In: Rendel, M. (ed.) *Women, power and political systems*, London, Croom Helm, 1981, 262 p.

The author singles out education from amongst the range of socio-economic factors influencing women's behaviour, as a strong determinant of women's participation in the modern sector of the labour force in Nigeria. The usual definition of labour force participation and problems of measurement in a developing economy are examined, and adapted to the Nigerian situation. Providing statistical evidence for her argument, the author points out that 'there is a very evident tendency for women in modern economic activities to be disproportionately crowded onto the lower rungs of the employment ladder'. There is a shortage of people in the middle occupational levels in Nigeria, but the orientation of the educational system (towards university and academic education) means that many, and especially women, do not have sufficient qualifications to take up these jobs. The author considers that more public policy research into factors limiting women's effective participation in the modern sector of the economy must be undertaken, and urges that public policy should be directed toward ensuring not only that there is adequate educational provision for women, but toward creating incentives to enable women to participate in development effectively.

24. Hoskins, M. W. *Women in forestry for local community development*. Washington D.C., Women in Development Office, September 1979.

The writer begins by outlining the rationale of the new emphasis away from industrial plantations, reserve and parkland management to community forestry. This rests on a number of environmental changes and increasing population that have reduced thousands of acres of bush and forest lands to desert. The new approach as articulated by the Food and Agricultural Organization is said to apply to any tree or shrub planting and care at the farm level to provide cash crops, and small processing of forest products at the household, artisan or small industry level to generate income. Hoskins analyses the many ways in which women feature in community forestry: they are the visible collectors and transporters of firewood, the basic fuel in most countries – for lack of firewood some women experiment with alternative fuels such as local plant stalks, dung or charcoal. They are also led by this lack to abandon nutritious foods such as soybeans and millet in favour of fast cooking ones such as rice; women who raise small ruminants around their compounds need forage; women need leaves and nuts to use in cooking and for herbal medicines. Some local taboos exist with regard to women and forestry, and superstition can be a source of difficulty. The case of Kenyan women who could not raise bees because of a taboo against women climbing trees is cited. Hoskins is aware that forestry projects can be problematic, because of competition for land, but suggests that this can be overcome by planting trees along roads, around the field or on any unused or unproductive land. In addition, the advantages of trees for prevention of soil erosion and rehabilitation of the soil by adding nitrogen and acting as wind-breakers is stressed.

III. Family and household

25. Bukh, J. *The village woman in Ghana*. Uppsala, Scandinavian Institute of African Studies, Centre for Development Research Publications No. 1, 1979.

A case study in a village in Ghana (Tsito) which illustrates the position of women in a patriarchal society subjected to pressures from various directions. Changes in traditional agriculture, caused by the introduction of cocoa, resulted in greater pressure on land used for food production.

A general impoverishment of land resources and reduction of nutritional value in crops grown has resulted from overcropping and the destruction of the forest by charcoal burners. The traditional family system, where men controlled the movements of women, has broken down and women have achieved more economic and personal independence, but the demands on them to fulfil new responsibilities have limited their freedom of choice so that their situation is not much improved. Women are caught between their traditional responsibility for children and their lack of control over necessary economic resources such as land, labour and money. A new type of small women-headed households which have to cope with subsistence responsibilities under pauperized conditions has emerged in the village. The author considers that the situation in Ghana has deteriorated in the five years to 1978 (when the report was written) and there has been a social and economic crisis of a dimension not experienced in Ghana before. Women alone cannot solve this crisis, but they must organize in grass roots groups so that they are in a position to demand their rights when any restructuring and reorganizing of Ghanaian society takes place.

26. Church, K. *A study of socio-economic status and child care arrangements of women in Medina*. National Council of Women and Development, Ghana, 1977.

The report is based on a sample of 100 in Medina, a suburb of central Accra. Of the women interviewed 73 were residing with a husband. There was a high remarriage rate as 29 of the women currently married had been divorced at least once. Fifty-nine per cent of the children stayed with both their parents and 30 per cent did not stay with their mothers. Whereas the majority of the husbands (70 per cent) were in salaried employment, only 14 per cent of the wives were in the modern sector. Half of the women in the sample were traders, some home-based and others working away from home, and none of these had any childcare arrangements, although in all cases the researcher noted that the presence of children was a constant strain upon their economic activities. Many of these women were so poor that they had no access to assistance with household chores, and even if daycare centres were provided, they could not afford to pay an economic rate. The few working mothers who expressed concern about childcare and domestic arrangements were amongst the educated and salaried groups, women who could afford housemaids and other domestic help. This group worried about the quality of childcare their children were receiving from the servants and complained about their own double career of home and work.

27. MacCormack, C. P. Control of land labor and capital in rural Southern Sierra Leone, and The compound head: structure and strategies. *Africana Research Bulletin*, Vol. 6, No. 4, 1976, p. 44.

These two papers are based on ten years of intermittent field work in the 1970s in six villages. The papers analyse the economic activities of Sherbro women and the implications of women-headed compounds in the larger social, economic and political context. In all of the 230 residential compounds investigated all adult women were economically active, contributing to farming, fish processing or trading. Women and men were not economically autonomous, but rather interdependent, in the whole productive process. In the fishing villages, men fished and wives bought the catch from them for smoke-drying and selling to middlemen/women or transported it to inland markets. Married couples kept separate accounts although they could co-operate in investments of mutual benefit and loans. In farming villages, the land is a corporate estate of cognatic descent groups and is farmed together by men and women for provision of the granary of their residential compound. Decisions to sell rice from the family granary for any reason are reached after consultations between husbands and wives. In 51 per cent of households the key to the granary was kept by husbands and in 49 per cent by wives, in this study. Farming women also engage in other income-generating activities such as distilling salt, and marketing food and petty commodities. Men on their part grow cash crops with the help of their wives. In addition to commanding the basic means of production in farming, land and fishing, Sherbro women can enjoy political power and resources as heads of descent groups. In this position they control access to land, organize labour, receive tribute and make marriage alliances. In two of the five farming villages surveyed, the head of the dominant descent group was a woman. MacCormack also notes that female-headed compounds in the villages are a significant feature of Sherbro society: Out of the 230 compounds surveyed, the following proportions were headed by women; 16 per cent in the coastal fishing villages; 23 per cent in the farming villages and 59 per cent in the capital of Kagboro chiefdom. This matrifocality bears no relationship to poverty and degradation, but is correlated with high social status and prestige. A compound head is the eldest living resident man or woman of any marital status; the compound itself is a basic unit of production and consumption and usually consists of constituent nuclear families or other blood relatives and unrelated clients or wards. Of the twelve case studies of women heads, some were living with strangers, some were widows, some were unmarried mothers employed in modern jobs like teaching. Some were wives of polygamous men who were living with other wives in other villages. In this study co-wives were found to engage in complementary work and to reciprocate in furthering each other's business so that if one was involved in fishing the other traded in farming products. The study highlights some important effects of modernization and commercialization of land on a peasant society. In 1976, some men and women invested money and labour in a relatively heavily capitalized rice farming venture arranged by a local member of parliament. Their profits ranged from 103 to 386 per cent, thus creating a large social class difference in the village. In addition, the mechanization of labour compensated for male labour, while the vast additional acreage added increased labour for women in weeding, harvesting, threshing and milling the rice. The women's labour-saving machines were either not available or too expensive. In that case a husband and wife found it cheaper to invest in the payment of a brideprice (£25–£60) to acquire a co-wife to defray labour. Lastly, MacCormack observed that the phenomenal prices for rice prompted the urban elites to advocate national legislation to privatize all farming land so that they could buy descent land and thus make the majority of Sherbro men and women landless proletarians.

28. Monsted, M. The changing division of labor within rural families in Kenya. In: Caldwell, J. C. (ed.) *The persistence of high fertility: Population prospects in the world*, Canberra, Australia University Press, 1977.

The paper analyses the division of labour in rural Kenya as affected by developments occurring since colonial days. These are the creation of white settlers and landless labourers and the recruitment of Africans as soldiers in the World Wars. Kenya's high annual birth rate of 3 per cent, in conjunction with the commercialization of land, has led to population pressure on the land and consolidation of land into private properties. These two developments have resulted in the allocation of work in the household and agriculture from men to women and the usurpation of women's traditional work, now commercialized, by men. Women have become the primary 'reproducers of labour' in the biological and social sense. With the support of their children, women bear the major burden of socialization, supplying of food, daily necessities and school fees for the children. Monsted's evidence to support the arguments put forward comes from an examination of 299 case studies of households with resident and migrant husbands. The studies were done during 1975 in eight districts from Western Nyanza and Rift valley provinces. Among the peasant families, whose landplots were generally less than four acres, 20 to 60 per cent used hired labour for ploughing or during the peak agricultural season. Women farmed in both cash and subsistence crops and also supplemented their incomes in most seasons by trading crops, undertaking casual labour or brewing illegal beer or liquor. Men's contribution in agriculture is in the form of ploughing and farm inputs such as seeds and fertilizers. Their non-farm activities are as farm labourers, small shopkeepers or migrant labourers. Their household contribution is limited to a few peak seasons and activities like house building and fencing. The middle to rich peasant families own large scale farms of 30–100 acres bought from previous European farms in the districts of Kericho and Trans Nzoia. Unlike the situation in the peasant homes, the husbands here contribute singly to all the children's needs and give wives petty cash. The husbands are schoolkeepers, shopkeepers or do some other permanent skilled work and/or own enough land to generate a surplus from the farm. Their wives engage in trading, shop management or are given land for their use. But the landless labourers who work for these rich commercial farms have forgone many of the benefits which they had during colonial days, such as food and a right to use a plot of a quarter of an acre for subsistence cultivation. In the pastoral households, where livestock has been the dominant factor in farming, Monsted found that women have expanded their work beyond the area of tradition into processing milk products and growing vegetables on small plots of land. In addition, women now work in agriculture on the husbands' land. But the husband is still the sole provider for school fees, farm inputs, clothing and household necessities.

29. Okonjo, K. Rural women's credit system: A Nigerian example. *Studies in Family Planning*, Vol. 10, Nos 11/12, 1979, p. 326–331.

The article examines a rotating credit system used by rural women in Nigeria to ensure the availability of cash to meet their family's financial needs, which has parallels throughout the world. This detailed study of women's behaviour reveals women's roles in the family and the economic priorities created by these roles in rural areas, and is indispensable information for understanding how women affect and are affected by the development policies pursued. An understanding of the particular credit system and its value to the women who organize it provides information useful for the design of projects which can work and are valuable to the women involved in them.

IV. Education

30. Callaway, A. Nigeria's Indigenous Education: The apprentice system. *Odu*, No. 1 1964, p. 62–79; and *Training young people within Indigenous small-scale enterprises: The Nigerian example*. Paper delivered to UNESCO seminar on planning out of school education for development, December 1971.

In an area where the indigenous apprentice system is absorbing a large proportion of young people with or without formal primary schooling, girls are very poorly represented in the locally owned and managed small-scale enterprises. In an Ibadan survey of 250 apprentices, only fourteen were young women, all apprenticed as seamstresses. By far the greatest number of girl apprentices are attached on an informal basis to women traders. Some girls who have not been to school learn older crafts of dyeing or *adire* cloth making. A young woman who completes a sewing apprenticeship is presented with a sewing machine by her husband if she is married, or by her parents or relatives if she is not.

31. Economic Commission for Africa. *Women as clientele of non-formal education*. Paper presented to the Regional Symposium on Non-Formal Education for Rural Development, Addis Ababa, August/September 1978.

Six areas in which rural women must be trained are delineated. In animal husbandry, training should focus on the growth and maintenance of the right type of pastures, construction of animal houses, identification of diseases and proper processing and storage of milk and milk products. In commerce and trade, women need to be trained informally in book-keeping techniques of management and identification of market demands. In handicrafts and other small-scale industries there is need for quality control and diversification of products. In food and nutrition, food taboos which deprive women of sources of protein should be dropped, and proper methods of food preservation, storage and transportation are necessary to avoid food wastages and superficial scarcities. In medical facilities, the extension of maternal and child health services as well as training of traditional midwives are advocated. Lastly, women should acquire skills to participate effectively in self-help community activities.

V. Demographic features

32. Akinla, O. Social obstetrics. In: *The role of family planning in African development*. Proceedings of a seminar held at University College, Nairobi, December, 1967.

    The article considers the interdependent relationship between maternal and child health and gives maternal mortality rates in Nigeria in comparison with those of the United Kingdom, India, Sweden, Morocco and Colombia. Between 1960–65 the four conditions which took the greatest toll of maternal lives in Lagos were in this order: severe anaemia, eclampsia, ruptured uterus and post-partum haemorrhage. The author points to the provision of ante-natal care and the education of women to take advantage of it, as the most urgent need in obstetrics in Nigeria.

33. Anker, R. *Demographic change and the role of women: A research program in developing countries*. ILO Working paper No. 69, Geneva, 1978.

    The paper sets out to examine the causes and effects of changes in women's roles and statuses and their interaction with demographic variables. Anker asks whether rising survival rates of children have reduced women's economic activity, or increased their labour. Have they reduced women's investment in the human capital development of their children and increased delegation of childcare responsibilities to other family members? In the case of falling fertility, the research intends to find out whether this leads to more productive and intensive work or to increased leisure. With respect to the roles and status of women, the question raised is what types of work have an effect on fertility and fecundity. Higher female educational status may not have a negative effect on fertility due to surrogate childcare or near proximity of work place and home. In rural areas, rates of mortality and morbidity of children may be increased by women's greater agricultural labour in the peak seasons and the author suggests that family planning programmes should pay attention to birth-spacing, so that children are born during the slack season. Lastly, the author examines factors related to sex segregation in the urban labour market and its effect on female roles. Three models which rationalize sex segregation in the labour market are critically examined. The author argues that the human capital model, which relates pay differentials to differentials in worker's productivity is not convincing, since sex differentials in physical strength, labour turnover and absenteeism are generally assumed rather than correctly appraised, and where they exist they are attributable to women's household roles and lack of relevant education and training. Overcrowding and segmentation models which explain that women are restricted to certain jobs for cultural reasons or because they lack skills are realistic and the author recommends research to overcome such obstacles for women. Future study should focus on collecting information on factors related to sex which affect productivity, on legal discrimination against women in employment, pay and working conditions, and on job processes, promotion and hiring.

34. Arowolo, O. O. Fertility of urban Yoruba working women: A case study of Ibadan City. *The Nigeria Journal of Economic and Social Studies*, Vol. 19, No. 1, 1977, p. 37–66. And: Female Labour force participation and fertility: The case of Ibadan City in the Western State of Nigeria. In: Oppong, C. et al (eds) *Marriage, fertility and parenthood in West Africa*, Canberra, Australian University Press, 1978.

These are some of the reports from *The Changing African Family Project* conducted in Ibadan in 1973. The analysis seeks to identify the major variables in economic and social transformation that are pertinent to modification of traditional childbearing practices. The studies show that female employment status bears little relation to fertility, the paradox emerging when women who are unpaid family workers have a lower level of reproductive performance than those in jobs which are assumed to have more role conflict with the demands of motherhood. Arowolo suggests that it could be that women in predominantly illiterate societies in the process of transition evolve adequate mechanisms for adjusting the traditional beliefs in large families to the demands of urban employment, that is extended family help and hired househelpers. In the 1977 report, the author identified rural-urban background differences in the women studied, and it was then that the postulated negative association between active participation in the labour force and fertility was borne out among Ibadan-born women. Higher levels of education were associated with higher fertility among Ibadan women of rural origin while education, especially post primary schooling, appeared to reduce the fertility of Ibadan-born women.

35. Caffrey, K. T. Eclampsia in Kaduna 1969–1971. *The West African Medical Journal*, Vol. 23, No. 2, 1975, p. 62–64.

The paper presents information on cases of eclampsia seen at the Ahmadu Bello University Hospital in Kaduna over a three-year period. Out of total admissions of 20,694 there were 269 suffering from pre-eclampsia and 133 from eclampsia. The incidence of multiple pregnancy was 8 per cent among eclamptics compared with 2 per cent in all hospital deliveries. Eclampsia was seen as a major obstetric emergency responsible for nearly 11 per cent of maternal and 18 per cent of foetal deaths. Forty-one per cent of the eclamptic patients underwent operative delivery, in comparison with only 9 per cent of all deliveries at the hospital.

36. Caldwell, J. C. Marriage, the family and fertility in Sub-Saharan Africa with special reference to research programmes in Ghana and Nigeria. In: *Family and Marriage in some African and Asiatic countries*. Cairo, Cairo Demographic Centre, Research Monograph Series No. 6, 1976. p. 359–371.

The paper draws on research undertaken in Ghana in 1962–64 and in Nigeria from 1973 onwards as part of the Changing African Family Project. It looks at aspects of contemporary marriage suggesting that much of the traditional family and marriage survives; at monogamy and polygyny, age at first marriage, the relationship between the married state and exposure to conception, and the nature of the family and family economics.

37. Caldwell, J. C. The economic rationality of high fertility: An investigation illustrated with Nigerian survey data. In: Caldwell, J. C. (ed.) *The socio-economic explanation of high fertility*, Canberra, Australian National University Press, 1976. Also in *Population Studies*, Vol. 31, No. 1, 1977, p. 5–28.

    Caldwell argues that the values and practices of traditional society, such as communal access to land and extended reciprocal family obligations continue to uphold a large family size. It is the influx of new imported styles of living obtaining among the urban-urbanized group which will bring a decline in fertility rather than purely economic considerations of parents.

38. Caldwell, J. C. Education as a factor of mortality decline: An examination of Nigerian data. *Population Studies*, Vol. 33, No. 3, 1979, p. 395–411.

    The paper is based on two surveys of the Changing African Family Project undertaken in 1973 consisting of 6,606 women in Ibadan City and another 1,499 women in the Southwest. Caldwell argues that women who are equally exposed to the advantages of medical facilities and urban living, make differential use of them depending on their maternal education and that this affects the levels of child survival. He advocates women's education as the major influence in the demographic transition. He backs his argument by considerable statistical data correlating child mortality with parental education, type of marriage, areas of residence and socio-economic and demographic data.

39. Chojnacka, H. Polygyny and the rate of population growth. *Human Resources Research Bulletin* (University of Lagos) No. 78/05, 1978.

    An analysis of survey data collected during 1977 and 1978 in 130 households of selected communities in the Southern belt of Nigeria. Between 29 and 50 per cent of the samples were polygynous households. A comparison is made between monogamous and polygynous unions on demographic and socio-economic variables. An important finding is the absence of any significant difference between the wives in the two types of unions with respect to completed fertility, but child mortality and age at marriage are significantly related to the type of union, which, in turn, is associated with socio-economic status. Child mortality is substantially higher in polygynous households and amongst illiterates. Similarly, polygynous households have lower levels of educational attainment and lower standards of living, as measured by per capita income. Polygynous unions prevailed amongst farmers, petty traders and manual workers and amongst Moslems and traditional believers. With respect to nuptiality, age at first marriage varied between 15–21 and 22–27 years for females and males respectively; it was lower among polygynous than monogamous unions for both husbands and wives. But the age-sex differential at first marriage was similar in both types of union. The author concludes that the major demographic consequence of practising polygyny is reflected in the very young nuptiality patterns for females which directly affects the rate of population growth.

40. Farooq, G. M. *Household fertility decision-making in Nigeria*. Working Paper No. 75a, Geneva, ILO, 1980.

    This is a report of a study based on a national household fertility, family planning survey conducted in 1971–73 in four states of former South-western Nigeria among a sample of 3,013 households. Among the social and economic factors relevant to household fertility decision-making is the level of females' educational attainment. It exerts the most pervasive influence on children born alive as well as on desired family size. Secondly, female higher education exerts important influences on the quality of female work participation and age at marriage which in turn influence actual fertility behaviour. Finally, the observation was made that the attitude to family limitation was positive when couples had achieved a sufficient number of live births.

41. Hauck, H. Weight changes during pregnancy in Awo Umawa, Nigeria 1960. *Journal of Obstetrics and Gynaecology of the British Commonwealth*, No. 70, 1963, p. 885–890.

    The paper presents weight gains of 350 cases of Ibo women attending the ante-natal clinic in 1960 with the aim of establishing their nutritional status. Estimates of mean gain throughout pregnancy were based on (1) comparison of mean weights of groups of pregnant and non-pregnant women of approximately the same height and age or (2) mean weekly gains of groups of women in the second or third trimester. In either method, the researcher estimated a gain of only slightly over 5 kilogrammes, which, he points out, is less than half the expected mean gain for British and American women. In as many as 30 per cent of the 58 cases observed for an average of 12 weeks in the third trimester, there was failure to gain or even actual loss of weight. A call is made for studies to determine the consequences to mother and child for low gains during pregnancy.

42. Hunponu-Wusu, O. O., et al. Demographic and fertility indicators among family planning acceptors in Kaduna, Northern Nigeria. *Savanna*, Vol. 3, No. 1, 1974, p. 77–84.

    A study carried out at the family planning clinic of Ahmadu Bello University Hospital Kaduna, which describes specific social characteristics of 448 acceptors. The characteristics of this group were: religion – Christians 57 per cent, Moslems 33 per cent; education – those with no schooling and primary schooling 38 per cent each, secondary schooling and above formed only 17 per cent; only 9 per cent of the group were Hausa and the largest single tribal group was that of Yoruba who made up 36 per cent. Most of the women become concerned about family size and spacing at the age of 26, and at least 35 per cent of the group had had six or more live births by that time.

43. Lucas, D. Some aspects of marriage, fertility and migration among women in Lagos. *Human Resources Research Bulletin* (University of Lagos) No. 3/001, 1974.

    The report is based on a survey made by the Human Resources Research Unit between January and March 1973 and is part of a series of bulletin reports of the research project on Occupation, Marriage and Fertility among Nigerian women in Lagos. The author looks at the effect of childbearing and marriage on women's labour force participation. There had been an influx of young females into Lagos, and the equalizing of the sex ratio could lead to a rise in the crude birth rate as the immigrant females begin childbearing. The effect of increasing standards of education on childbearing is not clear in this study. Women who had received secondary level education seemed to be forming more definite ideas of ideal family size, but less educated women seemed to be having fewer children than the educated ones. The author suggests that this could be due to prolonged breast feeding and poorer health and nutrition.

44. Oppong, C., Adaba, G., Bekombo-Priso, M., and Mogey, J. *Marriage, fertility and parenthood in West Africa*, Canberra, The Australian National University, 1978.

    A collection of papers from the XVth Seminar of the International Sociology Association Committee on Family Research, Lome, Togo, 1976, in two volumes. Volume one, Part 1 covers family and marriage systems, with studies on West Africa in general, the Kwara Nomadic Fulani, Egbado Yoruba, on Dakar, Cameroun, Zaire, and Benin. Part 2 looks at parents and children, childcare, with studies on West Africa, Ghana (2 studies) and a general study on the changing economic roles of children in comparative perspective. Part 3 is on family system and change and has work on the Bete, on Ghana (2 studies) and Nigeria (2 studies). Volume two, Part 4 looks at factors affecting fertility and in addition to some general studies, includes work on Nigeria (3), Ghana (2), and Ivory Coast (1), Part 5 covers family planning and birth control, with work on Sierra Leone (1), Nigeria (4) in addition to general papers in this topic area. The papers are in English or in French, with a summary in the other language.

45. Youssef, M., Buvinic, M., and Kudan, A. *Women in migration: A Third World focus*. Washington, D.C., Women in Development Office, 1979.

    The authors suggest that not much research has been focused on autonomous female migration as distinct from that of accompanying wives, nor has attention been paid to wives of migrants left in the villages. Their analysis of migration in Africa is based on East, North, Central and Southern Africa. These regions show the highest level of sex differentials in migration from rural to urban areas. But Ethiopia, Lesotho and Mauritania show total migration with little or no sex differential migration and perhaps little outmigration from rural areas in general. Men dominate migration especially between the ages of 20 and 34 years, but in the higher age group of 50 to 54 years females are found to dominate outmigration in all other countries except for South Africa, Botswana and Lesotho. Female dominated outmigration is also shown for the ages 15 to 19 in Kenya, Lesotho, Morocco, Rwanda and Libyan Arab Jamahiriya. South Africa, Botswana and to a lesser extent Tanzania reveal no female-dominated migration in any age group. Only North African countries feature in international migration on an inter-continental basis to any appreciable degree. Intra-continental migration is most characteristic of Ghana, Uganda, Rhodesia, South Africa and Tanzania (largely countries with political-economic crises) and is male dominated. Only in Togo and Malawi did the sex ratio of the migrants favour women. In other cases, women migrate to other countries as dependants. Most women migrants give family and marriage, or escape from traditional norms, cultural stigma of barrenness or unwanted pregnancies, as motives for migration. The authors suggest that women under-report the economic motives for their migration. The economic plight of autonomous female migrants is revealed and aggravated in lack of support networks, high levels of unemployment, even in unskilled jobs and hence the relegation of such women to trading and other low paying jobs. Because of the officially restricted single-sex migration settlements in South Africa and the *de facto* male migration pattern in other African countries, women-headed households linked to male migration is a major problem in the rural areas. This has resulted in an increase in uncultivated land, an increase in women's labour, and a decrease in crop production. The authors speculate that this problem has contributed to a breakdown of the family structure by fragmenting family authority and decision-making as well as leading to instability through divorce, and extra-marital relations. They point out, however, that the literature leaves the question of the impact of migration on marriage and fertility unanswered.

VI. Other

46. Fleuhr-lobran, C. Agitation for change in the Sudan. In: Schlegel, A. (ed.) *Sexual Stratification*, New York, Columbia University Press, 1978.

Research for this study was conducted in Khartoum between 1970 and 1972. The paper begins by outlining outstanding features of heterosexual relationships in Northern Sudan. Rural women are not as restricted in their movement as urban women. Rural women cultivate land, carry water from long distances and do not use the *tob* to conceal their bodies in public. It is a prevalent practice for women to undergo pharaonic circumcision which involves the excision of clitoris, labia majora and labia minora. But there is a gradual movement towards the practice of the *Sunni* form which is simply clitoridectomy. Circumcision, which is done before the age of ten years, is associated with decency, cleanliness and morality. Because of a strict sexual segregation in public gatherings, and a high cost of marriage in the city, boys and young men's sexual experiences are with prostitutes or temporary homosexual liaisons. The women's movement existed for a quarter of a century, and in that period most agitation has been against obedience laws which, for example, forced women to return to their husbands' homes after they had run away.

Some women threatened to commit suicide, to convert to Christianity, or repay their dowries rather than return to their husbands. This informal dissent was followed in 1946 by the formation of the Sudanese Women's League as a wing of the Communist Party. In 1951 the league was renamed the Sudanese Women's Union and started to publish a progressive magazine – *The Woman's Voice*. It opposed Islamic divorce, obedience laws and polygamy. It featured articles on personal and child health, and advocated maternity leave and equal pay for working women. It did not, however, deal with the issue of circumcision. Abolished during the Abboud regime, the Communist Party women in the league actively demonstrated in 1964 during the overthrow of that regime, and as a result won the vote. Nimieri's military regime enacted a number of progressive reforms in 1969 – the abolition of the obedience laws, raising the amount of alimony and support from one-quarter to one-half of a man's salary, giving women pensions and extending maternity leave from seven to forty days. But since 1971, Nimieri has abolished all unions and parties critical of his regime and the women's union has been replaced by the Women's Affairs Committee of the Sudanese Socialist Unit. The author criticizes this group for having little grassroots organization among women and for being preoccupied in arranging teas and receptions for diplomatic wives.

47. Strobel, M. *Muslim women in Mombasa* 1890–1975. New Haven and London, Yale University Press, 1979, 258 p.

This period of history covers the introduction, experience and legacy of colonialism in Mombasa. The impact was both economic and ideological: initially economic changes involved a shift to wage labour for large numbers of men, and denied women their former role in production. In ideological terms the control of male elders of Mombasa society over their dependants (wives, children and clients) was weakened as western values and concepts intruded into the society. The ideological impact of secular education, the mass media, and limited wage labour for women have been to some extent progressive, undermining some aspects of Moslem culture which confined women and fostered their dependence on men. But the progress has been circumscribed by the social relations and values rooted in colonialism and neo-colonialism. Despite the strength of the cultural attack on Moslem values, the author argues that the norm for social segregation of the sexes retained much of its vitality and fostered a female subculture which manifested the class and ethnic complexities of Mombasa society. These class and ethnic differences and their complex interaction over time prevented women from identifying exclusively with any particular division, and thus prevented them from organizing on more general lines. An extensive bibliography is included in the book.

Journals (Special issues on women)

African Studies Review, Vol. 18, No. 3, 1975.
African Urban Notes, Nos V and VI, 1976/77.
Rural Africana, No. 29, 1975/76.

Research on the Status of Women, Development and Population Trends in the Arab States: An Annotated Bibliography

by Soha Abdel Kader

Research on the Status of Women, Development and Population Trends in the Arab States: An Annotated Bibliography by Soha Abdel Kader

A. INTRODUCTION

This brief annotated bibliography of research on the status of women in the Arab region focuses largely on general studies on women's status, women and development, and demographic aspects, and is prefaced by a list of bibliographies which themselves provide an introduction to the wide range of recent work on women.

Generally speaking, analysts of demographic transition in the Arab region complain about the quality and quantity of data available though, as Allman (1978)[1] notes, there has been substantial improvement in the last decade. The main sources of demographic data are: censuses, vital registration statistics, sample surveys, and micro-studies (field work). The dearth of demographic data and its incomparability in terms of definition of terms and varying times of census data collection pose serious obstacles for the project of drawing a precise profile of demographic transition in the Arab region. These difficulties are most pronounced in relation to drawing a demographic profile of Arab women and particularly of their participation in socio-economic development. Despite the stated concern of many governments of the region for the integration of women in national development strategies, demographic studies focus only incidentally on women.

Other sources of research on the status of women in the Arab region are social science studies in the fields of sociology, psychology, political science, history, economics, law and the medical sciences. These studies are abundant, and a number of recent bibliographies give some indication of their range.[2] Much of the social science literature on women in the region deals with the status of women in Islam. The available studies are divided into two broad categories according to Ayad Al-Qazzaz (1977)[3]: studies which adopt a defensive posture, and maintain that Islam sustains rather than undermines women's rights, and those which adopt a critical posture, and see Islam as the cause of the low status of women and the inequalities between the sexes prevalent in the Moslem world.

As a general statement, we can say that just as there are deficiencies in demographic studies on the status of women in the Arab region, there are also deficiencies in social science studies on the status of Arab women. From these studies we have acquired some knowledge about certain aspects of women's lives in some parts of the Middle East and for some strata of the population. What is needed is to evolve a rubric within which information can be accumulated, unevenness of data assessed and the gaps filled. This means research which links population dynamics with changes in family patterns and the status of women, which takes into account the processes of socio-economic and cultural change, and which is interdisciplinary and where possible cross-cultural. Such research of course requires an improvement of both the demographic base and the social science research base.

The bibliographic entries are categorized as follows:

I. General, including bibliographies;
II. Women's work and labour force participation, including material on women and development;

III. Family and household;
IV. Education[4];
V. Demographic features.

Where necessary the items are listed alphabetically within subcategories.

NOTES

1. Allman, J. (ed.), *Women's Status and fertility in the Muslim World*, New York, Praeger Publishers, 1978.
2. Abdel Kader, Soha, *The status of research on women in the Arab Region, 1960–1978*, 1979 (Entry 48). Gulick, J., *An annotated bibliography of sources concerned with women in the modern Muslim Middle East*, Princeton, NJ, Princeton University Press, 1979 (Princeton Near East Paper No. 17). Al-Qazzaz, A., *Women in the Middle East and North Africa: an annotated bibliography*, Austin, Texas, Center for Middle Eastern Studies, University of Texas at Austin, 1977 (Middle East Monograph No. 2).
3. Al-Qazzaz, A., *Women in the Arab World, an annotated bibliography No. 2*, Sacramento, California State University and Association of Arab American University Graduates Inc., Detroit, 1975. And Al-Qazzaz, A., op. cit. (Entry 49).
4. Although there are only two entries in this category the topic is covered in a number of general studies. (See subject index p. 271.)

B. THE BIBLIOGRAPHY ON THE ARAB REGION

I. General

BIBLIOGRAPHIES

48. Abdel Kader, S. *The status of research on women in the Arab Region, 1960–1978*. Unesco, Division of Human Rights and Peace, January 1979.

This paper is an attempt to analyse critically social science research being undertaken on the role and status of women in the Arab Region. It is devoted to research trends since 1960 in the fields of history, religion, sociology, anthropology, economics, political science and law research. Where possible, reference is made to women's extra-familial and productive roles. The paper is divided into five main parts. Part I is an attempt to draw a general profile of Arab women based on available studies in the different fields. Part II is an assessment of the status of research on women in individual countries in the region. Part III deals with Arab literature. Part IV includes conclusions, criticisms and recommendations. Part V is a bibliography of English, Arabic and French studies divided by country and by language.

49. Al-Qazzaz, A. *Women in the Middle East and North Africa. An annotated bibliography*. Austin, Texas, Center for Middle Eastern Studies, University of Texas at Austin, 1977. Middle East Monograph No. 2.

The bibliography consists only of items written in English. The purpose of the compilation and annotation is 'to provide the English language speaker with as comprehensive a picture as possible of what is written on the subject'. The bibliography includes citations on studies on Bahrain, Egypt, Iraq, Jordan, Kuwait, Lebanon, Libyan Arab Jamahiriya, Oman,

Democratic Yemen, Sudan, Syrian Arab Republic, in addition to North African countries. More than 200 citations are included covering a large variety of topics. As the author notes in the introduction, 'the bibliography contains many items about the position of women in Islam' as they constitute the bulk of literature in English on the status of women in the Arab region and North Africa.

50. Gadalla, S. *Population policy and family planning communication strategies in the Arab States Region*. Vol. I Summaries of pertinent literature and research studies. Unesco, Paris, 1978.

    This volume includes 459 annotated citations of studies in Arabic, English and French covering the topics of population and demography, fertility and family planning behaviour, population policies and family planning programmes and Islam's view on population and family planning issues. Of these works, many deal with the region as a whole (85) or with a combination of countries within the region. Of the country-specific studies, most are related to Egypt (96), Tunisia (79), Morocco (31), and Syrian Arab Republic (30). According to the author, these four countries are known to be 'the leaders in the field of population and family planning research in the region'. A significant percentage of studies deal with Iraq (17 studies), Algeria (14), Jordan (14), Lebanon (12), and Kuwait (10). The author's purpose is to offer 'valuable insights into the nature and scope of the population problems and the various social, economic and cultural factors which should be taken into consideration in formulating and implementing population policies and family planning programs'.

51. Mahdi, A.-A. Women of Iran: a bibliography of sources in the English language. *Resources for Feminist Research/Documentation sur la Recherche Feministe*, Vol. IX, No. 4, Dec. 1980/Jan. 1981, p. 19–24.

    The author states that 'Iranian women have been unfairly neglected in the literature of the social sciences. There exist no nationally based historico-theoretical studies of women's situation in Iranian society. There are few analytical studies dealing exclusively with women's oppression in Iran.' The studies listed in the bibliography then are either descriptive accounts or only secondarily concerned with women, but they were chosen because they have some bearing on the study of women, containing either relevant information and statistical data, or because their conclusions have implications for the position of Iranian women.

52. Meghdessian, S. R. *The status of Arab women*, London, Mansell Information Publishing, 1980.

    Produced under the auspices of the Institute for Women's Studies in the Arab World (IWSAW) founded in 1973, at Beirut University College, Lebanon and based on their Documentation Centre, this bibliography contains over 1,600 entries and includes all Arab countries from the Middle East and North Africa. It covers books, articles, conference proceedings, published and unpublished papers, masters and doctoral theses, and bibliographies. Particular attention has been given to coverage of local material collected at international conferences, and work on subjects avoided until recently in traditional societies. Most entries are in English and French and the bibliography is arranged under general subjects and individual countries.

53. Population and Family Planning Board (Research Department) *Egyptian Population Studies: Annotated bibliography*. Vol. 1 (Arabic), 1978; Vol. II (English), 1979. Cairo.

    These two volumes were prepared by Dr. Sara El Lozy and are the first in a series of annotated bibliographies to be published periodically by the Research Department of the Egyptian Population and Family Planning Board. The introduction to this work suggests that the population problem is of such magnitude in Egypt that solving it necessitates 'the co-operation of all academic and executive institutions and the scientific study of population issues in their relationship with all other aspects of society'. Volume I in Arabic includes 2,212 citations covering: population trends, the family, housing, population structure, education, family planning, population distribution, fertility, health, labour force, migration, mortality. Volume II, in English, includes 1,064 citations covering the topics of: spatial distribution, trends in population, mortality, fertility, marriage and divorce in the family, migration, population characteristics, regional demography, historical demography, demography, economic and non-economic interrelations, policies, methods of research, production of population statistics, official statistical publications, bibliography, conferences.

54. Raccagni, M. *The Modern Arab woman: A bibliography*. Metuchen, NJ, Scarecrow Press, 1978. 237 p.

    A bibliography of materials in English, French and Arabic covering the period 1798 to 1976 with 2,989 citations, about a third of which are annotated. There is a general subject section and a geographical section.

55. United Nations Economic Commission for Western Asia. *Sources for Research on Population and Development in the ECWA Region*. Beirut, UNECWA Population Division, 1979.

    The first of a two-part bibliography covering sources of population literature relating to the Arab world. Partly the result of a comprehensive analysis of population research dealing with the Arab World prepared for the International Review Group for Social Science Research on Population and Development, the analysis necessitated the collection and consultation of over 1,000 references. This part covers non-Arabic sources, while Part II covers Arabic references. The two parts contain some 3,500 entries basically covering the period from 1960–78.

OTHER

56. Beck, L. and Keddie, N. (eds) *Women in the Muslim world*. Cambridge, Mass., Harvard University Press, 1978, 698 p.

    A collection of 33 original essays on women in the Moslem world. Divided into four parts, Part 1 is on general perspectives on legal and socio-economic change, with two papers on law reform and one on status and fertility patterns, followed by articles on social change in Morocco, Turkey, Tunisia, Algeria, Kuwait and Iran (2 studies). Part 2 gives a historical perspective with studies of Turkish women in the Ottoman Empire, two on Egypt, and one on women and revolution in Iran 1905–11. Part 3 deals with case studies – nomads, villagers, town and city dwellers, with 12 papers covering such groups in the following countries: Iran, Syrian Arab Republic, Lebanon, Morocco, Pakistan, Turkey, and Egypt. Part 4 looks at ideology, religion and ritual, and the countries on which papers appear here are Morocco, Egypt, North Africa, Iran and China. A useful and wide ranging collection full of information.

57. El Saadawi, N. *The hidden face of Eve: Women in the Arab World*. London, Zed Press, 1980, 212 p. (Translated by Dr. Sherif Hetata.)

    The author takes as a basic proposition that 'the situation and problems of women in contemporary human society are born of developments in history that made one class rule over another, and men dominate over women. They are the product of class and sex' (p. i). From this perspective she looks at what it is like to grow up as a woman in the Islamic world of the Middle East, and covers such topics as sexual aggression against female children, circumcision, prostitution, abortion, marriage, divorce, sexual relations, work, Arab women in history and Arab pioneers of women's liberation. Amongst her conclusions she argues that the emancipation of Arab women can only result from their own struggle so they must organize, and that wars of liberation and radical transformation associated with the establishment of socialist systems can speed the rate of change; that positive aspects in Arab and Islamic culture should be emphasized and negative discarded, pointing out that, at the time of the Prophet, women had rights of which they are deprived in most Arab countries today. She also points out that the portrait of the Arab women in past and contemporary literature does not reflect a true image but is incomplete, distorted and devoid of a clear understanding, since it is woman through the eyes of Arab men. A new introduction to this translation discusses the importance of the revolution in Iran for women.

58. Farman-Farmaian, S. Women and Decision making: with special reference to Iran and other developing countries. *Labour and Society*. Vol. 1, No. 2, 1976, p. 25–32.

    The author argues that laws which are designed to protect women and guarantee their rights will be largely ineffective when women are illiterate, do not know their rights, and are incapable of demanding them. To provide opportunities for these women and revise patterns of behaviour, which have not changed for centuries, education for women must be expanded. Parents must be motivated to send daughters to school, and facilities for women must be increased, with training and educational programmes to foster women's participation at all levels. For example, handicrafts training should include marketing experience as well as production, and women in rural areas should be trained to set up and run co-operatives and small businesses.

59. Minority Rights Group. *Arab Women*. London, Minority Rights Group, 1975, 20 p. (Report No. 27.)

An introduction by Ann Dearden is followed by brief descriptions of the situation of women in Egypt, Lebanon, Syrian Arab Republic. Iraq, Tunisia, Algeria, Saudi Arabia, Democratic Yemen, United Arab Emirates, Oman, Libyan Arab Jamahiriya, Bahrain, Kuwait, Qatar, Yemen Arab Republic, Morocco, Jordan, and Palestine. Some figures are provided and a short bibliography.

60. Population Council (West Asia and North Africa). *The Measurement of women's economic participation: Report of a study group*. Beirut, 1979. (Regional Papers.)

The study group was sponsored jointly by the Faculty of Health Sciences of the American University in Beirut and the Population Council. Members of the study group included research specialists whose aim was to discuss and offer suggestions on the problems of measuring women's economic participation. Indices and aspects which were considered important in this respect were: the conceptualization of work, measurement of work, time budgets, the role of education, resource allocation, mother-child relationships, and policy formulation and implementation. The paper includes research notes on the economic participation of women in Yemen Arab Republic, Aman, Egypt and Cuba. In addition, four articles offer methodological suggestions that in the researchers' opinions are likely to lead to improved assessment of the extent and magnitude of female labour force participation.

II. Women's work and labour force participation

WOMEN AND DEVELOPMENT

61. Ahmed, W. *Constraints and requirements to increase women's participation in integrated rural development*. A paper presented at the seminar on the Role of Women in Integrated Rural Development with Emphasis on Population Problems, sponsored by United Nations Food and Agricultural Organization. Cairo, October/November 1974. Mimeo.

The author argues that, as long as development programmes for women remain those considered appropriate to womanhood, such as housekeeping and mothercraft, it will be difficult to enlist much enthusiasm from either men or women. What are needed are development projects which include opportunities for women to participate in non-agricultural, income-producing activities such as decentralized manufacture of processed primary products, consumer goods, and light engineering goods. These are commodities which are labour-intensive, resource-based, and require simple technology, small investment and cheap or little fuel.

62. Badran, H. *Arab women in national development: A study of three Arab countries, namely Egypt, Lebanon and the Sudan*. A paper presented at the Conference on the Role of Arab Women in National Development. October 1972.

Although the number of women who work is increasing in these three countries, the author finds that the generally held opinion is that women should not work outside the home. Working women are largely limited to the agricultural and service sectors, in large part because their opportunities for education and vocational training are still small. The author argues that four basic factors affect a woman's contribution to national development: education, including non-formal education and vocational training; women's organizations; legislation; and the young child, and the availability of social services surrounding childbearing.

63. Farrag, O. L. Arab women and national development. *Les Carnets de l'Enfance*, No. 23, 1973, p. 87–97.

This paper is based on a discussion at the October 1972 conference on the role of Arab Women in National Development, and the author argues that because of the role that women play in shaping the personalities of the next generation, greater attention must be given to human resource development programmes that include women among their beneficiaries. Suggestions for change made at the conference and listed in the article are the following: more adequate education and training for girls, including vocational training opportunities and functional literacy teaching; training of pre-school educational personnel and an increase in the number of family planning centres. Further suggestions entail legislative changes at international levels in line with ILO standards, the encouragement of political awareness among women, support for women's organizations, the provision of opportunities for women workers to assume posts in administrative leadership, the development and improvement of programmes aimed at preparing girls for their role as mother and wife, the setting up of agricultural training centres, and the establishment of new, well-equipped nurseries.

64. Van Dusen, R. *Integrating women into national economies: Programming considerations with special reference to the Near East.* Report submitted to the Office of Technical Support, Near East Bureau, AID, 1977.

The purpose of this report is to review AID programming with a view to assessing the participation of and impact on women of development activities – especially those activities involving women of the Islamic Near East. Van Dusen recognizes the existence of a considerable literature on women and development and attempts to offer a summary and analysis of this literature. She does this within the context of four major hypotheses: (1) the literature on women in development is not policy orientated; (2) the obstacles to reaching women are almost insurmountable; (3) little is known about Near Eastern women and this is what Near Eastern governments want; (4) women in the Near East do not work and do not want to work. The paper includes an annotated bibliography on women in development and a general bibliography of the published works on the status of Near Eastern women generally, particularly after 1970.

65. Youssef, N. H. Social structure and the female labor force: The case of women workers in Muslim Middle Eastern countries. *Demography*, Vol. 8, 1971, p. 427–440.

The author examines the women's labour forces in Middle Eastern countries through a comparative analysis with studies of similar Latin American countries. She states that in terms of quantitative comparative data, Middle Eastern countries systematically report the lowest female participation rates in economic activities outside of agriculture. She says this behaviour represents a deviation from both the current experience of other developing nations and the historical experience of the now-industrialized West. The use of comparative data on female employment patterns in Latin American countries, which are at a roughly similar stage of economic development, shows that the low level and particular character of women's involvement in the work force in the Middle East can be explained by institutional arrangements contingent upon aspects of social structure. Five countries were selected for intensive analysis: Chile, Mexico, Egypt, Morocco, and Pakistan. One major aspect of social organization and its cultural adjuncts is emphasized: the interplay between the volitional avoidance by women of certain occupational sectors because of the social stigmatizing aspect, and the prohibition of occupational opportunities imposed by males. In the Middle East, the combined effects of this tradition of female seclusion and exclusion are confirmed by the detailed analysis of the structure of the non-agricultural labour force. Middle Eastern women are systematically absent from occupational and industrial sectors of employment which involve public activity and presuppose contact with males.

66. Youssef, N. H. Differential labor force participation of women in Latin American and Middle Eastern countries: The influence of family characteristics. *Social Forces*, Vol. 51, 1972, p. 135–153.

This article examines the different levels of women's participation in the non-agricultural labour force of developing countries; for purposes of limiting the investigation, the author has narrowed the comparison to Latin American and Middle Eastern countries, specifically Chile, Egypt, Morocco, and Pakistan, and to females of age 15 or more. The first part of the article is devoted to an examination of marital and fertility characteristics involving rates of marriage, divorce, delay of marriage, numbers of children, etc. It is concluded from the data that differences in marital and fertility rates are not sufficient to explain the higher amount of female participation in non-agricultural work in Latin American countries versus Middle Eastern countries. The author moves on to examine family and kinship organization: the similarities, the differences

– both historically and as related to religious influence, the effect on single, widowed, divorced and married women, and opportunities and alternatives available to women other than marriage and childbearing in Latin America and Middle Eastern countries. The conclusion is that the amount of participation of women in the non-agricultural labour forces of these countries is a function of both marital and fertility conditions, and social organization (kinship and family organization) of these societies.

67. Youssef, N. H. *Women and work in developing societies.* Berkeley, University of California, Institute of International Studies, 1974. (Population Monograph Series, No. 15.)

This book is concerned with women's participation in the non-agricultural labour force of developing countries. The study includes thirteen countries, six in Latin America and seven in the Middle East. While these countries are shown to be similar in their industrial and economic development, they differ in their social and cultural systems. By studying statistical data on marital and fertility rates, educational levels, controlling institutions and motivations, the supply and demand for women in the labour force, historical factors, and religious influences in these developing countries, Youssef concludes that the pattern for increased women's participation in the non-agricultural labour force is not repeating the pattern which was evident in the now industrialized Western countries. She isolates two overriding problems: high fertility is a major obstacle in raising the per capita income of these countries; and education in birth control methods does not control high fertility. Interpretation of the data revealed the following: there is a higher participation of women in the non-agricultural labour force in Latin America than in the Middle East, and differential female participation can be attributed to a number of factors, including education, economic need, historical background, family and social structure, and religion. Youssef notes that while one factor alone cannot explain the differences, the breakdown of strong family ties, largely due to the influence of the Catholic church in the education of women and its competition with males for a dominant role in female motivation in the Latin American countries can be seen as the most substantial factor for a higher participation of women in the labour force in Latin America. She concludes that in order to increase female participation in the labour force it is necessary to centre personal and social rewards and motivations in work rather than in traditional wife and mother roles.

68. Youssef, N. H. *Women and agricultural production in Muslim societies.* Paper presented at the seminar, Prospects for Growth in Rural Societies: With or Without Active Participation of Women. Princeton, New Jersey, 1974.

This empirical study utilizes United Nations statistical data to show that the female labour force in Moslem countries is very small in the agricultural sector. One explanation offered for this fact is that strict seclusion sanctions prevent women from such activity. Youssef suggests that there is evidence of girls doing unpaid farm work, and that the obvious presence of fifteen to nineteen year old women in the fields militates against this hypothesis. There could also be a problem in reporting, as men may be reluctant to report their women as working. Pakistan has a higher incidence of women agricultural workers than other Moslem countries. It is suggested that women are a marginal, expendable labour force and tend to exacerbate male unemployment. Given the sexual division of labour which is almost universal in agriculture, it seems that 'female' crops and specializations are a relatively minor component in the Moslem world. Youssef suggests that specifically female rural industries be developed to improve women's status and sense of selfhood, and to further their independence.

69. Youssef, N. H. Women in development: Urban life and labor. In: Tinker, I. (ed.) *Women and world development.* New York, Overseas Development Council, 1976, p. 70–77.

Urban women represent a significant force in developing countries. The author outlines the rationale for integrating women into development and discusses the issues to be considered and strategies to be implemented to realize the contributions which women can make to their cities. The adverse effects that development will have on women, as well as the positive contribution to economic production that women can make, are taken into consideration. 'When women's participation in the process of development is seen as a means of increasing real per capita income over time, and when the struggle for development is a race between capital accumulation and population growth, high fertility becomes a major obstacle to the improvement of living standards.' The author feels that lack of schooling and jobs for women results in high fertility; high fertility in turn limits education and job opportunities. This vicious circle is difficult to break when resources are limited. Finally, the author lists the various national legislation bearing upon the position of women which must be reviewed in order to ensure the integration of women into national development.

PROFESSIONAL/MANAGERIAL WORK

70. Kayhan Research Associates. *The employment of women in the higher echelons of the public and private sectors.* Report prepared for the Women's Organisation of Iran, December 1975, p. 76.

The study aimed at determining the degree to which women had succeeded in penetrating into the higher echelons of selected organizations, and to look at attitudes and problems associated with women's employment at higher levels, but also provides information on women's exployment in general as a background. Both statistical information and information drawn from personal interviews and discussions are used. The underlying assumption was that the expansion of work opportunities for women and an increase in their number in jobs at higher levels would be desirable. Amongst their conclusions, the authors state that expansion of the economy and expanding educational opportunities for women 'have recently provided and would continue to provide women with more opportunities for work' (in 1975). Various problems limiting opportunities are given – lack of education, education which is not suited to the demands of the market and the growing economy, a preference for male employees by male employers, traditional attitudes towards women amongst men and women, and, of course, women's responsibility for the home and childcare.

III. Family and household

71. Cairo Demographic Centre. *Family and marriage in some African and Asiatic countries*. Cairo, 1976. (Research Monograph Series No. 6.)

The monograph is divided into four parts. Part I looks at the methodology of comparative surveys on family and marriage in Arab and African countries. Part II includes individual survey reports for Egypt (4 studies), Sudan (1 study), Syrian Arab Republic (1), Uganda (1), and Zaire, Kinshasa (1). Part III includes comparative survey analyses for aspects of family life and marriage in four Arab and African cities – Cairo, Damascus, Kinshasa, and Tororo (Uganda) (5 studies) and a study on marriage and marital change in Tropical Africa and the Middle East. Part IV includes some general and country studies covering Ghana and Nigeria (1 study), and Egypt, Teheran, Jordan, Kuwait, Syrian Arab Republic and Tunisia, concluding with a study on marriage and remarriage in Islam.

IV. Education

72. El-Sanabary, N. M. *A comparative study of the disparities of educational opportunities for girls in the Arab States.* Unpublished dissertation, University of California, Berkeley, 1973.

The author is concerned with the disparities in educational opportunities for girls in Arab states. The article studies sixteen Arab states, with the following findings: more boys than girls receive and have an opportunity for technical and vocational education; girls have less opportunity for such training and are predominantly restricted to the humanities and social sciences; more financing is available for boys' education. The lag in educational opportunities is found to be a combination of various factors including a Moslem cultural barrier, stemming from traditions grounded in the Middle Ages, and the economic status of the states (with a predominance of rural areas, low industrialization, low income levels, and low female participation in the labour forces). A need is seen for education of girls to improve the female potential to contribute to the socio-economic progress of these states. The author suggests that the education of mothers, especially in the areas of health and general education, could lead to more widespread acceptance of education for girls, as attitudes could then be passed on to younger generations.

73. El-Sanabary, N. M. *The education of women in the Arab States: Achievements and problems, 1950–1970*. Unpublished paper presented at the Symposium on Near Eastern Women Through the Ages, University of California at Berkeley, March 1975.

This paper examines the educational status of women in Arab states, and includes (but is not limited to) data on Kuwait, Lebanon, Bahrain, Saudi Arabia, Qatar, Yemen, Egypt, Algeria, Morocco, and the Sudan. The author divides the article into several sections: origins of modern girls' education in the Arab world, a quantitative aspect, primary level education, diversification of educational curricula, women in secondary teacher education, higher education for women, and access to professional university education. These areas are approached from both historical and statistical standpoints, indicating attitudes, influences, progress, disparities between male and female opportunity, levels of enrolment, and comparisons among the Arab states in the area of education for women. The author points out that massive educational programmes have been initiated in most of these countries in an attempt to achieve an improved socio-economic status through use of women in the labour force. While, at a general level, the last twenty years have shown significant improvement in the status of education for women, efforts have been hampered on several levels. Lack of financing and of compulsory education, as well as a tendency to treat the education of women as a secondary problem and to centre women's education around the humanities and social sciences have been major contributory factors.

V. Demographic features

74. Allman, J. (ed.) *Women's status and fertility in the Muslim World.* New York, Praeger Publishers, 1978.

This is one of the very few recent publications that attempts to link demographic studies and social science research studies on the status of women in the Moslem world. The book is divided into two main parts. Part I, entitled Changing Fertility Patterns, includes studies on socio-economic determinants of fertility in Turkey, Egypt, Kuwait, Jordan, Algeria and Tunisia in addition to two chapters by the editor that analyse demographic transition, family planning and population policies in the Middle East and North Africa. Part II, entitled Changing Family Patterns and Women's Status, includes studies on family structure and relations and changes in roles of women in Isfaban, Iran, Turkey, Beirut, Tunisia, Morocco and Yemen. As the editor states in his preface, this collection of essays attempts to remedy partially the dearth of information on demographic change and to provide the reader with some recent approaches to the study of changing family patterns and women's status.

75. Cairo Demographic Centre, *Fertility Trends and Differentials in Arab countries.* Cairo, 1971. (Monograph Series No. 2)

This monograph is divided into three main parts. Part I is on levels, patterns and trends of fertility in Arab countries; Part II is on differential fertility in Arab countries, and Part III deals with policies and programmes relating to fertility control in Arab countries. Summarizing the findings and conclusions of the studies, Wunsch notes that the great deficiencies and incomparability in data available poses serious obstacles to any generalizations about the region.

76. Cairo Demographic Centre. *Aspects of manpower in Arab countries.* Cairo, 1972. (Research Monograph Series No. 3.)

This monograph is divided into three parts. Part I deals with country studies and the labour force in Morocco, Algeria, Tunisia, Libyan Arab Jamahiriya, Egypt, Sudan, Jordan, Syrian Arab Republic, Iraq and Kuwait. Part II includes seven studies on the demographic characteristics of the labour force in Egypt. This monograph makes a serious attempt to assess and estimate the rate of female labour force participation in the Arab region. Deficiencies in the techniques of census survey data collection affecting the accurate estimation of the size of the Arab female labour force are highlighted and analysed. Social and cultural variables affecting the increased participation of women in the labour force are also discussed. In part III one study by Hassan (p. 452–467) looks at 'The ecology and characteristics of gainfully occupied females in Cairo City'. This study empirically examines the hypothesis that working women in Egypt tend to seek residence in localities of close proximity to central business areas, close to their work, particularly in the absence of free highways, adequate parking space and private means of transportation. The hypothesis is found to be valid.

77. Cairo Demographic Centre. *Urbanization and migration in some Arab and African countries.* Cairo, 1973. (Research Monograph Series No. 4.)

This monograph is divided into two parts. Part I includes country studies in internal migration and urbanization in Morocco, Tunisia, Libyan Arab Jamahiriya, Sudan (2 studies), Egypt (4 studies), Jordan, Syrian Arab Republic (12 studies), Iraq (2), Kuwait, Nigeria (Lagos), and Liberia. Part II includes comparative studies on urbanization, migration at the present, and projections for the future, in the Arab region as a whole. As mentioned in the text of this report the studies included in this monograph deal with women in relation to migration and urbanization only. Sex is used by some of the authors incidentally as a variable in describing the socio-economic characteristics of rural to urban migrants. A more detailed analysis of the available tables, which include sex as a variable, may provide useful insights into the trends and magnitude of female migration in the Arab region.

78. Dixon, R. B. *The roles of rural women: Female seclusion, economic production, and reproductive choice.* Paper prepared for the Conference on Population Policy from the Socio-Economic Perspective. Washington, Resources for the Future, 1975. Mimeo.

This paper examines the potential demographic effects of a proposed women's co-operative programme in Asian and Middle Eastern societies. The author suggests that if small-scale, labour intensive, light industries that employ only women were established in rural villages, more young women would leave the seclusion of their homes. Conditions under which such programmes would have antinatalist effects, according to the author, include: non-agricultural employment, living quarters for unmarried women, co-operative ownership, acquisition of vocational skills, functional literacy training, provision of family planning information and child care for employed married women, peer group support and solidarity from co-workers, and a source of prestige and pride apart from marriage and children.

79. Ibrahim, S. E. *Internal migration in Egypt: A critical review*. Paper presented to the Population and Planning Board, Egypt, January 1980.

    An examination of the sex ratio of migrants over time which indicates that 'the earlier pattern of male dominance among migrants in the productive age group (20–50 years of age) is giving way to a more balanced sex ratio in the country as a whole' (p. 24).

80. United Nations Economic Commission for Western Asia. *Population situation*. Beirut, UNECWA, Population Monographs, up to 1980.

    A series of independent monographs on the population situation in each of the countries of the ECWA region. The monographs to date cover Democratic Yemen, Kuwait, Lebanon, Syrian Arab Republic, Qatar and the Arab Emirates in English, and Jordan, Bahrain and Yemen in Arabic.

81. Youssef, N. H. *Women's status and fertility in Muslim countries of the Middle East and Asia*. Paper presented at the annual meeting of the American Psychological Association, New Orleans, 1974.

    This informative paper relates the available information (including demographic data) on fertility rates of Moslem countries to the status and position of women in the Moslem social structure. Youssef has found that all Moslem countries exhibit higher fertility rates than those non-Islamic countries currently at comparable levels of economic-industrial development. She describes how the interplay between the socio-familial forces and the volitional responses of women restricts women to marital and maternal roles and prevents them from seeking higher education, economic independence, and participation in public life. All are seen to have an impact on the Moslem women's reproductive behaviour. The author also discusses how the institutional arrangements in Moslem society have not provided sufficient mechanisms to allow women to prepare themselves gradually for roles and activities outside the family. She concludes that the Moslem societies will have considerable difficulty redefining what specific types of extra-familial activities will be appropriate or acceptable for women to pursue, even if they are granted the opportunity to work and be educated. Without this redefinition, there is little expectation that the fertility rates in the Moslem world will decline.

Institutions undertaking research relevant to the status of women, population trends and development

1. *Cairo Demographic Centre*

   The Cairo Demographic Centre issued a series of monographs that include results of research studies undertaken by members of its staff.

Monographs 2, 3, 4 and 6 are annotated in the bibliography (entries 75, 76, 77 and 71 respectively).

2. *Institute for Women's Studies in the Arab World, Beirut University College, Beirut*

   This institute was set up in 1973. Since its establishment 'the stimulation of research on the role, status, conditions, traditions and developments pertaining to women and children in the region has been the Institute's basic goal'. In addition to a journal *Al-Raida* published in English and Arabic, the institute has conducted several research projects in co-operation with international institutions, particularly ILO and ECWA.

3. *The League of Arab States*

   Resolution 2828 of the League of Arab States, in 1971, established the *Arab Women's Commission*. Its aim is 'to improve and realize the full integration of Arab women in national development and to work for the protection of their different rights on equal basis'. The Commission was affiliated to the League's Social Development Department. In addition to organizing eight conferences (the first in 1972, the last in 1978), dealing with the topic of Arab women and development, the Commission also published *A Statistical Abstract for Arab Countries 1970–1975* covering demographic data on women in all Arab member countries. The abstract was published in Arabic, English and French.

4. *The Organization for the Promotion of Social Sciences in the Middle East (OPSSME)*

   This organization, established in 1974, has organized three workshops. The third was on Family and Kinship and was convened in Kuwait, in November 1976. It was co-sponsored and funded by Kuwait University and Unesco. Twenty-seven countries were represented amongst those who attended and papers dealt with the status of women, fertility trends and the participation of women in development processes.

Research on the Status of Women, Development and Population Trends in Asia: An Annotated Bibliography

by Kimi Hara

Research on the Status of Women, Development and Population Trends in Asia: An Annotated Bibliography by Kimi Hara

A. INTRODUCTION

Asia is a vast and diverse continent and it has proved impossible to cover all of the countries in this selective bibliography. The major focus of the selection is on Japan, the Philippines and Singapore, with some entries relating to other countries. A number of bibliographic works are included to suggest further lines of development of research on women in other countries of the area, and the general introduction at the beginning of this volume contains a brief overview of research concerns in the region.

The entries in the bibliography are divided into six major categories:

I. General, including bibliographies and theoretical or conceptual contributions, as well as more general studies of women's status;
II. Women's work and labour force participation, including material on women and the processes of development and individual country studies;
III. Family and household, containing chiefly general studies of this institution;
IV. Education;
V. Demographic features;
VI. Other, including material on health and government policy.

B. THE BIBLIOGRAPHY ON THE ASIAN REGION

I. General

BIBLIOGRAPHIES

82. Ayub, N. *Women in Pakistan and other Islamic countries: A Selected bibliography with annotations.* Pakistan, A Women's Resource Centre/ Shirkat Gah Publications, 1978.

    This book is an effort to define, describe and give structure to the existing body of literature – academic, periodical and popular, and is in three sections. The section on Pakistan is divided into topic areas such as education, health and legislation. The two other sections are on women and Islam, and women in other Islamic countries, the latter divided by country. This is a useful work since literature specifically on women in Pakistan is limited.

83. Chung, B. J. *The status of women and fertility in Southeast and East Asia: A bibliography.* Singapore, Institute of Southeast Asian Studies, 1976, 167 p.

    This annotated bibliography of 548 entries includes material on the status of women and fertility in six Southeast and East Asian countries: Indonesia, Malaysia, Philippines, Singapore, Thailand and Korea; and in Taiwan. The document starts with an overview of the status of women and fertility in the region, concluding that decision-making and role-planning in the family, the legal status of women and the relationship between fertility and the status of women have been relatively neglected. The work is an attempt to draw attention to the need for such studies by bringing together the studies which exist. It covers the social, familial and legal status of women as well as more general studies and women's status in relation to fertility.

84. Dasgupta, K. (ed.) *Women on the Indian scene: An annotated bibliography.* New Delhi, Abhinav Publications, 1977.

    This is an extensive bibliography of the literature available on various aspects of the status of women, economic, social, educational, cultural, political, and legal, including biographies of eminent women. It is a systematic survey of the literature seeking to present an overall view of the work already done in the field, and to identify the gaps in order to initiate further research. The bibliography is restricted to literature in the English language only, and has 822 publications and covers material published until June 1975.

85. Eviota, E. U. *Philippine women and development: An annotated bibliography.* Quezon City, Institute of Philippine Culture, Ateneo de Manila University, 1978, 27 p.

    This volume presents annotations of selected studies on Philippine women published by 1977, focusing on the involvement of women in such areas of socio-economic concern as work, employment, education, family, decision-making, health, and nutrition. A selected list of titles on women and world development in general is also included.

86. Regala-Angangco, O. D. et al. *Status of women in the Philippines: A bibliography with selected annotations.* Quezon City, Alemar-Phoenix Publishing House, Inc., 1980, 98 p.

    This volume includes books, monographs, brochures, pamphlets, unpublished dissertations, lectures, speeches, conference papers, laws and statutes and articles in periodicals, magazines and newspapers concerning the status of women in the Philippines. The scope is varied, encompassing values, attitudes, family, education, the economy, law and politics, from historical, psychological and social perspectives.

87. Research Unit on Women's Studies, S.N.D.T. Women's University Bombay, *A select bibliography on women in India.* Bombay, Allied Publishers, Private Ltd., 1975, 131 p.

    The bibliography covers books published up to March 1975 and lists unpublished theses. Journal articles since 1960 are included. The headings are: general, historical studies, biographies, status and role of women, women in marriage and the family, health and family planning, education, employment, social problems and women's welfare, the legal position of women, women's outside participation, different communities, art, folklore, and psychological studies.

88. Salmon, C. Essai de bibliographie sur la question feminine en Indonesie. [An attempt at a bibliography on the women's question in Indonesia] *Revue Archipel*, No. 13, 1977, p. 23–36.

    This bibliography consists of approximately 250 unannotated entries; in addition to the language of Indonesia, references are listed in French, English and Dutch. The classifications are as follows: general studies, religion, legal aspects, women, family and home, family planning, education, pioneers and heroines, feminist movements, women and work, contemporary problems.

CONCEPTS AND METHODS

89. Inciong, E. M. Woman labor: An unquantified resource? *Philippine Labor Review*, Vol. 1, No. 3, 1976, p. 69–73.

    The author questions the utility of present statistics in establishing sound programmes for women workers. As an example she cites the absence of a category for housekeeping in census data, indicating the opinion that housewives do not play a role in the economic structure. The author considers that women's labour force participation cannot be appreciated fully nor their problems dealt with unless the data gathering system is improved.

90. Mangahas, M. and Jayme-Ho, T. The economic status of women: An analytical framework. In: *The role of women in contributing to family income.* Proceedings of the regional workshop in Bangkok, 19–23 July 1976. Bangkok, Friedrich-Ebert-Stiftung, 1977, p. 45–67.

    The authors suggest an economic framework for analysing the economic status of women. It involves the determination of work and income conditions for female labour, the concept of full family income and its feedback effects on the demand for labour, and the manner in which economic conditions for women can affect future conditions through such demographic variables as fertility and family formation. The authors contend that an economic model becomes meaningful only when it is able to help attain equity within the society as a whole.

OTHER

91. Berger, M. Japanese women – old images and new realities. *The Japan Interpreter*, Vol. 11, No. 1, 1976, p. 56–67.

    The author examines whether the images of Japanese women commonly held by Americans – the exotic combination of doll-like beauty and apparent subservience have any relation to reality. His case for the invalid stereotype is presented with commentaries by Japanese women on their counterparts in the United States, showing that standards of strength and power differ as social and cultural values differ. For example, in Japan (1) although there are strongly defined sexual roles, both roles are considered important; (2) the so-called man's world, especially the white-collar world, is regarded by Japanese women with increasing scepticism; (3) legal and social discrimination is apparent, but few Japanese women seem to have any feelings of inferiority in their emotional relations with men; (4) the number of women recognizing, realizing and seeking a broader life-style within their reach is increasing.

92. Cook, A. H. and Hayashi, H. *Working women in Japan: Discrimination, resistance and reform.* Ithaca, Cornell, Industrial and Labour Relations Publications, 1980.

Although women account for 38 per cent of the labour force in Japan, the third largest economy in the world, the role of the female worker has been largely that of the dispensable employee. Women are subject to a different set of workplace practices from their male counterparts. In general, they do not share in the benefits and security of the lifetime employment system or in promotion opportunities. Japanese law requires equal pay for equal work, but comparison of wages is made difficult by occupational segregation of the sexes and the practice of retiring women by the age of thirty, often at marriage or childbirth. Cook and Hayashi trace the cultural roots of Japanese attitudes toward working women and discuss the economic conditions that sustain these attitudes. A detailed statistical description of women in the Japanese labour force is included in an appendix. Basing their study on an examination of current and pending legislation and interviews with working women, employers and legal experts, the authors devote a major portion of their book to legal cases involving issues of equal pay, forced early retirement and maternity and menstrual leave.

93. Croll, E. J. Social Production and female status: Women in China. *Race and Class*, Vol. XVII, No. 4, Summer 1976, p. 39–52.

It can be argued that some structural constraints inhibiting the further redefinition of the role of women still exist in Chinese society, for incomplete transformations in the mode of production encourage the persistence of certain ideological constraints, particularly in rural areas. But even where transformations in the mode of production are more complete, as in the urban areas in China, the author argues that ideological constraints remain. The experience and conscious analysis of the People's Republic of China indicates that not only is social production not a sufficient condition to explain social status, but that other factors interfere and discourage access to and control over the strategic resources of society. In the case of women it is ideological constraints above all which are seen primarily to obstruct the passage from social production to social status in China today.

94. Dube, L. *Studies on women in South East Asia: A status report.* A report prepared for Unesco, published in the series of the Regional Adviser for Social Science in Asia and Oceania, Bangkok, 1980, 77 p.

The report reviews research on women in ASEAN countries – Indonesia, Malaysia, the Philippines, Singapore and Thailand; provides a critique of some of the basic approaches found in the work; suggests directions for future research in specific areas of study; and provides an extensive bibliography.

95. *Fujin Hakusho.* [White Papers on Women] Nihon Fujin Dantai Rengo Kai Hen [Japanese Women's Federation] (ed.) Tokyo, Sodobunka, 1979.

Part I looks at parent-child relationships. As a result of the increase in the number of labourers' families, urban areas become overpopulated and both husband and wife must work to support the family, because of economic problems and housing shortages. The first part of this white paper considers women whose role inside the house is strictly defined, the problems of parent-child relationships and child-rearing, the lack of social security for children despite the increase in the number of working mothers in the population, and geographical solidarity on child upbringing. Part II considers the present conditions and demands of women. Topics covered are the decline in the rate of female labour force participation, population trends, statistical data on the rise in divorce rates, the existing conditions of prices of commodities, family finances and housing costs. The problems of self-employed women and housewives, women labourers and women in farming villages are enumerated. Other issues considered are social security and unemployment, the problems of old age, prostitution prevention law, women, education and culture, and women's social and political participation.

96. *Gendai Nihon Josei no Ishiki to Kodo* [Consciousness and Action of Modern Japanese women]. Fujin ni Kansuru Shomondai no Sogochosa Hokohusho [A collective survey report on various problems concerning women] Tokyo, 1974.

Problems of women's lives related to marriage, the family, household, employment, civic life and leisure are considered here with statistical data. Topics related to marriage are images of marriage, choosing the proper mate, and stability and failure of marriage; on family and household, the report looks at husband-wife relationships, parent-child relationships, women's old age, the household economy, and women's legal standing in homes. On employment, the report considers the post-war conditions of women's employment and trends in the female labour force, women's professional consciousness, the domestic life of couples who are both working, self-employed women's work and consciousness. Explanations about conditions and characteristics of civic activities, requirements for participation, and obstacles for involvement, the position and role of participating women are discussed. Women's leisure is considered from the point of view of time composition of women's life, recreation, aims for leisure and pressures from its pursuit.

97. Havens, T. R. H. Women and war in Japan, 1937–45. *The American Historical Review*, Vol. 80, No. 4, 1975, p. 913–934.

The author attempts to answer two questions about wartime Japanese society: (1) What were the experiences of women, Japan's largest social group, during 1937–45?, and (2) What were the implications of wartime life for Japanese society and modern society in general? Japanese women were the victims of considerable socio-economic change induced by the war. The precise impact of the war on Japan is complicated and involves two abnormal factors: first the military occupation by a conquering nation for six and a half years, leading to more rapid social reform than might otherwise have been the case; and secondly the extraordinarily rapid economic development after 1952, which had more impact in changing people's lives than the social engineering of the occupation. The wartime conditions of women are described with statistical data, which can be used as a stepping-stone toward more general conclusions about the connection between war and the history of society.

98. Jain, D., Chand, M. and Singh, N. *Women's quest for power.* New Delhi, Vikas Publishing House, 1980.

The book discusses five cases in which women have organized themselves in pursuit of better food, clothing, shelter and employment in India. The cases considered are: the Self-Employed Women's Association, Ahmedabad; the Anand Milk Producers Union, Kaira; the Lijjat Pappad Organisation (all three are women's co-operatives); women painters of Madhubani, who were involved in a government launched handicrafts programme; the 'Night Patrollers of Manipur' a self-help group of women dedicated to attacking alcoholism (amongst men). In each of the cases connected with employment, the women have provided themselves with an income, but done little to change their status. The study is interesting, however, since it provides information about what is happening to women as a result of industrialization, anti-women state policy and private profiteering, and indicates the ways in which women react to these phenomena.

99. *Japanese Women.* Report of Mid-Decade April Meeting of the 1980 National Conference of Non-governmental Organisations of Japan, United Nations Decade for Women 1976–1985. Tokyo, Executive Committee of the 1980 National Conference, July 1980.

A report of this independent movement for the improvement of women's status in Japan and their activities in the five years between International Women's year and 1980. The report outlines the problem areas, the recommendations, which they have made to successive governments and progress made. Of the Japanese National Plan of Action they state 'There is no doubt that the Government, in taking advantage of the circumstances is doing nothing more than hiding conveniently behind a disguise. As far as concrete policy is concerned the National Plan of Action is actually inadequate' (p. 11). They also give the results of a questionnaire survey on equality between men and women and the improvement of the status of women.

100. *Japanese women speak out. White Paper on sexism in Japan.* Tokyo, Task Force, 1975. (Address of Task force: c/o PARC PO Box 5250, Tokyo International Japan.)

Produced by a collective of women in International Women's Year, this is a collection of papers divided into four main categories: (1) Sexism in Japan, which includes 'The invisible proletariat – recession lay-offs in

Japan – "ladies first" ' by Kaji Htsuko; sexism in children's books by a women's group called Idobata, and 'The political participation of Japanese women' by Goto Masako, plus a paper on 'Thirty years of the "Women's Policy" ' by Iijima Aiko; (2) Women fight back – with articles on the abortion struggle in Japan by Nagano Yoshiko, and women in the anti-pollution movements by Matsui Yayori; (3) Victims of double discrimination – with papers on women in Okinawa by Kinjo Kiyoko, and 'To be female and outcaste in Japan' by Kitazawa Yoko; (4) Towards solidarity among Asian Women, with a discussion of Women at the Conference of Asians, and a paper on 'Foreign capital invasion and Thailand's textile workers'.

101. Khanna, G. and Varghese, M. *Indian women today.* New Delhi, Vikas Publishing House, 1978, 212 p.

A study of 1,000 Indian women, a representative sample from different areas of the country and different socio-economic strata. The women were interviewed and the topics covered were situational characteristics, e.g. religion, marital status, husband/father's occupation; marriage and married life, sex and family planning; socio-economic and cultural aspects of family life; parent-daughter relationships; fashion, social practices and issues. Amongst the issues for example attitudes towards inter-caste marriage, dowry, divorce, adoption, co-education, sexual freedom, premarital sex were sought. The women were also asked about the employment of women.

102. Kobayashi, T. and Yoneda S. *Fujin no Ayumi Hyaku-nen* [The centennial course of women] Nihon Fujin Dantai Rengo Kai Hen [edited by Japanese Women's Federation] Tokyo, Otsuki Shobo, 1978.

A reformist view on women who have been the foundation of Japan's rapid economic growth, their constant efforts to adapt to the ever-changing external conditions of Japanese societies in the last hundred years. The book describes the conditions of women living in the transitional period from the last stage of the closed, feudal Edo Period to the opening of the country to foreign trade, and the Meiji Restoration; the effects of the civil rights movement on women; the emergence of working women and the ill-treatment they received; the active participation of women under Taisho democracy; the tragedy of the Pacific war; how women fought during the period when equality of men and women declared by democratic movements was destroyed by the Occupation Army; how women were deprived of job opportunities and forced to take low-paying, part-time jobs under the influence of the Vietnam War and rapid economic advance.

103. Mattielli, S. (ed.) *Virtues in conflict: Tradition and the Korean woman today.* Seoul, The Royal Asiatic Society, 1977.

A collection of ten essays investigating the effects of the Confucian tradition on women in the Republic of Korea, about half of which are written from the perspectives of history and folklore, whilst the remainder deal with issues related to the status of women in the Republic of Korea today. Cultural conflicts engendered by the processes of development and modernization are dealt with in several essays. Other topics considered are psychological problems, legal status, educational experience and labour force participation.

104. Morosawa, Y. *Onna no Rekishi.* [History of women], Volumes 1 and 2. Tokyo, Miraisha, 1977.

Why, in primitive societies, did women become dependent on men? What was love and family to the ruling class in ancient times? Keeping these questions in mind the author analyses the reasons for the existence of a distinct form of love, the formation of the family type, and the role of women in such societies. The author explains the meaning of love and family for the ruling class and for the common people, and the inner structure of the family of the two classes in ancient societies; the nobility's form of love in the Heian Period; women of the Kamakura and Muromachi Period; the conditions of the Edo Period, where the feudal system was firmly established; and the meaning of love and family in Meiji, Taisho and Showa eras.

105. Pharr, S. J. Women in Japan today. *Current History*, No. 68, April, 1975, p. 174–176.

The author discusses the gaps in reality – the legal rights and traditional practices, which put women in unequal positions compared with men both inside and outside the family sphere – supporting the argument with statistical data. Women's education, work, marriage and political activity are considered. As far as education is concerned, many parents and daughters consider that the goal for girls is marriage and full-time housework, and seek an education which will fulfil this goal. For work, although in 1971 almost 39 per cent of Japan's total work force was women they held jobs with the least prestige and lowest pay. Democratization, urbanization and prosperity in post-war Japan have all had a major impact on family life, especially on the roles of family members. The sexual division of labour once clearly defined, is now breaking down among younger couples. In political activitity, Japanese women compared for example with American women, are far less involved in outside social activities and are less politically orientated. During the post-war period, there has been a constant clash between the laws and customs affecting women's status. The author considers that many of these problems have their roots in the history of Japan.

106. Ray, R., Chaudhury, R., Basa, K., et. al. *Role and Status of women in Indian society*. Calcutta, Firma Klm Private Ltd., 1978, 167 p.

A collection of fourteen scholarly essays in fields varying from literature and history to economics and political science. Three main groups emerge: (1) essays tracing historical change in the role and image of Indian women; (2) those dealing with women and education; and (3) those analysing the situation of the 'new women' in India. This third group, dealing by and large with urban, well-educated, ambitious, middle class women, as opposed to the mass of uneducated women, indicates that the problems this group face are not so different from those of women in developed countries. Once these women have entered the fields of law, medicine, engineering, and business, they experience delay in promotion, segregation in the workplace and above all, conflict between work and family life.

107. Romero, F. R. P. Is the economic emancipation of the Filipino working woman at hand? *Philippine Labor Review*, Vol. 1, No. 3, 1976, p. 21–32.

In her paper, Romero reviews the various protective legislative measures passed for the working woman, arguing that they operate against women, since employers do not want to hire female employees because they wish to avoid the requirements laid down by the state. The author enumerates several other blocks to achieving economic equality for women workers. These are (1) traditional and cultural constraints; (2) economic considerations; (3) government attitudes; and (4) the weakness of administrative machinery. She then suggests that if equality is to be approximated, a multi-faceted approach should be followed. The national programme of action must take into account political, social, economic, educational, and cultural factors, and as a starting point, research should be conducted to get an accurate and reliable assessment of the present position of working women.

108. Shiozawa, M. and Shimada, T. Documentary on Post-war women living alone. *Japan Quarterly*, Vol. 23, No. 4, 1976, p. 363–377.

This article discloses the social prejudice and psychological hardship accompanied by physical decline faced by one million single women, the victims of the Second World War. The war deprived these women, who were at the time in their late teens and early twenties, of the choice of marrying, one of the fundamental rights of a human being. Yet the social prejudice in Japan against single women, such as the traditionally held ideas on girls' education and ineffective equality of civil rights for men and women, are so strong that they create inferiority complexes in many of these women. They face serious problems in old age, since they have no children to turn to when their mental and physical abilities begin to decline. There is another group who received professional training and followed a different route. These career women show that conforming to the traditional pattern of marriage was not the only path for women. The authors try to clarify what made these particular women hard-working, successful, pessimistic and critical, by discussing a series of interviews with them. At the same time the article indicates the responsibility and obligation of the entire society for these women as a group.

II. Women's work and labour force participation

WOMEN AND DEVELOPMENT

109. Hara, K. *Economic Growth and woman's role in Japan*. A paper presented at the session on Sex Roles in Society, IX World Congress of Sociology, Uppsala, Sweden, 1978.

This paper deals with the relationship between economic growth and women's role in Japanese society. Structurally, women are allocated and utilized as an instrument to achieve economic growth. The traditional principle of good wife, wise mother education is still actively moulding young girls and their attitudes. Male planners have very little intention of allowing women to develop their abilities and potential in order to build a better society. Men have to be convinced by women of the need to restructure the society in which we live.

110. Illo, J. F. I. Constraints to rural women's participation in Philippine development: A report from the field. *Philippine Studies*, No. 27, 1979, p. 198–209.

This paper discusses the concerns of rural married women in Camarines Sur, and provides a framework for explaining the participation in development to which these concerns are related. It indicates that first, rural women share with their menfolk a common constraint, which is primarily structural. Secondly, the participation of rural women is influenced by the social and economic class to which they belong. Those in the lower class simply have to work on any job available. Upper class women are socially required to fulfil some desirable minimum home production time. They would otherwise be censured by society for reneging on their principal duties as mother and wife.

111. *Katipunan ng mga Bagong Pilipina*. [Trends in women's participation in National Development: The Philippine experience.] A paper submitted to the World Congress for International Women's Year, Berlin, Federal Republic of Germany, 1975.

This paper indicates that larger numbers of women work outside the home as a result of increasing industrialization, but that statistics show that sex discrimination in employment is still prevalent despite legislation which prohibits it. Women are the last to be hired and the first to be fired. If they are hired, they are bypassed for promotion. The paper claims that male-female inequality stems from the traditional notion that the home is still the only rightful place for women. It has been inculcated among Filipino women that they should view their world in terms of home and family. The report states that recent Philippine government efforts to improve the conditions of the female populace are insufficient and inadequate. Women themselves must form an effective organization and unite to achieve this end, and compel the state to improve their lot and involve them actively in national developmental efforts. Government programmes will not take root and bear fruit, unless there is active mass participation.

112. Montiel, C. *Indicators of the perceived level of effectiveness of low income women's organizations*. Final report submitted to the Philippine Institute for Development Studies through the Institute of Philippine Culture, Ateneo de Manila University. Quezon City, Department of Psychology, Ateneo de Manila University, 1979, 64 p. (Women in Development Studies 5.)

This study concerns low income women, who are members of community organizations. It asserts that the status of women in the development process may be gleaned from their participation in community organizations. Using the self-reliant model, the author presents women's assessment of their organization, particularly in terms of effectiveness in serving as a channel of communication between the members and government, in involving the people in planning organizational projects, and in undertaking activities aimed at solving community problems.

113. Palabrica-Costelo, M. and Costelo, M. A. *Low skilled working women in Cagayan de Oro: A comparative study of domestic, small-scale, and industrial employment*. Final report submitted to the Philippine Institute for Development Studies through the Institute of Philippine Culture, Ateneo de Manila University. Cagayan de Oro City, Research Institute for Mindanao Culture, Xavier University, 1979, 145 p. (Women in Development Studies 6.)

This study investigates the relationship between women and the development process, by comparing women in three occupational types – factory workers, domestic helpers, and workers in small-scale establishments. These types were chosen to approximate various development stages, namely traditional, transitional and modern. The women were compared in terms of their social and economic background, level of living, job satisfaction and occupational mobility, institutional participation, and social psychological measures.

114. Papanek, H. Development planning for women. *Signs – Journal of Women in Culture and Society* (Chicago) Vol. 3, No. 1, 1977.

This is a plea for the integration of women into development planning with strong arguments for its importance. Various political, attitudinal, conceptual and methodological problems which hinder the integration of women in the development process as equal partners with men are outlined and the author suggests a broader international context of research and experience as solutions to these obstacles.

115. Postel, E., Schrijvers, J. (eds.) *A woman's mind is longer than a kitchen spoon: Report on women in Sri Lanka*. Leiden, Research project Women and Development, June 1980, 146 p.

A report based on data collected by a Sri Lankan-Dutch team engaged on a project 'Women and Development' in 1977–78. The aim of the research was to describe and analyse the situation of women under changing social and economic conditions, and to give recommendations for a development policy aimed at the needs of women and their participation in society. A large amount of data on the condition of life of women in different sectors of Sri Lankan society is included.

116. Santiago, E. S. *Women in agriculture: A social accounting of female workshare*. Final Report submitted to the Philippine Institute for Development Studies through the Institute of Philippine Culture, Ateneo de Manila University. Los Banos, Laguna, Association of Colleges of Agriculture in the Philippines, 1980, 154 p. (Women in Development Studies 7.)

This study aims to identify the workshare, roles, and activities performed by women in the agricultural sector and to assess the impact of technology, food production, and related programmes on women's status. A survey of women in two rural areas, one in Bulacan, the other in Batangas, indicated substantial participation of women in all aspects of farm work. Findings also show that more of the men than women are displaced when land preparation is mechanized and that more men than women have access to agricultural extension services. The author also presents two case studies: an organization of village women and a member of this organization, in order to illustrate the organizational development of a formal women's group and its impact on the members, and the community in general.

117. Weekes-Vagliani, W. (in collaboration with Bernard Grossat) *Women in development:At the right time for the right reasons*. Paris, OECD, 1980, 330 p.

A secondary analysis based on survey data for ten ethnic groups in four developing countries aimed at identifying the moment at which the vicious circle of illiteracy, poverty, rapid and excessive population growth and hunger can be broken, and women incorporated into the development process. The results indicate that knowledge of certain factors is essential for the design of effective policies and programmes which will affect both young women and other groups in the population: ethnicity and family systems associated with ethnic groups, domestic life cycle patterns, the meaning of delayed marriage and economic autonomy in each setting. The timing of intervention in terms of domestic life cycle patterns is also crucial. The study looked specifically at determinants of age at marriage and family formation in Malaysia, Fiji, Sri Lanka and the Dominican Republic.

INDIVIDUAL COUNTRIES

118. Aganon, V. G. and Aganon, M. E. *A study of women workers in women dominated manufacturing establishments in Metro Manila*. Final report submitted to the Philippine Institute for Development Studies through the Institute of Philippine Culture, Ateneo de Manila University. Quezon City, Asian Labor Education Center, University of the Philippines System, 1979, 131 p. (Women in Development Studies 1.)

This study investigates factors which lead to the presence of more women workers in some manufacturing establishments. It compares the status of men and women employees of similar positions in the establishments surveyed and ascertains the contributions to and benefits derived from the work of these workers. Findings of the study indicate that to a certain extent sex is a major factor in the hiring of employees in the sample establishments: women are hired for jobs requiring good finger dexterity and patience, while men are assigned to heavy manual tasks. No discrimination between sexes in terms of salary and work conditions is indicated, but the study fails to arrive at conclusive findings, because men and women perform different functions.

119. Alcid, M. H. Women's participation in the labor force. *Philippine Labor Review*, Vol. 2, No. 1, 1977, p. 55–62.

The article examines significant trends in labour force participation of women, and the factors which influence such participation. Statistics available show that the number of women in the labour force is increasing in the Philippines, from 4 to 5 million over a ten-year period. In terms of age distribution, the groups with the highest participation rate are those between 25 and 44 years, and those between 45 and 64 years. In general, the unemployment rate of females is higher than that of males. Of the employed, most are absorbed in agriculture, followed by manufacturing and commerce. There are various determinants of female labour force participation, especially that of married women. Some are individual attributes, such as education; some refer to attributes of the family, such as the presence of young children and domestic help and the husband's income; and others are characteristics of the market in general, such as labour demand conditions and the nature of job opportunities.

120. Asian and Pacific Centre for Women and Development. *A Case study on the modernization of the traditional handloom weaving industry in the Kashmir Valley: the integrated development project for the Woollen Handloom Industry in Jammu and Kashmir*. New Delhi, Institute of Social Studies, 1980.

The objective of this study is to ascertain the impact on the employment and income of the traditional artisans, especially women, of the United Nations Integrated Project for the modernization of the traditional woollen handloom weaving industry in the Kashmir Valley. The new loom is far superior in terms of volume of production, productivity and finish, and the weaving process can continue uninterrupted, since the woven portion is automatically wound on. As part of this investigation, case studies of six weaving households were carried out. These studies show that in all cases there has been a sharp reduction in the employment of allied workers, mainly women, and that all the weavers have suffered a fall in their monthly income since they joined the Project. The expansion of this Project will lead to further unemployment amongst women, since only mill made yarn is to be used, women hand spinners would be the first victims and the chances of improving the status of women will be reduced. This review shows that the project appraisal criteria, personnel and procedures of United Nations agencies are not yet capable of coping with the need for a new economic order, nor the need to integrate women into the processes of development.

121. Gonzalez-Marbella, S. J. *Filipino women's entrepreneurship in small scale manufacturing industries*. M. A. thesis, Department of Sociology and Anthropology, Ateneo de Manila University, 1978.

This study describes the socio-economic backgrounds, motivations, role behaviour, and fertility patterns of married Filipino women engaged in small scale manufacturing in Metro Manila. Survey findings reveal that women entrepreneurs are highly educated, high achievers, and are generally first or middle born children. Reasons given by these women for venturing into business are the desire for greater monetary returns, and to have their own business or 'independence'. Findings also show that the busier the woman is with her business, the greater she feels the need to be freed from childrearing and close home management supervision tasks, the lower is her pregnancy rate, and the wider the interval between her pregnancies. When asked about their duties and responsibilities in general most of the women gave answers related to business performance followed by wife-mother duties.

122. Hackenberg, B. H., Lutes, S. V. and Angeles, T. *Social indicators of premarital and postmarital labor force participation among women in Region XI*. Final report submitted to the Philippine Institute for Development Studies through the Institute of Philippine Culture, Ateneo de Manila University, Davao City, Davao Research and Planning Foundation, Inc., 1980, 106 p. (Women in Development Special Studies 3.)

Aiming at exploring the impact of socio-economic growth on women, this study looks into the indicators, which are predictive of the labour force participation of women after marriage. The contention is that early socialization to wage work, before marriage, is indicative of the current employment status and of the occupational and social mobility of women. Poverty is also found to be a significant factor in determining post-marital labour force participation. Data for the study were gathered in a survey of single migrant women in three cities in South Mindanao in 1979, and from a 1977 socio-economic and fertility survey of households in Region XI.

123. Hara, K. Status of Japanese women: Career-mindedness of University graduates – problems in the compatibility of profession and home. *International Christian University Social Science Journal*, Vol. 13, 1975, p. 209–220.

This paper is an attempt to review some studies of career-mindedness and the compatibility of profession and home on the part of educated Japanese women, in the light of the changing socio-cultural milieu. In order to understand some of the problems peculiar to Japanese society, a short description of the social status of women in pre-war and post-war Japanese society is given. Industrialization brings about an increase in the labour force participation of women, but this increase is mainly in the categories of the unskilled or semi-skilled. In 1969, women in the administrative and managerial categories of labour constituted only 4 per cent of these workers, an increase of 1.5 per cent in ten years, and a problem for the career-minded, educated Japanese woman. The emergence of the nuclear family is a concomitant phenomenon of industrialization and urbanization. In 1930, the average family size was five persons, but in 1970 it was 3.73. Institutional care and protection of children are indispensable for working mothers, when they have to combine work inside and work outside the home.

124. Osako, M. M. Dilemmas of Japanese professional women. *Social Problems*, 26, October 1978, p. 15–25.

Despite advanced industrialization, Japanese professional women have been excluded from responsible positions in most private industries. They are placed on a career track separate from male employees and discriminated against in wages, promotion and retirement. Most working women, however, take this differential treatment for granted and view their employment as a temporary stage before marriage or childbirth. This acceptance is possible because of (1) the high cultural value placed on motherhood and collective goal achievement, and (2) the housewife's unchallenged authority at home, which discourages women from pursuing an independent career. In addition the norms of rewarding continuous employment (i.e. promotion and wages based on length of service – *nenko joretsu*) and the stress on group loyalty (as expressed by the long overtime put in by workers and active participation in the company's social activities) virtually deny women the option of combining familial and career roles. The home-orientated majority hinders the formation of effective public opinion advocating fair employment practices, thus perpetuating the *status quo* of the sexual division of labour. The author attempts to analyse how the sexual inequality experienced by Japanese professional women persists, despite recent changes or because of them, by examining the indices of social behaviour in their full empirical context.

OTHER

125. Blake, M. *A case study on women in industry.* Asian and Pacific Centre for Women and Development, April 1980.

This study discusses women in industry, including labour intensive and sophisticated technology industries and the traditional women-employing industries. From what is already known about women, this paper tries to identify the areas in which more information is required, the issues on which action might be taken, and a research methodology which integrates the process of education and mobilization of women with the process of fact-finding. In Asian countries, namely Hong Kong, Malaysia, Korea, Singapore, and Thailand, the establishment of labour-intensive, sophisticated industries such as the electronics industry, has created employment opportunities for women. The expansion of this branch of industry is due to the establishing of subsidiary plants of multi-national corporations with home bases in developed countries. These establishments are export orientated, labour-intensive and profit maximizing through cheap labour, which the Asian countries supply. The host governments in turn, are anxious to gain foreign investment for their own development programmes, and as a result the increased participation of women has not represented an improvement in the status of women. The author calls for research into employment structures, cross-cultural comparisons of protective legislation for women, industrial hazards and health, and the educational needs of women workers, with a view to action and policy change on legislation for women and discriminatory practices against women, and the education and organization of women workers. Basic to the paper is the attempt to arrive at processes which integrate the three goals of research, education and mobilization as these relate to women. What needs to be identified are the different socio-cultural elements, which contribute to the successful mobilization of women, and the processes of organization so that the determinants of the mobilization of women may be extracted.

126. Miralao, V. A. *Female employment and fertility in the Philippines.* Ph.D. dissertation. Cornell University, 1980.

Using data from the 1975–76 survey on the Role and Status of Women in the Philippines, the author looks into the association between female employment and fertility in two areas: (1) the contribution of women's premarital employment in delaying the age at first marriage and in shaping women's early family size desires, and (2) the manner in which work and fertility relationships might be modified by the nature of women's occupations and by the socio-economic condition and type of household. The study finds that female employment before marriage contributes significantly to a postponement in marriage. No conclusive evidence, however, is indicated on the influence of employment on women's fertility desires and expectations, and on the number of children borne. Examination of the work-fertility relationship by socio-economic group shows women's employment to be negatively associated with number of children among women in high income households, but positively among women in low income households. With regard to type of household, the study indicates that working women in extended households tend to expect fewer births than their non-working counterparts.

127. Patag, M. E. J. *Career choice correlates of Filipino women in traditionally male and female fields.* M. A. thesis, Ateneo de Manila University, 1980, 169 p.

This study seeks to ascertain the personality factors or traits, which characterize women who are in a stereotypically feminine field, such as teaching, and in a stereotypically masculine field, such as management, to see whether these women see themselves as possessing these traits. It also compares women's attitudes and feelings towards womanhood. Female graduate students in business administration and in education from three universities were interviewed. Findings indicate no significant differences in self-image between the two groups, but attitudes and feelings toward womanhood are positively correlated with women's career choices. Those with more liberal attitudes are in business, while those who are more conservative are found in education.

128. Zosa-Feranil, I. and de Guzman, E. A. Female participation in the labour force and fertility in the Philippines. *Philippine Labor Review*, Vol. 2, No. 3, 1977, p. 53–69.

This paper posits an association between female labour force participation and fertility. This contention gains more significance when seen in the light of the urban-rural locale as well as the nature of the economic activity. Findings show that working women in highly urbanized communities and those engaged in economic activities away from their homes, generally exhibit lower fertility, whereas women who perform economic activities entailing home or family arrangements display fertility levels comparable with those exhibited by their non-working counterparts. Although causal relationships are not clearly specified, observed association opens up the possibility that female labour force participation may reduce fertility to desired levels.

129. Feranil, I. *Women, work force participation and underutilization.* Final report submitted to the Philippine Institute for Development Studies through the Institute of Philippine Culture, Ateneo de Manila University. Manila, Population Institute, University of the Philippines System. 1979, 126 p. (Women in Development Special Studies 2.)

This study seeks to identify women workers and their employment situations. It focuses on the issues related to under-utilization – forms of under-utilization and the conditions that breed this situation. Using data from the UPPI 1975 work force survey, the author suggests that given a different approach to labour force data, females, like their male counterparts, may be seen as essentially economically active. Females, however, tend to suffer more from under-utilization, especially those in their thirties and forties, those never married, and wives of household heads.

III. Family and household

130. Boey, C. Y. Daughters and working mothers – the effects of maternal employment. In: Kuo, E. C. Y., and Wong, A. K. (eds) *The Contemporary family in Singapore: Structure and change*. Singapore, Singapore University Press, 1979, 306 p.

An examination of the effects of maternal employment on the female child in Singapore. The findings that have emerged from the study can be summarized as follows: (1) In general, daughters of working mothers are less traditional in their sex-role definition regardless of their social class background; (2) only among girls from a higher social class background is maternal employment associated with both a higher achievement motivation and a higher academic performance of the respondents; (3) the corollary that children of employed mothers seem to do more household chores than the children of non-employed mothers is not supported in the present study; (4) daughters of working mothers generally express less affection for their mothers than those of non-working mothers; (5) maternal employment is not associated with strict discipline of the daughters. The findings, however, indicate that where the mother has a positive attitude towards employment, she is less severe in her discipline than is the case with those who have a negative attitude.

131. Boulding, E. Familial constraints on women's work roles. *Signs – Journal of Women in Culture and Society*, Vol. 1, No. 3, Part 2, Spring 1976, p. 95–117.

The writer relates male and female roles – the female has the triple role of 'breeder-feeder-producer', while the male bears primarily the producer role. As early as the hunting and gathering societies, through agrovillages, the trading towns and the first urban civilizations more work has been done by the triple-roled women. Most of the 'breeder-feeder' role was not mass serviced, and women's hard work has often been belittled. With the fiction of males as the heads of households, the subsidiary position of women is further enhanced by the discrepancy of wage differentials in waged labour. The writer calls for equal rewards and equal opportunities for both sexes – for women to take the producer's role and men to take breeder-feeder roles.

132. Hollnsteiner, M. R. The Filipino family confronts the modern world. In: Gorospe, V. R. (ed.). *Responsible parenthood in the Philippines.* Manila, Cellar, 1970, p. 19–44.

The family has many functions for society as well as for the internal structure of the family itself. This paper deals with the Filipino family's response to the modern world in terms of: (1) the role of men and women; (2) the parent-child relationship; (3) extended kinship and the nuclear family. The stereotyped view of women's role is that of the good mother guarding her children and effectively managing the home. Men are considered to be chiefly the breadwinner and to represent authority. The parent-child relationship is characterized by closeness and affection between them. The preference for extended kin relationships in the largely non-kin world of the open community is decreasing in the modern environment.

133. Layo, L. L. Correlates of female income: Preliminary results. In: *The Role of women in contributing to family income.* Proceedings of the regional workshop in Bangkok, July 1976. Bangkok, Friedrich-Ebert-Stiftung, 1977, p. 122–136.

Using a sample of 581 working women, the author looks into the factors that affect female income and the relative importance of each factor in accounting for income differentials. Female income is viewed in terms of female income per month, wife-husband income ratio, and female-household income ratio. The following factors were identified as affecting female income: demographic – rural-urban residence, age, and civil status; economic – husband's income, household income and per capita income; work-related – occupation, industry, types of employment, number of years worked, number of hours worked per week, reasons for working and attitudes towards working women; education; and number of children.

134. Lynch, F. S. J. and Makil, P. Q. The BRAC 1967 Filipino family survey. In: Gorospe, V. R. (ed.). *Responsible parenthood in the Philippines.* 1970, p. 53–71.

The topic of the eleventh annual meeting at the Baguio Religious Acculturation Conference (BRAC) was the Filipino family. The survey was conducted in order to gather data on the Filipino family and to clarify the role of organized religion in the rapid population increase in the Philippines. Five aspects were considered: (1) church attendance and closeness to pastor; (2) family size; (3) family planning; (4) family roles; (5) non-traditional behaviour. Findings were as follows: The tendency to attend church services regularly is clearly associated with high educational attainment; educational attainment and the number of children are inversely associated; the tendency to favour family planning is associated with high educational attainment, frequent mass-media exposure, upper social status, and being a Protestant; the ideal father is a good provider and the ideal mother manages the household well; the good child is above all considerate of his or her parents. A preference for new ways of doing things is associated with high educational attainment, frequent mass-media exposure, youth, upper social status, and being a member of the Iglesia in Christo or a Protestant church.

135. Mani, A. Caste and marriage amongst the Singapore Indians. In: Kuo, E. C. and Wong, A. K. (eds). *The Contemporary family in Singapore.* Singapore, Singapore University Press, 1979.

A main finding in this analysis of caste and marriage amongst Singapore Tamils, is the lack of congruence between attitudes towards caste marriage and the actual observance of caste at marriage. It appears that the individual is given ample freedom to hold his own views. It may even be fashionable to condemn the existence of caste, but caste principles are adhered to when it affects one's caste status. As far as marriage is concerned, in Singapore, the caste groups tend to ignore minor hierarchical distinctions, but to emphasize the importance of belonging to several major levels. This is mainly because of the lack of prospective spouses in most castes.

136. Man Singh, D. and Bardis, P. D. (eds). *The family in Asia*. London, George Allen and Unwin, 1979, 431 p.

A collection of papers on the family in a number of Asian countries – Thailand, Afghanistan, India, Pakistan, Iran, China, Republic of Korea, the Philippines, and Japan. A theoretical overview of the Asian family and society is provided as an introduction, and in the conclusions, by the editors, and a brief outline of the situation in each of the countries is discussed to provide a comparative overview. The authors conclude by drawing together some general trends which could be observed in the diverse countries covered: trends towards (1) more egalitarian family relations and less sexual segregation, limited subjugation of women to an inferior status; (2) emphasis on individualism and independence; (3) greater differentiation and specialized functioning of social institutions; (4) birth control and family planning; (5) social mobility; (6) marital disruption and divorce; (7) neglect and improper care for the elderly; (8) formal education for children; (9) more governmental influence on family activities.

137. Porio, E., Lynch, F. and Hollsteiner, M. R. *The Filipino family, community, and nation: The same yesterday, today, and tomorrow?* Institute of Philippine Culture, Ateneo de Manila University, 1975.

The survey, sponsored by the Philippine Social Science Council (PSSC), covers fifteen large urban areas and attempts to gain opinions on a variety of important topics, with emphasis on the family, community and nation. Specific topics were: decision-making in family matters, activities shared by family members, priority given to child-rearing values, the working mother, perception of self, community, and the nation, and awareness of and perceived priorities among government programmes. The main characteristics in the Filipino family are that the relationship between spouses is egalitarian, and that children should be obedient to their parents. Respondents who are aware of a change in their personal circumstances in the previous year were predominantly negative in their assessment of what had occurred. They expected the future to be rather gloomy for themselves, but the Philippines as a nation to have good prospects. The Filipino is aware of the government's national development efforts, but can personally relate to only a few of them.

138. Singh, G. and Savara, M. *A case study on child care facilities in metropolitan Bombay.* Asian and Pacific Centre for Women and Development, 1980.

The objective of this study is to survey some creches in Bombay City, to understand how they operate and to elicit suggestions for making creches more useful. The study was restricted to the needs of urban women from the poorer socio-economic groups, those who could not utilize the private paid creche facilities. The survey of three creches run in Bombay City for the poorer sections indicates that there is a great demand and need for childcare facilities, which would allow women to work with greater concentration, attention, and less expenditure of energy. In all the cases studied, the women themselves were extremely reluctant to express their grievances, since they feared that the child might be removed from the creche or that they may be victimized at work. A well organized network of creches would reduce infant mortality, prevent malnutrition, and develop the basis for schools. It would also assist in increasing girls' participation in education, since it is usually older girl children who are withdrawn from school to replace their mothers. The success of such a programme lies in the development of community support and initiative in the scheme.

139. Vogel, S. H. Professional housewife: the career of urban middle class Japanese women. *The Japan Interpreter*, Vol. 12, No. 1, Winter, 1978, p. 16–43.

This article gives details on the lives and the social roles of some typical middle class Japanese housewives, indicating that their role in the family is distinct from that of American housewives. The data is drawn from an in-depth study of a sample of middle class Tokyo housewives. The vast majority of women desire marriage and see it as their primary, if not exclusive, life-long career, requiring training, special skills and endless devotion. Their essential job is that of mothering, of providing '*amae*' for the entire family. They put themselves into their tasks and their family relationships with professionalism since mothering is directly tied to their whole purpose in life and self-definition. Despite rapid economic growth and modernization after the Second World War, the sharp role differentiation between men and women has held firm, and the place and role of the Japanese housewife is clearly defined. To the Japanese, this division of labour is not viewed as social discrimination, but gives security and an all encompassing identity. Everyone has a role in Japanese society and the housewife's place is central to the family and basic to the preservation of solidarity.

140. Yu, E. and Liu, W. T. *Fertility and kinship in the Philippines.* Notre Dame, Indiana, University of Notre Dame Press, 1980, 286 p.

A study of the relationship between family processes and marital fertility, with a sample of 2,000 women from both rural and urban backgrounds, using sample survey and ethnographic techniques. The authors provide a brief historical and social background to Philippine society, and detailed information on reproduction and courtship, contraceptive knowledge and its use, folk methods of birth control, marital relationships and extramarital relationships, relationships between parents and children and the kinship structure. The authors conclude that population policies cannot be formulated in a vacuum, and that there cannot be emphasis on disseminating contraceptive methods without changes taking place in economic conditions, health care, socio-cultural values and psychological perceptions of the people in the society.

IV. Education

141. Hara, K. *What women students think – their academic work, profession and marriage.* International Christian University, 1963. (Japanese.)

This exploratory study was conducted by the Japanese Association of University Women in 1961. The subjects were 1,910 seniors in ten co-educational universities and eight women's colleges in the Tokyo and Kansai areas. Some of the findings are as follows: (1) Three-quarters of the subjects wanted to work after graduation, but only one-quarter wished to continue regardless of marriage or children; (2) 27 per cent considered an occupation to be a stop-gap until marriage or childbirth; while 25 per cent wished to stop for childbirth but to re-enter employment after the children grew up; (3) there are fewer stop-gap orientated students and more career orientated ones in national universities than in private universities; (4) when mothers are working, daughters tend to wish to maintain a career as well, and there is a significant difference between the two groups – those with mothers working and those with non-working mothers; (5) the ambiguous attitude towards their future, which was characteristic of 25 per cent of the subjects, may reflect changing social conditions.

142. Hara, K. *A survey of university women graduates – how they utilize their abilities.* Tokyo, Japanese Association of University Women, 1969. (Japanese.)

This survey was conducted in 1969 by the Japanese Association of University Women. The sample consisted of 4,466 women graduates from thirteen colleges and universities, both women's and co-educational. Some of the findings can be summarized as follows: (1) out of 1,881 women who responded in the study, 24 per cent continued working, but 43 per cent have had some work experience; (2) the average length of work experience was between four and six years; (3) the main reasons for discontinuing work were marriage, childbirth and child-rearing; (4) almost half of those who continued working were not married; (5) 14 per cent of graduates from private women's colleges continue to work whilst the figure for the national co-educational universities is 58 per cent.

143. Unesco. *Final Report of the Asian Regional Seminar on Access of Girls to Primary Education.* Paris, Unesco, 1978. 33 p. (ED 78/CON. 712/4.)

The report reviews the situation on girls and primary education in a number of countries in the region, in particular the sixteen economically developing countries. The conclusions are that (1) the majority of girls in these countries have no opportunity for primary education; and (2) parity between girls' and boys' access to primary education has almost been achieved in eight of these countries, but does not seem to be an attainable goal in the near future in the other eight. The major problems cannot be solved by education alone. The report also discusses problems in the achievement of equal access for girls to primary education, an experimental project in Nepal, and new approaches in several countries of the region. It concludes with some recommendations to improve the situation.

144. Yoshida, N., Hara, K., Sekiya, R. and Ujihara, S. *Problems related to women's higher education, occupation and home*. Institute for Democratic Education, 1961. (Japanese.)

This is a report based on 2,071 replies from women aged 25 to 55 who graduated from higher educational institutions, married and have had a profession. Some of the findings are as follows: (1) The degree of satisfaction from the two-track life has no relation to the type of family composition. Those living with a husband, however, felt happier in their two-track life than those without. (2) Two groups, one which feels extremely happy with the two-track life and the other which wants to give up the job as soon as possible, are compared. The former seem to enjoy their job, while the latter group are more pressured by economic need. (3) Whether they have domestic help or not seems to be related to the success of the two-track life. (4) Junior high school teachers and medical doctors seem to get less satisfaction from the double-track life than artists, specialists or researchers. (5) The respondents put greater value on psychological co-operation of family members and planned living than electrification of home chores in order to maintain the two-track life successfully. (6) One of the greatest obstacles to the two-track life is small children. The problems related to the traditional Japanese child rearing practices and mother-child relationship need to be re-examined in terms of compatibility of home and profession. (7) In the Japanese social structure, it is extremely difficult for mothers to get re-employed in the kind of institutions in which they desire to work after a few years of absence. Nevertheless, 67 per cent of those who were not working indicated a desire for such re-employment. This is no longer a personal problem but has become a social problem which requires a social solution. (8) To have more daycare centres established ranks first for the purpose of maintaining a two-track life, and there are many complaints concerning discriminatory treatment of women – a too early retirement age applied only to women, inequality in pay, and lack of promotion. (9) Many respondents insist that women should make extra efforts to make a two-track life possible, and 71 per cent of them are opposed to women returning to the home and abandoning their work outside.

V. Demographic features

145. Chang, C.-T. Nuptiality patterns among women of childbearing age. In: Kuo, E. C. Y. and Wong, A. K. (eds). *The Contemporary family in Singapore: Structure and change*. Singapore, Singapore University Press, 1979.

There has been a rising age for marriage amongst women in the years 1947 to 1970. There are three significant factors which determine the nuptiality patterns of the population: (1) The gap of nuptiality patterns among three major ethnic groups has narrowed because of the dying out of the traditional custom of child marriage among both the Malays and the Indians and Pakistanis. (2) Enrolment has increased tremendously for all students from primary school to higher educational institutions, especially in the case of female students. (3) Moslems tend to marry much earlier than others, but the proportion of Moslem marriages has been decreasing. The findings above have relevance to our understanding of the recent trend towards later marriage.

146. Concepcion, M. B. Philippine population problem. In: Gorospe, V. R. (ed.) *Responsible Parenthood in the Philippines*. 1970. p. 1–18.

This paper demonstrates the urgent population problems of the Philippines in various aspects. The population of the Philippines is 38 million and its annual growth rate is 3.5 per cent. Four reasons are given for this high level of population growth: (1) the death rate has declined rapidly; (2) the birth rate remained high; (3) a high birth rate and a declining death rate leads to an increase in the proportion of children and adults in the population relative to older people; (4) the number of births and birth spacing patterns influence the growth rate of the population. The growing population cannot all be provided with proper jobs, which leads to slow economic development, and problems are also found in education, urbanization, sanitation, and housing. The suggested way to control these problems is effective use of birth control, but this approach meets strong opposition based on the Filipino's cultural tendency towards having large families in order to offset high infant and child mortality rates, which have already been reduced by modern technology.

147. Hollnsteiner, M. R. Modernization and family planning. In: Gorospe, V. R. (ed.). *Responsible Parenthood in the Philippines*. 1970. p. 45–52.

Modernization is inevitably followed by cultural change, and this paper focuses on family planning under the pressure of cultural change. A wife may discontinue her participation in family planning if there are problems such as disapproving husbands, community censure, or unpleasant physical side effects. Couples are aware, however, that the proper knowledge of family planning brings them a better economic situation and frees them from the link between the sexual act and procreation. The Filipinos are slowly but definitely shifting in the direction of modern attitudes to family size. It takes a long time for the mass of people to acquire new behaviour patterns and value systems, but modernization, including family planning, offers attractive and even inevitable ways of achieving development and better family and living conditions.

148. Kuo, E. C. Y. and Hassan, R. Ethnic intermarriage in a multi-ethnic society. In: Kuo, E. C. Y. and Wong, A. K. (eds). *The Contemporary family in Singapore*. Singapore University Press, 1979.

This analysis of inter-ethnic marriage in Singapore reveals that the intermarriage rate has remained relatively stable over the past ten years since Independence. The data show that those who marry across ethnic boundaries, compared with all marriages, are more likely to (1) have been married before; (2) also marry across religious lines; (3) be from the lower or upper occupational groups. The latter two generalizations remain true even when the remarriage cases are excluded. The remarriage group is found to be most endogamous with respect to religion. This is probably due to the fact that a large proportion of remarriages involve Moslems, and are thus intra-religious. Their unique and unexpected findings related to the age factor are as follows: When remarriage cases are excluded – (1) the intermarried grooms are not different in average age from other grooms, who were single at the time of marriage (and the brides are only slightly older than their counterparts in the latter group); (2) the age distribution of grooms among the inter-ethnic marriage group is not much more variable than that of all marriage groups while that of the brides is more variable; (3) the mean age difference between husband and wife among the interethnic marriage group is smaller than that of the total marriage group and that between grooms and brides who were single at the time of marriage.

149. Lauby, J. *The effect of marriage, childbearing and migration on the labor force participation of women*. Final report submitted to the Philippine Institute for Development Studies through the Institute of Philippine Culture, Ateneo de Manila University. Manila, Behavioral Sciences Department, De La Salle University, 1979, 137 p. (Women in Development Special Studies 4.)

This study aims to determine the patterns in labour force participation of Philippine women compared with those of men. Using the life cycle approach, the author assesses how the employment status of women is affected by marriage, childbearing, and migration. In general, the findings are that these life events have very little impact on changes in women's employment status. Women as a whole do not seem to interrupt their work for marriage or childbearing. They are, however, seen as starting work at a later age and retiring earlier than men do.

VI. Other

150. Bagadion, B. Jr. and others. *Law in the mobilization and participatory organization of the rural poor: The Kagawasan case*. Quezon City, Institute of Philippine Culture, Ateneo de Manila University, 1979, 75 p.

This volume documents the formation of participatory organizations of the rural poor and the impact of law and legal resources in the development of these organizations. One such organization presented here is a women's group which sought to fight community health and nutrition problems through united action and co-operation. The authors describe the issues and incidents which led to the organization of the rural women and how these women joined other organizations in the struggle to solve community problems involving legal action.

151. Chew, S.-K. Educational and occupational attainment of Singapore's Chinese women and men. University of Singapore, Department of Sociology, *Sociology Working Paper No. 59*, 1977.

Singapore's Chinese females who have participated in the labour force tend to come from higher socio-economic backgrounds than males, but women's mean education and occupation are lower than that of men. Other findings reported are: (1) some degree of inheritance of English education from father to son and daughter; (2) high and significant zero-order correlation between father's English education and respondent's level of education as well as significant net effect of father's English education on sons' but not daughters' level of education; (3) differential effect of respondent's English education on occupation between the sexes in Singapore.

152. Everett, J. Matson. *Women and social change in India*. New York, St. Martin's Press, 1979, 233 p.

Arguing that the Indian women's movement is one of the more successful bourgeois feminist movements which has achieved objectives more rapidly and with less opposition than the women's rights movements in the United States and the United Kingdom, the author tries to answer three questions: Why did the women's movement emerge? How did it justify its demands? Under what conditions are women's movements successful in achieving objectives? The author discusses the British and American context, the emergence of the Indian women's movement in the Indian context, the ideology of the Indian women's movement, their campaign for political representation and for Hindu law reform.

153. Higuchi, K. The PTA – A channel for political activism. *The Japan Interpreter*, Vol. 10, No. 2, Autumn 1975, p. 133–140.

The PTA has been criticized as a useless organization oppressing: (1)

husbands of PTA participant wives; (2) children; (3) principals and teachers; and (4) average mothers. The activities of the PTA must have some substance if it is to refute these criticisms. The author questions whether the PTA, probably the largest and most broadly based women's organization, is serving the interest of women members and functioning as an innovative social force. The most outstanding merit of the PTA is that it provides women with valuable training, for example in public relations skills, with knowledge of the general working of organizations and societies, and leads them to question authority and look for change. No profound progress has yet been made however.

154. Japanese Government *National Plan of Action.* Headquarters for the Planning and Promoting of Policies Relating to Women. 1977. (Japanese.)

This is a report of the National Plan of Action proposed by the Headquarters for the Planning and Promoting of Policies Relating to Women, which endeavours to formulate a plan 'to elevate the status and welfare of women and thereby to contribute to the development and progress of the whole society' (p. 3). The problems behind the necessity for the plan are recognized, and substantial measures of action to be undertaken by the Government are proposed. (See also Entry 99.)

155. Lebra, T. S. Sex equality for Japanese women. *The Japan Interpreter*, Vol. 10, Nos 3–4, Winter, 1976, p. 284–295.

This article delineates three basic directions in which the movement for women's equality has led in Japan. The conclusion that all three are problematic in a broad social context seems to line sexual equality up with racial, economic and other types of inequalities. Progress beyond a certain point involves fundamental social change. The direction in which Japanese women could move towards sexual equality is trilinear. The three paths are identified as: (1) dimorphism, an extension and intensification of the tradition of sex inequality, the division of labour based on the sexes; (2) bimorphism, a newer type of equality in which each sex performs both domestic and occupational roles; (3) amorphism, an equality defined by both sexes based on their freedom of choice to adopt any role that suits their abilities and desires. The reality is the existence of the problem of status asymmetry between the sexes caused by dilemmas arising in all three directions and the ambivalent attitudes of women themselves. The author considers that at the present time, since the universality of male dominance is an undeniable fact, the range of direction in which equalitarian ideology can be implemented is limited in all cultures.

156. Omvedt, G. *We will smash this prison – Indian women in struggle.* Orient Longman, 1980.

A personal account of the author's involvement with and impressions of the budding women's movement in India in the 1970s. Different chapters document the life conditions and problems of various groups of women – agricultural labourers, college students, street-sweepers.

157. Matsui, Y. The crusade of Japan's women against the ravages of pollution. *Unesco Courier*, 28 August 1975, p. 12–15.

This article presents an optimistic view of the changing role of Japanese women, who are finally trying to counter the stereotyped image of subservient wife and protective mother, treated as inferior to men. A brief description is given of the issues related to two Minamata Disease outbreaks, when women played the leading role in both attacking the guilty companies, and in the movements against environmental pollution. The author also mentions that women have been active in the consumer movement and have played a significant role in bringing about changes in Japan's politics and society.

158. OECD. *Manpower policy in Japan*. Reviews of Manpower and Social Policies. 1973. 169 p.

This is one of eleven reviews of manpower and social policies in different member countries published by OECD on the basis of discussions and of reports from those countries. The main concern of this report is manpower, and it concentrates on the seniority wage system and lifetime employment. The reports do not specify whether they are dealing with male and female employees, but considering the stress on lifetime employment and the seniority system, women are virtually excluded from manpower policy. Women are treated as one of the special groups, such as middle-aged or older workers, young workers, physically handicapped people and farmers. Special attention should be paid to p. 152–153 where there is a discussion of the possibility of women participating in working life, which casts doubt on the participation of married women in the world of work drawing attention to the job re-entry problem.

159. Roco, S. S. Jr., Imperial, S. S. and Illo, J. F. I. *Bikol integrated health, nutrition, and population project: a problem of medium*. Quezon City, Social Survey Research Unit (Naga City), Institute of Philippine Culture, Ateneo de Manila University, 1979.

This report describes the Bikolanos' health beliefs, illness and health practices, nutrition status, family planning attitudes and practices, and the factors affecting the acceptability of the Barangay Health Aide as a health specialist. Respondents were married women with ages ranging from 17 to 78 years. Using the social soundness approach, the study findings point to the need to institute public health programmes in the Bikol River Basin.

160. Unesco Regional Office for Education in Asia. *Higher Education in the Asian Region*. Bangkok, Bulletin of Unesco, Vol. VII, No. 1, September 1972.

The report reviews broadly the development of higher education in ten countries of the Asian region, which are Afghanistan, Burma, Ceylon, India, Iran, Japan, the Republic of Korea, Malaysia, the Philippines, and Thailand. One of the problems is the medium of instruction. In formerly colonial countries, education has been conducted in the language of the mother countries, but today those countries are confronted with the problem of using their native language. Higher education is expanding rapidly, and the Philippines shows the largest number of students in higher education per 100,000 of population (1,751). This expansion has also enabled more women to enrol in universities. Emphasis has been placed on literature and the humanities rather than on science and technology, since the former can be taught without high expenditure. However, the emergence of new economic and social demands and the changing composition of the student population indicate the need for a more diversified structure, and the emphasis is now shifting from the humanities to science. The necessity for building a post-graduate level of institutions is urged, since, without it, a brain drain continues and the contribution of education to the development and welfare of the developing country will not be realized.

161. Yasay, F. C. *A study of population – career development*. Institute of Philippine Culture, Ateneo de Manila University, 1974.

The study was sponsored jointly by the National Economic Development Authority of the Philippines and the United States Agency for International Development, and traces the development of the careers of 123 Filipinos who were trained abroad in population or family planning related courses under the Overseas Participant Training Programs. The objectives of the study are: (1) to determine the behaviour of the participants and non-participants before and after the former underwent training abroad; (2) to elicit the opinions of the participants, non-participants, and agency administrators about the training programme in general and the individual participants' training in particular. The research applied two types of comparison: one compares the trained group with the non-trained group; the other the conditions of before and after the training. The findings of the survey are related to benefits derived from the training; differences between trainees and non-trainees; criteria used for selection of trainees; need for the same type of training; problems encountered by trainees. The study concludes with several recommendations, which include confining the overseas programme to learning opportunities not available in the Philippines, making efforts to select training centres, classifying the training, and rigid screening of the candidates.

Journals

Feminist International No. 2 on Asian Women '80 includes a large number of articles under the general headings (i) Japanese women: the life cycle; (ii) Women in Asia: a feminist perspective; (iii) Women and Japanese culture; and (iv) Japanese Feminism: Theory and practice.

Law and Society Quarterly, Vol. VI, Nos 1–4, Jan.–Dec. 1976 is a special issue dedicated to the Status of Women in Indian Society, and includes an extensive, though unannotated bibliography.

Manushi, a journal about women and society. (C1/202 Lajpat Nagar, New Delhi 110024.) Published in Hindi and English.

Pacific and Asian Women's Network. (529 Bauddhaloka Mawata, Colombo 8, Sri Lanka.) First publication of the Pacific and Asian Women's Forum, a network of women in 17 Pacific and Asian countries. Topics covered include education, breastfeeding/bottle feeding, Asian women factory workers, marriage in China, images of women in films, women in Fiji, Bangladesh and Pakistan. Original if short articles.

Research on the Status of Women, Development and Population Trends in Eastern Europe: An Annotated Bibliography

by Barbara Tryfan

Research on the Status of Women, Development and Population Trends in Eastern Europe: An Annotated Bibliography by Barbara Tryfan

A. INTRODUCTION

Women's problems are considered of considerable importance for scientific research in the countries of Eastern Europe, as demonstrated by the amount of material appearing in journals and other publications, selectively presented here. The struggle for women's rights in all fields of life has been reflected in the literature of these countries since the 19th century, but the climate for the successful achievement of equality for women has existed since the establishment of socialist states in this region. In all of these countries, the formal, legal, constitutional equality of women is guaranteed, and considerable steps have been taken in terms of integrating women into areas which were previously the domain of men – particularly in relation to educational access and to labour force participation and professional work – in comparison to the countries in the rest of the world. It seems, however, that these achievements in production and educational access have been accompanied by only minimal restructuring of other institutions,[1] with the family remaining a central socializing institution, and women having primary responsibility for childrearing and housework. The conflicts and contradictions of the dual role performed by women which this collection of bibliographies has demonstrated in other regions of the world remains a problem in countries formally committed to equality for women. It has even been suggested that women's access to higher education in these countries should be limited since their concomitant commitment to work and career may lead to a loosening of family ties.[2]

The material in this bibliography reflects the changing focus of studies on women in different time periods, and the continuing contradictions in women's status and position in these countries. The basic criteria of choice for inclusion is that the item should be representative of the types of evaluation of the women's question which have been or are being made against the background of social conditions in the particular countries. The underlying themes in this bibliography are related to women's rights and their implementation in the political, economic, social, familial and cultural spheres, although the borderline between each of the areas is blurred. Almost all of the entries are in the language of the country concerned; the very few exceptions are indicated by the phrase 'in English'. The countries covered are Bulgaria, The German Democratic Republic, Hungary, Poland, Romania, Czechoslovakia, the USSR and Yugoslavia.

The bibliographic entries are categorized under the following broad headings:

I. General;
II. Women's work and labour force participation, including work in the professions and women in rural environments;
III. Family and household, including general studies, rural and urban studies, and considerations of maternity and divorce;
IV. Education;
V. Demographic features.
VI. Other

Entries are in alphabetical order within subcategories.

NOTES

1. Heitlinger, A., *Women and state socialism: Sex inequality in the Soviet Union and Czechoslovakia*, 1979 (Entry 167).
2. Barbara Tryfan in the report from which this introduction was taken.

B. THE BIBLIOGRAPHY ON EASTERN EUROPE

I. General

162. Atkinson, D., Dallin, A. and Lapidus, G. Warshofsky. *Women in Russia.* Hassocks, Sussex, The Harvester Press, 1978, 410 p. (In English.)

A wide ranging collection of papers looking at all aspects of women's lives in the Soviet Union. Part I is on the historical heritage, and includes papers on women and the Russian Intelligentsia, and factory women; Part II looks at sex roles and social change, and includes work on sexual equality in Soviet policy, Bolshevik alternatives and the Soviet family, rural women, women in the industrial labour force and the professions, and equal pay; Part III considers women, society and politics, with studies on women and sex in Soviet law, educational policies and attainment, images of male and female in children's readers, social services for women, women in political roles, and women's issues in public policy debates. Despite recognizing the considerable advances in women's position and status in the Soviet Union, compared with other countries in the world, a general conclusion is that 'there is no question that in the Soviet Union the status of women remains in many ways inferior to that of men' (p. 386).

163. Bartoszewicz, C. Biological and cultural factors and the social position of a woman. *Bulletin of the Institute of Social Economy*, No. 2, 1972.

On the basis of Polish and foreign literature, the author presents the aim of scientific research works on the genesis, structure and dynamics of biological and cultural factors and the social position of women. Reviewing material on the issue for the past century, the author isolates the basic problem of correlating women's status and the conditioning of biology and civilization at two levels – macro and micro. The first refers to discrimination in the broad context of social changes; the latter to the co-existence of the family and professional roles.

164. Blekher, F. *The Soviet woman in the family and in society.* Jerusalem, Keber Publishing House, distributed Wiley, 1979. (English translation by Hilary and Ron Hardin.)

This study looks at the historical changes in the position of women in Russia, at marriage and family problems in the Soviet Union, at women at work in all areas of productive, cultural and social activity, and at the life style and work activity of Soviet women in day to day life. The major problem which emerges is the double load which Soviet women, fully integrated into the labour force, suffer since they have responsibility for domestic labour. A symposium in Minsk in 1969 made a number of recommendations to deal with the contradiction between the professional activity of women and their social roles of wife and mother, and the resulting moral, socio-demographic and economic losses that this contradiction engenders. Although these extensive recommendations are still under consideration, and form the basis for research on women, implementation seems very slow and the situation of working women has improved little in the intervening years.

165. Dziecielewska-Machnikowska, S. (ed.). *Woman in the developing socialist society.* Lodz, Lodz Publishing House, 1975, 182 p.

In nine articles the authors concentrate on the situation of women working in a large city industrial centre. There is a high level of employment of women, often with inadequate qualifications, and this leads to a number of problems outlined by these authors. The following problems are dealt with: women's situation on the labour market; their attitudes towards work, part-time employment, outside work and services; the professional activity of women who have children; aspirations and professional plans of women employees; women as breadwinners in the family among textile workers; social benefits for women; the situation of elderly women in multi-generational families; the leisure time of women textile workers and its use.

166. Ferge, Z. The relation between paid and unpaid work of women, a source of inequality – with special reference to Hungary. *Labour and Society*, Vol. 1, No. 2, April 1976, p. 37–52.

The author argues that although the status of women in Hungary has improved in the last two decades, historical disadvantages and patriarchal prejudices still impede women's access to positions of leadership. It is suggested that the approach to improving the status of women should not give priority to merely accelerating the rise of women into power, but should take the form of an organic development based on 'multiplying and diversifying social values so as to allow for the flourishing of individual differences' (p. 52).

167. Heitlinger, A. *Women and state socialism: sex inequality in the Soviet Union and Czechoslovakia.* Macmillan, London, 1979, 241 p. (In English.)

A comparative investigation of the record of two countries formally committed to equality between the sexes, in order to discover, if possible, the optimal conditions necessary for such equality in industrial societies. In looking at the USSR the author concludes that, as far as general observations on sex equality and the integration of women's productive and reproductive role is concerned, women's progress in the sphere of production has been remarkable compared with any country. These achievements in production and educational access have been accompanied by only minimal restructuring of other institutions, and the family remains a central socializing institution, with the woman having primary responsibility for child socialization and housework. Motherhood is regarded as a social function, whereas, in Western society, it is a personal matter. Women however, occupy a disproportionately small number of positions of authority, both in the economy and in political institutions. A similar situation faces the Czechoslovak woman. In her conclusions, the author considers state socialism, egalitarian ideology and sex equality, state policy, the sexual division of labour and social change – the case of population control, and socialism and the women's movement. She concludes overall that a state socialist transformation is insufficient to bring about the liberation of women – whilst women have entered the productive labour force in large numbers in Eastern Europe, they still suffer from inequality – and that women's liberation requires a dual process of entry into the national economy and relative withdrawal from the domestic economy. Structural changes must be accompanied by a cultural revolution aimed at eliminating sex-role stereotypes.

168. ILO. *Work and family life: the role of the social infrastructure in Eastern European countries.* Geneva, ILO, 1980.

A study based on monographs dealing separately with Czechoslovakia, the German Democratic Republic, Hungary, Poland and the USSR, covering facts and figures on employment, services for children of working women, special conditions of employment for parents of young children and information and advice for parents. The report contains a review of measures taken to create favourable social attitudes to working women, but a general conclusion is that 'family and domestic responsibilities, which are often largely borne by women, do indeed constitute in practice a formidable obstacle to the exercise of the right to work, even when this right is officially recognised, when women have access to adequate training and when the national employment situation is favourable'.

169. Jankowa, Z. A. *Soviet woman: Social portrait.* Moscow, 1978.

The book is devoted to present day problems of women's situation and role in Soviet society. The author suggests a system of helping women in the conditions of advanced socialism, which will favour the shaping and development of women's personality.

170. Kisielieva, G. P. (ed.). *Woman in work and at home.* Statistics Moscow, 1978.

The authors of this collective work look at the mutual interaction of the socio-economic role of women and their performance of the role of mother and wife.

171. Rannik, Z. (ed.). *Women's work and family.* Tallinn, Academy of Sciences, 1978.

In separate chapters of this collective work, several aspects of the role of the family in society are considered. Particular attention is paid to children's socialization and the combining of women's two roles in the family and in the society, and to the economic-consumption function of the family.

172. Regent-Lechowicz, M. *Evolution of women's rights in Poland and in the world of today.* Warsaw, Association of Common Science, 1975, 83 p.

The author takes up two basic ideas: the history of the struggle for women's rights, and women's rights in the world today. The major initiative of the United Nations aiming at improvement of women's condition, the genesis of International Women's Year, and the chief moments in the history of social and political liberation movements are discussed. Four problems are considered in detail: women's share in political life, their position in the family, access to education, and professional activization. Each chapter is devoted, in succession, to political, civil, social and economic rights and divided into two sections – Poland and other countries – to enable a comparison to be made of Poland's place in the evolution of women's rights.

173. Scott, H. *Women and Socialism: experiences from Eastern Europe.* London, Alison and Busby, 1976, 240 p. (In English.)

Based largely on research in Czechoslovakia, but also including illustrative material from other Eastern European countries, this study focuses on the conflict between the ideals of equality between men and women, and the reality of women's situation. The basic argument is that the experience of socialism in these countries has led to an institutionalization of existing inequalities, since there has not been a re-evaluation of sex roles, nor a new approach to the functions of the family. Women are still responsible for the home and family, and suffer discrimination in the work place, despite legal, educational and employment rights, which are the envy of Western feminist movements.

174. Sokolowska, M. (ed.). *Contemporary woman.* Warsaw, Book and Science, 1966, 378 p.

A collection of papers by representatives of different scientific disciplines – sociology, medicine, economics, psychology, pedagogics – prepared for a seminar devoted to women's problems. The keynote of the seminar was to show present day women's situation against the background of their advancing professional activization. The focus is on the problem of women's work, their health and biological features, and their time-budgets in different social and professional groups. Aspects of the women's question such as the material situation of single women, women approaching retirement age earning a living, and issues connected with co-existing in multi-generation families are also discussed.

175. Szpakowicz, H. *Almost all about women in the USSR.* Moscow, *Politics*, No. 24, 1975, p. 11.

The author uses statistical data from the Soviet monthly *Journalist* concerning women's employment structure in individual sectors of the national economy in the years 1928–73. He also looks at women's educational level, contracted marriages, birth rate, divorce index, and time-budgets of women employed in industry in selected regions.

176. Tryfan, B. *For an equal starting point.* Warsaw, People's Publishing Cooperative, 1974, 314 p.

The author attempts to evaluate the socio-economic factors, deep-seated in the peasant family and in the local community, which exercise a strong influence on the development of the child and, to an essential degree, determine his or her future career. At the same time, attention is devoted to the mother's role in the socialization process, and to attitudes towards girls' education.

177. Tryfan, B. *Women in agricultural regions of the world.* Warsaw, State Scientific Publications, 1979, 217 p.

The book is an attempt to formulate the woman question against the background of the changing structure of agriculture, and of general socio-economic processes going on in the world today. The author shows the significance of the countrywomen's role as food producer, shown in many studies carried out both in European and non-European countries. Particular attention is devoted to women's situation in developing countries, and to the indicators of discrimination against women, which is particularly conspicuous in agricultural regions. The book presents women's share in food production, their varieties of professional status in agriculture, and specific problems of development in particular countries. The influence of industrialization and demographic processes on countrywomen's employment structure is also discussed. In analysing the marital and maternal role of the woman, social policy programmes of selected countries of the world with respect to women are indicated.

178. Wieruszewski, R. *Equality of women and men in People's Poland.* Poznan, Poznan Publishing House, 1975, 234 p.

The book contains an evaluation of the achievements of three decades of full equalization of women's and men's rights. Emancipation is presented primarily, as equality of opportunity. The author defines equal rights as 'equality of rights' and 'equality towards the law', and equality as 'equal duties', giving the terms a broader meaning. The author argues for the necessity of additional rights for women, which should not be considered privileges.

179. *Women in Poland.* GUS, Warsaw, Main Office of Statistics, 1975.

The book contains seven parts. Part I includes data concerning women's age structure, fertility, life expectancy, and migration. Some of the data are projections, covering the period to the year 2000. Part II deals with education in all types of schools and universities, and with scientific degrees obtained by Polish women. Part III provides information on professional activities in specific sectors of the national economy. Part IV presents women's situation in the family. Part V deals with women's social and living standards. Part VI presents women's share in political, social and cultural life. In Part VII some international comparisons are presented.

II. Women's work and labour force participation

THE RURAL SECTOR

180. Bairamow, A. *Women and the development of Bulgarian rural areas.* Paper presented at the IV World Congress of Rural Sociology, 1976.

Both women's professional work and their role in the development of rural areas are evaluated in several aspects. Women still constitute half of the total number of persons employed in agriculture, but rapid mechanization in plant production, causes the number of women employed in this line of farming to fall. The need arises to retrain women in order to provide them with the possibility of employment in other areas. The number of women employed in animal production, in agricultural-food industry, in services, and in administration is systematically increasing. The author also discusses the problems of population reproduction and of manpower, of educating youth and of social and cultural life.

181. Burian, A. Women in the Czechoslovak agriculture and the problem of time budget. *Contemporary Countryside*, No. 3, 1971.

Referring to Czechoslovak studies which concentrate on the evaluation of time-budgets, the author analyses the time use of women employed in agriculture and compares the results with those of women employed outside agriculture. Considerable attention is devoted in the study to women's labour expenditure, with reference to men's expenditure in a rural environment. In view of the double role of a woman, the author considers the proportion of time used for farmwork and that for household duties. He formulates the concept of leisure time – a social category which was little or not at all known to earlier generations. The author presents data concerning women's time budget on a weekly scale, during and out of season. He also presents the use of time in two different periods of the year, taking into account various kinds of work in agricultural administration and in plant and animal production. The great difference which occurred between the group of women employed in administration and those employed in animal production can be explained by the fact that the administration employs mainly young and often single women, who are not yet absorbed by household and family tasks.

182. Cernea, M. Studies on a countrywoman's situation in Romania. *Contemporary Countryside*, No. 1, 1974.

The author studied the situation of countrywomen. It is generally believed that social changes in the modern society further women's emancipation and enrich their personality. It seems, however, that the process is more complex and not at all explicit. The rapid industrialization of present day Romania and the simultaneous collectivization of agriculture within less than 15 years (1949–62) exercised a many-sided influence on family structure and women's position in the family. The author considers some unexpected consequences of those processes. In the past decade, there is to be noted a feminization of Romanian agriculture, which employs nearly 49 per cent of professionally active persons, with women prevailing in the labour force. Collectivization of agriculture brought about a number of structural changes in the peasant family. Changes concerning women's position in a peasant family are investigated in three aspects: the economic role of the woman as a participant in the labour force in agriculture, wife's status, and maternity functions. The main changes aim at increasing women's economic independence in a peasant family, whilst the economic role of the woman as a producer increases. That is accounted for by the rapid advance of industry, which can absorb any number of production co-operative members, primarily men, of course. It can be said, then that feminization of agriculture is a consequence of changes in the macrosystem.

183. First-Dilić, R. *Production role of countrywomen in Yugoslavia*. Zagreb, Department of Rural and Urban Sociology of the Institute of Social Studies, 1976.

According to the author, women play a substitutional role in private farms and production co-operatives, replacing the male labour force flowing away from agriculture. Women's work, in general, requires lower qualifications and is marked by a lower level of pay and lower prestige. Countrywomen, in principle, have no alternative choices, farming is a social and economic necessity for them, and not the result of their own decision. As a result of the living and working conditions, which are more primitive than in towns, and the social isolation in the patriarchal rural environment, women agricultural workers acquire an awareness of their status very slowly. The author considers that in the future this situation will change, agriculture will acquire the status of a socially recognized profession, and the labour force employed in agriculture will become stabilized. Under these circumstances, this work will be undertaken as a result of a conscious choice and not a necessity for lack of other alternatives.

184. Fiszerowa, M. and Leszczyńska, H. *Woman – family – society*. Warsaw, Polish Agricultural and Forestry Publications, 1975.

This is the first brochure of the series of the Library of Rural Housewives Circles. (These circles are operating in 36,000 villages.) The aim of the series is to indicate the problems facing women employed in agriculture. The authors of the first brochure concentrated mainly on family matters, with particular consideration of children's education. At the same time they showed the family against the background of the environment, and the problems women have in organizing social action.

185. Fulea, M. and Cobianu, M. *Women's status and role in agricultural cooperatives in Romania*. Bucharest, Department of Sociology of the University in Bucharest, 1976.

The economic status of women members of production co-operatives was analysed on the basis of regional sociological studies and statistical data. Women's social and political status is closely correlated with the position of the female labour force in the socio-professional structure of co-operative farms and in that of the rural environment, in line with the existing organizational scheme and development outlook. The study covers women's promotion process to managerial posts, the extent to which this takes place, the level of ideal and real aspirations, women's effectiveness in performing managerial functions, and a consideration of the social climate in terms of enabling these processes.

186. Illiewa, N. *Social changes in rural areas of Bulgaria: Development of women's personality*. Sofia, Institute of Sociology of the Bulgarian Academy of Sciences, 1976.

The author analyses women's share in the evolution of farming, and other factors influencing women's social status. There has been both a relative and an absolute decrease in the rural population of Bulgaria. Women have as a result taken on different work in the structure of the rural labour force, and there has been at the same time an increase in women's education and qualifications. Changes have also occurred in rural living conditions, bringing them closer to the urban living standard. This is reflected in the electrification of rural areas, in modern home equipment, in the reduction of traditional duties, and the acquisition of urban models of life. These processes are accompanied by a development of cultural positions and an increase in women's share in artistic activities. The author also discussed particular features regarding the use of time by rural women, especially leisure time, women's education and the correlation between time-budget, age, and educational level.

187. Krucék, Z. *Features of the contemporary rural family in the Socialist Republic of Czechoslovakia*, Prague, Economic Research Institute of Food and Agriculture, 1977.

The present day process of structural change and of scientific and technical development in agriculture influence the structure and function of an agricultural family. The once homogeneous peasant family is gradually undergoing a disintegration and changing into a heterogeneous family as far as employment of the family members is concerned. About 30 per cent of children born in rural areas remain in agriculture, nearly 40 per cent take up work in industry, and the rest work in other sectors of the national economy. This change in the kind of employment is rarely accompanied by a change of place of residence, and an increasing proportion of the rural population works in cities. As a result, the way of life of rural families begins to change and become similar to that of urban families. The abolition of private ownership of the means of production, and the decline of private farms account for new social and moral rules for family unity. The family lost the function of a private owner and producer and became a consumption unit and an organizer of the life of its members. The social significance of the family has increased in recent years, and the relationship between the material and cultural side of family life has moved further towards an emphasis on the cultural aspect in both urban and rural families.

188. Krucék, Z. *Positions of selected bio-social groups in agriculture*. Prague, Economic Research Institute of Food and Agriculture, 1976.

On the basis of comparative studies on the population of various economic sectors, it can be shown that there are differences between groups of agricultural workers, connected with age and sex. Some specific features of social groups appear, which concern groups of countrywomen, young workers and retired people.

189. Majorek, B. *Promotion*. Warsaw, 1967, 102 p.

This is one of few publications on women's situation in the socialized sector of agriculture. In the years 1965–66 the editorial office of *Agricultural Worker* published a survey on the work and life of women employed in state farms. The book contains interesting statements by women participants in the survey, which reflect changes in the professional and civil role, in education and qualifications of women employed in this sector of the economy.

190. Müller, J. and Fleischer, K. *Women's position in the agriculture of GDR*, Leipzig, Karl Marx University, 1976.

A review of studies on the adaptation of women to mechanization processes in agriculture, and to technical professions connected with these processes. Some general conclusions are that, in 1974, the number of women employed in agriculture amounted 401,000 and their social status was a result of the process of development, characterized by a movement into industrial methods of work. Concentration, specialization and further socialization of production strengthens the role of the individual in collective work; professional/technical training aims at a general improvement in the use of technical advances.

191. Patruszew, V. D. *Problems of countrywomen's non-professional duties*. Report to the IV World Congress of Rural Sociology 1976.

This USSR study on the subject of women focused on the comparison of women's leisure time with men's, with particular consideration of women working in agriculture. The study indicates the need for social policy directed towards the elimination of the differences which still exist. According to the analysis of empirical data, at present, women's worktime in *sovkhozes* and *kolkhozes* is somewhat shorter than that of industrial women workers. In the last two decades the number of countrywomen's working hours decreased, but the number of working days on a yearly scale increased. Countrywomen devote much time to work on the homeplot, which is their second workshift. In recent years, the amount of time designated for work on the homeplot decreased, but it still remains an essential problem. Over the whole year, women employed in agriculture have less time off than men.

192. Peszewa, R. *Harmonious development of countrywomen in Bulgaria*. Sofia, Institute of Sociology of the Bulgarian Academy of Sciences, 1976.

It is argued that the harmonious development of women employed in agricultural production is a prerequisite for social progress. In Bulgaria each new phase of integration and modernization of agriculture is actively shared by women. In this process of change, their social qualities have developed. A new generation of women agricultural producers, which is experienced in the building of a modern society and its culture, has grown up. The author maintains that harmony was achieved between women's professional interests and aspirations and the sphere of their non-productive activity and that this latter activity becomes a rich and inexhaustible production reserve.

193. Příkrylova, A. The development of professional activity forms of women in the agriculture of the Socialist Republic of Czechoslovakia. *Rural Sociology*, Prague, No. 13, 1977, p. 29.

Women have always held a vital position in social and economic life in Czechoslovak agriculture, since they make an important contribution to the labour force. Agricultural development through concentration, specialization, integration and mechanization of production processes imposes the necessity of employing women in all production areas. Structural changes in agriculture account for a gradual reduction in the proportion of women therein.

194. Příkrylova, A. and Kohn, P. *Women's wages in agriculture*. Prague, Economic Research Institute of Food and Agriculture, 1979.

Wages and earnings of women employed in agriculture are a vital element of their living standard and of their social status. The authors present the wage level structure of women working in agriculture, according to age groups, qualifications and functions performed. The horizontal aspect of professional earnings differentiation is more evident than the vertical. Differences between men's and women's earnings are presented in detail, and the elimination of differences in wages is described as a complex problem, related to the overall improvement of women's professional status. The authors refer to Soviet suggestions, which emphasize the specific biological and family functions of women in the sphere of earnings.

195. Répássy, H. *Characteristic features of women's employment in agricultural regions of Hungary*. Budapest, Institute of Economic Planning, 1976.

In Hungary, studies of women's employment in rural communes indicates that women's professional activity in agricultural regions is on a lower level than in towns, as regards socially organized work, and the level of 'dependants', i.e. women maintained by their husbands, is higher. For various reasons this term has a different meaning in town and country, since rural districts provide less opportunity for employment, and there is little choice in the kind of work available.

196. Ryvkina, R. W. and Kariakina, J. M. *Comparative characteristics of mobility and professional career of various demographic groups of rural population*. Novosibirsk, Academy of Sciences, Siberian Branch of the Institute of Economics, 1976.

In the Soviet Union, the Siberian Branch of the Soviet Academy of Sciences, amongst other institutions conducts studies on women's situations. These problems were taken up by the Department of Urban and Rural Social Problems of the Institute of Economics and Industrial Engineering, and research was carried out on professional mobility and success in work of countrywomen of different generations, in comparison with analogous populations of men. Differences in professional mobility according to sex were found. Women, on the whole, are less mobile than men, and young female workers less mobile than older ones.

In all population groups, vertical mobility dominates over horizontal and the population of ascendent mobility is twice as numerous as that of a descendent mobility. Women's share in professional work is half that of men and a woman's professional career is, on average, shorter than that of a man. Essential differences have also been noted in the employment dynamics of men and women, according to generation the starting point in professional work among youth is higher than it was among older people. The results suggest a basis for the direction of further studies.

197. Steinberger, G. and Unterbeck, D. *Development of the socialist rural family type in the German Democratic Republic*. Report to the IV World Congress of Rural Sociology, 1976.

The character of structural and functional changes within the family in GDR depends on the total development of socialist production. Advances in the division, organization and conditions of work have brought about essential changes in women's and men's social status. Focus is put on the quality of family functions, which are seen as a crucial condition for the development of the social structure.

198. Tryfan, B. *Social status of a countrywoman*. Warsaw, Book and Science, 1968, 345 p.

Studies on the situation of a present day countrywoman aimed at showing the picture of her changing role in the family and in the environment under the impact of socio-economic changes brought about by industrialization and urbanization. The evolution of social relations in rural districts introduced new elements into a countrywoman's life, reflected by an increase in her prestige, authority and position. In comparison with a family living in town, however, changes in rural areas are much less advanced, since they are limited by the fact that small scale peasant farming as a whole remains in conflict with the concept of modern participation in life.

199. Tryfan, B. (ed.). *Pure waters of my emotions*. Warsaw, Book and Science, 1975, 589 p.

This is the second part of a three volume publication: 'Memoirs of countrywomen'. The collected material comes from a competition for countrywomen's memoirs, organized in 1970 by the Institute of Rural and Agricultural Development of the Polish Academy of Sciences, together with the Central Union of Agricultural Circles. This volume is devoted to problems of marriage, maternity and family. As distinct from the other two volumes of the cycle, dealing with professional work and culture as well as with the social and civil role, this volume contains memoirs, relating for example to selection criteria of the marriage partner, and family interference in personal matters.

200. Tryfan, B. *Situation of a countrywoman against the background of social and economic changes in agriculture in three decades of People's Poland.* Warsaw, Central Union of Agricultural Circles, 1976.

The problem of countrywomen is presented in the context of the problem of women in general, and of changes in the rural environment. The text also contains presentation of Polish research works on countrywomen, compared with other publications dealing with women.

201. Tryfan, B. *Role of the countrywoman*. Warsaw, State Agricultural and Forestry Publications, 1976, 166 p.

The book aims at presenting the family, professional and civil role of present day women working in rural areas. Questions such as the contracting of marriage, number of children in rural families, division of roles in the family and in the household – the division becoming increasingly, in the author's view, an equal partnership – are discussed. The book also provides projections for the future, and potential solutions to the problems of rural women of a social or organizational nature.

PROFESSIONAL/MANAGERIAL WORK

202. Dziecielska-Machnikowska, S. and Kulpinska, J. *Women's promotion*. Lodz, 1966, 138 p.

The study looks at women who perform managerial functions in their workplace, and the problems of promotion. The limitations on women's promotion to high positions in the hierarchy are discussed in relation to inter-personal relations in a production plant, and the demands of women's role in the family.

203. Kozlowska, H. and Strzeleck, J., *Problems of women managers*. Warsaw, Supreme Cooperative Council, 1970, 114 p.

The subject taken up in this book is entirely new – the authors present the problems of women's professional and social promotion, taking the example of consumers' co-operatives. They reveal the mechanisms for promoting women and the reasons which impede their assumption of managerial posts. The data was generated from proceedings of debates of women holding the highest managerial posts in consumers' co-operatives, and questionnaires filled in by women performing the highest functions.

204. Strzemińska, H. *Women's professional work and their time budget*. Warsaw, State Economic Publications, 1970, 291 p.

Dealing with the problem of women's professional work, the author indicates that its effectiveness and social usefulness are influenced not only by the organization in which they work and material incentives, but also by inter-personal relations at the working place, and the way of using leisure time, which helps to regenerate physical and psychic strength. The main subject of the book is the connection of time-budget and professional work.

OTHER

205. Charczew, A. G. and Golod, S. J. *Women's professional work and the family*. Leningrad, 1971.

The authors consider problems of women's professional activity from the perspective of philosophy and sociology, and emphasize motives for taking up employment, and the role of working women in the family. An analysis is carried out of statistical and empirical data on a macro-scale, as well as in selected enterprises and families.

206. Dachowa, A. and Danielewska, S. *Working women – obligations of the working place*. Warsaw, Supreme Council of Trade Unions, 1974, p. 43.

In Poland, women working outside agriculture constitute 41 per cent of the total number of employed women. With them in mind, the Supreme Council of Trade Unions published this brochure containing information on the professional status of working women, on work and health protection, and on help in bringing up children.

207. Dech, Z. *Women's professional work in Poland in the years 1950–1972, and its economic and social aspects*. Warsaw, Book and Science, 1976, 289 p.

The aim of the book is to show the dynamics of women's employment in People's Poland, and to confirm the value of professional work for women's development. The first chapter of five is devoted to general characteristics of employment policy in Poland in the years 1950–72. The second deals with women's professional activity in relation to employment dynamics within the country, and in comparison with other countries of the world. The extent of women's employment in the national economy and women's situation on the labour market is discussed in the third chapter and the fourth contains an evaluation of women's employment structure, with particular emphasis on the phenomenon of the feminization of some professions. The fifth chapter looks at selected aspects of women's work, for example their usefulness in production, work discipline, and the influence of employment on the family situation.

208. Kotlar, A. E. and Turczaninowa, S. J. *Employment of women in an enterprise: A statistical-sociological outline*. Moscow, 1975.

This is a monograph, based on sociological investigations in a number of enterprises noted for the high concentration of women in their labour force. The authors consider basic rules for the rational employment of women in a socialist system. One chapter is devoted to the influence of women workers' situation on their social and professional activity.

209. Kulczycka, B. Women's professional activity. *Statistical News*, No. 5, 1975.

The author analyses the employment structure, according to sex in single age groups, in different sectors of the National economy, related to educational level. The index of professional activity decreases with age in non-agricultural work and increases in agriculture.

210. Luszczycki, I. H. (ed.). *Women's production activities and the family*. Minsk, 1972.

This collection of publications was developed on the basis of data prepared for the national symposium of Soviet Republics sociologists. It covers a wide range of problems, linked with using women in the national economy.

211. Oledzki, M., Kochanowska, J. and Szumlicz, T. *Economic and social conditionings of women's further professional activization in Warsaw.* Warsaw, 1974, 93 p.

The authors characterized the demographic situation of Warsaw in the years 1960–80, considering the population structure according to sex and age, and the resources of the female labour force compared with those countrywide. They presented the state of employment and labour market of women in the capital, as well as women's activities in other towns. In the last chapter, they look at the economic and social factors, which will influence women's professional work up to the 1980s.

212. Oledzka, A. *Women – time budget – multishift work.* Warsaw, Supreme Council of Trade Unions, 1975, 175 p.

The author takes up the problem of the economic and social consequences of women's multishift work. She considers the advantages and drawbacks of this employment from within valid legal regulations. She finds that, from the viewpoint of women's interests, the multishift work renders it difficult to combine the family and professional role. She presents different aspects of the work and leisure time budgets of women employed in the multishift system, for example the influence of the system on performing household duties, on the organization of child-care, and on satisfying their own needs and aspirations.

213. Padowicz, W. *Professional activity, employment and education of women in some countries.* Warsaw, Institute of Labour and Social Affairs, 1974, 50 p.

On the basis of a wide range of statistical information, the author presents data on women's professional activity, motives for taking up employment, employment structure in individual economic sectors, and on women's professional training. All the data contain a reference to Poland. Problems are shown in the dynamics of changes and in a comparative scheme.

214. *Polish women of '76.* Warsaw, National Publishing Agency, 1976, 102 p.

The publication was prepared by the editorial staff of the weekly *Woman and Life* and is consequently a journalistic report portraying the present day Polish woman, who combines the roles of wife, mother and worker. Parts of this brochure contain discussions on essential problems of education, professional work, and authority of women.

215. Przedpelski, M. *Women's employment structure in People's Poland.* Warsaw, Polish Scientific Publications, 1975, 267 p.

The author's aim was a systematization of studies carried out so far on women's professional activization against the background of the social and economic changes, which have occurred, in Poland, in the last thirty years. The author considers that the basic factors contributing to changes in women's labour market participation are the processes of industrialization and the expansion of education. The author evaluates the phenomenon of the professional activization of women in Poland in four chapters of his book. Chapter two is of particular significance in connection with the main determinant of change – industrialization. This deals with the influence of industrial development on the increasing employment of women, women's share in labour force resources, and the employment structure in individual sectors of the national economy. The next chapter presents changes in women's labour force participation, with regard to professional specialization, educational level, and the age structure of professionally active women. The last chapter of the book is devoted to the outlook for professional activization of Polish women.

216. Szyszkan, N. M. *Women's work in the conditions of a developed socialist society.* Kishinev, 1976.

The author takes up theoretical aspects of women's employment, its social nature, forms and conflicts, as well as privileges associated with it in the society under study. The particular emphasis is on the influence of women's employment in socialized enterprises on social and demographic processes. He shows the search for ways to raise women's labour productivity in Socialism. Statistical data and results of sociological studies in the USSR are used in the book.

217. Wrochno, K. *Problems of women's work.* Warsaw, 1971, 149 p.

The author presents the problem of the new social position of women, against the background of changing working and living conditions. She presents the role of present day woman through the prism of law and social awareness. She deals with aspirations for equal rights in the field of education and social activity, with emphasis on feminization of some types of schools and some professions.

218. Zukalova, O. *Socio-economic position of women in socialist Slovak agriculture.* Bratislava, Institute of Philosophy and Sociology of the Slovak Academy of Sciences, 1976.

The author devotes much attention to the problem of time-budget, noting some of its characteristic features in agriculture. Social changes, which have influenced the change of status and duties of men and women within the family, actually played a minor role in agricultural families. The results of studies on work time structure of men and women from different social groups confirms the fact that, in spite of a smaller range of women's professional duties out of the home in comparison with men, the total scope of women's duties, taking into account their household and family duties, is larger in all social groups, both on working days and on holidays.

III. Family and household

RURAL/URBAN

219. Dumitru, M. D. *Family evolution in the modernization process of Romanian agriculture*. Cahiers du CENECA, Paris, 1968.

In Romania, studies on women's situation are an integral part of studies on the family and this author has produced several such studies, putting particular emphasis on the division of work and prestige in marriage. In this work the author evaluates changes, which took place in the countryside, as a consequence of social and economic transformations in Romania. The functions performed by Romanian women farmers, members of production co-operatives, are given special attention.

220. Jancu, F. *Changes in structure and function of a Romanian peasant family*. Bucharest. Report to the IV World Congress of Rural Sociology in 1976.

The decreasing function of the family in production brought about changes in the relations between generations. Young family members obtained a greater independence in making decisions, in selecting their work, and in choosing their marriage partner. This is reflected in women's position in the family. On the other hand, the migration of rural populations, particularly men, to other work, leads to a differentiation of the structure of rural families in terms of the work performed and to a special role for women in peasant-worker families.

221. Jankowa, Z. A. *A city family*. Moscow, 1978.

The author considers the rules governing the functioning of an urban family in socialist society, trends towards structural changes, and the standard of living. Particular attention is given to the labour force work and family functions performed by women, to social and individual forms of satisfying cultural needs, and to assumptions of help for the family.

222. Markowska, D. *Family in rural community – continuity and change*. Warsaw, People's Publishing House, 1976, 274 p.

The book is devoted to the evolution of a rural family. The author develops and explains the term 'traditional peasant family', and characterizes its place in the relative-neighbour system in the local and national community. The book consists of three parts: the first covers the turn of the 19th century, the second the inter-war period (1918–39), and the third the rural family after the Second World War. The author looks for the elements which survived or are considered valuable traditions in the present day family, as well as those which clearly make the contemporary rural family different from the peasant family in previous generations. Considerable attention is devoted to women's situation in marriage and in the family.

MATERNITY

223. Bubik, A. *Women's rights connected with pregnancy, childbirth and maternity.* Katowice, 1976.

This study provides information on work related to social and living problems. The author discusses work prohibited for women in Poland, the ban on giving notice and dissolving employment contracts during pregnancy and maternity leave, rights in case of dissolving of employment contract, maternity leave, breaks for baby nursing, taking time off, care allowances, unpaid leave for women bringing up small children, and women's part-time employment.

224. Kurzynowski, A. *Employment continuity and maternity.* Warsaw, State Economic Publications, 1967, 182 p.

On the basis of results of studies carried out in the Section of Sociology of the Institute of Social Management, the relationship between maternity and labour force participation of women was analysed. The author maintains that non-interruption of work due to childbirth and maternity duties has become the model of women's behaviour. He points out that work and family are no longer alternative values for women, but that both are part of the whole of women's social role. The book includes data on women's employment in Poland in the years 1950–70, with special consideration of married women. The problem of work continuity after childbirth is considered in relation to the sector of the economy, the type of working place, the specific work of the mothers, their education, qualifications, years of service and amount of wages.

225. Radziński, T. *Rights of working mothers.* Warsaw, Supreme Council of Trade Unions, Warsaw, 1973, 113 p.

Against the background of the acquisition of rights in the Polish legislature by women, beginning in 1924, the author presents the basic regulations on maternity protection. These regulations cover the rights of pregnant women and women lying in with respect to employment and health, as well as questions connected with childcare, in the form of monetary and material allowances.

DIVORCE

226. Bogacka, H., and Sobieszak, A. Reasons for divorces in the light of a survey study. *Statistical News*, No. 5, 1975.

The increasing rate of divorce in Poland (1.19 per 1,000 inhabitants in 1973) has led to studies on the reason for this phenomenon. Ten per cent of divorce cases, examined in 1973, were covered by the investigation. In evaluating the question from the woman's point of view, several aspects are emphasized. The age of women who filed a complaint was, at the time of contracting marriage, somewhat lower in rural areas than in urban centres. Meanwhile, at the moment of filing a complaint the age of countrywomen is higher than that of townswomen. Chief amongst the reasons for divorce were unfaithfulness (24 per cent) and alcoholism (23 per cent).

227. Czujkow, L. W. *Marriages and divorces.* Moscow, 1975.

The work deals with the setting up and stability of a contemporary rural family. The author analyses the connection between setting up of marriages and divorces. On the basis of ample empirical data and considerable statistical information, the author presents characteristics of partners contracting marriage for the first time, and aspects of divorce cases.

OTHER

228. Charczew, A. G. (ed.). *Family as subject of philosophical and sociological studies.* Moscow, 1974.

In considering theoretical and methodological aspects of research work, the authors take up the subject of conditions and possibilities for educational influence in the family in a socialist society. The relationship between education in the family and that within other social groups, and the dependence of personality development on living conditions, material security and the degree of cultural and moral development of parents is discussed.

229. Charczew, A. G. (ed.). *Change of women's situation and the family.* Science, Moscow, 1979.

This collective work includes the results of basic investigations by leading specialists of the USSR and of other countries working on problems of family relations. The Soviet authors consider the problems of duties performed by the woman, employment structure, women's social role and demographic family development, child socialization, and the emotional factors involved in forming a family.

230. Charczew, A. G. *Marriage and family in the USSR.* Moscow, 1979.

The author considers the complex set of problems concerning the development of marriage and family in a socialist society, with emphasis on problems of stabilization and the social functions of a Soviet family currently and in the future.

231. Charczew, A. G. and Mackowskij, N. S. *Present day family and its problems.* Moscow, 1979.

The authors analyse the social and demographic conditions of families in socialist and capitalist countries. They also characterize motives for contracting marriages, mutual relations between spouses, problems of durability and consolidation of a family, and of children's education. The problem of internal conflicts and reasons for divorces was also taken up.

232. Gordon, L. A., Klopow, E. W. *Man after working hours.* Moscow, 1972.

The authors present basic types of everyday behaviour of workers in large cities. While discussing the participation of family members in housework, they evaluate the role of wife and husband, mutual relations, children's education, and family ties. They also look at the correlation between certain types of behaviour and living standards.

233. Hebenstreit, W. Women and children in the GDR. *Time*, No. 18, 1975.

Women play an essential role in the country's economy, since 84 per cent of their total number, aged 15 to 60 are studying or working professionally. In order to help working mothers, a system of social benefits was developed. This took the form of maternity leaves extended to 18 weeks, rest-leaves, financial allowance on the occasion of childbirth, credits for young married couples to fit out their apartment. Mothers, who are bringing up at least three children, benefit from the right to a four-hour working day with full wages.

234. Jurkiewicz, N. G. *Soviet family, functions and stability conditions.* Moscow, 1970.

On the basis of sociological studies carried out in Minsk, a well-known Soviet lawyer took up the problem of the concept of a present day family, its functions, motives for contracting marriages, and the conditions for the stability of marriage.

235. Komorowska, J. (ed.). *Changes in the Polish family.* Warsaw, Publishing Institute of the Supreme Council of Trade Unions, 1975, 448 p.

This collection contains 19 chapters grouped in four sections: (1) History of the Polish family; (2) the family in literature, folklore and mass information media; (3) present day family realities; (4) the family in other countries. The author of the introduction deals with the problem of the erasing of differences between families of various social strata and environments, and between town and country. The women's question is strongly emphasized in the chapter 'Family of the nineteenth century', where women's moral qualities and their role in supporting national awareness in the family at the time of Poland's partitons are discussed. In the chapter entitled 'Sex and custom changes' the problem of role changes for both sexes, within the family, is formulated. In the third part of the book, the reader finds a consideration of changes in family planning, evaluation of the evolution of criteria for marriage choice, analysis of family structure and function, opinions of young men and women on role division in the family, present day family customs, intergenerational ties, and a discussion of pathological phenomena and their connection with the increase of women's professional activization.

236. Lobodzinska, B. Family and professional women's roles in the world. *Family Problems*, No. 5, 1972, p. 49–54.

The article is a report of the XII International Seminar on Family Studies, held in Moscow in 1972, under the auspices of the Soviet Sociological Association. The debates concentrated on the conflict between family and working women's roles, against the background of the change in marital roles connected with the increasing proportion of married women working.

237. Wasilieva, E. K. *The family and its functions.* Moscow, 1975.

On the basis of a secondary analysis of population censuses and research results, the author evaluates the influence of selected socio-economic factors on family development, and the influence of the family on social processes. Attention is devoted to successive phases of family life cycle, with particular consideration of an urban family. The family role in the professional preparation of young people is also considered.

238. Wawrzywola-Kruszyńska, W. *Marriage and the social structure.* Wroclaw-Warsaw-Cracow-Gdansk, Ossolineum, 1975.

The author takes up an interesting and previously little considered topic of spouses becoming alike in heterogeneous marriages. The author denies the accepted theory of free marital choice and indicates determinants, which limit the freedom of choice, based on survey studies carried out in the years 1964–67 in several Polish towns. In the author's opinion, the factor exercising the strongest influence towards monogamy is education.

239. Wiloch, B. (ed.). *Mothers and daughters.* Book and Science, Warsaw 1971, 276 p.

The collection contains the most valuable memoirs sent for the competition announced by the editorial office of the women's weekly *Friend*, under the title 'Two Generations'. These memoirs concern firstly the relationships of women of the interwar period, showing the difficulties in access to education, unemployment, and hard living conditions of many families from worker and peasant environments. Secondly, memoirs of young women, whose path to promotion and personal success is quite different, are presented.

240. Yankova, Z. A. (ed.). *Problems of sociological studies on the family.* Moscow, Institute of Sociological Research, 1976.

This is a collection of articles dealing with present day problems of family life. Particular emphasis is put on the reproduction, educational and socialization functions of the family, as well as the internal and external requirements of family stability.

IV. Education

241. Andrzejak, S. Graduates of higher schools in three decades of People's Poland. *Statistical News*, No. 7, 1974.

In discussing the development of higher education in Poland, the author emphasizes women's share. A particular increase of women's share was to be noted in the lines of studies which were traditionally considered to be men's areas. In 1945, women constituted 2.8 per cent of all the graduates in specialized technical studies, and in 1973 the figure for women was over 20 per cent.

242. Andrzejak, S. Women's education. *Statistical News*, No. 5, 1975.

The author takes up the problem of promotion through education, comparing school attendance in 1930 and today, as well as differences between women and men, and between town and country. As early as

1950, in primary schools, the sex structure of the school population was the same as the sex structure of the total population of Poland. In the secondary schools, however, two phenomena are noted: a reduced gap between boys and girls; and a prevalence of women acquiring formal higher education.

243. Mrozowska, K. *A hundred years of Polish women's activity in education and science.* Warsaw, Polish Scientific Publications, 1971.

The author presents the story of the struggle for women's access to education at all levels. Referring to the tradition of progressive women activists of the epoch of positivism, striving for greater access to education for girls, she discusses the achievements of outstanding women representatives of emancipation in education. She also discusses Polish women who played a prominent role in the development of science in the world context, e.g. Maria Sklodowska-Curie. The struggle for girls' schools in different periods of Polish history is also presented in the book.

244. Tatara-Hoszowska, W. *Educational problems of girls in Peoples' Poland.* Warsaw, State School Publications, 1970. 195 p.

The author discusses objectives and methods of girls' education against the background of changes occurring in all fields of life in Polish society. In principle, the problem is presented in connection with women's professional activization, and with the necessity of adjusting their interests to the needs of the national economy. The author discusses the structure and organizational forms of educating girls at all levels.

V. Demographic features

245. Bielowa, V. A., Bondarskaya, G. A., et al. *How many children will there be in a Soviet family?* Moscow, Statistics, 1977.

This collective work contains the results of a study on women's opinions as regards the number of children per family. Differences in the actual number of children per family were related to social factors, such as educational level or place of residence.

246. Bondarska, G. A. *Birth rate in the USSR: the ethnographic-demographic aspect*. Moscow, 1977.

On the basis of data of censuses of 1969 and 1977, and of her own studies, the author analyses specific features of changes connected with the birth rate among different nationalities inhabiting the territory of the USSR. She studies the influence of factors such as urbanization, educational level and ethnic differentiation on the birth rate.

247. Borisow, W. A. *Perspectives of birth rate*. Moscow, 1976.

The author deals with the dynamics of the birth rate increase in the USSR and in other countries, quoting the results of the latest investigations.

248. Gierasimowa, J. A. *Family structure*. Moscow, 1976.

The demographic structure of the family is analysed on the basis of various survey studies.

249. Mantorska, T. *Reproductiveness in Poland compared with that in selected European countries*. Warsaw, GUS/Main Office of Statistics, 1972, 58 p.

The brochure consists of two parts: The first contains an introduction and discussion of three problems – childbirth, characteristics of women at progenitive age, fertility and number of children per family. The second contains 22 tables illustrating the problems presented. There is a comparative analysis of the situation in selected European countries related to demographic problems in Poland, as far as the procreative function of women is concerned.

250. Romaszczewskaja, H. M. (ed.). *Family demographic problems*. Moscow, Science, 1978.

The work contains an evaluation of the demographic, economic and social situation of a Soviet family. Using the results of an investigation into the living standards of the population, the living standards of families were analysed. Particular attention was paid to the social and demographic structure of families in housing projects.

251. Smolinski, Z. *Statistical analysis of the number of children women have*. Warsaw, GUS/Main Office of Statistics, 1974, 179 p.

The aim of the publication is to show the basic elements of demographic change in Poland; the number of children that women have. The problem is presented historically, beginning in 1939, with reference to all social and professional environments. The analysis is related to ideal, planned and desired numbers of children, and the reasons which cause reproductiveness to slow down. Future projections for these demographic patterns are also given.

252. Smolińska, Z. Women. *Statistical News*. No. 5, 1975.

The article contains information on the sex structure of the population of Poland. There is a statistical prevalence of women in older age groups, but in the group up to 35 years of age men predominate, and there are 95–98 women for each 100 men. Fewer girls are born each year than boys, and they are more vital. Women's average life expectancy is 73.8 years, and men's 66.8. Projections suggest that the proportion of women will continue to decrease and in the year 2000 men will predominate in the age group up to 50 years.

253. Stpiczyński, T. Women's internal migrations in Poland. *Statistical News*, No. 4, 1975.

The author presents the population structure according to sex and place of birth in the years 1921–70. It seems that in 1970, 52 per cent of townswomen and 39 per cent of countrywomen had changed their place of residence at least once in their lives. Generally speaking, women's mobility increased much more than men's which is confirmed by the fact that, in 1974, women constituted 52 per cent of migrants.

254. Sysjenko, V. A. (ed.). *The Family Nowadays*. Moscow, Statistics, 1979.

The work is devoted to the demographic structure of the family, stability of marriage, ties connecting spouses, and attitudes of parents towards procreation.

255. Volkova, A. G. (ed.). *Family demographic development*. Moscow, Statistics, 1978.

The following topics are discussed in this book: the evolution process of the family as the basic reproduction unit, rules of contracting marriages, women's fertility, and grown-up children's separation from parental authority. Demographic aspects of contracting marriages, divorces, the passing away of one spouse, motives for limitation of birth rate, and the role of ethics in marriage are also covered.

VI. Other

256. Butarewicz, L. *Health protection of a working woman*. Warsaw, Polish Medical Publications, 1975, 153 p.

The author's aim was to show health care for working women in a biological, demographic, social and economic framework. When considering women's growing professional activization, the author presents the biologically distinct character of a woman, selected problems of physiology in particular fields of work, and demographic processes conditioning family and professional roles. He deals in detail with the organization of women's health protection in Poland and in selected countries in the rest of the world. He discusses some gynaecological ailments and pregnancy complications caused by performing specific work duties. He also looks at the question of sick leave for women employed in industry, the development of benefits for maternity protection, and the advance of the social infrastructure in this respect.

257. *International Women's Year: Selected publications on women's question with filmography*. Warsaw, Association of Universal Science, 1975.

This is a collection of major publications and filmography on women, focusing on problems of women's civil rights in Poland and in the world, women's position in the family, in professional work, their role in science, creative art, literature and fine arts, and their share in social and political life.

258. Kwaśniewska, K. *Women's reading habits*. Warsaw, 1973.

The author reports the results of studies on the attitude towards books and the development of a habit of reading of women from different environments. An increase in the amount of reading overall tends to suggest that cultural interests are increasing. The book provides, not only numerical data on reading habits, but also information on the structure of interests. It is suggested that there have been qualitative changes in psyche, personality, and aspirations in the women investigated as a result of the influence of books.

259. Podbierowa, E. *Women's position in the acts of international law.* Poznan, 1975, 231 p.

The author attempts to show women's social status in the light of legal acts, and considers that formal equal rights, granted within the valid regulations, are not tantamount to actual equal rights, since the regulations are not fully observed everywhere. The book contains a rich collection of data on legal norms in various countries of the world and on some principles of their functioning. It consists of five chapters, which deal with the following: (i) development of the idea of equal rights for women since the social and liberation movements of the 18th and 19th centuries; (2) problems of women's personalities; (3) protection of women's rights in legislation, women's political rights and their development worldwide; (4) women's economic and social rights, primarily, access to professional careers, equal pay for equal work, acquiring qualifications; and (5) the situation in work of older women and mothers bringing up children. The author also looks at cultural rights, such as access to education at all levels, women's share in high school teaching and their chances for acquiring qualifications, and describes the activities of the Commission of Women's Rights at the United Nations.

260. Salwa, Z. *Rights of working mothers*. Warsaw, Supreme Council 1970, 95 p.

The major regulations up to 1970, putting in order matters concerning working women, are discussed in the work. Women's rights as regards work and health protection, maternity leave, facilities granted on account of bringing up children, are presented against the background of the development of women's legal protection in the interwar period and after the Second World War.

261. Wasilkowska, Z. *Law in women's lives*. Warsaw, 1967, 212 p.

In this work, legal acts, which regulate women's situation in the family and professional work in People's Poland, are collected together. Although some of the regulations have been expanded in the new work code, issued in 1975, the information presented here is of great importance in connection with the development of legislation.

Institutions undertaking research on women

In recent years, several centres have been set up in Eastern European countries to study women's status, with respect to access to education, demographic processes, women's share in migration and its influence on women's professional activization, evaluation of women's social roles and development of relationships in the family. These centres are:

EASTERN EUROPE

In the USSR

The USSR Academy of Sciences, especially its Siberian Branch Office, where sociological research, concentrating on the family and women's problems, is carried out under the guidance of Professor T. Zaslawska; The Institute of Sociological Research of the Academy of Sciences in Moscow, the Institute of International Workers' Movements in Moscow, the Institute of Economics in Moscow, the State University in Tartu, the Institute of Philosophy in the Estonian Academy of Sciences in Tallinn, the Institute of Art, Ethnography and Folklore in Minsk, the Institute of Philosophy and Law in Minsk, the Institute of Economics and Industrial Production Organization in Novosibirsk. All these centres participate in studies on women.

In Bulgaria

The Bulgarian Sociological Association in Sofia, the Bulgarian Academy of Sciences Institute of Sociology and Institute of Economics.

In the German Democratic Republic

The Institute of Social Sciences attached to the Central Committee of SED, Academy of Sciences of the GDR in Berlin, the University in Rostock, Karl Marx University in Leipzig.

In Hungary

The Hungarian Academy of Sciences in Budapest, the Institute of Economic Planning in Budapest, the Institute of Sociology at the University of Szeged.

In Poland

The Institute of Rural and Agricultural Development of the Polish Academy of Sciences, the Institute of Philosophy and Sociology of the Polish Academy of Sciences, the Institute of Social Economy, the Institute of Agricultural Economics, the Institute of Inland Trade, the Institute of Labour and Social Affairs in Warsaw.

In Romania

The Department of Sociology at the University in Bucharest, the Academy of Social and Political Sciences.

In Czechoslovakia

The Czechoslovak Academy of Political Sciences in Prague, the Institute of Philosophy and Sociology of the Slovakian Academy of Sciences in Bratislava, the Economic Research Institute of Food and Agriculture in Prague.

In Yugoslavia

The Department of Rural and Urban Sociology of the Institute of Social Research in Zagreb, and the Institute of Sociology of the University of Ljubljana.

Problems of women's status in Eastern European countries are the subject of activity of some international organizations. *The European Coordination Centre for Social Studies* in Vienna is supporting several scientific research studies with European socialist countries participating. Poland, Hungary, the Federal Republic of Germany, France, Austria and Sweden are participating in studies on (1) models of family life in European countries; (2) divorces; (3) the situation of countrywomen, with particular emphasis on dual occupation families.

The *FAO European Working Group for Household Problems* is looking at women's status in the family, and the topics covered here are women's contribution to the family income, the management of financial resources in the household, educating women for the needs of household, and women's non-school education, in all European countries.

In Poland, two international seminars were held in 1976 and 1979, which gathered together experts in the field of women's role in the household. The changing role of women in the agricultural environment was the subject of debates in Section 14 of the *IV World Congress on Rural Sociology*, held in Poland in 1976, and nine papers from East European countries were presented there, showing the main research lines and the major problems concerning an improvement of women's status in this region, with reference to the situation in other countries.

Sociologicky Casopis (Sociological Review), Vol. 12, No. 1, 1976, published by the Institute for Philosophy and Sociology of the Czechoslovak Academy of Sciences six times yearly. This issue is devoted entirely to women, and includes papers on women's position in the family under socialism, the historical development of the political participation of women and an analysis of basic functions and possible dysfunctions of the family in Czechoslovak society. A short bibliography is also included.

Research on the Status of Women, Development and Population Trends in Latin America: An Annotated Bibliography by Maria del Carmen Feijoo

Research on the Status of Women, Development and Population Trends in Latin America: An Annotated Bibliography by Maria del Carmen Feijoo

A. INTRODUCTION

The aim of this bibliography is to present some selected aspects of recent research on the relationship between women and development in Latin America. An interdisciplinary approach is taken paying special attention to conceptual developments arising in various fields which can throw new light on the traditional analysis of the dynamics of population from a demographic perspective. Specific demographic analyses referring to levels of female participation in the labour force and to fertility were explicitly excluded, since they are easily obtainable through the Latin American Population and documentation systems (DOCPAL) journal *Resúmenes de Población*, which has a predominantly demographic approach and is widely diffused.

The criteria used for the selection of the items to be included in the bibliography, which is not an exhaustive review, were that the studies described should indicate recent approaches exploring new trends in research. Within this framework, particular attention is paid to the relationship between the following aspects of women's experience: (1) female participation in the labour force; (2) women's status within the household; (3) processes of differential structuration of households; (4) national and international migratory flows and the role played by women in these phenomena. Several bibliographies of wider temporal and thematic approach are included at the beginning of the bibliography, which may be of use to readers wishing to pursue concerns other than those covered in the current work.

The majority of academic centres in Latin America, the universities, do not yet officially recognize studies about women, and the researcher interested in such work must trace data from various sources. Despite this lack of formal academic recognition, the subject is in fact frequently the focus of discussion and analysis amongst social scientists in the region, and a wide variety of studies are produced. The chief source of contributions to the study of women are periodic meetings, taking place either in Latin America, or in other countries, often under the aegis of the United Nations or one of its agencies. A second type of meeting arises from the initiative of national or regional institutions. Meetings of both types frequently result in the publication of volumes covering the material presented, and commentaries and evaluations of the results of such meetings. A list of some crucial meetings and journal editions and other publications, which reported on their deliberations, follows the bibliographic entries on page 180 and is itself followed by a short list of other relevant journals.

The entires in the bibliography fall into four main categories, subdivided according to the specific concerns of scholars in the region who have been included, and these are:

I. General, including bibliographies and conceptual and methodological studies;

II. Women's work and labour force participation, including research on women and development, studies on individual countries, and general studies on this topic;

III. Family and household, including rural and urban studies and work on women family heads;

IV. Demographic features, with studies on demographic aspects of the family and on migration.

The entries are listed in alphabetical order within subcategories.

B. THE BIBLIOGRAPHY ON LATIN AMERICA

I. General

BIBLIOGRAPHIES

262. Buvinic, M. *Women and world development: An annotated bibliography*. Washington, Overseas Development Council, 1976.

This bibliography focuses on the effects of socio-economic development and cultural change on women and on women's reactions to these changes. The objective is to disseminate information widely, especially on unpublished studies. The material is broken down into nine subject-categories and subdivided according to geographic area. The nine categories are: general studies on women in development; the impact of society on women's roles and status; the individual in society; socio-economic participation of rural women; education and women; women's work and economic development; women and health, nutrition and fertility/family planning; women's informal and formal associations; women, law and politics. The book provides a list of other bibliographies and a list of special issues of journals and periodicals devoted to the theme. It includes 381 annotated entries of articles and books.

263. CEPAL. *Lista bibliográfica sobre la mujer en el desarrollo de América Latina.* [Bibliographical list on women and development in Latin America.] Jointly produced by the División de Desarrollo Social, the Programa de Integración de la Mujer en el Desarrollo and of the Centro Latino Americano de Documentación Económica y Social. 1979.

This bibliography is part of a major project, which aims at systematizing the available information on women and development in Latin America, so as to guide future research and to disseminate documents of limited circulation. It contains almost 500 entries, organized according to the following schema: international co-operation, economic and social policy, economic conditions and systems, institutional frameworks, culture, society, education, labour, demography, population, health, nutrition, science, geographical information and scope.

264. DOCPAL. *Resúmenes sobre población en América Latina*. [Summaries on population in Latin America.] Santiago de Chile, Vol. I, 1977.

The documentation system on population in Latin America, created by United Nations Latin American Demographic Centre (CELADE) in 1976, aims at enhancing the flow of information about population within the region. It organized three basic services on a regional level: the DOCPAL periodical; the elaboration of specialized bibliographies through computerized searches; and the reproduction of documents. *Resúmenes de población en América Latina* is a periodical of summaries, beginning in 1976 and published twice a year. The purpose is to keep population specialists up to date on recent documents, whether published or not, in their areas of interest, and to facilitate locating information on population in Latin America. It includes topical, geographical and author indexes, as well as a list of books, conferences, editorials and periodicals.

265. Grau, N. E. *La mujer en la sociedad latinoamericana: su papel y su situación*. [Women in Latin American society: their role and situation.] Mexico, Universidad Autonoma Metropolitana, 1977.

This annotated bibliography aims at providing a general overview of the existing literature on various aspects of women's life, and at making evident the need for increasing the number of scientific studies on the subject and of diffusing the existing ones. General and specific works by Latin American authors on the situation of the Latin American women, which were published in Spanish during the 1970s are included. The material reviewed is divided into three sections: participation of women in the labour force, women in social organizations, and ideology and education of women; it includes an appendix with a bibliography on women for various regions of the world. It was published in connection with the seminar Primer Simposio Mexicano-Centroamericano de investigaciones sobre la mujer.

266. Knaster, M. Women in Latin America: the state of the research, 1975. *Latin American Research Review*, Vol. XI, No. 1, 1976, p. 3–74.

This article is a review of research activities in the period 1970–75. It is a summary of a more comprehensive bibliography providing a general overview of the state of the art, summarizing research questions, concepts and objectives. The author concludes that Latin American research proposals suggest two general questions, (1) should the focus be on liberation for women or for the people (sex or class)? and (2) how is research on the subject to be done? The bibliography is divided into published and unpublished sources and articles are presented in alphabetical order. The reference for the more extensive bibliography (which contains 2,534 entries) is Knaster, M., *Women in Spanish America: An annotated bibliography from pre-conquest to contemporary times*, Boston, Mass., G. K. Hall and Co., 1977.

267. Recchini de Lattes, Z. and Wainerman, C. H. *Bibliografía preliminar sobre la participación de la mujer en la actividad economica en América Latina*. [Preliminary bibliography on the participation of women in the economic activity of Latin America.] Buenos Aires, *mimeo*, 1976.

This bibliography lists studies on participation of women in economic activity in Latin America carried out both in the region and outside. It includes about 250 references, organized by countries with a general section on Latin America. The authors highlight the preliminary character of the bibliography and warn of the limitations imposed by the lack of direct access to some of the materials.

268. Saulniers, S. S. and Rakowski, C. A. *Women in the development process: a select bibliography on women in sub-Saharan Africa and Latin America*, Austin, University of Texas, 1977.

This bibliography on women in Africa and Latin America includes 2,844 titles of books, articles, conference documents, pamphlets, and unpublished materials written between 1900 and 1976. It is divided into chapters according to the following subjects: status and roles of women, legislation, family, politics, social organizations, economy, social change, and development. Three annexes provide complementary information on women and development, a listing of bibliographical sources consulted, and the titles and publication places for the periodicals used.

CONCEPTS AND METHODS

269. Aguiar, N. *Casa e modo de produção*. [Home and mode of production.] Paper presented at the Seminário A mulher na força de trabalho na América Latina. IUPERJ, Rio de Janeiro, *mimeo*, 1977.

The author suggests that an analysis of the composition of the productive activities of women, including market and household tasks, can enable a differentiation of these productive activities to be made which will allow them to be incorporated into the concept of the labour force. Such an analysis requires a classificatory system allowing the disaggregation of different types of social organization of production. Existing classificatory systems are concerned with manufacturing and industrial activities, and do not consider other types of social organization of production. Distinction within productive activities will allow a more precise evaluation of the relation between capitalist industries and other types of domestic or handicraft production making the same kind of products. Female labour is particularly important in some branches of capitalist industry, such as the food industry, in which part of the production is undertaken by domestic workers. In order to verify this hypothesis the census should offer possibilities for discriminating among different types of social organization, instead of putting them together in the so called informal labour market.

270. Larguia, I. and Dumoulin, J. *Hacia una ciencia de la liberación de la mujer*. [Towards a science of the liberation of women.] Barcelona, ANAGRAMA, 1976. See an earlier English paper on the same subject. Some aspects of women's labour. *NACLA's Latin America and Empire report*, Vol. IX, No. 6.

This text is a theoretical analysis of female oppression using a Marxist method of analysis. The approach reveals that the role played by women responds to the necessities of the dominant economic system varying in pre-capitalist, capitalist and socialist systems. Under capitalism, if women work away from their homes and have to manage household matters, their working day is about 12 to 14 hours. Their occupations reproduce in the capitalist sphere the tasks traditionally associated with the reproductive role: women will be teachers, nurses, servants, and so on. The housewife should not be regarded now as a women who does not work, but as a fundamental element in the production and reproduction of the capitalist system: she manages the family budget, and is a consumer in the market; her domestic work turns goods into use values necessary to restore the labour force of the household's members, although it is a socially invisible task.

271. Recchini de Lattes, Z. and Wainerman, C. H. *Información de censos y encuestas de hogares para el análisis de la mano de obra femenina en América Latina y el Caribe: Evaluación de deficencías y recomendaciones para superarlas*. [Information from censuses and household surveys for an analysis of female labour in Latin America and the Caribbean: Evaluation of the deficiencies and recommendations for solution.] Santiago de Chile, CEPAL, 1979.

This report aims at a systematic analysis of the difficulties in measuring female labour force participation. The analysis is based on all censuses and some household surveys taken in Latin America and the Caribbean in 1970. The conceptual frameworks utilized in the analysis of women's participation in the economic sphere are reviewed: the 'New Home Economics' approach; macro-analysis on economic development and female labour force participation including the 'U' model hypothesis; empirical studies about women's participation in the market according to age, marital status, number of children, family cycle, educational level, migration and urban-rural residence; time-use studies and the Marxist approach to housework. The authors describe the origins of the labour force concept and evaluate existing difficulties with the information coming from surveys and censuses, suggesting ways to deal with these problems. An exhaustive and up-to-date bibliography on the subjects discussed in the paper is presented at the end of each chapter. It includes three appendices, two showing the type of questions and instructions covering 'condition of activity' in censuses and surveys in the region; the third is a summary showing available information, different variables and tabulations with data published and obtainable in the region.

OTHER

272. Barbieri, T. M. de. Notas para el estudio del trabajo de las mujeres: el problema del trabajo doméstico. [Notes for the study of women's work: the problem of domestic work.] *Demografía y Economía*. Vol. XII, No. 1, p. 34.

The article reviews the conventional studies on female participation in the Latin American labour force, which exclude unpaid domestic work (housework). It analyses some of the theoretical elements related to domestic work, understanding that the latter represents the main form of economic activity for a majority of adult women in developing contexts. Focusing on housewives from urban salaried sectors, the author analyses the specific features of domestic labour and its articulation with salaried work, concluding with a discussion on the extent to which domestic labour follows the law of value. The article can be set within the recent trend of Marxist discussion on the role of domestic work in various modes of production.

273. Collective of women of Latin America and the Caribbean, *Women of Latin America*, Paris, des Femmes, 1977, 321 p. (In French)

Introduced by a group of women concerned to define the specific nature of a Latin American and Caribbean feminism, avoiding the dangers of a mechanical application of models developed in other cultures, this collection of papers looks initially at the history of women's struggles in Latin America and the argument for wages for domestic labour. This is followed by a series of studies relating to individual countries covering the situation of women in Guadeloupe and Martinique, Bolivian women and the class struggle, the history of Chilean women, the status of women in Colombia, Cuban women and the process of liberation, peasant women and the struggle for liberation in Ecuador, women's wages in Mexico, women and Puerto Rican society, the liberation of women in El Salvador, the situation of women in Uruguay today, and maternity and women from the exploited classes in Venezuela. A short, but useful, bibliography is included.

274. Cubitt, T. A. Latin American Women. *Journal of Latin American Studies*, Vol. 12, Part 1, May 1980, p. 169–184.

The author reviews seven books on women in Latin America, assessing their contributions to empirical data, methodology and theory on the study of women. Although all seven increase knowledge of women in Latin America, they do not necessarily contribute to a developing theoretical framework. The author concludes that women's opportunities in Latin America are limited, and the limitations come from the structure of economic opportunities available, which is itself determined by the development of the peripheral capitalist economy, which requires the existence of non-capitalist modes of production subservient to the interests of the dominant mode, in order to assure the process of capital accumulation. Women are largely participating in non-capitalist modes, with the result that they experience extremely poor conditions. The books reviewed are Roberts, G. and Sinclair, S. A., *Women in Jamaica: Patterns of reproduction and family*, Millward, NY, KTO Press, 1978, 346 p. Lewis, O., Lewis, R. M. and Rigdon, S. M., *Four women: Living the revolution*, Urbana, CA, University of Illinois Press, 1977, 443 p. Kelley, J. Holden, *Yaqui women: Contemporary life histories*, Lincoln and London, University of Nebraska Press, 1978, 263 p. Henderson, J. D. and Henderson, L. Roddy, *Ten notable women of Latin America*, Chicago, Nelson-Hall Publishers, 1979, 257 p. The Wellesley Editorial Committee (ed.), *Women and national development: The complexities of change*, Chicago and London, The University of Chicago Press, 1977, 346 p. Lavrin, A., *Latin American women: Historical perspectives*, Westport and London, Greenwood Press, 1978, 343 p. Barrios de Chungara, D. with Viezzer, M., *Let me speak! Testimony of Domitila, a woman of the Bolivian Mines*, New York and London, Monthly Review Press, 1978, 235 p.

275. Graciarena, J. Notas sobre el problema de la desigualdad sexual en sociedades de clase. [Notes on the problem of sexual inequalities in class societies.] In: CEPAL *Mujeres en América Latina. Aportes para una*

discusión. [Women in Latin America: Contributions to a discussion.] Mexico, Fondo de Cultura Economica, 1975.

The author distinguishes three basic perspectives in the literature on the situation of women – 'populationist', 'developmentalist' and 'egalitarianist'. The purpose of the article is to demonstrate how the fragmentary and isolated nature of these approaches prevents a complete understanding of the problem; as a consequence, programmes aimed at enhancing the position of women, based on women turn out not to be feasible. Although sexual differentiation is one of the main pivots around which society is structured, it is neither autonomous nor the only one, being closely linked to other dimensions, such as the internal and external power structures, the development of the productive forces, the social division of labour and the various social classes. The key question is that of determining whether women face greater discrimination as women or as members of a social class, ethnic or regional group. The hypothesis that sexual differentiation is secondary to discrimination by social class for lower class women is suggested. Other relevant questions are put forward: what is the significance of the struggle for sexual equality in a class society where there is no social equality? How are inter-sexual differences situated vis-à-vis more general social inequalities?

276. Jelin, E. La mujer y el mercado de trabajo urbano. [Women and the market place of urban work.] *Estudios CEDES*, Vol. I, No. 6, 1978.

This paper deals with a specific area within the general field of the relation between women and development: the type of economic activity women perform in urban areas and, specifically, that of lower-class women in underdeveloped capitalist societies. Three analytically separate dimensions related to female employment are discussed: (1) supply constraints, linked to the position of women within the household, and therefore to the composition of the household, the sexual division of labour and the relationship between domestic and market production; (2) general labour market conditions prevalent in peripheral capitalist societies; (3) specific, explicit and implicit employment policies for women – including discriminatory practices and the sex segregation of occupations. Without precluding the consideration of female participation in the labour force, the essay sets domestic work and reproduction tasks within the framework of social production. Studies on the subject should incorporate a historical perspective, disaggregate the concept of economic activity and explicitly consider the household as a mediating structure of women's position in the labour market, paying more attention to: historical changes in household structures and the varying position of women in them; varieties of household structures, including 'non-nuclear' patterns, analysing the internal division of labour in relation to both domestic production and outside employment; the transformation of the household along its domestic cycle and the life cycle of its members. At the micro-level Jelin points out the usefulness of the 'life cycle' concept and the 'life history' technique.

277. Navarro, M. Research on Latin American women. *Signs – Journal of Women in Culture and Society*, Vol. 5, No. 1, 1979, p. 111–120.

This article provides a general overview of relevant examples of recent scholarship on women by Latin American social scientists. Several centres make women one of their major concerns, for example: Centro de Estudios de Población (CENEP), Argentina; Centro de Estudios del Estado y Sociedad (CEDES), Argentina; and Associación Colombiana para el Estudio de Población (ACEP), Colombia. The author points out that most Latin American social scientists working on women are not feminists, and the general framework into which the majority of the studies of women fall is that of dependency theory, where researchers focus on women and development in terms of a peripheral capitalist economy.

278. Stolcke, V. Mulheres e trabalho. [Women and work.] *Estudos CEBRAP*, No. 26, São Paulo, 1980.

Within the debate on the roots of feminine subordination, 'productivist' approaches, i.e. those where only activities related to material production are considered as socially valuable, have ignored the fundamental role played by women in the reproduction of class societies. Furthermore, these approaches do not capture the specific nature of the subordination of women. It is argued here that the condition of women is fundamentally determined by the role marriage and family play in the reproduction of social inequality. The entire relationship between the condition of women, the family and class society has to be understood, in terms of the different meanings these institutions have for different social classes and their role in the reproduction of social classes and of the relations of domination between them. The author also suggests that the reproduction of class relations is achieved through the control of female sexuality 'which seems to me to be the root of the subordination of women and the determinant of all other manifestations of subordination'. From a critical perspective, the article revises Marxist thought and strategies for the liberation of women, analyses the ideological supports of class society and the ways in which these institutions perpetuate the subordination of women. On the other hand, the author indicates the mistake of attributing female subordination to her exclusion from productive work and therefore in fostering her incorporation into 'social production'. Finally, there is a description of the history of agricultural female workers in the coffee plantations of São Paulo and the relationship between family and working class, emphasizing the fact that for those women, wage work is a necessity and not a choice so that their integration into wage work did not alter their domestic role, which continues to influence their performance as well as their level of remuneration.

II. Women's work and labour force participation

WOMEN AND DEVELOPMENT

279. Chaney, E. M. and Schminck, M. C. Las mujeres y la modernizacion: acceso a la tecnologia. In: *La Mujer en América Latina*, Mexico, Sepsetentas, Vol. I. See also in English, Women and modernization:

access to tools. In: Nash J. and Safa, H. I. (eds). *Sex and class in Latin America*. New York, Praeger, 1976.

The authors suggest the existence of evidence that the situation of women worsens as the modernization process advances. Access to the inanimate instruments and power on which our modernization depends has been differentiated on the basis of sex. An example of the type of processes described is that of the changing roles of women in the textile industry, as its technology developed and advanced, where they are in charge of the tasks with the least skill requirement. The authors argue that the introduction of advanced technology in developing economies displaces women from their positions. In Latin America, two out of every five working women are domestic servants, street vendors, prostitutes, low-wage clerical workers and, in some countries, petty traders. They briefly analyse the roles of women in the modernization process in Chile and Peru, which follow the pattern described above. Lastly, they point out that if the status of women deteriorates as development advances, exceptions are not lacking, maintaining, however, that even if women are able to enjoy the benefits of development more than other minorities, their participation and power as a group becomes more restricted.

280. Recchini de Lattes, Z. and Wainerman, C. H. Empleo femenino y desarrollo económico: algunas evidencias. [Female employment and economic development: some evidence.] *Desarrollo económico*, Vol. 17, No. 66, 1977.

Reviewing studies of the relationship between female participation and economic development with a wide geographical and historical coverage, the authors point out that these studies coincide in suggesting the existence of a curvilinear U pattern of relationship. Female participation is high both in the early and late phases (the former characterized by domestic unpaid production and the latter by extra-domestic paid labour) diminishing in the intermediate phases. The existing evidence for the Latin American region, however, by no means corroborates fully the U pattern. These discrepancies may be only apparent and could result from theoretical and methodological problems in both concepts (participation and development). While synchronic studies suggest the existence of a linear association, some diachronic studies reveal unclear patterns that do not allow for generalization. The available studies of cases over long periods indicate a curvilinear association. The authors consider that the U pattern is, at this moment, only a reasonable conjecture to be taken as a starting point, and that future work will require efforts on more disaggregated theoretical and empirical levels, particularly through case-studies, in order to grasp the historical and structural specificity of each case.

281. Safa, H. I. The changing class composition of the female labour force in Latin America. *Latin American Perspectives*, Vol. IV, No. 4, p. 15, 1977. See also in Spanish, Modificaciones en la composición social de la fuerza laboral femenina en América Latina. *Estudios de Población*, Vol. I, No. 11, 1976.

The article attempts to explain the changes in the pattern of female participation in the labour force in Latin America as resulting from the development of industrial capitalism and the decline of the family as a productive unit. Reviewing various studies on the subject, the author concludes that the prevalent type of development does not favour the incorporation of proletarian women into the labour force; rather, the growth in female employment tends to benefit middle and upper class women. The paper analyses the role of women in the different stages of development of industrial capitalism, concluding that in the new division of labour, men provide the labour power, while women reproduce and maintain it. Capital reinforces this division by praising the role of women at home, even if the history of the participation of women shows that they never stopped working, be it at home or in the market place. In Latin America, the model of dependent industrial development favoured female employment less than in advanced societies. Educated elite women have entered the labour force in increasing numbers, but employment for working class women has stagnated or declined. Finally, the author points out that for the majority of Latin American and North American working class women, work is not an option, but a necessity. Thus, the discussion of motivational aspects and of individual factors in female labour force participation is of secondary importance.

282. Saffiotti, H. I. B. *Relaciones de sexo y de clases sociales.* [Relationship between sex and social class.] In: *La Mujer en América Latina.* Mexico, Sepsetentas, Vol. II, 1975.

The hypothesis suggested is that partial socialization of working women is an efficient mechanism through which capitalist society is able to mobilize, to a greater or lesser extent, reserves of female labour, according to conjunctural situations. It distinguishes between the social condition of women in highly industrialized countries, and their situation in underdeveloped nations. In order to understand the nature of relations between the sexes the author presents the results of research carried out in the city of Araracuara (State of São Paulo, Brazil) among low income sectors. The results show that almost half of the working women interviewed had occupations requiring little skill and were badly remunerated, in work such as domestic service. Once another member of the family is able to replace them in their function of generating a monetary income, these women return to their ideal as housewives. The unfavourable conditions of employment, as well as the virtual imposition of a double day, hinder the development of a greater commitment to paid employment.

283. Wolfe, M. La participación de la mujer en el desarrollo de América Latina. [The participation of women in the development of Latin America.] In: CEPAL. *Mujeres en América Latina: Aportes para una discusión.* [Women in Latin America: Contributions to a discussion.] Mexico, Fondo de Cultura Economica, 1975.

This article attempts to clarify the usage of the terms 'women and development'. Its key concern lies in the understanding of development as a process of which women should be a part. Reviewing the Latin

American situation, it shows that the process of economic growth did not contribute to the liberation of women, but accentuated the unfavourable aspects of their situation. Educational expansion, in which both sexes have participated equally, is the most favourable aspect of development. Analysing secondary data for the region as a whole, however, the conclusion is drawn that for equal educational levels, women occupy lower categories in the occupational structure and receive incomes that are lower than those of men. The fact that domestic service maintains its importance as a source of employment for women reflects the inability of this type of development to offer them more satisfactory participation in the labour market. The author highlights the fact that studies of participation do not take into account systematically the enormous volume of non-remunerated labour undertaken by women, a fact that fails to be reflected in calculations of labour force participation or of the national product.

INDIVIDUAL COUNTRIES

284. Arizpe, L. Women in the informal labour sector: the case of Mexico City. In: Wellesley College, Center for Research on Women in Higher Education and Professions, (ed.). *Women and national development: the complexities of change*. Chicago, University of Chicago Press, 1977. See also in Spanish, La mujer en el sector de trabajo informal en la ciudad de México: un caso de desempleo o elección voluntaria. [Women in the informal sector in Mexico City: a case of unemployment or voluntary choice.] *Estudios de Población*, Vol. I, No. II.

The paper describes the increasing importance of informal employment in developing countries and the large number of women in this sector. The existence of a very large informal labour sector is associated with the functioning of national economies, trying to determine the occupational alternatives for women in marginal activities in Mexico City. It presents information about female participation in the labour force in Mexico and in Mexico City, and concludes that the lack of formal employment opportunities, especially for women over 30, forces them to enter informal activities, which tend to create their own demand. Entering domestic service or becoming a street vendor are not voluntary choices, but the only possible alternative to escape unemployment.

285. De Riz, L. El problema de la condición femenina en América Latina: La participación de la mujer en los mercados de trabajo. El caso de México. [The problem of the female condition in Latin America: The participation of women in the labour market. The case of Mexico.] In: CEPAL, *Mujeres en América Latina: Aportes para una discusión.* [Women in Latin America: Contributions to a discussion.] Mexico, Fondo de Cultura Economica, 1975.

The problem of the female condition in Latin America is viewed from the perspective of the difficulties of female participation in the labour force. The author's hypothesis is that the decisions affecting female incorporation into the labour market have different weight according to women's socio-economic status. Two types of markets (to some extent un-competitive) exist for each sex in Latin America. The available data confirm this duality of labour markets. The paper includes an analysis of agriculture, manufacturing and services in Mexico, based on data from the IX Population Census (1970). Finally the author expresses doubts about the possibilities of increasing female participation in a labour market, which has already shown an inability to absorb male labour supply in a productive way.

286. Franco, R., Llona, A. and Arriagada, I. La mujer en situación de extrema pobreza: El caso de Chile. [Women in a situation of extreme poverty. The case of Chile.] In: Covarrubias, P. and Franco, R. (eds). *Chile, Mujer y sociedad*, Santiago, UNICEF, 1978.

The authors describe some characteristics of Chilean women in a situation of extreme poverty, and discuss whether the roles attributed to women have been modified among poor people. They review several formulations of poverty; and describe some characteristics of poor women (age, education, labour force participation) in relation to poor men and relatively better off women. Data from the 'Map of Extreme Poverty' drawn on the basis of the 1970 Census data, that includes information on the population of the strata (sex, province, rural-urban residence, labour force status) is used in the study. The authors consider that the statistical information shows the existence of notorious differences not only between poor women and those who are relatively better off, but also in relation to poor men. They remark that it is impossible to explain the situation of these women without inserting them in the families to which they belong, since the differences mentioned before only make sense when the functions women perform in the domestic group are taken into consideration. See also on the same subject. Arriagada, I. Las mujeres pobres latinoamericanas: un esbozo de tipologia. *Estudios de Población*, Vol. II, Part II, 1977. [Poor Latin American women: a sketch of a typology.]

287. Gonzalez Salazar, G. La participación de la mujer in la actividad laboral de México. In: *La Mujer en América Latina*. Mexico, Sepsetentas, Vol. I p. 108–134. 1975. See also in English, Participation of women in the Mexican labour force. In: Nash J. and Safa, H. I. (eds). *Sex and class in Latin America*, New York, Praeger, 1976.

On the assumption that the scarce participation of women in economic activity is one of the determining factors for their social inferiority in underdeveloped societies, the article presents data from the 1970 Population Census on the participation of women in the labour force in Mexico. The author concludes that higher educational levels of women foster the achievement of higher status, and thus allow for greater occupational flexibility and a better incorporation into the labour market. She considers that although their participation in the labour force is not a panacea, it is an important goal for women, together with a greater control of reproduction.

288. Madeira, F. and Singer, P. Structure of female employment and work in Brazil, 1920–1970. *Journal of Interamerican Studies and World Affairs*,

Vol. 17, No. 4. See also in Portuguese, Estructura do emprego e trabalho feminino no Brasil: 1920–1970. *Cadernos CEBRAP*, 13, 1975.

The authors suggest that the structure of female employment depends on the level of development achieved by a society. In Brazil, the industrialization process of the past fifty years has determined the following fundamental changes: (a) a growing shift of population away from agriculture, due to the transition from subsistence production – the central activity of women – to commercial production; (b) changes in urban manufacturing activities, resulting in the substitution of traditionally 'female' artisans by factories; (c) an expansion of social services (education, health, social security, public administration) fostered by industrialization, creating a new massive source of employment for women. Nevertheless, labour opportunities are smaller than the number of women in the urban population, so that many of them are engaged in domestic service. Changes produced by development have thus had contradictory effects on the status of women. It was estimated that in 1970 more than three-quarters of the economically active female population remained at the margin of waged production. The article includes information based on the Brazilian censuses.

289. Pico de Hernandez, I. and Quintero, M. Datos básicos sobre la mujer en la fuerza trabajadora de Puerto Rico. [Basic data on women in the workforce of Puerto Rico.] In: *La Mujer en América Latina*, Mexico, Sepsetentas, Vol. 2, 1975, p. 114–131.

The paper provides information on the following subjects: Puerto Rican women in the labour force, the female employment structure in Puerto Rico, employment in the public and private sectors, income differentials, and the sub-utilization of women. The sources from which the information is extracted are not cited.

290. Prates, S. and Taglioretti, G. *Participación de la mujer en el mercado de trabajo uruguayo. Caracteristicas básicas y evolución reciente.* [Participation of women in the labour market in Uruguay: Basic characteristics and recent development.] Paper presented at the Seminaria A Mulher na forca de trabalho no América Latina. IUPERJ, Rio de Janeiro, *mimeo*, 1978.

The paper analyses the basic characteristics of female participation in the Uruguayan labour market, taking the following moments as references: the main phase of the import substitution model (around the late 1950s); the crisis in the mid-1960s and the recent stagnation. Quantitative and qualitative aspects of female participation in the labour market are analysed, including: the size of the economically active female population in relation to the total economically active population; refined participation rates; participation rate by age, skill and type of occupational category, using data from the national censuses of 1963 and 1975 and from the national household surveys carried out during the intercensal period. The authors consider that their conclusions lead to a questioning of the validity of the U curve hypothesis in the Uruguayan case, particularly the conceptualization of social change as a transition from tradition to modernity. Finally, they ask about the significance of the growing female participation rate in Uruguay, at times of stagnation.

291. Recchini de Lattes, Z. Las mujeres en la actividad ecónomica en Argentina, Bolivia y Paraguay. [Women in economic activity in Argentina, Bolivia and Paraguay.] *Demografía y Economía*, Vol. XIII, No. 1, 1979, p. 37.

The article attempts to further the understanding of the relationship between female participation and development, focussing on the trends in Argentina, Bolivia and Paraguay, since the Second World War. It revises the formulation of the U curve, suggesting that the female participation curve is an aggregation of various curves, each corresponding to a specific sector or occupation and increasing or decreasing in accordance with changes in the economic structure. It presents demographic and socio-economic indicators for these countries for the period 1947–76. The conclusions support the thesis that an adquate formulation of the relationship between female participation and economic development requires the qualification and disaggregation of the data. Although the study dealt exclusively with the concept of female participation, it also demonstrated that as aggregate data are analysed according to specific dimensions, the interpretation of participation differentials becomes more coherent.

292. Recchini de Lattes, Z. *La participación económica femenina en la Argentina desde la segunda posguerra hasta 1970*. [Female economic participation in Argentina from the Second World War to 1970.] Buenos Aires, CENEP, 1980.

This paper uses census information to analyse the intensity and direction of the demographic and socio-economic transformations in Argentina from the Second World War up to 1970, related to female participation in the labour force. The analysis is limited to the individual variables of age and urban/rural residence, the former incorporating changes produced throughout the life cycle of the cohorts. The author studies insertion in the labour market and the changing female composition of the various sectors and occupational categories, and summarizes the relevant literature on female participation and development. She points out that the female labour force increased notably during the period studied, and that this increase in participation in the 1960s could be interpreted as the beginning of an ascending phase of the U curve in Argentina with the following characteristics: (1) the most important increase occurs in periods of the life cycle associated with such events as marriage and childbirth; (2) the most significant change takes place between ages 35 and 54, when the youngest cohorts enter the labour market for the first or second time; (3) female participation decreases in the primary and secondary sectors and increases in the tertiary sector – public administration and social and community services absorb the major part of the increase, followed closely by personal services and commerce. In conclusion, the author suggests that the important social changes which occurred during the period studied gave rise to an increased participation of women in economic activity, especially of the youngest cohorts and in occupations requiring relatively high qualifications. A retrogression in this tendency is highly unlikely; new increases in participation and a continuous feminization of certain occupations might be expected.

293. Ribeiro, L. and Barbieri, T. de. La mujer obrera chilena una aproximacion a su estudio. [Chilean women workers, an attempt to study them.] In: Covarrubias, P. and Franco, R. (eds). *Chile, mujer y sociedad.* Santiago de Chile, UNICEF, 1978.

In the authors' opinion the problem of women is generally presented at a highly abstract level and refers to an ideal pattern. Neither 'the woman' nor 'the Latin American' nor 'the Chilean' woman exist. In each class situation, the daily reality of women and the principal foci of tension should be examined. The research deals with workers in manufacturing industry. The data were gathered as part of an exploratory study in which workers and managers from three Chilean provinces were interviewed. The authors analyse the situations which arise from the triple condition of worker, wife and mother, and the difficulties that female labour pose to managers and workers. The main conflicts affect mothers and housewives, a majority among the workers interviewed. Neither in relation to childrearing nor to housework do they receive any help from factory or state; both institutions consider the family as a private area, with which they should not interfere. Despite these difficulties, female labour is essential both from the point of view of the productive system and the needs of women themselves. The authors conclude that this conflict between production and reproduction can only be solved at the social level.

294. Rodrigues, J. Martins. *A mulher operária. Um estudo sobre tecelas.* [The working woman: a study of female textile workers.] São Paulo, HUCITEC, 1979.

The study analyses the meaning that factory work has for a woman, attempting to understand the relationship existing between this specific form of participation in capitalist relations of production and the sex of the agent. Given its numerical importance in the São Paulo labour force, the author chose to concentrate the study on female workers in the textile industry; the empirical research was done in a textile mill in a city of the state of São Paulo. The meaning of the activity of the worker is analysed on two levels, one referring to her functions within the working class family in relation to the reproduction of the labour force; the other, in relation to the general attitudes and expectations, not only of the worker herself, but of the family head as well.

295. Sautu, R. *The female rural worker in Argentina, Bolivia and Paraguay.* Paper presented at the IX World Congress of Sociology, Uppsala, 1978. *mimeo.*

The study analyses female labour in the context of the employment patterns prevailing in the various regions of the countries studied. These result from agricultural systems and land tenure patterns and, at a more general level, the social organization of economic production. The author concludes that the key determinant of female participation is the probability of accumulation of family capital, which in turn is related to the size of the property and the land tenure system. As the size of the property decreases, there is a decline in the use of wage work, while family labour and female participation increase. In the rural sector, poverty and female labour seem to go together. In Argentina, the economic activity of women appears to be under-registered, since the social definition of economic production excludes subsistence activities, and women who help their families seasonally are not recognized, either legally or statistically.

296. Schmink, M. Dependent development and the division of labour by sex: Venezuela. *Latin American Perspectives*, Vol. IV, No. 1–2, 1977, p. 153–179. See also in Spanish, *Revista Mexicana de Sociologia*, Vol. 39, No. 4, 1977, p. 1193–1227.

The study uses the dependency framework to look at the structure of female employment in Venezuela, showing that, contrary to optimistic positions proclaiming the existence of a positive relationship between female economic activity and higher levels of economic development, changes in the economic system can reduce female participation in economic activity. When analysing the effects of dependency on the structure of the labour force the author indicates that the very rapid growth of service industries – with occupations largely filled by women – is the result of demographic changes and variations in the structure of production. Venezuela is seen as a paradoxical case of dependent development due to its petroleum reserves. Despite the growing participation of women in the labour force, female employment is increasingly concentrating in certain jobs in the service industries.

297. Silva, J. A. et al. Participación de la mujer en la fuerza de trabajo. [Participation of women in the labour force.] *Revista Paraguaya de Sociología*, Vol. 13, No. 36, 1976, p. 143–172.

Although female participation in Paraguay has increased in absolute terms, the rate of increase is lower than that for the male labour force. In 1950, female participation represented 23 per cent of the labour force, while in 1974 the figure was 20 per cent. Maximum participation occurs at an early age, except for brief periods at home, lasting longer in rural areas, given the characteristics of the productive structure. In 1972, the service sector and the manufacturing sector (including crafts) employed more than half of the female labour force, the majority of whom were independent workers. Labour opportunities expanded between 1962 and 1972, with a growth of female wage workers in industry. Educational levels for working women are higher than those of men: 67 per cent have primary level and 22 secondary level education. This increased participation of women in education responds to the requirements of the labour market: women enjoy important social benefits, which sometimes hinder their recruitment due to higher costs.

298. Tienda, M. Diferenciación regional y transformación sectorial de la

mano de obra femenina en México, 1970. [Regional differentiation and sectoral transformation of female labour in Mexico.] *Demografía y Economía*, Mexico, Vol. XI, No, 3, 1977.

The Mexican Population Census (1970) data constitutes the basis for this analysis of the influence of socio-economic development on female participation in the occupational structure and, specifically in the different productive sectors. The initial hypothesis, suggesting a positive relationship between the 'federal entity's level of development' and female labour force proportion, is tested with two regression models. According to expectations, the bivariate model indicates that 63 per cent of the variation can be attributed to differences in the level of development, while with the multivariate model, an additional 15 per cent of employment's variation is explained. The sectoral analysis reveals that the development index explains about 40 per cent of the variation in the dispersion of female participation in production, in relation to the standard level of women in the labour force. This suggests that the level of dispersion of female employment and development are negatively correlated, reinforcing the idea that development lowers the influence of sex in the distribution of women in the industrial structure. Nevertheless, significant variations in the intersectoral magnitudes can still be observed.

OTHER

299. Barrera, M. *Participación laboral femenina y diferencias de remuneraciones según sexo en América Latina.* [Female labour participation and differences in remuneration according to sex in Latin America.] Santiago de Chile, OIT/PREALC, 1978.

The author looks at two main subjects: the female rate of participation in the labour force and wage differentials between female and male workers in Latin America for the 1960–70 period. He analyses female work, the difficulties in measuring it and the structure of the economically active population. Several sources are used in the analysis: census, samples, household surveys, statistical annuals and various other studies. The author remarks that female employment and work conditions link in a very special way the world of labour to the social structure (family characteristics; social stratification system; productive forces). In connection with income, a high proportion of women are included in the lower strata; the percentage of women in the higher levels being very low. The author suggests the need to study specific subjects such as: female segregation in Latin American labour markets; the relationship between values and social ideologies in relation to the sexual division of labour; statistical information about female activity in rural areas; wages; sex segregation of occupations; employers' opinions and attitudes; and domestic paid and unpaid work.

300. Blay, E. Alterman. *Trabalho domesticado: a mulher na indústria paulista*. [Domestic labour: women in industrial development.] São Paulo, ATICA, 1978.

The basic hypothesis is that, whatever the level of technological development or of the political system, the social division of labour keeps sex as the criterion for the incorporation of individuals into the labour market. Empirical research includes skilled female workers in São Paulo industries. The first part of the volume describes the theoretical perspective from which skilled work is analysed. The second presents research results on female labour in more and less industrialized regions, and in urban and rural areas. The third part shows – through qualitative analysis – the social status of women in different societies. The fourth section studies the process of industrialization in Brazil, emphasizing aspects connected with female labour. The way in which skilled women are incorporated into industrial work is illustrated with data from field research. Finally, the socio-economic characteristics of female workers and their attitudes towards work are discussed on the basis of data from the same source.

301. Carvalho, M. L. de and de Silva, R. M. R. *O Trabalho feminino en áreas rurais na América Latina: Una revisao da literatura.* Paper presented at the Seminário A mulher na forca de trabalho na América Latina. IUPERJ, Rio de Janeiro, *mimeo*, 1978. [Female labour in rural areas in Latin America: A review of the literature.]

The author reviews existing bibliographies on the female labour force in Latin American rural areas from the point of view of the insertion of women and family into the social organization of production. The paper highlights the fact that studies on female participation in the labour force – either based on census data or on ethnographic research – fail to capture the reality of female labour. This problem is even more complex when dealing with rural areas, because of the heterogeneity of the organization of productive units. The authors try to identify the most important theoretical contributions and the principal difficulties in the study of labour force in rural areas.

302. Elizaga, J. C. *Participación de la mujer en la mano de obra en América Latina: la fecundidad y otros determinantes.* [Participation of women in the labour force in Latin America: Fertility and other determinants.] Santiago de Chile, CELADE, 1977.

The participation of the Latin American woman in the labour force is among the lowest in the world, a tendency confirmed by recent developments. The basic hypothesis is that fertility has a weak effect in explaining differentials in participation, so that a reduction in fertility does not result in an important increase in participation. The analysis takes into account factors at an individual level (civil status, education and income) and at the societal level (the structure and modernization of the economy). In terms of education, the relationship is a positive one, with Argentina and Chile possessing the highest levels of instruction and female participation. But as the supply of labour increases with the qualifications of women, demand remains a necessary condition for increasing their effective participation. Nevertheless, intersectoral changes and the modernization of the economy have been associated with a transitional stage in the participation of women, with an initial decrease and a subsequent increase.

303. Garcia, B. and Oliveira, O. de *Reflexiones teorico metodológicas sobre el estudio de la relaciones entre el trabajo de la mujer y la fecundidad en la Ciudad de México.* [Theoretical and methodological reflections on the study of the relation between women's work and fertility in Mexico City.] Paper presented at the Reunión del Grupo de Trabajo sobre procesos de reproducción de la población, 5° Guaruja. *mimeo*, 1977.

The paper presents theoretical and methodological guidelines for the analysis of female participation in the labour force and its relationship with fertility. These guidelines are to be used in the project on Internal Migration, Occupational Structure and Social Mobility in the metropolitan area of Mexico City. First, the authors discuss both the connections between participation and fertility – and the particular aspects of them that go beyond the analysis of their interrelation. There is then a brief bibliographic review of studies connecting the family, or household with fertility. The last chapter discusses hypotheses and the presentation of work plans on female labour and fertility, with special reference to the household.

304. Kirsch, H. La participación de la mujer en los mercados laborales latinoamericanos. [The participation of women in the labour markets of Latin America.] In: CEPAL, *Mujeres en América Latina: Aportes para una discusión.* Mexico, Fondo de Cultura Economica, 1975.

The author considers that the economic activity of women in Latin America is, to a great extent, a function of their degree of dependence on men, or of the role traditionally played by them within the family. Data is presented on the participation of women in the labour force for different years and countries, as well as information on educational levels and other socio-economic variables. The author concludes that under the prevailing forms of development participation of women in the labour market has not increased, and that the probability of any significant changes depends on substantial reforms of the production and consumption structures, the distribution of income and the power structure.

305. Paiva Abreu, A. R. de. et al. *A força de trabalho feminina em áreas urbanas na América Latina. Uma revisão da literatura.* [The female labour force in urban areas of Latin America. A review of the literature.] Paper presented at the Seminário A mulher na forca de trabalho na América Latina. IUPERJ, Rio de Janeiro, *mimeo*, 1978.

The paper is an attempt to systematize the theoretical frameworks utilized in the analysis of the urban labour force incorporating the most recent contributions. It includes data on the rate of female activity, by countries, for 1960 and 1970, and on the distribution of active women in the main sectors of activity. It discusses the problem of female labour in the context of the concept of marginality and the relationship between marginal employment and the process of capitalist accumulation. The authors highlight the necessity for increasing the number of empirical studies from which the mode of insertion of female labour in the different modes of production and the historical manifestation of their interrelationship could be determined.

306. Safa, H. I. Class consciousness among working-class women in Latin America: Puerto Rico. In: Nash, J. and Safa, H. I. (eds). *Sex and Class in Latin America*. New York, Praeger, 1976.

The author points out that incorporation into the labour force as such has had no significant influence on women's position. In fact it has resulted in a double burden. She analyses women's maternal roles in relation to the lack of class consciousness, with data from a shanty town in the heart of the San Juan (Puerto Rico) metropolitan area. It is suggested that there is a pronounced matrifocal emphasis in shanty town families, and in addition to the material aspects of domestic work, women perform an extra function for the oppressed urban proletariat by contributing to the existence of a domestic sphere, to which it is possible to retreat.

307. Uthoff, A. and Gonzalez, G. Mexico and Costa Rica: some evidence on women's participation in economic activity. In: Standing, G. and Sheehan, G. *Labour force participation in low-income countries*. Geneva, ILO, 1978.

The study is based on the results of samples from the Mexican Census of 1960 and 1970, and the Costa Rican Census of 1963 and 1974. The factors that have an influence on the female rate of participation are: women's age; educational level; marital status and number of children. During this period the economic participation of women between 15 and 19 years decreased in both countries, probably because of an enlargement of educational activity and the concentration of participation in the 20–39 age group. Education is positively associated with the rate of female activity except in the 15–19 age group. In both countries, marital status affects female participation: married women present the lower rates, while, in the other categories, the rates of activity are similar. Fertility is quite a significant factor in explaining the different levels of participation; it is the existence of a child rather than the number of children that produces lower levels of female activity. Another general conclusion indicates that the rate of female participation has globally increased in both countries.

III. Family and household

RELATED TO WORK

308. Angulo, A. and Rodriguez, C. L. de. Female participation in economic activity in Colombia. In: Standing, G. and Sheehan, G. (eds). *Labour force participation in low-income countries*. Geneva, ILO, 1978.

Using a multiple regression model, the authors analyse the impact of a set of independent variables on the number of hours women work and the number of children. 'Hours worked' was chosen instead of female participation rate because of the incidence of temporary work – especially in the traditional sector – on the economically active population. Women's educational level is used to differentiate modern from traditional. The measure used in the analysis of fertility is the number of children below five years, which is expected to be negatively associated with the number of hours worked. Results indicate that association is non-significant in both sectors. Women dedicated to unpaid housework present higher fertility rates. Age, duration of marital union and women's educational level are the variables which explain fertility better. Relation with the head of the household, type of marital union and occupational position have a fundamental influence on the rate of female participation in economic activity.

309. Cancian, F., Goodman, L. and Smith, P. Capitalism, industrialization and kinship in Latin America. Major issues. *Journal of Family History*, Vol. III, No. 4, 1978.

This essay attempts to define some major issues for the study of the history of Latin American kinship. In particular it focuses on the following problems: (1) studies of dependence and the world economic system; (2) research on industrialization and the family in Europe and North America, and (3) resource exchange theory. It posits two general propositions which need to be clarified by future research: first that industrialization has effects on the family in Latin America that differ from its impact in Europe and North America, because of the colonial or dependent capitalistic nature of Latin American economies; and secondly that different regions, classes and ethnic groups in Latin America have different kinship relations insofar as these groups exist under different historical circumstances. The authors discuss theoretical and methodological orientations and suggest examples of formal hypotheses for the examination of kinship and family in the Latin American historical context. The hypotheses suggested are of three kinds: based on resource control, on family activities and on cultural patterns.

310. Chinchilla, N. Familia, economia y trabajo de la mujer en Guatemala. [Family, economy and the work of women in Guatemala.] *Demografía y Economía*, Vol. XII, No. 1 (34) 1978.

The paper discusses existing approaches to the study of the relation between family and economy, and postulates that a Marxist perspective, explaining differences and similarities in family structure under different productive relations and stages of accumulation, can provide an improved analysis. The author reviews the historical evolution, regional differences and present situation of the family in Guatemala. The absence of work alternatives in rural areas forces the ejection of family members to urban areas. One of the most important functions of the family in a class society is to constitute a labour force reserve and to assume the responsibility for those who cannot work, and of whom the state does not take care. The family becomes a socio-economic guarantee for those who lack any other support, single mothers, widows and the divorced. The study looks at households headed by women, an increasingly frequent exception to the standard family structure. Field work on the Guatemala case enables the formulation of the following hypotheses: (1) with the penetration of capitalism, the productive function of the family decreases as workers are forced to sell their labour as individuals rather than as family units; (2) scarce labour demand and an unequal distribution of income increases the socio-economic function performed by the family and the ideology supporting it, and that is why, with some exceptions, the role assigned to women by the dominant ideology continues to be based on the biological function of reproduction.

311. Lustig, N. and Rendon, T. Condición de actividad y posición ocupacional de la mujer y características socio-económicas de la familia en México. [Condition of activity and occupational position of women and socio-economic characteristics of the family in Mexico.] *Demografía y Economía*, Vol. XII. No. 1 (34), 1978. See also a summary in English in *Signs – Journal of Women in Culture and Society*, Vol. 5, No. 1, 1979 p. 143–153.

The aim of this article is to study the participation and status of women in the labour force, taking into account the pronounced differences existing in Mexico between sectors, families and persons. The hypothesis is that female participation would be greater in the non-agricultural than in the agricultural sector, both because of the characteristics of the women involved and the pre-capitalist conditions of production in the latter. The article analyses female rates of participation in the labour force, according to the type of economic insertion of the head of household (agricultural and non-agricultural) and the level of domestic income, with data from the *Encuesta sobre ingresos y gastos familiares en México*, carried out in 1968. (Enquiry on family income and expenditure in Mexico.)

312. Peek, P. Family composition and married female employment: the case of Chile. In: Standing, G. and Sheehan, G. (eds). *Labour force participation in low-income countries*. Geneva, ILO, 1978.

The author tries to test the following hypotheses: (1) young children do not have a negative effect on female participation in the informal sector; (2) the inverse situation occurs in the modern sector; (3) young children have not only negative but also positive effects on female participation in the labour force. Data are from a 1964 sample. The explanatory variables are: spouse's age, education, children's ages, family income and branch of activity of the head of household. The hypotheses are confirmed for the traditional sector of the economy through regression coefficients. Contrary to what was expected for the modern sector, the positive effect of a high number of children on female participation is almost as intense here as in the traditional sector.

313. Recchini de Lattes, Z. and Wainerman, C. H. Marital status and women's work in Argentina: A cohort analysis. *Genus*, Vol. XXXIV, 1978.

Utilizing data for Argentina, the study illustrates how cohort analysis could increase our understanding of the changes in female economic participation over the last two decades, as well as that of the relationship between female participation in the labour force and the dynamics of marital status. The study of the Argentine case between 1950 and 1970 shows the heuristic value of cohort analysis, the importance of including the dynamics of the marital status of the members of the cohort through their life cycle, and the need for differentiating female marital status beyond dichotomous classifications. The application of the technique revealed the changes operating between 1950 and 1960 and 1960–70. During the first period, all cohorts twenty years of age and older decreased their participation; in the second, the participation of the various cohorts increased. When analysing the marital status of those cohorts whose participation increased, only the rates for married women increased significantly, although those who contributed more to the increase in the female labour force were the widowed and the divorced women. Finally, with the economic behaviour of the various cohorts analysed during the same period of the life cycle, the findings suggest that the changes related to the dynamics of the population in terms of marital status play a crucial explanatory role.

314. Silva, L. M. da. *A participação da mulher casada na força de trabalho: compatibilidade entre suas atividades extra-domésticas e o número de filhos*. [The participation of married women in the labour force: compatibility between their extra domestic activities and the number of children.] Paper presented at the Seminario sobre Participación femenina y familia, CLACSO, Montevideo, *mimeo*, 1979.

The object of this study was to analyse the participation of married women in the labour force and the compatibility between their roles as mothers and as partakers in economic activities. The empirical analysis is based on data from a sample of 3,612 homes in Belo Horizonte, Brazil. Women represent 54 per cent of the population studied. The micro-economic theoretical approach of reproductive behaviour incorporates the principles of the consumer and firm theories. The assumptions of the analysis are that the decision concerning the size of the family is taken within the family unit; the demand for children is a function of the satisfaction these will bring for the parents; and the salary the wife perceives represents the value of the time dedicated to activities in the labour market, or the opportunity cost of the time spent in other activities. Data are analysed applying a multiple regression model estimated through the minimum square method. The author does not consider the study as conclusive, insofar as the hypotheses are confirmed only for that part of the population included in the formal sector of the economy, and for the nuclear family model, without considering female headed households.

315. Wainerman, C. H. *Concepciones acerca de la mujer en la familia y en el mercado laboral de la Argentina*. [Conceptions of women in the family and in the labour market in Argentina.] Paper presented at the Seminario sobre Participación femenina y familia, CLACSO, Montevideo, *mimeo*, 1979.

The article's thesis is that although demographic, economic, and sociological factors are important determinants of the magnitude and structure of the labour force, in order to understand the behaviour of women toward work, ideological orientations with respect to the productive and reproductive roles of women have to be considered. The paper reports results of a research project aimed at unravelling the dominant values regarding women's work in Argentina. Since the labour force participation of women requires her assumption of an additional role (which usually conflicts with the reproductive one) the analysis includes views of the woman herself, about her position within the family, and about her relationship with males. The study chooses historical moments, in which substantial changes in the civil, labour and political status of women in Argentina took place: 1910, 1930, 1950, and 1970. The sources of data for this normative and ideological analysis are textbooks (especially reading books used in primary schools), mass communication media, religious texts and legal documents.

316. Wainerman, C. H. Educación, familia y participación económica femenina en la Argentina. [Education, family and female economic participation in Argentina.] *Desarrollo Económico*, Vol. 18, No. 72, 1979.

The availability of women for the labour force is the result of a series of characteristics related to their articulation of the mother/housewife role with that of salaried worker. The study focuses on two characteristics of the supply of women, education and family situation. Using information from the national census of 1970, the study aims to identify the manner and extent to which education and family situation are associated with the propensity of women to participate in economic activity. It shows that formal education operates as a recruitment criterion for entrance to the labour force, and that a high investment in education not only favours entry to the market, but retains women for more time in it. The presence of a male companion at home, rather than the presence of children is associated with women refraining from participating in the labour force. In 1970 in Argentina, women with a higher propensity to participate in the labour force were: those on the higher end of the educational scale and those without a companion (in the following order: separated and divorced, unmarried, widows, and married without children). A very high propensity to participate is also shown among women who are unmarried, separated, divorced and widowed when they have small children. These women need to participate, regardless of their educational level and the occupational position they might attain.

317. Wainerman, C. H. The impact of education on the female labour force in Argentina and Paraguay. *Comparative Education Review*, Vol. 24, No. 2, Pt. 2, June 1980, pp. 180–195.

The author attempts to identify which females, in different educational levels and family situations, have a greater propensity to participate in the labour market and to evaluate how formal education and marital status influence this propensity. Data are drawn from the latest available censuses of Argentina (1970) and Paraguay (1972).

318. Weiss-Altaner, E. Economia clasica, familias y actividad femenina. [Classical economics, the family and female activity.] *Demografía y Economía*, Mexico, Vol. XI, No. 1 (31) 1977.

The article reviews and compares the classical and neo-classical approaches to the study of society and outlines the economic determinants that modelled the family as an institution. It focuses on the use families make of their time by expressing it in terms of the labour theory of value. In this context, the author discusses the sexual division of labour; its role in economic reproduction; and the links between feminism and capital. Topics for future research are then suggested. Although the article does not deal specifically with Latin America, it does incorporate into the analysis conceptual elements developed in research projects and analysis of secondary data for Latin America. It also includes an ample bibliography on the subject.

RURAL

319. Alasia de Heredia, B., García, M. F. and García, Jr, A. R. *El lugar de la mujer en unidades domésticas campesinas.* [The place of women in the rural domestic unit.] Paper presented at the Seminario A mulher na forca de trabalho na América Latina. IUPERJ, Rio de Janeiro, *mimeo*, 1978.

This paper analyses the social relations within the households of petty producers connected with sugar plantations in north eastern Brazil, focusing on the place occupied by women in these units. There is no generalized female condition; women's status varies according to social groups and particular situations within households. In this case, it illustrates how tasks performed at the *rocado* are socially regarded as *trabalho* (work) while the ones performed at home, though similar, are not considered work. The social definition of work gives meaning to the sexual division of labour, justifying the male-female opposition. The relationship between *casa* and *rocado* organizes the tasks ascribed to 'work' and to 'no-work' throughout the life cycle of the domestic group. The model of domestic authority, which establishes the way in which household and social universes are articulated, comes into play in the '*casa-rocado*' division.

320. Deere, C. D. Changing social relations of production and Peruvian peasant women's work. *Latin American Perspectives*, Vol. IV, Nos. 1 and 2 (Issues 12 and 13), 1977, p. 48–69.

The paper analyses the way in which the development of capitalism affects the economic participation and social status of women, suggesting that the analysis of changes in their socio-economic position should be based on the empirical evaluation of the interaction between the forces and relations of production, which transform both rural society and the life of rural women. Evidence is presented from a historical case study of the Northern Peruvian Sierra, showing that in the hacienda system, the appropriation of female labour appears to be less severe than under other forms of exploitation. However, in-depth analysis reveals that the *hacendado* (landowner) possessed a contractual right to appropriate female labour without pay for the production of goods and the provision of services, be it in the latter's home or in the hacienda. It was female labour, which was particularly subject to unlimited appropriation, making evident that the sexual division of labour was used in the hacienda system as a means of increasing the rate of exploitation. In the 1940s, the creation of a stable market for milk led to the development of the first capitalist agricultural enterprises in the area of Cajamarca. These changes in the relations of production had contradictory effects on female labour. On the one hand, although women became wage-workers in the *tambo*, their servile obligations to the hacendado remained. By 1970, women comprised a third of the wage earning permanent agricultural force in the department, all of them being *tamberas.* On the other hand, the expansion of capitalist enterprises accentuated the prevalence of the *minifundio*, whose limited productivity prolongs the working day of both men and women and makes them seek external sources of income. The Agrarian Reform of 1969 accentuated these unequal tendencies of capitalist development. Women improved their employment opportunities in the co-operatives, although their status did not increase at the same rate, for their roles as wives, daughters or sisters of other members encouraged patriarchal family relations within the productive unit. The author concludes that the passage from the hacienda system to capitalist development is a dialectical process of social transition, based on the resolution of contradictions, in which the socio-economic condition of women both improves and deteriorates. Although exploited as wage earners, women were also oppressed under servile relations of production.

321. Deere, C. D. The differentiation of the peasantry and family structure: a Peruvian case study. *Journal of Family History*, Vol. III, No. 4, 1978.

The purpose of this essay is to explore the relationship between peasant family structure and organization, and the changing patterns of Latin American incorporation into the world economy. The thesis developed is that there is no direct linear link between family structures, the social formation and the world economy, but that the relationship is indirect and interactive. The essay demonstrates that the historical process of Latin America's incorporation as a peripheral of the world capitalist system is important for the analysis of the family as a social unit, which both contributes to and is determined by the overall process of change. The paper examines the implications of the transition from the hacienda system to agrarian capitalism, with reference to the social differentiation of the peasantry. Material conditions govern the process of decomposition of the peasantry over time as well as the possibility for its expanded reproduction, but family structure is not determined solely by economic factors. The thesis is developed in an historical analysis of the development of capitalism in agriculture in the Peruvian department of Cajamarca. The question of whether the growth of the nuclear family preceded of followed industrialization cannot be tackled independently of the particular relations of production in which the peasant family was integrated.

322. Deere, C. D. La división agrícola del trabajo por sexo: un estudio de la sierra norte de Perú. [The division of agricultural work by sex: a study of the northern Sierra in Peru.] *Estudios de Población*, Vol. II, Part II, 1979.

The article presents an analysis of the relationship between the sexual division of labour in agriculture and social differentiation among the peasantry, within the context of the contradictions created by rural poverty in the Department of Cajamarca (Northern Peruvian Sierra). Utilizing data from a survey of peasant families, it shows the significance of the rural woman for agriculture and the importance of her contribution to the labour force of the peasant family unit. Major differences in terms of the participation in agriculture appear: greater participation of women *vis-à-vis* men is related to the objective conditions of rural poverty. As the family loses access to its subsistence means of production, the importance of agriculture decreases and the need to generate income outside the plot increases. Agriculture then becomes less a masculine occupation and more a family activity, with every member contributing with his or her labour time, and sharing to a greater or lesser extent in decisions now tending to fall on women, who have added an additional preoccupation to their traditional domestic responsibilities.

323. Folbre, N. Population growth and capitalist development in Zongolica, Veracruz. *Latin American Perspectives*, Vol. IV, No. 4 (15), 1977.

This detailed empirical study of Zongolica, a *municipio* (county) of the state of Veracruz, Mexico, analyses the penetration of capitalist forms of agriculture and demographic change, since the end of the 19th century up to the 1970s. During this period, Zongolica – originally an agricultural economy – developed into an important coffee producing region. The study compares fertility data from Zongolica with that of Orizaba, the nearest urban centre, concluding that there is a trend toward increased family size in the first *municipio*. What is the basis of family size decisions in areas like Zongolica? Large families, in rural areas, rather than a source of poverty, become a way to fight against it and to secure future family income. Though families benefit from a large number of children, the increase in the supply of labour eventually depresses wages resulting in a benefit for capitalists. These changes, so different from the ones produced in Europe and the United States, show that the decomposition of the peasantry under the influence of modern capitalism is evidently not the same as under the classical development of capitalism in the 18th and 19th centuries.

324. Leon de Leal, M. *Mujer y capitalismo agrario*. [Women and agrarian capitalim.] ACEP, Bogota, 1980. Several chapters and advance reports of this project are available in previous publications: Leon de Leal, M. and Deere, C. D. Planteamientos teoricos y metodológicos para el estudio de la mujer rural y el proceso de desarrollo del capitalismo colombiano, [A theoretical and methodological plan for the study of rural women and the process of development of Colombian capitalism.] Paper presented at the Seminario sobre Participación femenina y familia, CLACSO, Montevideo, *mimeo*, 1979. Estudio de la mujer rural y el desarrollo del capitalismo en el agro Colombiano. *Demografía y Economía*, Vol. XII, No. 1 (34), p. 4–36, 1978; See also in English, *Signs*, Vol. 5, No. 1, 1979, p. 60–77.

This book is the final report of a large scale research project, begun in

1977, on rural, female labour in Colombia. The book aimed at understanding the position of women in the rural sector, in the framework of the changes in the Colombian social formation. Its theoretical framework focuses on the interaction between the way in which a given social formation is incorporated into the process of accumulation on a world scale and the national processes of class formation. It analyses the international social and sexual divisions of labour and the interrelations among them. The authors suggest linking changes in the relations of production and in class formation to the sexual division of labour in the production and reproduction processes of the peasant family. The division of labour by sex represents a strategy of the peasant home rather than an individual strategy or a rationalized option of each of its members. The authors describe the general features of capitalist development in the Colombian rural sector and its articulation in the four regions studied – Fredonia, Sincelejo, El Espinal and Garcia Rovira. These case studies suggest that women in a capitalist system act as reserve labour, be it in haciendas, in capitalist enterprises or in peasant units employing wage workers. The use of female labour is linked to two interrelated factors: low wages and the exploitation of family labour. Other chapters focus on women in the coffee region; the formation and changes in cattle *latifundia* and their effects on the organization of the peasant family; the transformation of the domestic unit and female rural labour in an area of advanced capitalist development; the sexual division of labour in the minifundia peasant unit; the dynamics of the peasant unit in two regions; and finally, proletarianization and agricultural labour in the small-holder economy and the sexual division of labour. The study demonstrates that the peasant woman is economically active and that her rates of participation are far superior to those reported statistically. Furthermore, regional historical processes affect men and women in different manners. The analysis of female labour in the productive unit highlights the importance of the participation of women, even if only as family help, rather than as directly responsible for the exploitation of the unit as well as for its relationship to the socio-economic position of the peasant family. The most important analytical tool for measuring female labour and analysing its importance in the rural sector of an underdeveloped country is, then, the examination of rural capitalist development as a historical process.

325. Lisansky, J. Women in the Brazilian Frontier. *Latinamericanist*, Vol. 15, No. 1, Dec. 1979, p. 1–4.

This report focuses on the impact of land conflicts in the Brazilian Amazon on women in the frontier town of Santa Terezinha over the past two decades. These were between squatter farmers and large companies installing government supported investment projects in cattle, mineral and timber production. It looks at the changes in women's work, roles and status as peasant families make the transition from a farming life to life in a frontier town, in a region dominated by large cattle-raising companies. One conclusion is that the economic pressures on families, resulting from increasing dependence on low-paying and irregular company employment, contribute to increasing instability in all types of marriage unions in the town, and to 15 per cent of households being headed by a woman. In general, the author concludes that women have gained little in status, material wealth, or security from the changeover from peasant subsistence production to the major strategies for economic survival practised in the town.

326. Young, K. Modes of appropriation and the sexual division of labour: a case study from Oaxaca, Mexico. In: Kuhn, A. and Wolpe, A-M. (eds). *Feminism and Materialism*. London, Routledge and Kegan Paul, 1978.

The study investigates the relationship between women's productive and reproductive roles, attempting to understand the mechanisms through which women were excluded from positions of control over social resources and socialized into accepting their subordinate position. It analyses the sexual division of labour as a system which assigns and excludes agents from productive positions and social roles in the organization on a sex basis, thus creating a system of reinforcement in the social construction of gender identities. Given the changes in economic relations, as a result of the process of capitalist development from 1870 to 1970, the study attempts to determine the consequences of these changes in two small agricultural communities of a mountainous zone of Oaxaca, Mexico and their effects on women. It attempts to demonstrate not only that these economic changes limited or expanded the access of women to economic roles, but the manner in which they affected women's reproductive roles. Transformations in the domestic units are analysed, showing that in the case of women belonging to poor families, the need to generate a monetary income for the family – through increasing the number of income-earners – puts more emphasis on women's reproductive capacity.

URBAN

327. Covarrubias, P. and Munoz, M. Algunos factores que inciden en la participación laboral de las mujeres de estratos jabos. [Some factors which influence the labour participation of women in marginal stratas.] In: Covarrubias, P. and Franco, R. (eds). *Chile, mujer y sociedad.* Santiago de Chile, UNICEF, 1978.

The article analyses the elements that either hinder or stimulate female participation in economic activity. Attention is focused on the participation of women in marginal strata in Santiago. Census (1960) and sample information suggest that: The participation of married women, either legally or by common law, in the labour force is more limited than that of single women; it is the age and not the number of children that influence female participation among married women; education exercises great influence and the rate of participation grows as it increases; professional skill is directly related to participation, its influence being greater than that of education; women work in a higher proportion when they belong to extended families; women, especially married women, work because of urgent economic need in the household.

328. Jelin, E. La bahiana en la fuerza de trabajo: producción simple y trabajo asalariado en Salvador, Brasil. *Demografía y Economía,* Vol. VIII, No.

3, 1974. See also in English, The bahiana in the labour force in Salvador, Brazil. In: Nash, J. and Safa, H. I. (eds). *Sex and class in Latin America*, Praeger, New York, 1976.

The aim of this article is to analyse the economic participation of women in Salvador, a city of the Brazilian northeast, explicitly introducing domestic activities into the analysis. The participation of women in domestic activity is compared to the participation of women in the various sectors or organizations of the market economy, such as simple commodity production, the capitalistic firm, and public administration or the state. The data are based on a survey carried out in 1970–71, on a sample of approximately 1,000 cases representative of the adult population (18 years and over). The article includes data on the participation of women for the four sectors of economic activity, showing that participation in the labour force depends on age and position within the family. As a conclusion, the author criticizes the academic and censal definitions of 'economic activity', 'economically active population' and 'participation in the labour force', since domestic activity and the crucial role played by women in it are not taken into consideration. Furthermore, the type of productive participation of men and women, their variations, and their determinants can only be understood by studying the relationship between the social division of labour and the intra-familial sexual division of labour. The need to study the family in relation to the organization of production and social classes is thus emphasized. Finally, the author suggests that there is no universal concept of relations between the sexes, but rather class relations of domination and exploitation that affect women in a differential manner, depending on the class and the family structure to which they belong.

329. Lomnitz, L. and Lizaur, M. Perez. Kinship structure and the role of women in the urban upper class of Mexico. *Signs*, Vol. 5, No. 1, 1979, p. 164–168.

The article describes the results of a study of the kinship structure of an upper class family in Mexico City. The investigation was extended over five generations, which included 118 nuclear families descended from a small merchant of the state of Puebla, one of whose sons migrated to Mexico City at the end of the 19th century and became one of the pioneers of Mexican industry. The authors find that women acted as unifying elements in the family, as they played a crucial role in the transmission of information, the most basic and elemental exchange within the clan. Prominent female figures acted as centralizing forces and their prestige was based on their knowledge of the family's history. In recent years, the role of women in family businesses has acquired greater importance, although their active participation is far from evident and maternity still remains their main preoccupation. The material included facilitates the understanding of the dynamics of kinship in complex societies, the interrelationship between kinship and class, the nature of relatives, and the specific role women play in the social system of the urban middle and upper classes.

330. Pecht, W. La mujer casada y el mercado de trabajo: grado de

participación en las areas urbanas. [The married women and the labour market; degree of participation in urban areas.] In: Covarrubias, P. and Franco, R. (eds). *Chile, Mujer y sociedad*. Santiago, UNICEF, 1978.

The study analyses the participation of women – either married to or cohabiting with a spouse – in Chile. The analysis proves that there is an association between participation and (1) level of fertility and education (female attributes), (2) income level and occupational status (husbands' attributes). The results of the study indicate that bi-variate associations between fertility, education and income and female participation in the labour force seem to exist, but that they become more complex when the simultaneous effects of various interrelations are considered. The author works with data from household surveys of 1970 and 1971 available at CELADE. It includes data on 'married' urban women between 25 and 34 years, according to income and occupational level of head of household and fertility levels, with comparative data for various Latin American countries.

331. Rodrigues, A. M. *Operário, Operária. Estudo exploratório sobre o operariado industrial da grande São Paulo.* [Working men and women: an exploratory study of industrial workers in São Paulo.] São Paulo SIMBOLO, 1978.

This book describes the methodological and conceptual issues for the psycho-social study of workers on which a following paper is based (Entry 333).

332. Rodrigues, A. M. *Mulher e familia entre operários e funcionários públicos: uma comparacao*. [Women and family: a comparison between wage workers and public employees.] Paper presented at the Seminario sobre Participación femenina y familia, CLACSO, Montevideo, *mimeo*, 1979.

The author compares the results of her empirical research on wage workers and public employees. The survival strategies and world views of both groups are compared in an attempt to suggest hypotheses that could guide future qualitative research. As components of the survival strategies, the composition of the domestic group, the sexual division of labour and the distribution of roles within the family are analysed. The author warns that a thorough understanding of the subject requires a consideration of the history and material conditions of each social group and their habits and ethos. Only such an approach will lead to an understanding of the totality of their representations and practices.

333. Schmink, M. *The plight of poor women in the Latin American metropolis. An exploratory analysis of policy issues.* New York, The Population Council, *mimeo*, 1980.

In the belief that in most countries the situation of women in rural areas and in the so-called marginal urban sectors has worsened during the recent years, several regional meetings, held by the United Nations, called for more adequate data collection, research and analysis of women's situation in these contexts. This report is intended to contribute to filling in the gaps in knowledge about crucial aspects of the situation of poor women in the Latin American metropolitan areas, i.e. women's access to urban services, given the fact that women often predominate in disadvantaged urban groups. The report is composed of a series of exploratory studies which deal with different aspects of the plight these women confront daily and over their lifetime. Its multiple aims intend to explore the outlines of women's role in the urban economy of Latin America and provide an analytical framework for understanding this role; to draw together scanty information related to women's access to urban services and the implications of these findings for the welfare of poor women and their families; and to point to policy directions which arise out of the tentative findings of these exercises. It studies in more detail the case of the urban transport sector, based on a pilot study of transport conditions in three poor neighbourhoods in Belo Horizonte, Brazil, carried out in 1979. The final chapter of the report is an exploratory essay, concerned with the design of programmes directed at low income populations.

WOMEN FAMILY HEADS

334. Barroso, C. *Sòzinhas ou mal acompanhadas: A situação da mulher chefe de familia*. [Alone or in bad company: The situation of women family heads.] Paper presented at the Seminario A mulher na forca de trabalho na América Latina. IUPERJ, Rio de Janeiro, *mimeo*, 1978.

The paper analyses the situation of female family heads, women who, because of marriage dissolution, abandonment, absence or non-existence of the husband, are responsible for their economic survival and that of their children. It highlights the growing proportion of homes headed by women in the world, and discusses some of the published data, emphasizing the need for perfecting the collection of data in the census. The author questions the use of the residential unit as a criterion for determining the web of social relations called the family. The conclusion is that a close relationship exists between poverty and homes headed by women in the Third World.

335. Nieves, I. Household arrangements and multiple jobs in San Salvador. *Signs*, Vol. 5, No. 1, 1979, p. 134–142.

In the shanty towns of San Salvador, (Republic of El Salvador) the consanguineous household contributes more to the welfare of its members than any other type of domestic organization by allowing its adult women to become economically active and collaborate in maintaining the group. The author defines the household as a group of individuals living together who might or might not correspond exactly with the family. Of the sample in the study, 73 per cent was organized on the basis of conjugal or affinity ties, including homes with and without conjugal family units, and those with more than one conjugal family unit (extended family homes of all kinds). Twenty-one per cent of the sample was composed of people related by blood ties. This information nevertheless, does not reflect changes registered in the composition of these units in response to changes in their socio-economic environment.

The author considers that the consanguineous domestic group has a greater capacity for internal modification than that of groups formed around ties of affinity of one or more couples. The consanguineous group is able to absorb migrant relatives, as its limits and composition are not strictly defined, and might be modified in response to specific needs, such as child care. Extended families or multiple family homes, making up 11 per cent of the sample, offer these advantages as well. These domestic arrangements are complemented by social networks among women for taking care of the children and providing other necessities.

336. Merrick, T. W. and Schmink, M. *Female headed households and urban poverty in Brazil*. Paper presented at the workshop 'Mujeres en la pobreza: que sabemos?' Belmont Conference Center, *mimeo*, 1978.

The authors analyse households headed by women, in order to discover how they manage and their relationship with urban poverty in Belo Horizonte (Brazil). The poverty group accounted for 41 per cent of female-headed households. Poor households with female heads depend much more on the head's earnings, than those headed by men. About half of the female heads are employed in the informal sector while only 15 per cent of male heads are in that situation. The disadvantageous earnings of women derive from the comparative lack of access to formal positions in the urban labour market. Poor female-headed households not only have more dependants to support, but also make use of a smaller proportion of its potential adult labour force. The informal sector is a treacherous substitute for welfare; it provides a survival strategy, but, at the same time, confines women to a subsistence level of existence and increases the probability of their being caught for life in the vicious circle of poverty.

337. Recchini de Lattes, Z. *Participación femenina y dinámica familiar en la Argentina, 1960–1970*. [Female participation and the dynamics of the family in Argentina 1960–1970.] Paper presented at the Seminario sobre Participación femenina y familia, CLACSO, Montevideo, *mimeo*, 1979.

The analysis deals with the growth of female participation between 1960 and 1970. This is basically attributed to the increase in participation of married women and to the growing proportion of widowed and divorced women, who have historically presented high rates of participation. It aims at explaining these changes, disaggregating by cohort the information about the position of women in the household (female heads, etc.) and type of domestic unit (nuclear and extended). The analysis of these three dimensions is used to interpret changes in the rate of participation and the occupational distribution of women.

IV. Demographic features

338. Arizpe, L. *Indígenas en la ciudad de México. El caso de las 'Marias'*. [Indigenous peoples in Mexico City: The case of the 'Marias'.] Mexico, Sepsetentas, 1975.

This book describes and analyses the characteristics of the migratory flow of *mazahuas* and *otomies* Indians from four rural communities to Mexico City. The study tries to explain the invasion which took place at the end of the 1960s of the Mexico streets by Indian women ('Marias') selling fruit. The 'Marias' play a very passive role in relation to migration and choice of occupation, husbands, fathers or brothers having taken the decision. Migration is not an individual experience: migrant families are linked to their rural communities by kinship or marital ties and by a permanent exchange of money and information. A three parameter model was used to solve the theoretical problem of agents (who migrates?) and motives; a personal and familial parameter; economic, political and cultural local conditions; and the historical characteristics and the national economic and political structure. Even though this level does not reach the migrant as an individual, it establishes the basic conditions affecting him/her. The model does not show a mechanical causal relation among variables, but a causal nexus of which migration is one possible effect. The study offers data from field work in four communities of Mexico and Queretaro as well as information from secondary sources. The origin of 'las Marias' can be traced in the migration of Indian families to Mexico City, as a result of both changes in their communities and the industrial development of the metropolis. The 'Marias' are a consequence of the incapacity of heads of households to support their families. The wife has to work, but because of her ethnic origin there is practically no demand for her labour, and the only way of earning a living is as a street vendor. The author points out that this situation is not only determined by the migrant's ethnic status – structural conditions of unemployment and underemployment clearly play a role.

339. Arizpe, L. *Migración, etnicismo y cambio económico. (Un estudio sobre migrantes campesinos a la ciudad de México).* [Migration, ethnicity, and economic exchange. (A study of peasant migrants in Mexico City.)] Mexico, El Colegio de Mexico, 1978.

The author considers rural-urban migration as a distinctive phenomenon of countries in peripheral capitalist regions, in the second half of the 20th century. This book has several aims: (a) to describe and explain the migration of Indian peasants to Mexico City through a case study of a 'minifundist' Indian agricultural area in central Mexico; (b) to apply a historical and structural perspective at community and group levels; (c) to develop new concepts to explain migration at the local level and new uses of the anthropological method. Two communities offering contrasting patterns of migration and social and occupational incorporation of migrants to the city are studied. One chapter of the book is devoted to migration, family and kinship. The interrelation between various aspects of kinship and migration are shown to have emerged as mechanisms to regulate human organization within the migratory phenomenon. Kinship rules the way in which persons and groups are organized during the process of migration and incorporation into urban life, but it does not cause migration. On the other hand, the combination of economic, social and political factors at the origins of migration determine the importance of kinship. The greater the poverty and marginality of migrant families, the greater the dependence on kinship ties. When there is more economic independence, families can replace those ties with the new ties of *compadrazgo* with city inhabitants.

340. Arizpe, L. Mujeres migrantes y economía campesina: análisis de una cohorte migratoria a la ciudad de México, 1940–1970. [Women migrants and the peasant economy: analysis of a cohort of immigrants to Mexico City, 1940–1970.] *América Indígena*, Vol. 38, No. 2, 1978, p. 303–326.

The fact that, with the exception of Peru and Guatemala, migration to cities in Latin America is predominantly female seems to confirm one of Ravenstein's laws. The current explanation (limited work opportunities in rural areas) takes attention from some of the most interesting aspects of the phenomenon: capitalist penetration in a peasant economy produces an internal polarity in the community and affects different groups differentially. The study of a sample of 70 migrants (Mexico City, 1970) from a survey on Migration, Occupational Structure and Social Mobility, leads the author to consider migration, not from an individualistic perspective, but in relation to the domestic group. The position of female migrants in the peasant household as well as their class origins are introduced. Using the life-histories of migrants, Arizpe analyses the employment and mobility alternatives migrants face in the cities and the strategies they develop when just arrived. The results of the study show that it is impossible to generalize about the motives and modes of migration. The analysis of the economic processes of each particular region is, evidently, necessary to understand migratory flows. To understand the intermediate motives of the phenomenon, which define the internal composition of the migratory flows, two mediating structures (class and domestic group) have to be examined. The influence of the domestic group on the decisions taken by women indicates that the family is still a basic unit in dependent capitalist societies.

341. Arizpe, L. *La participación femenina en el agro y la selectividad de las migrantes*. [Female participation in agriculture and the selectivity of migrants.] Paper presented at the Seminario sobre Participación femenina y familia, CLACSO, Montevideo, *mimeo*, 1979.

The paper explores some characteristics of migrants (age, marital status, education) and their motives to migrate, in order to explain both the role played by women in peasant families and migrants' selectivity. Migration is seen as a compensatory mechanism against the pressures toward the transformation of rural economies and the proletarization of their members. The analysis of the changes, suffered by production units in Latin American peasant economies during the transition from subsistence farming to capitalism, shows that the age at which daughters migrate is conditioned by the family's economic situation. If the income is very low the elder daughters tend to migrate very young. This pressure is not so clearly determinant in the case of intermediate daughters, who may even prolong schooling. However, families having more means of production or dedicated to commercial and handicraft activities also send women to cities. Though there is always a personal, imponderable element in the decision to migrate, the analysis of this phenomenon shows that the majority of women migrate as the result of a paternal decision or domestic pressure. The analysis indicates that the selectivity of migrant women can be explained by women's status and by changes in the sexual division of labour that take place within the household with the unequal incorporation of peasant communities to the capitalist system.

342. Arizpe, L. La migración por relevos y la reproducción social del campesinado. [Migration for relief and the social reproduction of the peasantry.] In: Balán, J. (ed.). *Migration and development* Paris, Unesco, 1981.

Rural-urban migration is analysed from the point of view of the decomposition of the peasant economy and the strategies adopted by 'minifundist' families to survive and reproduce themselves. The relevant question is how peasant families manage to survive, despite the destruction of their domestic economies and why they continue to increase their population, notwithstanding the fragmentation of their plots and the ever-increasing deterioration of the conditions of life. On the basis of data from two peasant communities in Mexico, the author shows how the social reproduction of the peasantry operates through a strategy of 'stage-migration' by which, through the permanent and consecutive migration of the children, the peasant family gathers resources to cultivate the land and reproduce itself. Through the 'stage-migration', peasants guarantee the return to the rural household of part of the wealth the city extracts from them.

343. Burch, T. K., Lira, L. F. and Lopes, V. F. (eds). *La familia como unidad de estudio demográfico*. [The family as a unit of demographic study.] San Jose, CELADE, 1976.

This book gathers together 15 articles concerned with demographic variables which influence the size, structure and characteristics of families. The studies give a general perspective on: (1) the present condition of demographic research on the family; (2) the difficulties arising from the deficiency of data; (3) the relevance demographic analysis has for certain social effects. Chapters are grouped in three sections: the conceptual and methodological aspects; size and structure of the family; and family structure and fertility. The book presents an annotated bibliography, with general studies on the sociology of the family; family and household; methodological studies; studies on the size and structure of households; family's social change; kinship relationships; family life-cycle and family structure and fertility.

344. Bustamante, F. La migración femenina en Chile. Algunas hipótesis sobre causas y características. [Female migration in Chile. Some hypotheses of causes and characteristics.] In: Covarrubias, P. and Franco, R. (eds). *Chile, mujer y sociedad*. Santiago, UNICEF, 1978.

The article studies migratory differentials by sex in Chile, with data from the 1970 Census. It considers migratory flows as the result of the dissolution of traditional social links in peripheral areas and the liberation of part of the population from their previous attachments. Female migration adopts two main forms: as part of a family group or alone, depending both on the structure of the zone of origin and the transformations of the rural family. The great number of young female migrants to cities expresses the transformation of a mode of production as well as a change in the relationship between family and economy.

345. Chaney, E. M. *Domestic service and its implications for development*. Paper presented at the Primer simposio Mexicano-Centroamericano de investigación sobre la Mujer, El Colegio de Mexico-UNAM, Mexico, *mimeo*, 1977.

The study approaches the problem of women in Latin America from the perspective of the women themselves. It deals with the situation of migrants in Lima and includes information on 50 interviewed migrants whose structural characteristics coincide with the profile of the typical domestic servant as obtained in another study. The central hypothesis is that modernization in Latin America, especially in urban areas, reduces the alternatives for women, and particularly for migrants. Women's alternatives are fewer than men's, either migrants or natives. The second hypothesis states that the inability of poor women to control fertility also explains why they are relegated to the lowest positions in the traditional labour market. Working mothers from four different occupations, including heads of households, are studied in order to explore these subjects. The article discusses domestic service and its relation to development, its trends and significance. It is seen as a permanent rather than a transitory phase. The migratory process is described; the migrant usually travels with a 'godmother' who presents her to an employer. At the *patrona*'s household she is socialized into the basic rules of urban life.

346. Garcia, B. and de Oliveira, O. Una caracterización socio-demográfica de las unidades domésticas de la ciudad de México. [A socio-demographic characterization of domestic units in Mexico City.] *Demografía y Economía*. Vol. XIII, No. 1 (37) 1979.

The importance of the household as a socio-demographic unit of study has been clearly established in Latin America. This study aims at showing the importance of the household in the analysis of the participation of the population in economic activity. The hypothesis is that responses to contractions or expansions in labour force demand are organized at the household (instead of the individual) level. The paper presents data on kinship composition, size and life-cycle stage of households in Mexico City. It studies differences in the internal composition of households, according to the position of the head in the economic structure: the relationship between household composition and occupational status, and the influence of these factors on the economic participation of other members of the unit. Data analysed are from a survey on internal migration, occupational structure and mobility in Mexico City. Findings about composition and size lead to the conclusion that the relatively large nuclear family was the predominant type of household in Mexico City (1970). Nevertheless, among the subgroup of female headed households, there is a significant proportion of non-nuclear domestic types (extended families), bigger in size than nuclear families because of the presence of other relatives.

347. Garcia Castro, M. and Lopes Cavalcanti Oliveira, Z. *Migrant women: the role of labour mobility in the process of production and reproduction*. Rio de Janeiro, *mimeo*, 1978.

This paper deals with female migration. The authors review the bibliography produced in Brazil relevant to the development of a theoretical model concerned with mobility, production and reproduction of the labour force, and the system of domestic production. Another section presents quantitative information on migrant women. The paper is especially concerned with productive relations in rural areas, and suggests the use of a historical and structural model in the analysis of women's situation.

348. Jelin, E. *Migración a las ciudades y participación en la fuerza de trabajo de las mujeres latinoamericanas: el caso del servicio domestico*. [Migration to the city and participation in the labour force of women in Latin America: the case of domestic service.] Buenos Aires, CEDES, 1976 (Estudios Sociales No. 4.)

The report analyses the migration of Latin American, especially lower-class, women from rural to urban areas and their occupational alternatives in the cities. Rural-urban migration trends in the region are discussed as a framework for the study of the productive insertion of migrants into the cities. The author offers certain hypotheses to explain the role played by women in the family and in the labour market. She points out that women migrate to Latin American cities more often than men; some women arrive alone, looking for jobs, while others arrive with their families (husbands, children, other relatives) and devote their main effort to housework. The qualitative difference between women who 'work' and those who do not 'work' – which at first appears important – disappears when we consider that the former enter the urban labour force mainly as paid domestic servants and the latter perform unpaid domestic services for their own families. The author believes that housework and domestic production, differential participation in the labour force, the existence and use of paid domestic service, and the unequal division of labour between men and women, are interrelated phenomena that can be fully understood, only if conceptualized as specific aspects of the organization of households. Household organization is intimately related to the organization of production, and studies to be carried out in the future will have to consider them from the point of view of the mechanisms that reproduce the economic system as a whole. The author postulates that households develop a 'strategy for survival' that includes the differential participation of its members in the outside world and the division of labour within the household. Migration to the city should be seen not as an individual event, but as part of the strategy of survival of the rural household. Systematic research on the survival strategies of domestic units, focused on the alternatives available, not to the individual, but to the household group, will provide the analytic development necessary to understand female migration and women's position, both in the labour market and in domestic production.

349. Lira, L. Aspectos sociologicos y demograficos de la familia en Chile. [Sociological and demographic aspects of the family in Chile.] In: Covarrubias, P. and Franco, R. (eds). *Chile, mujer y sociedad*, Santiago, Unesco, 1978.

The paper has as its objective the description of sociological and demographic characteristics of families in Chile. It analyses different types of families and life conditions in urban and rural areas. It establishes a typology of families that includes lower, middle and upper class urban families, and peasant and middle class rural families. Information from the 1970 Census on the proportion of households according to composition, and vital statistics for Chile and other Latin American countries are presented. Final conclusions emphasize the existence of a variety of family types, according to socio-economic and demographic characteristics. The author also draws attention to the great contrasts existing between very rich and poor families in different regions.

350. Safa, H. I. La participación diferencial de mujeres emigrantes de América Latina en la fuerza de trabajo de Estados Unidos. [Differential participation of women emigrants from Latin America in the labour force in the United States.] *Demografía y Economía*. Vol. XII, No. 1 (34) 1978.

The author's intention is to compare the migratory and labour profile of women in Latin American cities with that of migrant women to the United States. Attention is focused on the Puerto Ricans, Cubans, Colombians and Dominicans in the metropolitan area of New York, and on how the migrant population has been affected by changes in the labour market and in its socio-demographic composition. As in Latin America, the percentage of female migrants is higher here than that of males. This has to do with the nature of the labour market in New York, that demands female labour. The majority of the Latin American migrants are attracted by the possibility of finding employment in industry, mainly in the garment industry – the one which offers employment to the higher proportion of women in the country. This industry has traditionally been the biggest source of employment for Puerto Ricans. During the crisis of the 1960s the Puerto Ricans and other ethnic minorities were the first to be dismissed. From 1950 to 1970, and for various reasons, the rate of participation of Puerto Rican women in New York city decreased. In contrast with Puerto Ricans, Cubans, Colombians and other Latin American women registered a higher rate of participation in the labour force. This high proportion of women in the labour force is discussed by the author in connection with the 'machismo' hypothesis. This concept does not take into consideration the fact that in Latin America, peasants and lower-class women have always contributed to family income, either in the labour force, in household production activities or in the informal sector of the economy.

351. Sautu, R. Formas de organizacioń agraria, migraciones estacionales y trabajo femenino. [Forms of agrarian organization, migration conditions, and female work.] *Revista Paraguaya de Sociologia*, Vol. 16, No. 46, 1979, p. 49–62.

The article analyses female labour in the rural area in north-western Argentina. Industrial crops prevail in this zone. The statistical information indicates that the female rate of participation in rural labour (agriculture and cattle-breeding) is very low. The data do not agree with visual impressions and anthropological studies suggesting female participation in agricultural production. This participation differs widely, according to the various zones and the particular type and volume of agricultural production and level of development. On the basis of data from different sources, the paper analyses the relationship between the type of organization of economic production, employment patterns and spatial mobility of the population. It describes female and family labour in the zones producing tobacco (Misiones, Corrientes) cotton (Chaco, north of Santa Fe, Santiago del Estero), and sugar (Tucuman, Salta y Jujuy). The household is here the production unit. The cyclical incapacity to accumulate a surplus explains why more productive labour methods are not introduced. This situation results in seasonal and temporary female and male migration, operating as a mechanism to compensate for the small family income. If the economic situation improves, instead of working in the harvest, women turn to domestic work and return to rural labour when needed. Women are at a disadvantage – their work is not acknowledged in the census nor in the legal structure.

Some important meetings on women in Latin America and their results

Two meetings, one in Buenos Aires, and the other in Santiago de Chile, in 1974 were of particular importance to work in this area, producing a considerable number of studies of some originality.

1. A meeting on the subject 'Perspectivas femeninas en investigación social en América Latina' took place at the Instituto di Tella in Buenos Aires, under the sponsorship of the Social Science Research Council (New York) in March, 1974. Three volumes appeared compiling some of the material presented at this meeting: Elu de Lenero, M. (ed.), *La mujer en América Latina*, Mexico, Sepsetentas, 1975 (two volumes); Elu de Lenero, M. (ed.), *Perspectivas femeninas en América Latina*, Mexico, Sepsetentas, 1976; and Nash J. and Safa, H. I. (eds), *Sex and class in Latin America*, New York, Praeger, 1976.

2. Also in 1974, the Vice-Rectory of Communications and the Institute of Sociology of the Universidad Catolica de Chile organized a seminar entitled: La mujer Chilena, hoy. Certain of the papers presented, together with some from other sources, were included in Covarrubias, P. and Franco, R. *Chile, mujer y sociedad*. Santiago, UNICEF, 1978.

3. A seminar on 'Participación de las mujeres en el desarrollo de América Latina' was organized in Caracas by various United Nations organizations in 1975. The volume emerging from that meeting is useful for the analysis of the situation in the region and of the changes that take place during the process of

development. CEPAL, *Mujeres en América Latina: Aportes para una discusion*, Mexico, Fondo de Cultura Economica, 1975.

4. A conference entitled 'Women and development' took place, under the auspices of several associations of North American scientists, including the 'Latin American Studies Association' in 1976. This meeting, dedicated to the discussion of the situation of women in the Third World, included many contributions to the study of female status in Latin America. Some of the most important studies were published in: *Signs – Journal of women in Culture and Society*, Vol. III, No. 1, 1977; a collective volume – Wellesley College, Center for Research on Women in Higher Education and the Professions; *Women and national development: the complexities of change*, Chicago and London, University of Chicago Press, 1977; and the Colombian magazine *Estudios de Población*, Asociación Colombiana para el Estudio de la Población, Vol. 1, Part II, 1977.

5. The 'Primer Simposio Mexicano Centroamericano de Investigaciones sobre la Mujer' gathered under the auspices of the Universidad Autonoma de México and El Colegio de México in that city in November 1977. *Demografía y Economía*, Vol. XII, No. 1 (34), devoted a special issue to the meeting and *Signs – Journal of Women in Culture and Society*, Vol. 5, No. 1, 1979, reproduced some of the papers presented.

6. The seminar 'A mulher na força de trabalho na América Latina' gathered in Rio de Janeiro under the auspices of IUPERJ in November 1978. Its aim was to provide new criteria for the collection of data to enable a better statistical record of the different types of female work in the 1980 Census.

7. A workshop on 'Participación de la mujer en el proceso de desarrollo' under the auspices of the Instituto Nacional de Cultura of Peru and the Institute of Social Studies of Holland took place in Lima in 1978.

8. The first formal meeting of the working group on 'Participación femenina en el mercado de trabajo' within the CLACSO working group about 'Ocupación y desocupación' took place in Montevideo in December 1979. The subject of the meeting was female labour force participation and the family.

Special journal issues and other publications

Pescatello, A. (ed.), *Female and male in Latin America*, Pittsburgh, Pennsylvania, University of Pittsburgh Press, 1973, is one of the first important volumes in the period, now available in Spanish *Macho y hembra en América Latina*.

Women in Latin America, An anthology from *Latin American Perspectives*, Riverside, California, 1979.

Journal of Comparative Family Studies, Vol. IX, No. 1, Women in the family and employment, a cross-cultural view.

Journal of Family History, Vol. III, No. 4, 'The family in Latin America', 1978.

Latin American Perspectives, Vol. IV, Nos. 1–2 (issue 12/13): 1977, 'Women and class struggle'.

Three other journals (amongst others) produce work on women:

Boletin Documental sobre Las Mujeres, a quarterly journal with articles on the liberation of women in Latin America, published by Communicación intercambio y desarrollo humano en América Latina (CIDHAL), who have also published two English anthologies of articles from the *Boletin*.

Fem, Mexico (Av. Mexico 76–1, Col. Progreso Tizipan, Mexico 20,DF). Essays, theoretical analyses and articles on the history of feminism, and reports on the status of women in Mexico and Latin America in general. A. Foppa was one of the journal's editors.

Mujer y Sociedad, Peru, (Ica 441–A–Of. 401, Lima, Peru.) A feminist journal.

Selected Studies on the Status of Women, Changes and Continuities in the Sexual Division of Labour in Family and Society, Women's Education/Labour Force Participation and Demographic Trends in Northern America and Western Europe from 1975:
An Annotated Bibliography
by Janet Holland

Selected Studies on the Status of Women, Changes and Continuities in the Sexual Division of Labour in Family and Society, Women's Education/Labour Force Participation and Demographic Trends in Northern America and Western Europe from 1975: An Annotated Bibliography by Janet Holland

A. INTRODUCTION

Much of the research on women has been generated by or is a result of the resurgent women's liberation movements in these countries and the topics investigated cover every aspect of women's condition and experience. One substantial general area in which a considerable amount of research takes place is that of women and labour force participation at all levels. Empirical studies indicate exactly where women are located in the economy, in the lower reaches or in the higher levels of both economy and polity. Theoretical and analytical studies look at labour market segmentation and the interrelationship between unpaid domestic labour and paid work.

This bibliography is an attempt to illustrate selectively the type of work on women which is taking place in and about the countries covered here. I have relied on a range of cross-cultural studies and material relatively readily available to provide both information and an indication of the range of work on the status of women since 1975. Some items are in the language of the country of origin, and this will be indicated. The criterion for selection is that the work illustrates a type of study which is taking place in the United Kingdom and the United States and most probably in the countries of Northern Europe.

The organization of the entries, for ease of access given the large number in this section, is slightly different from that in the rest of the bibliographies. The work is first divided into four broad areas: Cross-cultural, United Kingdom, United States and Western Europe. Within these four categories the major categories of research used in the rest of the bibliographies appear:

I. General, including bibliographies;
II. Women's work and labour force participation;
III. Family and household;
IV. Education;
V. Demographic features (not covered in sections on U.K. and Western Europe);
VI. Other.

These are subdivided as relevant with reference to research in the geographical region covered. Within these subdivisions, the alphabetical order of authors prevails.

B. THE BIBLIOGRAPHY ON NORTH AMERICA AND WESTERN EUROPE

1. CROSS-CULTURAL STUDIES

I. General

BIBLIOGRAPHIES

352. Ceulemans, M. and Fauconnier, G. *Mass Media: The image, role and social conditions of women: A collection and analysis of research materials.* Paris, Unesco, 1979.

An extensive survey of research on the image, role and social condition of women as portrayed by the media (radio, television, film and press) in North America, Western Europe, Oceania, Asia, Africa and Latin America. The report is published in English, Spanish and French and contains a useful, comprehensive bibliography.

353. Evans, M. and Morgan, D. *Work on Women: A guide to the literature.* London and New York, Tavistock Publications, 1979.

A guide to the rapid accumulation of writing and research on women, which has accompanied the growth and spread of the women's movement and contemporary feminism in the west. The focus is on contributions to feminist writings, which illustrate the issues and direction of current research and debate. Chiefly orientated towards literature on the industrially advanced societies in the west, with a particular bias towards the United Kingdom and the United States, it also includes comparative material on women in socialist and developing countries. The selection is organized around institutional structures, which directly affect women's lives: education, employment, domestic labour, welfare, politics, the law, medical care, the media, and each section is prefaced and interspersed with brief discussions locating the work in contemporary debate.

354. Gallagher, M. *The portrayal and participation of women in the media.* Paris, Unesco, 1979.

A review and analysis of research and action programmes around the world, looking at both the portrayal of women in the mass media, and their participation. The author notes that, despite clear cultural variations in emphasis, certain themes and trends recur in each region of the world, and the picture is remarkable only for its consistency, when countries are compared. As far as cultural differences are concerned, in those countries where, in the author's view, women have made greatest progress toward social, economic and political equality (e.g. China, Cuba and some countries in the Eastern Bloc) the mass media in general reflect government commitment to policies towards women formulated on economic imperatives. In capitalist economies, the media have tended to respond to other, commercial pressures, which characterize women's participation primarily in terms of consumerism. A bibliography is included.

355. Oakes, E. H. and Sheldon, K. E. *A guide to social science resources in women's studies.* Santa Barbara, Ca., Clio Books, 1978, 162 p.

The authors aimed to produce a succinct evaluation of social science literature on women for teachers of women's courses. 'The annotations describe the contents and thesis of the resource and critically evaluate it in terms of its use as an undergraduate text' (p. xi). There is an emphasis on international material (in English) and the chapter headings are anthropology, economics, history, psychology, sociology, and contemporary feminist thought. Each chapter has a number of subdivisions and an introduction.

356. Parker, F. and Parker, B. J. *Women's Education – a world view: Annotated bibliography of doctoral dissertations.* Greenwood Press, 1979.

This study focuses on world-wide education of girls and women in and out of school and attempts a comprehensive listing with annotations of books and reports published in the English language, and doctoral dissertations on all aspects of women's education in a variety of careers.

357. Ritchie, M. *Women's studies: a checklist of bibliographies.* London, Mansell, 1980.

Contains over 500 bibliographies presented under the headings: General (including special issues of periodicals), anthropology area studies, arts, criminology, economics, education, geography, health and medicine, history, language, law and women's rights, literature, politics, psychology and psychiatry; religion, science, sex roles, and sociology. A keyword index is provided.

358. Safilios-Rothschild, C. *Sex role socialization and sex discrimination: A synthesis and critique of the literature.* US Department of Health, Education and Welfare, National Institute of Education, 1979.

The bibliography covers American literature between 1960 and 1978, providing an extensive review and critique under the following major headings: sex role socialization and the sex typing of behaviours; same sex and cross-sex influences on sex role socialization; women's achievement and achievement motivation; women's educational and vocational choices; sex role socialization patterns in selected societies; sex discrimination in primary, secondary and higher education; occupational sex discrimination; the case of Black women, race and sex discrimination; sex discrimination theory and research; sex and other stratification systems.

359. Stineman, E. (with the assistance of Loeb, C.) *Women's studies: a recommended core bibliography.* Libraries Unlimited, 1979.

The bibliography is intended as a support for a women's studies curriculum for undergraduate students. It provides an annotated and indexed core collection, organized around traditional disciplines, of English language publications. Each of the annotations is researched and designed to link the item with whatever may be relevant, in previous works, or in works by others. There are 1,763 entries, and indices for author, title and subject.

360. Vreede-de Stuers, C. *De vrouw in de buitenlandse werknamers, een beschrijvende bibliografie.* Rijswijk: Ministrie van Cultuur, Recreatie, en Maatschappelijk Weck, Netherlands, 1976.

A comprehensive annotated bibliography on women migrants in Western Europe (in Dutch). See a brief English summary 'Women migrants in Western Europe' in *Canadian Newsletter of Research on Women*, Vol. VII, No. 2, July 1978, p. 90–94. The author concludes that (1) the female migrant has not been given proper attention in her own right as she is seen in relation to husband or family; (2) she faces double discrimination, as migrant and as woman; and (3) the rare studies which do focus on women are only partial analyses, paying insufficient attention to the way in which women experience their migration and to what extent the changes in their life have influenced their thought and action.

OTHER

361. Bensadon, N. *Les droits de la femme des origines a nos jours.* Paris, Presses Universitaires de France, 1980, 123 p.

The author looks at the nature of myths about women, and at the role of women in a range of historical epochs, for example in the Roman Empire and in Greek antiquity, and outlines the two main struggles for women's rights – the struggle against sexual and against social taboos. This is followed by a brief discussion of the rights of women in a number of countries: the Federal Republic of Germany, the United Kingdom, Italy, Senegal, China, USSR, United States, Canada and France.

362. Boulding, E., Nuss, S. A., Carsons, D. L. and Greenstein, M. A. *Handbook of international data on women.* New York, Sage Publications, John Wiley and Co., 1976.

A handbook of data on women collected by national governments at the request of the United Nations. Indicators of the status of women in a large range of countries are presented in the following categories: general economic activity; economic activity by status, by industry, by occupation; literacy and education; migration; marital status, life, death and reproduction; political and civic participation. Details of the derivation of the indices presented, and the inevitable limitations of the data are discussed. This book provides an extremely broad and extensive source book of comparative data on the status of women in a large number of countries.

363. Commission for the European Communities. *Men and Women of Europe. Comparative attitudes to a number of problems in our society.* Brussels, December 1975.

Results and analyses of a survey carried out in the nine countries of the

EEC in May 1975 to mark International Women's Year. Amongst the topics covered in a questionnaire, which went to representative national samples totalling 9,500 individuals in all, were: the importance attached to women's status compared to men's; perceptions and evaluation of change in women's status; judgements of opportunities for women; aspirations; attitudes to paid employment; social reforms required to improve women's status; attitudes to politics and social participation; levels of satisfaction, feelings of happiness, and attitude towards the EEC. The CEC Office on Women's Employment have also begun a catalogue of research projects in process, planned or recently completed on women's employment and all related topics. Part 1 covers Belgium, Denmark, Luxembourg and the United Kingdom, containing 250 items. Part 2 covers Federal Republic of Germany, Italy, France, Ireland and the Netherlands.

364. Edholm, F., Harris, O. and Young, K. *Conceptualising women. Critique of Anthropology*, Vol. 3, Nos. 9/10, 1977, p. 101–130.

This article takes as its starting point the work of Meillassoux, C. (*Femmes, Greniers et Capitaux*, Paris, Maspero, 1975) on the interrelationship between production and reproduction. The authors try to clarify the concept of reproduction, in which the biological and social have been conflated. They want to distinguish three types: (1) social reproduction; (2) reproduction of the labour force; and (3) biological reproduction. They also discuss the multiple levels of functioning of the sexual division of labour, where allocations are mediated by a powerful ideological operator 'the social construction of gender identity'.

365. European Social Development Programme. *The changing roles of men and women in modern society: Functions, rights and responsibilities.* Seminar organized by the Division of Social Affairs of the United Nations office at Geneva, in collaboration with the Netherlands Ministry of Cultural Affairs, Recreation and Social Welfare, New York, UN, 1977. (SOA/ESDP/1977/2) in 2 volumes.

In the first volume, papers include: 'Women's progress within social development', by Ferge, Z. – data on policies, progress and implementation in a number of European countries is presented, and the author is critical of some demands of women's movements. 'Current changes in the roles of men and women', by Jaakkola, R., which considers two problems (1) a general frame of reference for the social status of men and women and the presentation of data for Finland, (2) socio-political means of promoting male/female equality. 'Recent changes in women's situation in Europe: A critical evaluation' by Kozakiewicz, M. – summing up losses and gains of emancipation, the author suggests that in countries where judicial or practical progress has been made, secondary and side-effects have appeared, which have engendered new inequalities. He looks at education, the professional status of women, and the relationship between household work and professional work using European data. In volume two, 'Background paper: the changing roles of men and women in Europe', E. Sullerot reviews the economic, familial and civil/political roles of European women and men, trying to identify social trends (particularly towards a similarity of roles) and the historical context of change in modern Europe.

366. Giele, J. Z. and Chapman Smock, A. *Women: Roles and status in eight countries*. New York, John Wiley and Sons, 1977, 443 p.

Women's status in Egypt, Bangladesh, Mexico, Ghana, Japan, France, the United States and Poland is explored in the papers in this book, mainly by sociologists. A multisectored approach to the position of women is taken, and in each chapter their status is described in terms of historical background, legal and political systems, work, family life, health and fertility and cultural participation, with a wealth of information provided. The editors provide an introduction and conclusion which attempt to integrate the chapters on different countries, and argue that societal complexity and sexual equality are related in a curvilinear fashion, with life options in the various sectors of human activity linked to 'modernisation' of the relevant cultural and structural features of society. From this broad historical perspective, the middle stages of development are viewed as the most problematic for women's equality, since industrialization tends to disrupt the pattern of men and women's roles, making women more dependent on men, and men less dependent on women's economic activity. Change in women's status is seen as the result of the interplay of change in the various sectors of activity.

367. Iglitzin, L. B. and Ross, R. (eds). *Women in the world: A comparative study.* Santa Barbara, Ca., Clio Books, 1976, 427 p.

A collection of papers resulting from a symposium in 1974 at the University of California, which covers in Part 1: conceptualizing the cross-cultural study of women, looking at the partiarchal heritage – African women and modernization, and female political participation in Latin America. Part 2 is on women in Europe and the United States, with studies on Italy, Ireland, France, Federal Republic of Germany, United Kingdom and the United States. Part 3 is on women in the developing countries and covers Ghana, Iran, Algeria, Colombia, Mexico and Hong Kong. Part 4 on women in nations mobilized for social change, looks at Yugoslavia, USSR, Israel, China (2 studies) and Scandinavia (2 studies).

368. Janssen-Jurreit, M. *Sexism: The male monopoly on history and thought.* Pluto, 1981, 384 p. First published in German as Sexism/Über die Abtreibung der Frauenfrage. Munich-Vienna, Carl Hanser Verlag, 1976, 756 p.

A large scale work, which deals with sexism in history, in political theory and politics, in the economy, in biology, in sexuality and in the structuring of identity. The author locates the source of sexism, not in production relations nor in a 'natural' division of labour, which put power in the hands of men, but in women's monopoly over the childbearing process, the only monopoly, as she says, which results not in power but in helplessness and subjugation. She surveys the early German, British and American feminist debates and exposes the varieties of patriarchal responses to them. Chapters include: a critical study of 19th century social-evolutionist theories, as well as those of the early socialists – especially Marx and Engels; a history of the suffrage movements around the world; and an account of the development and perpetuation of labour systems based on the division of sexes. There are also discussions of the ways in which gender in the German language can and has been used to denigrate women, on sexual aggression and clitoridectomy and female infanticide.

369. Leghorn, L. and Parker, C. *Women's worth: Sexual economics and the world of women.* London, Routledge and Kegan Paul, 1981.

A densely documented picture of the economic position of women around the world, supporting the argument that women's contributions are invisible in the economic balance sheets drawn up on the basis of a valuation of identifiable material products. The authors consider the relative merits of tradition and modernity for the position and status of women, pointing out the potential positive impact of development (voting rights, nominal equality) and the negative impact (loss of economic independence in subsistence agricultural communities), but also that a return to tradition (as in Algeria or Iran) is often also accomplished at women's expense. The fundamental factor is that the basic power relations remain the same. Three types of power, which women can hold are distinguished: minimal, token and negotiating, and the authors suggest that women's status and position are not static or progressing but may wax and wane among the three categories as the priorities of the societies, in which they live, change.

370. Mathieu, N-C. Biological paternity, social maternity: on abortion and infanticide as unrecognised indicators of the cultural character of maternity. In: Harris, C. C. (ed.). *The sociology of the family*. Keele, Sociological Review Monographs, 1979.

The author develops the argument that the biological level of explanation is only applied to women – women are seen as mediators between the natural and the social by virtue of physical reproduction, and the social or cultural level of explanation is applied to men. She stresses, with examples from anthropology, the social nature of maternity. The examples indicate that even when the information is available for this interpretation, it is viewed from a male perspective, and whilst paternity is regarded and presented as a socio-cultural category in these studies, maternity is not seen in that way.

371. O'Brien, M. *The politics of reproduction.* London, Routledge and Kegan Paul, 1981, 240 p.

A critique of traditional political thought which analyses the process of reproduction, elaborating a selection of the conceptual concerns of feminist theory, and offers criticisms of some influential works in the area of feminist studies, including de Beauvoir, Millett, Firestone and Reed. The author argues that these writers rely on existing 'male-stream' theories, which are inimical to women. She then considers the relation of creation to procreation as a determinant of the social forms of separation of the public realm and politics from the private realm and the family, discussing what she calls the idealist ideology of male supremacy. This is followed by a critical analysis of the conflation of production and reproduction in Marx's work, where the reproductive dynamic is arbitrarily awarded to the process of production – the materialist ideology of male supremacy. The author argues that only feminism is at present a major progressive force in Western history and that there must be a new approach to the study of history and politics based on the radical perspective of feminist thought.

372. O'Connor, K. and McGlen, N. E. The effects of government organisations on women's rights: An analysis of the status of women in Canada, Great Britain and the United States. *International Journal of Women's Studies*, Vol. 2, No. 6, Nov. Dec. 1979.

The development of the legal, political and economic status of women in the United States, United Kingdom and Canada is reviewed briefly. The laws of all three countries can be seen as deriving from 'common law', but the women's rights movements and the acquisition of rights vary and particular rights emerged at markedly different times. The authors suggest that differing governmental structures play a major part in these differences, and in particular the division between federal and state (provincial) authority, which has meant that in some cases women acquire rights earlier than might otherwise have been the case, but also some women achieve such rights later. This situation arises because central government is reluctant to impinge on provincial rights and this has a negative impact for women in conservative and traditional provinces or states. In the United Kingdom, where central government is the sole guarantor of women's rights, laws have been later in coming than in Canada and the United States, and this may have contributed to greater frustration and radicalization of British women during some periods.

373. OECD. *Equal opportunities for women.* Report prepared by the Working Party on the Role of Women in the Economy, established by the OECD Manpower and Social Affairs Committee in 1974. Paris, 1979.

The basic aim of this report is to bring out the gaps that have appeared or grown wider in recent decades between existing laws, policies and institutions in member countries on the one hand, and the aspirations of women and the reality of their working lives on the other. Chapter I describes the social and economic changes which have made employment more necessary and more feasible for women and led to their increasing participation in the labour force, and gives data on this changing participation for a number of OECD countries. Chapter II on education and training locates the main source of inequality in education, in the role prejudice which exists in society and which the educational system reflects, and examines the interrelation between educational policies, practices and choices and opportunities for women in the labour market. Policy trends for education in four countries are examined in relation to other areas of public policy, and the implications of a policy of equality in education are discussed. Chapter III concentrates on policies acting directly on conditions of employment, in approaching the question of equality in pay and employment, and covers a wide range of member countries in this light. Chapter IV discusses various time arrangements, which can facilitate women's participation in the labour market, enabling people to combine family and work responsibilities. Chapter V reviews different national approaches towards and arrangements for childcare for working parents. Chapter VI, based on information from fifteen countries, reviews the most important aspects of social security systems, which have not kept pace with social and economic change and have led to inequality of treatment for women. Various solutions to these problems, with attendant advantages and disadvantages, are discussed. This report provides a useful source book of information from OECD countries on the position of women. A bibliography and references would have made it more useful.

374. Newland, K. *The sisterhood of man.* New York, W. W. Norton and Co., 1979, 242 p. A Worldwatch Institute Book.

From a starting point of a background in government and economics, and from a convinced feminist perspective, the author looks at problems and areas of change in the roles and status of women around the world, concentrating on concerns which women have in common rather than on the problems facing any one country, and providing a great deal of factual information. Topics covered are women, the law and change; education and equality; health; media and women; politics; work, wages and families. No explanation, interpretation or analysis of the material presented is offered.

375. Reiter, R. R. (ed.). *Towards an anthropology of women.* London, Monthly Review Press, 1975, 416 p.

A collection of essays directed towards overcoming male bias in anthropological studies, suggesting the need for radical investigation and redefinitions and providing guidelines and examples of directions for an anthropology of women. The first three papers look at male bias in the interpretation of the biological and cultural evolutionary record, three more look at sexual equality in groups organised along kinship lines (the Kung of Southern Africa, Australian Aborigines, and the Káfe of Highland New Guinea). Two articles consider theories of the origin of gender relations. Rubin, G. 'The traffic in women: Notes on the "political economy" of sex', analyses how the female of the species becomes an oppressed, domesticated woman, and constructs a critical theory of the process of female subordination through a reading of Marx, Engels, Freud and Lévi-Strauss. Other papers look at contemporary West European peasant groups and aspects of the changing role of women in Third World countries, including a paper on rural women in China. Countries on which there are studies, apart from those mentioned above, are France, Spain, Italy, Colombia, the Dominican Republic and Nigeria.

376. Schlegel, A. (ed.). *Sexual stratification: A cross-cultural view.* New York, Columbia University Press, 1977, 371 p.

A collection of papers mainly by anthropologists, which explore aspects of women's lives in Morocco, Sicily, India, Sudan, Ivory Coast, Ghana, Yugoslavia, Barbados, Israel and among the Bantu, Hopi and Bontoc societies. The chapters deal with the topic on a non-comparative basis, but the editor, in her introduction and conclusion, reviews existing literature on gender stratification, extracts basic themes and attempts to link the chapters in a loose theoretical framework. The emphasis is on the need to identify differences between the sexes in control over the individual's own activity, and that of others and the importance of analysing this control in the major sectors of human activity – family, politics, economics, education, sexuality, reproduction and culture, rather than trying to make a global assessment of the relative status of men and women.

II. Women's work and labour force participation

PROFESSIONAL/MANAGERIAL WORK

377. Bartol, K. and Bartol, R. Women in managerial and professional positions: the United States and the Soviet Union. *Industrial and Labour Relations Review*, Vol. 28, No. 4, July 1975, p. 524–534.

The article looks at data on women in the United States and USSR in managerial and professional positions. The conclusion is that women in the USSR have not achieved the level of equality often attributed to them, but they have made significant progress in attaining professional and managerial positions. Even allowing for the higher labour force participation of Soviet women, the proportions of female economists, engineers and physicians in the United States are small by comparison. The differences in managerial positions are less dramatic, but still Soviet women are in a better position than women in the United States in terms of inroads into the male domain of management. The authors suggest that the example of public support for equal employment and of women in a wider range of professional work in the USSR could be usefully followed by the United States.

378. Rosenthal, M. M. Perspectives on women physicians in the USA through cross-cultural comparison: England, Sweden, USSR. *International Journal of Women's Studies*, Vol. 2, No. 6, Nov. Dec. 1979, p. 528–540.

The paper examines the patterns of female enrolment in medical schools, choice of specializations, pay and structure of practice and numbers of women in professional positions of decision-making power in the four countries considered. Despite considerable differences in the organization and functioning of medicine in these countries and the proportion of women in this profession (e.g. United Kingdom 20 per cent; USSR 80 per cent) some similarities are uncovered. Women are encouraged (or more openly permitted to apply for medical training) when their society requires their participation in the labour force and the medical profession for particular economic or social reasons. The case of the USSR suggests that when the need subsides women are subject to dis-recruitment; there is a remarkably similar pattern of choice of specialism, and women go into medical rather than surgical areas i.e. lower status areas; few women are in positions of leadership or decision makers in medicine. Problems of childbearing and caring and the broken career patterns of women are suggested as possible reasons for some of the observed similarities between these countries, and the author suggests that 'to legitimize alternate career models seems a sensible way to encourage rather than frustrate the participation of women in medicine' (p. 538).

379. Symons, G. L. *Managerial women in France and Canada: A comparison.* Paper presented at the CSAA annual meeting Montreal, June, 1980.

The paper compares aspects of the work and private lives of a sample of 64 women managers in France and Canada. It looks at career histories, socialization experiences, co-ordination of work and family life, sponsorship, impact of sex ratios in work setting, and the effect of the presence of women in powerful positions on equality of opportunity. It is part of a larger cross-cultural study comparing the condition of women managers in anglophone Canada, Quebec and France.

OTHER

380. Cook, A. H. Working women: European experience and American need. In: Cahn, A. Foote (ed.). *Women in the US labor force.* New York, Praeger, 1979, p. 271–306.

After outlining the problems which all working women face, and the provisions which must be made for taking into consideration the special circumstances of their involvement in the labour force, if the aim of equality between the sexes is to be met, the author looks at compensatory programmes for market re-entry and training in Austria, Australia, Federal Republic of Germany, and Sweden. She concludes that 'only when a genuine commitment to equality exists, as it does in Sweden, will the political parties, the unions, the employers and the officials of the labour market institutions initiate a thorough programme designed to bring women into all sectors of employment' (p. 288). Experiences in childcare are also compared in Australia, Austria, France and Sweden as a basis for comparison with the United States.

381. Darling, M. *The role of women in the economy.* A summary based on 10 national reports, Paris, OECD, 1975, 127 p.

A general overview and synthesis of reports from Australia, Belgium, Canada, Denmark, Finland, France, Italy, Japan, Sweden and the United States. The information provided is easily comparable; a useful reference work.

382. ILO. *Womanpower: The world's female labour force in 1975 and the outlook for 2000.* Geneva, ILO, 1975, 40 p.

The paper presents a statistical picture of women in the labour force in

1950, 1975 and projections for the year 2000. The data relate to the world's eight major areas, Africa, Latin America, Northern America, East Asia, South Asia, Europe, Oceania and USSR, and 24 standard regions. Levels and patterns of female labour force 'activity rates' and the influence on these of the married woman's role are discussed. The relative importance of women workers and their distribution among the principle economic sectors, occupational groups and status groups are briefly reviewed, along with characteristic patterns of female dependency. See also ILO. Women's participation in the economic activity of European market economy countries. (Statistical Analysis) Geneva, 1979, 30 p. This covers the female labour force in European market economy countries in mid-1975, trends and future prospects; the distribution of women workers by major sector, occupational status and major occupational group, and the proportion of the labour force they represent in each group, and special characteristics of the female labour force. ILO data and statistics from national publications are presented. See also for Third World countries (1) ILO Office for Women Workers Questions, *Women, technology and the development process*, Geneva, 1978, 8 p. Where three sorts of problems are outlined: (a) unequal access of women to formal education and training, especially in scientific and technical skills; (b) evidence is examined which indicated that women continue to 'manage' the subsistence economy with traditional techniques, new technology frequently aiding men's work; and (c) the introduction of new techniques in a shifting occupational hierarchy continues to displace women into low skill, low productivity jobs, depriving them of the opportunities to upgrade their skills and acquire technical know-how. And (2) *Women in industry in developing countries*, Vienna, ILO, Oct. 1978, 15 p., which presents data on the magnitude of the problem, a section on relevant ILO conventions, recommendations and standards. This summarizes ILO research and projects, covering recently completed and work in progress.

383. Manley, P. and Sawbridge, D. Women at work. *Lloyds Bank Review.* January 1980, p. 29–40.

The authors compare the pattern of female employment in the United Kingdom with that in the major developed European economies. They conclude that (1) over the past 20 (and particularly the past 8 years) there has been a shift toward female labour in the composition of the British work force to a degree more marked than in other European countries of comparable size and/or economic development; and (2) that the proportion of part-timers is much higher in the United Kingdom (i.e. 1 in 5 compared with, for example, Federal Republic of Germany 1 in 10, and Italy 1 in 20) the majority of these workers being married women. They suggest factors leading to the increase in part-time work in the United Kingdom – a favourable institutional climate, the growth of the tertiary sector and in particular public sector employment, and more important, the need, actual or perceived, on the part of married women themselves.

384. Morgan, F. *The European Community and work for women.* Supplement No. 2 to *Women of Europe*, revised version Dec. 1978, 23 p.

This booklet gives statistics on women's position in the EEC, but is mainly concerned with describing the various actions of the European Commission to advance the position of women at work, in school and in the family. It describes various policy documents which are directed toward this end (directives, resolutions etc.) and gives a bibliography of Commission publications.

385. OECD. *The 1974–1975 recession and the employment of women.* Paris, OECD, 1976, 32 p. Also in Amsden, A., Entry 406.

The report examines the impact of the 1974–75 recession on the employment of women, by looking at a number of labour market indicators such as unemployment, employment and labour force participation rates for men and women. It covers selected member countries including Austria, Denmark, France, Finland, Federal Republic of Germany, Italy, Netherlands, Norway, Sweden, the United Kingdom and the United States. The conclusions are that women were affected differently from male workers, in that those concentrated in the service sectors were insulated from the harshest effects of the recession, but those in industry experienced greater employment losses than men. In the areas where women were traditionally under-represented, the effect has been to slow the growth of their employment and thus has restricted women's opportunities.

III. Family and household

386. Adams, C. Teich, and Winston, K. Teich. *Mothers at work: Public policies in the United States, Sweden and China.* New York and London, Longman, 1980, 312 p.

The authors suggest that the basic distinction between the approach in American public policy and that of the two other governments considered here is that women's programmes in Sweden and China proceed from the assumption that marriage, motherhood and employment are potentially compatible activities for women as well as men, given the appropriate social organization, whereas American policy assumes a fundamental incompatibility between these roles, and women wishing to combine them must bear privately the costs of such decisions. They compare the three countries in their policies for working families – covering childbearing/maternity benefits and services; family planning, contraception and abortion; childcare, socializing housework; and welfare and family assistance. They look at women's politics and policy change, national economic policy and women in the labour force and the family in political culture.

387. Aldous, J. and Dumon, W. (eds) (with K. Johnson). *The politics and programs of family policy*. Notre Dame. University of Notre Dame Press, 1980, 289 p. See also an article by Dumon and Aldous; European and US political contexts for family policy research. *Journal of Marriage and the Family*, Vol. 41, No. 3, 1979, p. 497–505.

A collection of papers from the Notre Dame International Seminar on

Family Policy, March 1978. The meeting was originally planned to analyse the potential for American family policy of the European experience, but also demonstrated that existing American family policy in terms of welfare legislation, has implications for European family policy. Several papers provide background information on the kinds of family programmes which have developed in different national contexts in Europe, and a detailed paper on the Nordic countries, with special reference to Sweden is also included. In a section on the United States two papers discuss (a) a description and evaluation of American family policy, and (b) the fiscal and organizational constraints which operate on it. A final paper makes a comparison between family policy in the United States and Europe and discusses the politics of the issue.

388. Jordan, B. *Birth in four cultures: A cross-cultural investigation of childbirth in Yucatan, Holland, Sweden and US.* Eden Press Women's publications. Montreal, 1980.

The author examines a number of bio-social features of birth, for example the local conceptualization of pregnancy and birth, the nature of the decision-making process, and support systems available to the woman giving birth. She gives a detailed description of a Mayan birth process, which involves intense physical and emotional involvement of a whole group of helpers, including the father, and which contrast, with the American, Dutch and Swedish practice. The author argues that 'society's way of conceptualizing birth constitutes the single most powerful indicator of the shaping of the birthing system' (p. 34). This shared view of childbirth (for example in the United States it is seen as a medical procedure, in Yucatan as a tense but normal part of family life, in Holland as a natural process, and in Sweden as an intensely personal, fulfilling achievement) guarantees that participants have similar views about the course and management of birth, and furnishes resources for dealing with 'trouble'. The author contends that a successful attack on American obstetrics cannot be mounted from a purely medical viewpoint, but must take into account the cultural definition of the event, and that more research to provide a basis for change must be undertaken, research which is system orientated, cross-cultural and bio-social.

389. Kamerman, S. B. and Kahn, A. J. (eds). *Family policy: government and families in fourteen countries.* New York, Columbia University Press, 1978, 522 p.

A collection of papers on family policy focusing on countries (a) with an explicit, comprehensive family policy – France, Czechoslovakia, Hungary, Norway, Sweden; (b) with explicit but more narrowly focused family policy – Austria, Federal Republic of Germany, Poland, Finland and Denmark; and countries without any explicit family policy, where the notion of such a policy is rejected – United Kingdom, Canada, Israel, United States. The authors come from various disciplines; economics, sociology, psychology, medicine, social work, political science and public administration, and take differing views of the problem.

390. Kamerman, S. B. Work and family in industrialised societies. *Signs* –

Journal of Women in Culture and Society, Vol. 4, No. 4, 1979, p. 632–650.

The author suggests that a resolution between the work/family dichotomy may be emerging in certain more advanced industrial societies, through policy support, which could lead to the integration of the two, despite continuing physical separation. She describes developments in social or family policy models in five European countries, France, Federal Republic of Germany, German Democratic Republic, Hungary, and Sweden. The countries have a similar level of industrialization and high (some still rising) rates of female labour force participation. Four basic policy alternatives are discussed and the degree to which the countries covered approximate to these alternatives, although no country is a 'pure' model. The policy alternatives are (1) income maintenance to replace income forgone of parent who withdraws from the labour force to look after child/ren under three years of age; (2) subsidized provision of out-of-home child care; (3) income maintenance to permit parents to purchase childcare whilst working; (4) combination of income maintenance and subsidized child care facilities provided sequentially. The author considers that one major result of increased female labour force participation could be, given adequate social and family policies, the restructuring of work and family tasks and responsibilities so that all adults regardless of gender can participate equally in both domains.

391. Lipman-Blumen, J. and Bernard, J. *Sex roles and social policy: A complex social science equation.* London, Sage Publications Ltd., 1979, 404 p. (Sage Studies in International Sociology 14.)

This is a collection of papers posing the question of what, if anything, can social science research contribute to the formulation of social policy on sex roles. The first section looks at the difficulties of making the connections between research and policy, including, amongst others, papers on 'Where research and policy connect: the American Scene' by S. S. Tangri and G. L. Strasburg; on 'Demographic indicators of the status of women in various societies' by N. H. Youssef and S. Foster Hartley, and on 'A paradigm for predicting the position of women: policy implications and problems' by R. Lesser Blumberg. Part II looks at the deliberate use of policy to change sex roles and has papers on Sweden by A. Baude, Eastern Europe, by H. Scott, Norway, by H. Holter and H. Ve Henriksen, Jordan, by N. T. Es-Said, and India by V. Mazumdar. Part III looks at women as policy-makers, with chapters on French women policy-makers by C. du Granrut, women as voters by J. Bernard, and women as change agents by C. Safilios-Rothschild. The last section deals with unresolved issues and the future.

IV. Education

392. European Bureau of Adult Education, (in conjunction with the International Council for Adult Education) *Continuing education for women.* Special Issue of the Newsletter, 5/6 January 1979, 56 p.

Contains a number of short articles on continuing education for women in France, Austria, Belgium, Federal Republic of Germany, United Kingdom, Ireland, Italy, the Netherlands, Denmark, Finland, Sweden, Portugal, Spain, Switzerland and Yugoslavia. Special programmes and activities, often organized by and for women are reported, journals and organizations are listed.

393. Finn, J. D. Sex differences in educational outcomes: A cross-national study. *Sex Roles*, Vol. 6, No. 1, 1980, p. 9–26.

Through their organization and curricula, schools either promote separate roles for males and females or operate to minimize differences. This study describes sex differences in science and reading achievement and attitudes for nation-wide samples of 14 year old children in the United States, Sweden and England. Largely the same sex differences appear in all three countries – male and female pupils have similar reading skills, whilst girls have more positive reading habits; males perform better than females in science, with the smallest difference observed for biology; males have more positive attitudes toward science, except that females believe science to be at least as important a topic as boys do. There is no noticeable increase in sex distinctions with one more year of schooling (in the United States from grade 8 to 9). In English co-educational schools, however, girls show a deceleration in science and vocabulary achievement relative to their male peers. Girls in English single-sex schools exceed their male counterparts in reading and several science subjects. The hypothesis is that the role of successful female teachers and peers, and the absence of social pressure from boys, may facilitate girls' learning in these areas. A study of specific school practices and the ways in which they determine sex discrepancies is proposed.

394. Kelly, A. (ed.). *The missing half: Girls and science education.* Manchester, Manchester University Press, 1981.

A collection of papers from a range of political and ideological perspectives devoted to a consideration of girls and science education. The papers are divided into categories: (1) theoretical interpretations, which range from a biological basis for sex differences in achievements in science, to a consideration of the impact of patriarchy on these patterns, but are related to a common empirical base, a study by Kelly of international sex differences in science achievement of 14 year olds. (2) Research studies which (a) look at the way choices are made, at groups of girls who defy convention and study science, (b) undertake a consideration of what goes on in science lessons, (c) compare male and female results in science examinations, and (d) consider the image of science. (3) Reports of personal experience: descriptions from pupils and teachers of their experiences in science lessons, and suggestions for methods whereby teacher training institutions could sensitize their students to sexism in schools, and immediate suggestions for science teachers.

V. Demographic features

395. Hiorns, R. W. (ed.). *Demographic patterns in developed societies.* London, Taylor and Francis, 1980, 208 p.

A collection of papers on demographic trends in developed societies including Western Europe and North America. Papers include: J. Thompson and M. Britton, 'Some socio-economic differentials in fertility in England and Wales'; N. B. Ryder, 'Components of temporal variations in American fertility'; D. J. Van de Kaa, 'Recent trends in fertility in Western Europe'; D. A. Coleman, 'Recent trends in marriage and divorce in Britain and Europe'; G. Wunsch, 'Sex differentials and cause of death in some European countries'; A. M. Adelstein and J. S. A. Ashley, 'Recent trends in mortality and morbidity in England and Wales'; and J. M. Winter 'The fear of population decline in Western Europe 1870–1940'. The papers not only provide classic expositions of available material, including new and improved sources of data, but also incorporate new methodology whilst retaining the historical perspective.

396. Kirk, M. *Demographic and social change in Europe: 1975–2000*. Liverpool, Liverpool University Press, published in association with the Council of Europe, Strasbourg, 1981, 167 p.

A review of the work done by the Committee for Population Studies of the Council of Europe over the past five years. The questions the report looks at are: (1) What will be the probable size and structure of the population of member countries from 1975–2000? (2) What processes have been and continue to be at work to bring about the demographic trends of the next 25 years and what are their possible implications for the next century? (3) What is the significance of changes in population size and structure within this time scale for the economic and social systems of particular member states?

397. McIntosh, C. Alison. Low fertility and liberal democracy in Western Europe. *Population and Development Review*, Vol. 7, No. 2, June 1980, p. 181–207.

The last two decades have seen a rapid decline in fertility rates in Europe, and there is increasing convergence amongst countries to a level where the replacement of population in the long run is no longer assured. This paper argues that the policy responses of Western European governments are only tenuously related to demographic trends, and that reluctance to implement comprehensive pronatalist policies is attributable to uncertainty over the social consequences of zero or declining population growth and over the efficacy of measures to stimulate fertility. But the major source for lack of decisive action in this area is the result of the political pluralism which characterizes liberal democracies. The article looks at the differing orientations towards population growth which have developed in France, Sweden, and Federal Republic of Germany, discusses the implications of low growth as perceived by a select group of high level government decision-makers and their advisors in these countries, reviews policy measures introduced so far, and explores some of the most important variables, which shape the perceptions and actions of policy-makers with regard to population policy.

398. Niphuis-Nell, M. (ed.). *Demographic aspects of the changing status of*

women in Europe. Leiden, Martinus Nijhoff Social Sciences Division, 1978, 155 p. Proceedings of the Second European Population Seminar, The Hague/Brussels, December 13–17, 1976.

A collection of papers based on four themes, and with an introduction by the editor which analyses the various approaches taken by the authors, and provides an explanatory framework for their positions. The themes are: marriage and marriage dissolution; marital fertility; extra-marital fertility; and geographic mobility. Amongst the papers R. W. Hommes looks at the measurement of the status of women; W. A. Dumon at divorce; J. Piotrowski at marriage and marriage dissolution in Poland; Z. Pavlik and J. Zborilova at changes in Czechoslovak marital fertility; A. Pinnelli at marital fertility and the status of women in Europe; P. Testy at extra-marital fertility and its occurrence in stable unions in Western Europe; H-J. Hoffman-Nowotny at sociological and demographic aspects of the changing status of migrant women in Europe; and S. Vanistendael gives a report of a symposium on demographic aspects of the changing status of women in Europe.

VI. Other

399. Caplan, P. and Bujra, J. M. (eds). *Women united, women divided.* London, Tavistock Publications, 1978, 288 p.

A series of papers on women's solidarity in a wide range of societies, in India, East and West Africa, Australia, China, the West Indies and the United Kingdom. The crucial variable considered in providing an explanation for differing degrees of solidarity was sex segregation, found to be present in varying degrees in all of the societies studies. In the introduction, Bujra suggests 'a mediating concept to build a bridge between the biological fact of women's existence and the infinitely varied forms of her social existence' (p. 20) that is domestic labour, which is socially productive labour expended in the context of the domestic unit.

400. Epstein, C. F. and Coser, R. L. (eds). *Access to power: cross-national studies of women and elites.* London, George Allen and Unwin, 1981, 259 p.

A collection of comparative papers from a number of European countries and the United States, describing, quantifying and analysing problems faced by women in pursuing high level careers in politics and business. The countries covered are the United States, France, the United Kingdom, Norway, Finland, Austria, Federal Republic of Germany, Poland and Yugoslavia. Two introductory chapters by each of the editors provide a cross-cultural framework for the studies, although several of the individual papers include two or three comparisons. A general conclusion is that ideology plays an important role in creating conditions favourable for women's entry into high level positions, as much as legislative or other attempts to make organizational structures more receptive to their inclusion.

401. Lovenduski, J. and Hills, J. M. (eds). *The politics of the second electorate: Women and public participation*. London, Routledge and Kegan Paul, 1981, 280 p.

Essays outlining the political behaviour of women in 20 countries, representing an effort to marry current research on women to traditional political science preoccupations with the study of governments, legislatures, parties and electoral behaviour. In each chapter, material is included on national women's suffrage movements and the contemporary economic and social position of women. Differences and similarities in type and degree of political involvement of women emerge in the reports, although a steady increase of activity by women in all political spheres is charted, and these are discussed by the editors in their introduction and conclusion. The countries covered are: United Kingdom, the United States, Canada, Australia, France, Spain, Federal Republic of Germany, Italy, Sweden, Finland, Eastern Europe, USSR and Japan.

402. Mednick, M. T. S., Tangri, S. S., and Hoffman, L. W. (eds). *Women and achievement: social and motivational analyses.* Washington and London, Hemisphere Publishing Corp. 1975.

A collection of 25 articles divided into three sections – Section 1 social variation and constant themes; Section 2 achievement related motives; and Section 3 achievement patterns, which combines a focus on cross-cultural and intracultural variation with a thorough look at motivational constructs underlying achievement behaviour. It includes papers by I. K. Broverman, S. R. Vogel, D. M. Broverman, F. E. Clarkson, and P. S. Rosenkrantz on 'Sex role stereotypes: a current reappraisal', S. S. Tangri on role models, H. Holter on sex roles and social change, M. Horner and others on achievement motivation, and C. Safilios-Rothschild on 'A cross-cultural examination of women's marital, educational and occupational options'.

403. Rendel, M. (ed.) *Women, power and political systems.* London, Croom Helm, 1981, 262 p.

A collection of papers from two meetings of the International Political Science Association study group on Sex Roles and Politics in 1979. The editor indicates, in the introduction, the way in which the subject of women and politics has been treated by political scientists, the errors and omissions in this work – the most fundamental being the exclusion of studies of the family and labour – and suggests the ways in which the chapters in this book contribute to gaps in the field. Countries discussed in the papers include the United States, United Kingdom, Brazil, Nigeria, Czechoslovakia, Finland, Turkey, Tanzania, and topics cover participation in the armed forces; women and the formulation of public policies: education and labour force participation; demography, political reform and women's issues; technology and the social control of women; women's employment networks; and the impact of women in positions of power (MPs, judges) on the situation of women.

404. Williams, J. E. Sex-trait stereotypes in France, Germany and Norway. *Journal of Crosscultural Psychology*, No. 10, p. 133–156.

Previous studies in the United States, United Kingdom and Ireland indicated a high degree of cross-national generality in sex trait stereotypes, that is the psychological traits differentially ascribed to women and men. This article reports on similar studies on university students in France, Federal Republic of Germany and Norway, who were given translated versions of the Gough-Heilbrun Adjective check list and asked to report on those traits more frequently associated with men, with women or with neither sex in their respective countries. The results suggest a high degree of similarity in the findings of the three continental groups and the three previous English speaking groups. Although some minor differences appeared among countries, the author considers that the results were sufficiently similar to 'permit the hypothesis that there are common sex-trait stereotypes which exist in all Western countries and perhaps even in countries of greater cultural diversity'.

405. Wolchik, S. L. Ideology and Equality: The status of women in Eastern and Western Europe. *Comparative Political Studies* (Beverley Hills) Vol. 13, No. 4, 1981, p. 445–476.

The author argues that women in socialist states have greater access to higher education and employment, but remain at the fringes of economic and political power and are hindered by a traditional division of labour in the home. The pattern is explained by reference to the differential commitments of socialist elites, who tend to promote improvement in the status of women only when it contributes to higher priority goals such as modernization. Women are losers in the conflict with other goals. In the non-socialist countries women can influence public opinion and values through independent women's groups and organizations and in that way can bring women's issues into the national political arena.

2. UNITED KINGDOM

I. General

406. Amsden, A. H. (ed.). *The Economics of Women and work*. Harmondsworth, Penguin Books, 1980, 409 p.

A series of readings by economists on women and work. Four major schools are represented and their treatment of the topic contrasted: these are the neo-classical, institutional, Marxist and radical approaches. Part 1 deals with market work, homework and the family, including a paper by I. V. Sawhill on 'Economic perspectives on the family' and one by J. Humphries on 'Class struggle and the persistence of the working class family'. Part 2 looks at job segregation by sex and women's lower pay, with two papers on discrimination by B. R. Bergmann, and B. Chiplin and P. J. Sloane, and papers on theories of labour market segmentation. Part 3 is on women's employment and the economy, including papers on unemployment, and the relationship between wives' labour force behaviour and income and consumption patterns in the family. An introduction to the various approaches and an assessment of their contribution to understanding women and their work is provided by the editor.

407. Barker, D. Leonard and Allen, S. (eds). *Dependence and exploitation in work and marriage*. London, Longman, 1976, 265 p. and *Sexual division and society: Process and change*. London, Tavistock Publications, 1976, 286 p.

In the first volume, a series of both empirical and theoretical papers look at the interrelationship between paid work and domestic labour and the ways in which marriage relationships are shaped by male dominance and the labour market. Amongst the topics covered are the dual labour market, homeworkers, the political economy of domestic labour in capitalist societies, and a case study of French upper middle class families in terms of marriage, role division and social cohesion. The papers in the second volume deal with aspects of social relationships consistently neglected by sociologists, questioning existing assumptions about gender and sexual divisions from a variety of perspectives – Marxist, feminist, interactionist. One group of papers is concerned with the ways in which different agencies reinforce sexual differentiation by processes which mediate the dominant ideological presuppositions of a society differentiated along sex lines, covering marriage, divorce, medicine, social security and education. Others deal with gender relationships, changing in China, and unchanging in communes in England.

408. Delamont, S. *The sociology of women: An introduction*. London, George Allen and Unwin, 1981.

This relatively elementary sociological text contains a wide range of material on the United Kingdom, and on racial and ethnic groups, which is organized biographically, that is in age sequence of the various stages a women goes through in her life. The author takes a feminist perspective in the sense of being anti-sexist and seeking autonomy for women.

409. Fransella, F. and Frost, K. *On being a women: A review of research on how women see themselves*. London, Tavistock Publications, 1977, 237 p.

The authors aim to find out what women say, think and feel about themselves, and review sociological and psychological studies which have reported on this. They also intend to make people aware of how uncommon it is actually to ask women what they think about themselves. The underlying conceptual framework employed for sifting the evidence is Kelly's personal construct theory. Some of the topics covered are personality, sex-role perceptions, self-esteem, sexuality, mental health, and maintenance of and resistance to change of sex stereotypes.

410. Garnsey, E. Women's work and theories of class stratification. *Sociology*, Vol. 12, No. 2, 1978, p. 223–243.

Stratification studies in general exclude the study of inequalities based on the division of labour by sex and this paper attempts to identify the ambiguities which arise from the *ad hoc* treatment of this issue in the literature, at individual and aggregate levels of analysis. The author argues that a systematic approach would require reconsideration of the assumption that the class position of the family is determined by the occupation of the male head of household – evidence is provided here illustrating the inadequacy of this assumption. It would also require an examination of the collective effects of women's employment on the occupational system, which would itself require consideration of the processes by which women's work in the labour force and in the household articulate. An adequate analysis of the division of labour between men and women and the inequalities associated with it might provide insight into some basic causes of change in the occupational and class structure.

411. Kuhn, A. and Wolpe A-M. (eds). *Feminism and materialism*, London, Routledge and Kegan Paul, 1978, 328 p.

A collection of papers which attempt to confront theoretical problems which arise in various kinds of work being done in women's studies or feminist theory, and to provide a coherent basis for an understanding of women's position, by outlining the foundation of a systematic approach to the analysis of that situation with reference to women's relation to modes of production and reproduction. Two themes recur – the family and the labour process, and a number of concepts emerge as crucial in the development of an adequate explanation of women's position – patriarchy and ideology chief amongst them. Amongst the papers in the collection are R. McDonough and R. Harrison 'Patriarchy and relations of production', which attempts to define patriarchy as a concept, which can be used in specific historical contexts in opposition to a universalistic definition; L. Caldwell on 'Church, state and family: the women's movement in Italy'; V. Beechey on 'Women and production: a critical analysis of some sociological theories of women's work'; J. West 'Women, sex and class' (See Entry 415); and A-M. Wolpe, 'Education and the sexual division of labour. See also K. Young (Entry 326).

412. Roberts, H. (ed.). *Doing Feminist research*. London, Routledge and Kegan Paul, 1981.

A collection of papers aimed at presenting a number of accounts of sociological work undertaken by sociologists who have been influenced by feminism, the feminist critique of sociology, or both. The accounts point to theoretical, methodological, practical and ethical issues raised in such projects. H. Roberts looks at background issues in doing a piece of feminist research; A. Oakley at problems in adopting the standard criteria for interviewing – based she thinks on a masculine view of reality at odds with viewpoints of women as social actors. J. Pettigrew reviews her research on landowning Sikhs (Jats) in the Punjab, and the problems of access to material, because of her position as a woman married to a Jat. David Morgan looks reflexively at his own work and position as a male sociologist, and points out that although women do not need to be told the significance of gender, men do. C. Delphy looks at the flaws and inadequacies in studies of class which fail to explain the class position of women, and C. Llewellyn develops the discussion of stratification, with details of her experiences working on a major study of (male) social mobility; P. Woodward and L. Chisholm discuss the problems they had working on the second national survey of 1960 graduates. A final chapter by D. Spender discusses the part played by publications in shaping a discipline and suggests that the 'gatekeeping' function of editors is one which should be carefully considered.

413. Sharpe, S. *Just like a girl, how girls learn to be women*. Harmondsworth, Penguin Books, 1976.

A study of 249 fourteen- to fifteen-year-old working class girls, from English, West Indian and Asian families. 'The book is intended as a descriptive and analytical account of the situation of young girls in Britain today, set in a historical and social context and illustrated by the girls themselves' (p. 8.) The author looks at changes over the last 100 years, the social construction of sex differences, the media, contradictions in female education and myths about women's roles and abilities. She discusses the occupational aspirations and expectations of the girls in the sample, their response to being asked which sex they would have chosen to be (75 per cent female, 25 per cent male), and black girls in Britain today. Amongst her conclusions, the author noted that many of the white girls in her group were concerned with their social and marriage prospects to the detriment of their other prospects, whereas most of the West Indian girls and almost all of the Asians expressed relatively high educational aspirations but were less openly enthusiastic about married life or motherhood. She points to the power of ideology which reinforces sex roles and is passed on in the family, school, media, organizations like the church and in the economic organization of home and work. The struggle against this ideology is an integral part of the women's movement, in addition to changing economic conditions, and the author discusses some of the ways in which ideas of femininity and masculinity can be changed.

414. Spender, D. *Man made language*. London, Routledge and Kegan Paul, 1980.

The main argument in this study is that 'the English language has been literally man made and still is primarily under male control' (p. 12), and that since language is fundamental to existence as a human being, it is through patriarchal language that much of women's subordination is formed. The author reviews language and sex research, particularly stereotypes of women's language and talk, providing evidence which counters, amongst others, the myth that women talk more than men. For Spender women are silent, a muted group for whom the meanings embedded in (the English) language are partial and false. The author suggests, by discussing a range of different illustrative instances that through the symbolic representation of the patriarchal order in language, women and their experience is negated and denied. Only if women find and develop their own forms of language and ways of encoding meanings can they move towards autonomy and self determination.

415. West, J. Women, sex and class. In: Kuhn, A. and Wolpe, A-M. (eds). *Feminism and Materialism*, London, Routledge and Kegan Paul, 1978, p. 220–253.

The author looks at the implications of female employment for women's class position, as opposed to the sociological approach of taking the family as the main determinant of women's class position. She criticizes the allocation of women to a class on the basis of the family (i.e. the husband's occupation), since it cannot deal with (1) unattached or non-dependent women, (2) stratification by gender; and (3) stratification within the family. Various other points are made, for example, what is the impact on the material level of the family of women's wages; women's place in the division of labour is specific not only because of women's domestic labour, but is also specific within the general division of labour outside the home. The notion of women as a class is rejected and the importance of women's location in the social division of labour and in employment for their class location is reiterated.

II. Women's work and labour force participation

PROFESSIONAL/MANAGERIAL WORK

416. Cooper, C. and Marshal, J. The changing pattern of British executives' wives. *Management International Review*, Vol. 17, No. 1, p. 37–46.

This paper examines the changing role of the British manager's wife and what that might mean for the future of the manager, his wife, and the organization. It is based on research carried out among British managers and their wives into the satisfactions and pressures of organizational life. Past, present, and future profiles of manager's wives are developed at different stages of the life cycle, for example early marriage, child-bearing/rearing, and the 'empty nest' phase. The consequences of change in these roles is examined in detail.

417. Lannon, J. Male versus female values in management. *Management International Review*, Vol. 17, No. 1, 1977, p. 9–12.

It has been observed and documented in the United Kingdom that the progress of women achieving acceptance has been slowest in management of industry and commerce. Many reasons are suggested for this, for example insufficient training, disruption in career progress, prejudices of male managers, women's low aspirations. Some of these are borne out by evidence, others are not. This paper looks at the differing 'cultures' or organizations, defining culture as the set of norms made up of beliefs in the way authority should be exercised, how much individual eccentricity is allowed or encouraged, the way in which work should be organized, and the realtive emphasis on efficiency as a criterion of success. The authors suggests that what should be considered within this structure is the appropriateness not of men and women, but rather of male and female traits, arguing that every management is made of a collection of these traits, with some kinds of organizational cultures requiring more female traits than male ones.

418. Silverstone, R. and Ward, A. (eds). *Careers of professional women*. London, Croom Helm, 1980.

An examination of the career structures and experience of women in seven professions and semi-professions: accountancy, architecture, dentistry, medicine, nursing, physiotherapy and teaching. In each case historical material, figures for current participation rates and details of women's experience in each type of work are given, and the problems and difficulties which women encounter in terms of (a) discrimination, (b) combining career and domestic responsibilities, and (c) availability of and access to training and re-training facilities. Further reading, extensive in some cases, is provided, and some comparative material for the United States and European countries is also included. The editors describe the emergence of a bimodal career pattern for women in the United Kingdom and the United States (although the total proportion of women working in the latter is lower) in which a period of reduced participation in economic activity over the childbearing period is interposed between periods of higher employment activity. In the rest of the EEC countries, a more traditional pattern of withdrawal from outside employment on marriage or the birth of the first child is maintained. Recommendations are made in each chapter for reforming the work of women in the professions discussed, and these relate mainly to opportunities for part-time training and employment for both men and women, re-training, equal promotion opportunities, improved career guidance and counselling, and additional childcare facilities. The editors consider that, in addition to changes in these areas, increased paternal participation in childcare is a prerequisite for an improved position of women in the occupations discussed.

419. Wheeler-Bennett, J. *Women at the top: Achievement and family life*. London, Peter Owen, 1977.

The book contains interviews with fifteen women in high level positions in a range of areas. They talk about their career patterns, experience of work and home life, and expectations for the future. All endorsed the necessity for a supportive spouse to enable them to succeed in their field, and pointed to the major curb on success and achievement for women as that of women's prime responsibility for the family, childcare and the home.

OTHER

420. Barber, J. and Downing, H. Word processing and the transformation of the patriarchal relations of control in the office. *Capital and Class*. Special Issue 10, Spring 1980, p. 64–99.

'We've tried to show in this paper that traditional, previously effective forms of control in the office which have their roots in patriarchy, are, within the context of the present crisis in the accumulation process, becoming redundant. Microelectronically based equipment is seized by capitalists as a solution offering a new form of control which enables them to cheapen labour and intensify production' (p. 96.) The authors argue that microelectronics in the office is a specific attack on women's work, and that the introduction of word processors (and other equipment) into offices should be seen not as part of a technology which is autonomous, driving forward by its own momentum, but related to and crucially part of capital's strategy to continue to reproduce itself. There is a brief outline of the historical development of office hierarchy, women's role in the office and employee strategies for controlling time and employers countervailing strategies to increase control over labour and productivity. Figures are given for expected female job loss, as a result of technological change in the office.

421. Bird, E. *Information technology in the office: the impact on women's jobs*. Manchester, Communication Studies and Planning Ltd., and Equality of Opportunity Commission (EOC), 1980, 90 p.

An investigation funded by the EOC which looks at the consequences of new technology for women employed in the office sector (33 per cent of all women workers). It is based on a literature review, questionnaires to 51 firms using word processors and office computer terminals, and case studies of ten organizations using the new technology. Detailed projections for displacement of female jobs to the year 1985 are given and a general conclusion is that there will be a shift in the balance of opportunities for men and women, with a decrease in availability of typing work (usually done by women) and an increase in sales work (chiefly done by men) and that this is an example of a trend which is expected to become more pronounced in the future 'partly because more of the new jobs will be skilled and at present more men than women have the required skills' (p. 6.) See also J. Morgall, 'Typing our way to freedom: Is it true that new office technology can liberate women?' in *Feminist Review*, 9 Autumn 1981, p. 87–101.

422. Boston, S. *Women workers and the Trade Unions*. London, Davis-Poynter, 1980.

A history of women workers and the Trade Unions in the United Kingdom from the early 19th century to the present day. The development of the organization of women workers is located in the context of broader social, biological and economic factors, which have determined women's position in society. Attention is drawn to the struggle which women have had to be recognized by male trade unionists, to be accepted as members of unions, and to be treated as equal members when within the unions. The author argues that the attitude of male unionists towards women, reflecting the dominant capitalist and sexist ideology of society, has allowed chauvinism to override trade union sense, and contradicted not only the socialist aims of most unions but also the logic of the trade union movement itself. Recurrent themes run through the analysis offered in this book, equal pay, or the absence of it; the role and need for specific legislation for women; and whether women should be separated from men or not in unions or in structures within unions.

423. Bruegel, I. Women as a reserve army of labour: a note on recent British experience. *Feminist Review*, No. 3, 1979, p. 12–23.

The paper examines the argument that female labour is particularly 'disposable' in times of economic crisis, and therefore of use to capital as a reserve army of labour, in the light of the experiences of women workers in Britain in the years 1974–78. The conclusion is that the reserve army of labour model holds, but not in the simple version, which needs qualification. Women's employment opportunities over the period have been protected from the worst effects of recession and crisis by the continuing expansion of the service sector during the period, but individually, women have been more susceptible to redundancy when compared with men in similar circumstances. (See also Entry 385 for other countries in OECD, and Entry 480 for the USA.)

424. Department of Employment (DE) *Women and work: a review*, and *Women and work: Overseas practice*. Manpower papers Nos. 11 and 12, London, HMSO, 1975.

Following on from Manpower Paper 9 (1974) which gave an aggregate statistical picture, and No. 10 (1974) which explored individual differences between the sexes in relation to work, paper No. 11 uses relevant research to illustrate certain aspects of the employment situation for women and of the prevailing attitudes to women's employment of employers and women themselves. It deals particularly with practical issues which arise for women who work and run a home and for those who interrupt employment, and later return. Paper No. 12 gives an indication of trends and thinking on women and work by drawing selectively on examples from other countries – the USA, Canada, and Sweden in particular, but with information on ten European countries with respect to relative positions on equal pay.

425. Holland, J. *Work and women: A review of explanations for the maintenance and reproduction of sexual divisions*. London, Institute of Education, Bedford Way Papers No. 6, 1981, 61 p.

A critical review of a range of literature on women largely from the United Kingdom and United States, taking as its starting point women and work. The author looks at explanations for sexual divisions, which are located at (a) the personal or psychological level, including psychoanalysis; and (b) the structural level, built into the institutions and practices of society. The latter section examines studies of sex role socialization and the development of male and female stereotypes in the family, in the school and at work. Further sections consider the possibility of a 'reality' principle operating in women's occupational decisions, and discuss the maintenance of sexual divisions in terms of the workings of the capitalist system or the principle of patriarchy, and the role which the state plays in the reproduction of this fundamental division in society. The monograph includes an extensive bibliography.

426. Hunt, A. *Management attitudes and practices towards women at work*. London, HMSO, 1975.

A study for the Office of Population Censuses and Surveys, Social Survey Division, of 223 establishments employing over 100 people in the following industries: Food manufacture, engineering, textiles, transport, commerce, and distribution. The aim was to find out in what fields differences in conditions and opportunities exist between men and women and to define attitudes to these differences. The report is based on the answers of formulators (212) and implementers (222) of personnel policy. One main conclusion was that 'A majority of those responsible for the engagement of employees start off with the belief that a woman applicant is likely to be inferior to a man in respect of all the qualities considered important' (p. 12). The generally negative attitude of these managers towards women employees indicates one of the basic problems for improvement in women's occupational and promotion possibilities.

427. Mackie, L. and Pattullo, P. *Women at work.* London, Tavistock Publications, 1977, 192 p.

The authors examine women's work, its radical differentiation from men's, in all respects, and the routes by which women arrive in their place in the labour force. Provides considerable information on the topics of housework, education, low pay, professions, training, the family, legislative rights and the trade unions.

428. Porter, M. Worlds apart: the class consciousness of working class women. *Women's Studies International Quarterly* (Oxford), Vol. 1, No. 2, 1978, p. 175–188.

A tentative analysis of the relations between trade union ideology, as experienced by husbands, and class imagery expressed by wives in a small sample of married working class couples. There is a brief review of the literature on class imagery and consciousness and women's studies – indicating the lack of work on working class women and their ideas of class or sex. One conclusion is that either the sexual division in the working class, which precludes women from the resources of institutions or ideology, can lead to women being more radical, in the sense of challenging the structure behind appearances, and more class loyal, than men.

429. Purcell, K. Militancy and acquiescence amongst women workers. In: Burman, S. (ed.) *Fit work for women.* London, Croom Helm, 1979, p. 112–133.

The author questions the stereotype of women wage workers as less interested in conditions of work and pay because of domestic commitments. Her paper demonstrates how the domestic role ascribed to women tends to handicap them in employment and trade union activities, but argues that considering the available empirical evidence and the social framework, within which women operate, the belief in the widespread existence of the passive woman worker is a myth.

430. Smith, D. Women and Trade Unions: the US and British experience. *Resources for Feminist Research*, Vol. X, No. 2, 1981, p. 53–59.

A review of five historical surveys of women in the trade unions in the United Kingdom and the United States, including Boston, S. *Women workers and The Trade Unions*. London, Davis-Poynter, 1980, Entry 422. Others reviewed are P. S. Foner, *Women and the American labor movement: From Colonial times to the eve of World War I,* New York, The Free Press, 1979; J. J. Keneally, *Women and the American trade unions*, Montreal, Eden Press Women's Publications, 1978; S. Lewenhak, *Women and trade unions: An outline history of women in the British trade union movement,* London, Ernest Benn Ltd., 1977; and M. Tax, *The rising of the women: Feminist solidarity and class conflict, 1880–1917*, New York, Monthly Review Press, 1980.

III. Family and household

431. David, M. E. *The state the family and education.* London, Routledge and Kegan Paul, 1980.

The central argument here is that the family and the education system are used in concert to sustain and reproduce the social and economic *status quo* – specifically they maintain the existing relationships within the family and the social relations within the economy, the sexual and social division of labour. The theoretical framework draws on Marxism, the educational system being seen as part of the activities essential for the reproduction of the conditions of capitalism, and feminism, specifically the attempt to locate the analysis of female disadvantages in capitalism to the sexual division of labour and the position of women in the family. The twin themes of the work are the relationship of the family to the educational system, and family issues within the educational system. Historical material on legal and policy changes with respect to education is examined, in the light of this framework, with particular emphasis on the development of parental rights and duties towards schooling.

432. Equal Opportunities Commission (EOC). *Women and low incomes.* A report based on evidence to the Royal Commission on Income Distribution and Wealth. Manchester, EOC, 1977.

This statement of evidence to a Royal Commission was concerned with the problem of poverty and low income, as experienced by women in the United Kingdom, examining the situation from the point of view of inequality based on sex, in terms of income and state benefits. Women's incomes were shown to lag behind those of men and the problem of low pay was seen as primarily one of low earnings amongst women. A series of recommendations were made, including dispersal of women throughout all sectors of the economy, to counteract the tendency for them to be concentrated in low wage level industries and at the lower levels in other industries; guaranteed access to fringe benefits for women; access to training and a consideration by employers of the problem of enabling their female employees to have minimum disruption of careers as a result of childbirth and childcare responsibilities. After detailing the discrimination and difficulties, which women experience in connection with state benefits, the report recommends, amongst other things, that the concept of women's dependency should be modified, and women should be treated as men's equals under the social security laws and regulations; that the concept of head of family should be eliminted, so that either men or women could draw benefits as need arises; and that special attention should be given to the needs of certain disadvantaged groups, amongst which women predominate. Although the report provides a range of information on women's position, it points out that there is a paucity of research on women's incomes, reflecting the low priority attached to this area in the past, and that more research must be undertaken.

433. Hunt, P. *Gender and class consciousness*. London. Macmillan, 1980, 210 p.

The author looks at the effects of gender related experiences and ideologies on the development of class consciousness and practice and explores the integration of domestic and industrial production, and how the two sexes are differently related to this double production process in general structural terms and in terms of the family life-cycle. Another concern of the study is with ideological conceptions, which obscure the interdependence of industrial and domestic production, chiefly by emphasizing gender differences between men as breadwinners and women as homemakers. The research is structured around long conversations with three types of households: (1) married couples with no children, and both wage earners; (2) married couples, one of whom is a full-time houseworker, with children; (3) married couples, both wage earners, with children. The author draws the following conclusions: both men and women share the ideological conception of family life as a private, non-socially productive domain, despite the fact that domestic production is an integral part of social production; behaviour in the families interviewed reinforces the ideology of male breadwinner, female homemaker, even in cases when their own practice is counter to the norm; the author found what she calls 'production class consciousness' amongst ex-full-time houseworkers who returned to or entered the labour force – they made more positive demands in the industrial place of work, which were non-instrumental and emphasized pleasant conditions and satisfactions other than pay. She suggests that this could be the result of a lack of familiarity on their part with the procedures and practices of trade unions and from being shielded from the instrumental nature of capitalist relations of production due to privatization in the family setting.

434. Lambert, L. and Streather, J. *Children in changing families: A study of adoption and illegitimacy*, London, Macmillan, 1980, 196 p.

An investigation based on the National Child Development Study, undertaken by the National Children's Bureau – a study of all children living in England, Scotland and Wales who were born in the first week of March 1958. The present work looks at the illegitimate and adopted children in this sample at age 11, considering changes in their background and development since the age of seven. Two parallel studies (Crellin, E., Pringle, M. L. K. and West, P., *Born Illegitimate*, Windsor, NFER, 1971; and Seglow, J., Pringle, M. L. K. and Wedge, P. J., *Growing up adopted*, Windsor, NFER, 1972) describe the children up to age seven. The authors consider the environmental factors which are associated with child development, and the role and function of the family in contemporary society, before looking in detail at the adopted and illegitimate children compared with the legitimate children in the total group in terms of the following factors: parental care situation, social class and family size, low income families, housing conditions, height of the child, school attainment and social adjustment. Detailed statistics and analyses are included in an appendix. Various differences between the groups with different birth statuses were found in terms of school attainment and social adjustment, but these often disappeared, when other social class and environmental factors were held constant. The authors conclude that some children were fortunate and lived in an exceptionally favourable environment, and many of the adopted children were among this group. For other children, living in families with poor housing and low income, and experiencing the difficulties, mainly associated with low status, were far more pressing and ever-present problems than whether their parents had been married when they were born.

435. Molyneux, M. Beyond the domestic labour debate. *New Left Review*, No. 116, July–August 1979, p. 3–27.

A critique of the underlying assumption of much of the domestic labour debate that the labour of the housewife is a functional consequence of capitalism. The author criticizes in detail the work of C. Delphy, who argues for a domestic mode of production parallel to the capitalist mode; and J. Harrison, who argues that domestic labour is part of a client mode within the capitalist mode of production. Molyneux stresses the importance of the reproduction of labour power, and of taking women's total situation into account in its historical and cultural specificity, in order to understand women's subordination. Much of the domestic labour debate is seen as economistic, hoping to explain everything by stressing one aspect of the total picture. The domestic labour debate also ignores, in the author's view, the interplay between women's work in the home and waged work, and the 'material effectivity' of such ideologies as that of 'mothering', in depressing women's position in the labour market.

436. Oakley, A. *Housewife*. Harmondsworth, Penguin Books, 1976. First published by Allen Lane in 1974.

This is part of a general project which looks at women's attitudes to housework in industrial society at the present time, the historical background to the role of housewife, cross-cultural patterning of the sexual division of labour and ideologies of women's domesticity. This volume deals with the historical background, ideological material, and case studies of four contemporary housewives. Oakley looks at women's roles in the pre-industrial society, the changes brought about by industrialization with the separation of work from home, and the increasing permeation through the layers of 19th century English society of the doctrine of female domesticity. This doctrine, passing from the middle classes to the working classes, often clashed with the economic reality of working class women's lives. The author considers two cultural myths which sustain the role of housewife and its exclusive allocation to women and the actual and ideological components, which help to sustain these myths: the myth of the universal, natural and necessary division of labour by sex and its relegation of women to a domestic role in the family group, and the myth of motherhood as the sole means of self realization for women. For change to occur, she suggests that a revolution in current cultural ideologies of gender roles is required. See also by the same author, *Sex, gender and society*, London, Maurice Temple Smith, 1972, which looks at general sex differences and similarities, with special reference to cross-cultural variations in male and female roles; and *The sociology of housework*, London, Martin Robinson, 1974, which provides a more detailed analysis of the survey from which the four housewives' case histories are taken.

437. Poster, M. *Critical theory of the family.* London, Pluto, 1978, 233 p. (First published by The Seabury Press, New York, 1978.)

Section one of this book reviews critically what the author sees as the major theories of the family – those of Freud, Parsons, Erikson, Engels, Reich, the Frankfurt School, Lacan and the family therapists. The basic position taken is that the crucial questions about the family concern the psychological level, types of emotional structure, which change as the family changes, and generate changes in the deepest needs of individuals. The second part outlines four models of family structure from the early modern period to the present, drawing on the history of the family in Europe. These are the bourgeois family in the mid 19th century, both the aristocratic and peasant family of the 16th and 17th century and the working class family of the early industrial revolution. The author argues that the bourgeois type of family is the most prevalent in the United States today, and that it is 'on shaky ground' (p. 199). He suggests a critical (or normative in his definition) theory of the family in which analysis proceeds at three levels: (1) the family as a psychological structure – the level which defines the family and indicates the contribution which the study of the family can make to social science; (2) daily life; and (3) the relation to society. The latter two levels are conceptualized as supplementary to the first. The theory outlines the limits, to which any family structure reinforces or eliminates hierarchies of age and sex.

438. Wilson, E. *Women and the welfare state.* London, Tavistock Publications, 1977, 208 p.

The book looks at the development of welfare state intervention in the United Kingdom from the early 19th century to the present day, related to the changing position of children, women and the family. The author argues that an appreciation of the way in which women have been defined by welfare policy is essential to an understanding of those policies and the welfare state itself. Women are defined in terms of their role in the home of servicing the worker and bringing up children.

IV. Education

439. Dale, R., Esland, G., Fergusson, R. and MacDonald, M. (eds). *Education and the State Vol. 2: Politics, Patriarchy and Practice.* Barcombe, Sussex, The Falmer Press and Open University Press, 1981, 420 p.

Both volumes are collections of readings, most of which have been published previously. The first examines elements of the large scale political and economic structures, which affect educational provision, and this second volume deals with schooling and the politics of culture, sexual divisions and patriarchy, the social construction of childhood and the family, and the politics of teaching. The section on patriarchy includes 'Women and production: a critical analysis of some sociological theories of women's work' by V. Beechey (also in Kukn and Wolpe Entry No. 411), which identifies and criticizes various theories of women's position both in the family and in waged work; 'The official ideology of education for girls' by A-M. Wolpe, where curricular provision is shown to reinforce two structures of inequality, those of gender and social class; 'Schooling and the reproduction of class and gender relations', by M. MacDonald, arguing that the reproduction of gender relations is part of bourgeois hegemony; 'Patriarchy, racialism and labour power' a brief excursion by P. Willis; 'The unhappy marriage of Marxism and feminism; towards a more progressive union' by H. Hartmann, who considers the arguments concerning patriarchy and capitalism as sources of sexual inequality and puts forward the possibility of a synthesis; 'Socialism and feminism: women in the Cuban revolution', by N. Murray, who indicates that in a socialist country, where men and women are treated ideologically as equals and where women play a considerable role in the economy, gender divisions and inequalities still exist, especially in the domestic sphere.

440. Deem, R. (ed.) *Schooling for women's work.* London, Routledge and Kegan Paul, 1980, 200 p.

A collection of papers which demonstrate with studies of varying orientations 'that the reproduction in schooling of gender categories, of class, of the sexual division of labour, and of the relations of patriarchy, plays a significant part in the maintenance of the subordinate position of women in our society, whether in paid work, public life or the family' (p. 11). Amongst the papers are J. Shaw, 'Education and the Individual: schooling for girls, or mixed schooling – a mixed blessing?' arguing that co-education schools are disadvantageous to girls; M. Fuller on 'Black girls in a London comprehensive school, and J. Harding on 'Sex differences in mathematical performance: a review of research and possible action'.

441. Deem, R. State policy and ideology in the education of women 1944–1980. *British Journal of Sociology of Education*, Vol. 2, No. 2, 1981, p. 131–143.

An examination of changes in state policies and ideologies about women's education, linking them to the dominant political ideology, the economy and general social policy. The author traces the gradual evolution of policies and ideologies which encouraged women's education and labour force participation through the period of social democracy from the late 1960s to the early 1970s, and considers the consequences for women of the collapse of the social democratic ideal and the decline in consensus about education since the early 1970s. The limited impact of legislation on sex discrimination is discussed and the author concludes that although some aspects of educational inequality for women have been remedied, many remain in a political, economic and ideological climate which increasingly emphasizes women's place in the home, and that such inequalities can only be tackled by the development of an alternative set of social and economic policies, which challenge the social relations of capitalism and patriarchy.

442. Department of Education and Science (DES). *Curricular differences for boys and girls*. London, HMSO, 1975 (Educational Survey 21.)

In 1973, members of Her Majesty's Inspectorate investigated to what extent curricular differences and customs contributed to inequality of opportunity for boys and girls. They looked at primary, middle and secondary schools and Further Education. Their general conclusion was that 'some curricular differences do unfairly and unnecessarily militate against the personal development of career prospects of girls'. The main findings were that (1) in 98 per cent of the schools studied, the sexes were separated for some aspects of their work; (2) in 28 per cent of secondary schools preemptive patterning of curricular in the first three years mean that there is really no choice at age 13 (the point where pupils 'choose' their courses for public examinations or the final phase of schooling); (3) in the fourth and fifth year in secondary schools there are significant differences in the subjects studied by boys and girls – boys take physics and chemistry to a much greater extent than girls, girls are more likely to take modern languages, art and music; (4) opportunity for girls is restricted by the nature and availability of composite (package deals) and optional courses (vocational, recreational, practical, aesthetic courses); (5) mixed schools tend to underline rather than blur the distinctions between the sexes. The Inspectors conclude that traditional assumptions about girls and boys are worked out through the curricular patterns of secondary schools with support for them from most teachers, parents and pupils. They consider that any differences which continue to exist should be based on genuine choice; choice equally offered to all with the necessary interest, ability, determination, and not choice based on traditional assumptions about the 'proper' sphere of interest and influence for boys and girls.

443. National Union of Teachers (NUT). *Promotion and the woman teacher.* London, NUT, March 1980, 75 p.

The NUT made a questionnaire survey of one per cent of women teachers in 1976 (which proved to be representative of the body of women teachers as a whole on certain basic criteria) in order to (1) draw a picture of women teachers as a body; (2) investigate theories advanced about the motivation and promotion orientation of women teachers; (3)

to see if there was evidence for the complaints about discriminations, which the union had been receiving; and (4) to see if they could explain the low status of women in the profession. A review of existing studies in the area demonstrated that obvious factors such as the large proportion of women working part time, the concentration of women in the primary sector, and the low proportion who are graduates, were not sufficient to explain the discrepancy in women's and men's career patterns in teaching. The survey found that women teachers do not fit the stereotypical image – only 33 per cent of the sample could be described as married women with children below school leaving age; and that women showed no sign of 'low promotion orientation', but still had difficulty gaining promotion. The study concluded that there were three main types of discrimination experienced by these women teachers: outright sex discrimination, discrimination against older teachers, and discrimination against married women.

444. Walden R. and Wakerdine, V. *Girls and mathematics: the early years*. London, Institute of Education, 1982, 73 p. (Bedford Way Papers No. 8.)

A report of a two year investigation aimed at examining some of the basic assumptions underpinning teaching and learning of mathematics in the early years of schooling, by systematic observation of the production of mathematics learning through the social relations in the classroom. The authors observed classrooms in two nursery and two primary schools, with the aid of video equipment, and conducted three small studies to consider (a) differential uses of space made by boys and girls; (b) gender awareness; and (c) time sampling of activities to see if stereotypical use of time was made by boys and girls. Contrary to the prevalent conception that girls perform less well in mathematics than boys, the authors argue that there is a discontinuity in girls' mathematics performance and at primary level they perform better than boys. So much so that the 11+ examination for allocation to secondary level education (now abolished) had differential male and female norms so that girls would not substantially outnumber boys in selective grammar schools. At secondary level girls' failure in mathematics is neither consistent nor uniform, and as studies in the United States have shown, hinges on the failure to choose to take mathematics courses in a school system, in which this subject is not compulsory. Amongst their conclusions the authors suggest that explanations for the discontinuity in girls' mathematics performance in terms of stereotyping are too static to capture the variability and non-stereotypical behaviours which they observed, and that explanations in terms of the production of gender identity through classroom practices might prove more satisfactory. Elements in these interactive practices to which they point as relevant are (1) teachers' cues in language, as to the masculinity or femininity of tasks, (2) teachers' own lack of confidence in their mathematics ability leading them to endorse and encourage the confident amongst the children (most frequently girls in the primary and nursery schools observed), (3) the use in primary schools of stereotypically female activities (weighing, measuring, shopping) for mathematics teaching, superceded in secondary schools by a content of mathematical tasks and activities largely stereotypically masculine, and (4) teachers as role models for girls (but not boys) in the primary and nursery schools.

445. Wolpe, A-M. *Some processes in sexist education*. London, Women's Research and Resources Centre Publications, 1977, 42 p.

This pamphlet contains two papers 'Education the road to dependency' and 'Sexuality and gender roles in a secondary school'. The first argues that schools maintain and reproduce ideologies in general and the ideology relating to women's roles in particular, through the curriculum, through the school organization, and through teachers as agents. The curriculum has two components, which embody the feminine ideology (1) particular subjects are related to the adult female role, i.e. domestic science and handicrafts; (2) the manner in which disciplines such as mathematics and science are taught contains a 'profoundly unconscious' ideology, which emphasizes the application of the knowledge to the division of labour between male and female. The second discusses sexuality on the basis of empirical observation, arguing that pupils are 'rehearsing' sexual forms of behaviour, either directly, or through observation, unrecognized by the staff in the early secondary years, and that the staff contribute to a clarification of these roles either as agents in the presentation of the curriculum, or through their own behaviour.

V. Other

446. Burns, R. B. Male and female perceptions of their own and the other sex. *The British Journal of Social and Clinical Psychology*, Vol. 16, part 3, September 1977, p. 213–220.

The semantic differential technique was used on adult Open University students, to discover their perceptions of their own and the opposite sex. Analysis of the test data revealed the conventional stereotypes of masculinity and femininity despite what the author calls presumed changes due to current social pressures. There was considerable agreement on the characteristics of males and females, and most discrepancy occurred between a sex's perception of itself and its belief about how the other sex perceived it. These latter inferred perceptions produced extreme stereotypes.

447. Dixon, B. *Catching them young 1: Sex, race and class in children's fiction*. London, Pluto Press, 1977, 141 p.

The central questions posed in this analysis are what are the attitudes, values and opinions found in the most popular children's fiction; how will these attitudes contribute to the ideas and beliefs which children form during these early years of their lives; and what is the picture of the world conveyed through this fiction? Looking at both American and British children's literature, the author surveys the material for the major attitudes expressed, finding sexism, racism and an overwhelming middle class bias towards social divisions in children's fiction. Part 2 of this work in a separate volume looks at political ideas in children's fiction.

448. Hartnett, O., Boden, G. and Fuller, M. (eds). *Sex-role stereotyping*. London, Tavistock Publications, 1979, 241 p.

A collection of papers from a conference held in 1977, under the auspices of the British Psychological Society, representing a variety of approaches, including historical surveys, critiques of previous research, theoretical papers, and recent empirical studies. The first three papers represent an overview of research on sex differences and sex-role stereotyping, including a consideration of cognitive differences by D. Griffiths and E. Saraga. Part 2 focuses on motherhood and the cognitive attribution of meaning that women bring to the experience. Part 3 looks at attitudes towards success and failure and includes a paper by C. Ward critical of previous studies in this area. Part 4 deals with sex role stereotyping in education with a paper by R. J. L. Murphy on sex differences in examination performance asking whether these reflect differences in ability or sex role stereotypes, and concluding that 'the socio-cultural influence plays the bigger part' (p. 166). Part 5 considers androgyny, and Part 6 is a paper by R. B. Ekstrom on several programmes in the United States designed to reduce sex role stereotyping in many areas of the school curriculum and organization. One general theme, which emerges from this collection, is the distinction between male and masculine and female and feminine – i.e. between sex and gender, the biologically and socially determined, with the latter considered amenable to change. See also Chetwynd, J. and Hartnett, O. (eds), *The sex role system*, London, Routledge and Kegan Paul, 1978, in which the editors suggest that the sex role system has the following interacting characteristics: (1) Assignment on the basis of sex to one or two different and mutually exclusive series of personality traits, creating male and female dichotomous stereotypes; (2) the allocation on the basis of sex into activities considered useful or necessary for the maintenance or survival of the social unit – the sexual division of labour; (3) male attributes are invested with higher value than the female. Papers in the collection look at biological explanations for sex stereotyping, socialization into sex roles, the influence of the school, work, and welfare and tax systems.

449. Leeson, J. and Gray, J. *Women and medicine*, London, Tavistock Publications, 1978, 240 p.

The authors suggest that three major barriers exist between doctors (usually men) and other health workers (usually women) and between doctors (middle class professionals) and patients (predominantly working class non-professional) and these are class, profession and sex. They look at women as providers of health care, both as doctors and other health workers, and women as patients, including conditions and diseases specific to women, and the way in which the medical profession and health service deals with them. Other topics reviewed are the role of the trade unions and the labour movement, with respect to women and health, and alternative ways of approaching this area. The authors argue that, in the male dominated medical profession, medical encounters are profoundly influenced not only by the symptoms presented, but by the sex of the participants, and this sex stereotyping is strongest in gynaecological and psychiatric settings. Some American comparisons are included in certain sections of the book.

450. McRobbie, A. Settling accounts with subcultures: A feminist critique. *Screen Education*, No. 34, Spring 1980, p. 37–49.

The development of cultural studies over the past 15 years in the United Kingdom has had as central strands youth culture and the sociology of youth, but the emphasis has been on male youth cultural forms. This article explores questions about youth culture and subculture by attempting a feminist rereading of P. Willis' *Learning to labour* (Saxon House, 1977) and D. Hebdige, *Subculture: the meaning of style* (Methuen 1979).

451. Nava, M. Girls aren't really a problem . . . *Schooling and Culture*, Issue 9, Spring 1981, p. 5–10.

The author draws attention to the lack of provision for girls in the Youth Service in the United Kingdom and suggests that this is primarily due to the fact that girls have not constituted the same 'street problem' as boys. Girls are regulated to a greater extent than boys in the home, and when they are on the street, by boys. The article examines recent developments in feminist youth provision for girls.

452. *No Turning Back*. Writings from the Women's Liberation Movement, 1975–80. London, The Women's Press, 1981, 266 p.

A collection of writings by activists from varying political positions within the British Women's Liberation Movement, indicating the diversity of campaigns, and a combination of practical and theoretical issues. Topics covered are women and the state, sex and class, work – paid and unpaid, minds and bodies, male violence and culture.

453. Oerton, S. J. *The feminist press in Britain since 1970*. Unpublished MA dissertation, University College Swansea, University of Wales, 1981.

The feminist press in Britain is first examined in relation to its historical and social genesis, and the types of magazines and papers are defined and categorized by examining the concepts of sexism and feminism and distinguishing between the various political stances present within the women's liberation movement. The feminist press is then placed in the wider social and political context and its alternative or minority nature is assessed. As a channel for communication for the women's liberation movement in the United Kingdom it is judged as successful: 'the feminist press is a remarkable example of a medium of communication, which serves to meet its readers' needs and desires' (p. 141). Finally, in outlining the economic and administrative structure of this press, the author indicates the intractable financial and organizational difficulties which it faces.

454. Richards, M. P. M. Innovation in medical practice: Obstetricians and the induction of labour in Britain. *Social Science and Medicine*, Vol. 9, 1975, p. 595–602.

During the past decade, in the United Kingdom, there has been a rapid increase in the use of induction and acceleration techniques for normal labour and delivery. The paper tries to analyse some of the historical, social and technical processes, which underlie this change in practice. Induction techniques carry some risks and seem to have no clear advantages for doctors or patients. The author suggests that widespread adoption of these methods reflects a tradition in obstetrics that favours interventionist procedures which involve close control over patients and appear to be 'scientific'. There is little evidence, however, that such techniques have been adequately assessed or can be said to represent rational medical practice.

455. Roberts, H. (ed.) *Women health and reproduction*. London, Routledge and Kegan Paul, 1981, 196 p.

A collection of papers which documents the lack of power women have in relation to their own bodies and their own fertility, but also suggests that there are areas where women could seize the means of reproduction, and take control of their bodies and their lives. Papers include H. Roberts on male hegemony and the structures through which male power operates in the field of birth control; a careful historical account of the way in which obstetricians began to take over control of childbirth in the 18th century by M. Connor Versluyen; H. Graham and A. Oakley on the difference between an obstetrician and a mother's view of childbirth; J. Rakusen on Depo-Provera and the lack of access which women have to information on which to base decisions concerning their health; P. Bart on an illegal abortion collective in Chicago, and K. Gardner on 'well woman' clinics. G. Young, a general practitioner, discusses the inadequacies of medical education and training and suggests possible improvements, and J. Hanmer looks at sex predetermination, artificial insemination, and the maintenance of male-dominated culture, exploring technological developments in reproduction.

456. Smart, C. *Women, crime and criminology: A feminist critique*. London, Routledge and Kegan Paul, 1976, 208 p.

A critique of the study of crime and deviancy indicating that there is very limited consideration of women's criminality, and studies which do make reference to women are explicitly based on an inadequate perception of the nature of women, relying on a determinate model of female behaviour. Other studies refer to women implicitly, or give them token recognition. They are often categorized with juvenile delinquents or mentally abnormal offenders, a classification which the author sees as symbolic of women's traditional civil and legal status. The author documents and criticizes a range of studies looking at both classical and contemporary work on female criminality, prostitution, rape and sexual politics, the treatment of female offenders, and women, crime and mental illness. An analysis of the types of crimes committed by female offenders indicates fallacies inherent in a reliance on official statistics and demonstrates the inadequacy of the common argument that female emancipation increases female crime rates. Throughout the book, the author considers the treatment of women as offenders and victims by the criminal law, the police, the courts and the legal system. A basic conclusion is that more research is required to map the dimensions of female criminality located in the wider moral, political, economic and sexual spheres which influence women's status and position in society, including a reappraisal and reinterpretation of existing material in the light of a reconceptualization of the role of girls and women in the community.

457. Smart, C. and Smart, B. (eds). *Women, sexuality and social control*. London, Routledge and Kegan Paul, 1978.

An introduction indicates the areas in which control of women operates: the reproductive cycle, the double standard of morality, women's subordinate legal and social status, and the separation of work and home. The collection of papers covers legal non-intervention in the private sphere as an aspect of the structural coercion of women; the social control of women in general medical practice; a historical analysis of the myth of male protectiveness and the legal status of women (by A. Sachs, see also Entry 516); prostitution and the ideology of male sexual needs; a study of the sexual codes and conduct of teenage girls by D. Wilson; sexist assumptions and female delinquency; and two papers on rape.

458. Stacey, M. and Price, M. *Women power and politics*. London, Tavistock Publications, 1981, 214 p.

The authors consider that, although it is generally true that women are not in positions of power (a concept which they discuss in some detail but used here in its most general sense), in a surprisingly short period of time in this century, a large number of women have become involved in politics, leaving the private domain to enter the public domain. The issue is examined cross-culturally, historically and in the context of contemporary social and political arrangements. The authors look at the social relations of the family, the development of the centralized state and the separation of industrial production and the office from the home. They argue that women are not equally and universally oppressed, and that some women oppress others, concluding that 'the oppressions of patriarchy, of capitalism, and of state power interlock and are mutually sustained, and all have to be opposed' (p. 188).

459. Vallance, E. *Women in the house*. London, Athlone Press, 1979.

A detailed study of women in parliament in the United Kingdom both at the present time and historically. The author poses the basic question; why so few in the United Kingdom, (3 per cent in 1981, a very low proportion compared to the rest of Western Europe) and looks at various factors which might contribute to this situation. The major causes are located in the general position of women in British society, in attitudes towards women, particularly to the possibility of their wielding power, and their own self perceptions. A further important contributory factor, however, is the electoral system and the selection process for parliamentary candidates. The author contrasts this system with that of

European countries, with proportional representation, rather than a first past the post system, and especially the Scandinavian countries where the representation of women in parliament ranges from 17 to 23 per cent. 'It is the combination of social awareness and official recognition of women's claims and the electoral system itself which has facilitated Scandinavian achievement in this sphere' (p. 165). A useful chapter which details a comparison with the situation in the United States and European countries, including Scandinavia, also includes a range of additional comparative material on the status and position of women in these countries.

460. Moi, T. Representation of patriarchy: Sexuality and epistemology in Freud's Dora. *Feminist Review*, No. 9, Autumn 1981, p. 60–74.

A close analysis of Freud's account of his treatment of 18-year-old Dora, which reviews previous feminist critiques of this work and argues (1) that Freud's counter-transference contributes decisively to the failure of Dora's analysis, and (2) that the report demonstrates a deeply unconscious patriarchal ideology, revealed most clearly in Freud's definition of the feminine as the negative of the masculine in his view of Dora and the feminine epistemology she is supposed to represent.

3. UNITED STATES

I. General

BIBLIOGRAPHIES

461. Ballou, P. K. Bibliographies for research on women. *Signs – Journal of Women in Culture and Society*, Vol. 3, No. 2, Winter 1977, p. 436–450.

The author discusses some of the significant bibliographical works on research on women, which have appeared since 1970, under the headings of general, history, literature, anthropology and area studies, economics and employment, education, politics and the law, sociology, psychology, health and future needs.

462. Sokoloff, N. J. Bibliography on the sociology of women and work, 1970s. *Resources for Feminist Research/Documentation sur la Recherche Feministe*, Vol. VIII, No. 4, 1979, p. 48–74.

The focus is on women and work in the United States with some references to Canada and deals with (1) general information and data on women and work, (2) feminist critiques of the sociology of women and work, (3) mainstream sociology's approach to women and work including status attainment, (4) dual labour markets, (5) radical sociology's approach to women and work, including Marxist theory of the labour market, (6) early Marxist feminism, and (7) later Marxist feminism. Published and unpublished material (usually conference papers) is included, and each section is prefaced by a brief introduction. No annotations, but a useful bibliography.

OTHER

463. Beere, C. A. *Women and women's issues: A handbook of tests and measures*. San Francisco, Jossey-Bass, 1979.

Descriptions of a collection of tests and measures used in a wide range and number of studies on women, including stereotypes. Results of studies, where the instruments have been used, are given and critical comments made on their use and usability.

464. Blau, F. D. and Jusenius, C. L. Economists approaches to sex segregation in the labour market: An appraisal. *Signs*, Vol. 1, No. 3, part 2, 1976, p. 181–199.

The paper attempts an appraisal of the contribution of economic theory to an understanding of the causes of sex segregation and pay differentiation between men and women in the labour market. Three points are taken as given: (1) sex segregation of considerable magnitude exists in the labour market; (2) women are segregated by occupational categories and within occupations by industry and firm; (3) aggregate male/female pay differentials exist. They review and assess a number of neo-classical approaches to wage differentials and sex segregation, including the competitive model (overcrowding) and human capital variants, and the monopsony model. The authors conclude that the major contribution of the neo-classical school has been to suggest plausible reasons for male/female pay differentiation, but the implications of these analyses for understanding the linkage between pay differentials and sex segregation were found to be less satisfactory. The authors favour an institutional approach derived from internal labour market analysis which can help, they argue, to trace these linkages.

465. Chase, I. D. A comparison of men's and women's intergenerational mobility in the United States. *American Sociological Review*, Vol. 40, No. 4, 1975, p. 483–505.

A comparison of what the author calls 'the main forms of intergenerational mobility for each sex in the US – occupational mobility for men and mobility through marriage for women' (p. 502). Using a variety of methodological techniques on a nationally representative sample, and on subsamples and cohorts, the author concludes that women have greater mobility both upward and downward through marriage than men have through occupations. In addition women more readily cross boundaries between major status groupings of white collar, blue collar, and farm workers, but men are more likely to 'inherit' their father's status, and there is greater association between the status of fathers and sons than of fathers and daughters. An analysis for historical trends revealed little evidence either for increasing fluidity, or for rigidity in the mobility patterns on the author's criteria for either sex.

466. Daniels, A. K. *A survey of research concerns on women's issues*. Washington, DC, Association of American Colleges, 1975, 43 p.

A review of the current (1975) state of interest in research on women's issues, asking two major questions; (1) how will research affect social policy in areas of life that relate to women; and (2) what research questions can provide the information required to promote positive changes in social policy. The review 'sketches a rough outline of the central questions within each major area, indicates some of the work that has been done and suggests new directions that might be taken' (p. iv). It covers the women's movement and its consequences, socialization and the educational system, work, marital status and family, health and life-cycle issues, and other general issues of practical concern to women – e.g. politics, finance. In considering the findings of research on women, one of the author's conclusions is that 'not until greater numbers of women are in decision-making positions within funding agencies and on advisory and review boards will research priorities change significantly' (p. 33).

467. Deckard, B. S. *The women's movement: Political, socio-economic and psychological issues*. Harper and Row, New York and London, 1979. (Second edition.)

The study deals in Part I with American women today, covering sex stereotypes as political ideology; the nature of women – psychological theories; self fulfilling prophecy – sex role socialization; family, myth and reality, middle class and working class versions of the family; exploitation of working women; the obstacle course that professional women have to run; and women and the law. Part II looks at women's place throughout history, primitive, slave and feudal societies; capitalist and socialist societies; the history of women's struggle for emancipation and the new liberation struggle since 1960; current issues and theories in the women's liberation movement.

468. Eichler, M. The origin of sex inequality: A comparison and critique of different theories and their implications for social policy. *Women's Studies International Quarterly*, Vol. 2, No. 3, 1979, p. 329–346.

The paper identifies, differentiates, describes and criticizes four theories purporting to explain the origins of sex inequality, giving examples of the work of at least two proponents of each. The theories are classified on the basis of the logic of the explanation, rather than the nature of the sex difference defined as most important, and are evolutionary theory, biological theory, economic theory and cultural theory. The general criticism is that these attempted explanations in terms of constants cannot explain the variability which is observable in the type and content of male/female differentiation over time and space, and the author argues that such theories do not provide justification for policy statements, which are often based on one or another or a combination of the theories. The theories themselves are all ethically neutral in the sense that they could be used to argue either for the *status quo*, or for changes in women's position, and are therefore irrelevant to policy issues. The author considers that gender relations should be explained in terms of specific historical, social, political, economic, cultural and biological factors that obtain at one point in time in a particular society, not in terms of universals.

469. Eisenstein, Z. R. (ed.). *Capitalist patriarchy and the case for socialist feminism.* New York, Monthly Review Press, 1979, 394 p.

A representative collection of work on socialism and feminism, which aims at developing a fuller understanding of the relationship between patriarchy and capitalism. Sections of the book contain articles on motherhood, reproduction and male supremacy; a socialist feminist historical analysis; capitalist patriarchy and female work; patriarchy in revolutionary society (Cuba, and China); and socialist feminism in the United States. Articles of particular interest are (1) H. Hartmann, on 'Capitalism, patriarchy and job segregation by sex' arguing that the present status of women on the labour market and the current arrangement of sex segregated jobs is the result of a long process of interaction between patriarchy and capitalism, illustrating the argument with historical data from the United States and United Kingdom, and stressing the role of male workers in this process; and (2) B. Weinbaum and A. Bridges 'The other side of the paycheck: Monopoly capital and the structure of consumption', defining the economic aspect of women's work outside the labour force, and calling them 'consumption workers'. The argument is that this work is structured by the state and by capital and is alienating and exhausting.

470. Fausto-Sterling, A. Women and science. *Women's Studies International Quarterly*, Vol. 4, No. 1, 1981, p. 41–50.

Two interconnected questions are explored here: (1) why are there not more women scientists, and (2) what would scientific inquiry and subject matter consist of if there were equal numbers of male and female scientists. The latter question also relates to the issue of how to change forms of scientific inquiry and teaching in order to achieve full entry of women into science. The author suggests that the reconstruction of the real history of women in science is in its earliest stages, and points out that examination of the evidence indicates that the assertions that women are less mathematically able and scientifically creative than men are more myth than fact. Science is a social construct and full equality for women in science would profoundly alter the structure of scientific practice itself. This issue of the journal is on *Women and Futures Research*, and also includes an article by J. Rothschild on 'A feminist perspective on technology and the future' (p. 65–74) which suggests three avenues for exploration (1) the need to look to the past, and to present pre-industrial cultures to uncover women's role in technological development; (2) to take from the theory and experience of the current feminist movement; and (3) to consider a future based on alternative technologies and alternative modes of social and economico-political organisation.

471. Giele, J. Z. *Women and the future: Changing sex roles in modern America.* New York, The Free Press, 1978.

The author reviews changing sex roles in the United States in the context of politics and liberation; women, men and work; the family, family policy, education and the symbolic portrayal of males and females. A rather optimistic stance is taken, with such changes as have occurred seen as having the potential for initiating the dramatic and radical transformation that would be required for full equality for women and the development of a 'new Adult ideal' which would incorporate the human qualities of both male and female. Each chapter on the topic areas outlined above is accompanied by a comprehensive bibliography.

472. Hubbard, R. and Lowe, M. (eds). *Genes and gender II: Pitfalls in research on sex and gender.* New York, Gordian Press, 1979.

Volume I dealt with the myth of genetic determinism and the way it is used to exploit women in American society. Information is introduced to refute this myth which can be seen as flowing from Wilson's socio-biological theory (E. O. Wilson, *Sociobiology: The new synthesis*, Cambridge, Harvard University Press, 1975). This first volume gave facts about what is known of the action of genes in the development of bodily structures and functions, and the way in which hormones work, and indicated ways in which biologists, psychologists and other scientists have distorted these facts to justify the inferior social roles assigned to women and the low value placed on their cultural, social and economic contributions. This second volume develops the critique of socio-biology with papers on 'Universals and male dominance among primates: A critical examination'; 'Social and political bias in science', examining animal studies and their generalization to human behaviour; 'Aggression and gender', 'Sociobiology and Biosociology', asking whether science can prove the biological basis of sex differences in behaviour; 'Methods limits and problems in research on consciousness', and 'Trans-sexualism: an issue of sex-role stereotyping'. The book offers strong criticisms of sex difference research in terms of the theoretical framework within which it is conducted, the specific research methodologies used, and the ways in which results are interpreted and used, suggesting that 'most of the difficulties derive from the fact that true objectivity is not possible for human beings rooted in cultural traditions' (p. 144).

473. Laws, J. L. *The second X: Sex role and social role.* New York, Elsevier, 1979, 405 p.

'The aim of this book is to trace the systematic consequences of being born female' (p. 1). Reviewing and criticizing a wide range of work on women, the author looks at (1) woman as worker and sex segregation, which she sees as a major organizing principle of life in American culture; (2) woman as housewife, including unpaid domestic labour and the consumer role; (3) woman as object, concerned with female sexuality; (4) woman as girl/child, which considers sex typing, sex role socialization, and traditional and contemporary theories of women's psychology; and (5) woman as androgyne – a combination or reconciliation of femininity and masculinity. A considerable range of literature in these areas is reviewed, and each chapter is accompanied by a comprehensive bibliography.

474. Maccoby, E. E. and Jacklin, C. N. *The psychology of sex differences.*

Stanford, Stanford University Press, 1974, paperback 1978. In two volumes, I Text, 391 p., II Annotated Bibliography, 627 p.

A massive, scholarly work, assembling a large body of evidence concerning sex differences and similarities in aspects of psychological functioning. The annotated bibliography contains over 1,400 entries. The authors dispel a range of myths about sex differences, for example that girls are more suggestible, that boys are more analytic, and that girls lack achievement motivation; support one or two others, e.g. that girls are more verbal, boys better in visual spatial ability, and are more aggressive; and they suggest that others, such as competitiveness, and dominance, have too little evidence to establish them. Amongst their conclusions, the authors state that 'societies have the option of minimising, rather than maximising, sex differences through their socialization processes' (p. 374).

475. Rohrbaugh, J. B. *Women: Psychology's puzzle.* London, Sphere Books, 1981. (First published by The Harvester Press, 1980.)

A critical review of a large amount of research on women, examining the major themes and studies relating to five key areas of female psychology and gender differences – biology, personality, social roles, bodily functions and mental health. After examining the formal theories and studies, the author compares them with women's own opinions and experiences. Focusing on the experience of American women, the author argues that the prevailing myths about female psychology distort the reality of women's everyday experience, and she considers the implications of being female in a world where stereotypes determine the place of women in society.

II. Women's work and labour force participation

PROFESSIONAL/MANAGERIAL WORK

476. Brown, L. K. Women and business management. *Signs – Journal of Women in Culture and Society*, Vol. 5, No. 2, 1979, p. 266–288.

A review essay analysing the present state of research primarily from the United States on women as managers in business, commerce, and industry.

477. Dellacava, F. A. and Engel, M. H. Resistance to sisterhood: The case of the professional woman. *International Journal of Women's Studies*, Vol. 2, No. 6, 1979, p. 505–512.

An analysis of questionnaires mailed to a random sample of female lawyers and academics in New York City indicates that professional women feel estranged from, and marginal to other women. The author suggests that this is a result of structural constraints rather than prejudice and that women who assume deviant roles (even high status ones in professions) perceive other women as a negative reference group. There are two reasons for this: (1) their perception of success requires them to over-conform to the expectations of the world of the male professional;

(2) they have a need to see themselves as special and unique in order to deal with the internal conflict they experience as a result of either not following the traditional female role model, or fulfilling these roles in a manner defined by the larger society as inadequate.

478. Kanter, R. M. *Men and women of the corporation.* New York, Basic Books, 1977, 348 p.

The author develops a theory of the working of a corporation, demonstrating how the careers and self images of managers, professionals and executives and of secretaries, manager's wives, and women looking for advancement, are determined by the distribution and exercise of power. She defines power as efficacy, the ability to mobilize resources, rather than domination, and indicates that in a large bureaucracy, power is 'a virtual requisite for effective performance in jobs with accountability for others, and subordinates have good reason to prefer to work for powerful leaders' (p. 6). The women's issue is an important sub-theme in the study, which is based on extensive investigation of one large corporation over a period of five years.

479. Pepitone-Rockwell, F. (ed.). *Dual-career couples.* Beverly Hills/London, Sage Publications, 1980, 294 p.

An examination of dual career couples from the perspective that the traditional family model no longer meets the needs of couples in the 1980s. Part I: The development of dual career couples, contains an article by R. and R. N. Rapoport (who coined the phrase 'dual-career family'), which reviews the major research studies in the field, including their own. Part II looks at marriage and family issues, including theoretical and empirical studies on wives' employment and family role structure, benefits and costs of dual career marriages, situational constraints and role strain, time management and coping strategies, and spouses contributions to each others roles. Part III on career issues, has articles on four forms of career co-ordination by couples in the same or different fields, on laws affecting dual-career couples, and on effective employment search strategies for dual-career couples. A further paper compared professional psychologist pairs, compared with psychologists not married to each other looking at advancement constraints, job satisfaction and salary differences.

OTHER

480. Almquist, E. M. Women in the labour force. *Signs*, Vol. 2, No. 4, 1977, p. 843–855.

A review of the three previous years of sociological research on the status of women. The article combines previously unanalysed data from the US Bureau of the Census *A statistical portrait of women in the US* (Current Population Reports, Special Studies Series P-23, No. 58, Washington DC, Government Printing Office, 1976) and findings from recently published research. It looks at the following aspects. (1) Changing patterns of female labour force participation; (2) women's levels of status attainment; and (3) sex discrimination as revealed in differential income levels between men and women. The rate of improvement in women's position in the labour market is 'glacial', and sociological research, the author argues, pitched as it is at the macro sociological level, is contributing little to change this situation. Suggestions for future research are that the processes through which women reach their overall position in the labour force as revealed by previous studies, should be investigated in more detail. For example, specific occupations should be studied to see how women fare in different fields, and specific jobs investigated to reveal whether employers pay women less than men for the same work, or whether they assign lower wages to 'female' than to 'male' jobs. The attitudes of 'gatekeepers', those who make decisions about women's employment and pay should also be investigated. The article provides a review of some of the relevant literature.

481. Blaxall, M. and Reagan, B. (eds). *Women and the workplace: The implications of occupational segregation.* Chicago, University of Chicago Press, 1976, 326 p.

The overall aim of the papers in this collection was to (1) analyse occupational segregation as an interlocking set of institutions with sociological, psychological and economic aspects, and with deep historical roots; and (2) to consider what policy changes might be needed to achieve a society free from denial of job opportunities on the basis of sex. (p. ix). Sections deal with the social institutions of occupational segregation, including a paper on occupational segregation and the law, by M. J. Gates; the historical roots of occupational segregation, with a comparison of public policy in the USSR and the United States by G. W. Lapidus, and H. Hartmann on 'Capitalism, patriarchy and job segregation by sex' (see Entry 469); the economic dimensions of occupational segregation, with Blau and Jusenius appraising economists' approaches to sex segregation in the labour market (see Entry 464) and Ferber and Lowry on women as a reserve army of labour (see also for the United Kingdom, Breugel, Entry 423); and combating occupational segregation, which looks at policy issues involved in reducing occupational segmentation.

482. Cahn, A. F. (ed.). *Women in the US labor force.* New York, Praeger, 1979, 309 p.

A collection of papers which has the aim of reviewing women's overall role in a full employment economy and their particular problems in fulfilling that role. Overviews are provided by two economists, and the following chapters are the contributions of economists, lawyers, educators. The editor provides a summary of the arguments presented here (p. 1–22). Topics covered are: (1) overcoming barriers, looking at legal rights to equal opportunity employment, *de facto* job segregation, under and unemployment amongst groups of women, and women in non-traditional occupations. (2) Support services and adjusted conditions – the family and employment, economic aspects of childcare and part-time work. (3) Education and employment, considering facilitation of career education, vocational education and apprenticeship. (4) Key factors: tax treatment and media images. (5) International comparisons (see A. H. Cook Entry 380).

483. Kanter, R. M. Some effects of proportions on group life: Skewed sex ratios and responses to token women. *American Journal of Sociology*, Vol. 82, No. 5, 1976–77, p. 965–990.

The paper develops a framework for understanding the social perceptions and interaction dynamics that centre on 'token' individuals, using the example of women in an industrial sales force dominated numerically by men. Three perceptual phenomena are associated with tokens: visibility, which generates performance pressures; polarization, which leads the dominant members of the group to heighten their group boundaries and exaggerates the differences between 'tokens' and 'dominants'; and assimilation, which leads 'tokens' to be trapped in stereotypical roles and behaviours. The analysis is generalizable to other token members of groups, for example blacks in predominantly white groups, and the author points out that the negative effects of token status lead to certain policy conclusions. Numbers appear to be important in shaping outcomes for disadvantaged groups, and members of under-represented categories need to be added to existing groups in sufficiently large numbers to counteract the effects of tokenism.

484. Ritter, K. V. and Hargens, L. L. Occupational positions and class identifications of married working women: A test of the asymmetry hypotheses. *American Journal of Sociology*, Vol. 80, No. 4, 1975, p. 934–948.

A study of 566 married women, which indicates that traditional assumptions that wives derive their class positions and identifications exclusively or predominantly from the occupational positions of their husbands, does not hold for working wives.

485. Roby, P. Sociology and women in working class jobs. In: Millman, M. and Kanter, R. M. (eds). *Another voice: feminist perspectives on social life and social science*. New York, Anchor Books, Anchor Press/Doubleday, 1975, 382 p.

The author reviews research on women in blue collar, industrial and service jobs in the United States from 1890 to 1970. She discusses current research (1975) in some detail, covering womanpower, women's liberation, unions and equal employment studies. A programme for research directed towards the creation, improvement or abolition of social policies (if necessary) in order to improve the living conditions of women employed in blue collar jobs and their families is suggested, including historical, demographic and ethnographic research on working conditions, and specific studies on their wages and working conditions, possibilities for desegregation of jobs, training and promotion opportunities.

486. Sidel, R. Urban survival: *The world of working class women*. Boston, Beacon Press, 1978, 180 p.

The author's objective is to give 'eight working class women an opportunity to communicate with us directly about the problems of survival in the city today' (p. 2). The city is New York and the women represent a diversity of age, ethnic background, race, occupation, educational level and marital status.

487. Sokoloff, N. *Theories of women's labour force status: A review and critique*: Sociology Department, John Jay College, City University of New York, 1979, 67 p.

A wide variety of explanations have been suggested in attempting to understand women's disadvantaged position in the labour market and this paper reviews and evaluates five current sociological theories: status attainment, dual labour markets, Marxist theories of monopoly capitalism, Marxist feminist theories of the home, and Marxist feminist theories of patriarchal capitalism. The conclusion is that any adequate theory of women's position in the American labour market must relate women's market position to their position in the home, and look at the interrelationship between capitalism and patriarchy. See also by the same author *Between money and love: The dialectics of women's home and market work*, New York, Praeger Publishers, 1980.

488. Syzmanski, A. The effect of earnings discrimination against women on the economic position of men. *Social Forces* (Chapel Hill) Vol. 56, No. 2, 1977, p. 611–625. And the following article by Villemez, W. J. Male economic gain from female subordination: A caveat and reanalysis, p. 626–636.

The first article analyses data from the 1970 census to examine the question whether males benefit economically from earnings discrimination against women. The author concludes that they do not. The second article is a methodological critique of the first. The author then analyses the data once again and concludes that 'proper measurement and analysis shows apparent gains for all males from the economic subordination of females' (p. 633.)

489. Wolf, W. C. and Fligstein, N. D. Sex and authority in the workplace: The causes of sexual inequality. *American Sociological Review*, Vol. 44, No. 2, April 1979, p. 235–252.

On the basis of data from the Wisconsin Study of Social and Psychological factors in Socio-economic Achievement, the authors look at the causes for women being prevented from achieving positions of authority in the workplace. Three causes are considered: (1) women's qualifications, (2) behaviour and policies of employers, and (3) attitude and behaviour of the women themselves. Although a substantial amount of sex difference in aspects of authority can be explained by the level of women's qualification, it is not the most important factor. The authors suggest that the most important cause of women's lack of representation in positions of authority in the workplace is the behaviour and policies of employers.

III. Family and household

490. Bose, C. Technology and changes in the division of labor in the American home. *Women's Studies International Quarterly*, Vol. 2, No. 3, 1979, p. 295–304.

Popular ideology indicates that technology has helped liberate women from the household, but the author argues that just as women's workload declined, technology allowed them to take on new burdens. The specific impact of various levels of technology on the division of household labour are examined – industrialization, utilities, appliances and convenience foods – and the effects are measured in three ways: (1) potential reallocation of women's time, (2) the new division of labour amongst members of the household, and (3) labour market aids for housework. The conclusion drawn is that most past change in work content has occurred from non-technological sources, and that household division of labour seems to be increasing. Liberation from this burden is more likely to come through the provision of labour market services for the household.

491. Eekelaar, J. M. and Sanford, N. K. *Family violence: an international and interdisciplinary study*. Toronto, Butterworths, 1977, 572 p.

A collection of studies in the following categories: Part One, family violence: psychological and social perspectives. This includes a paper on 'Media, violence and the family' by L. A. Beaulieu. Part Two, violence between adults: legal and social responses, includes 'The law's response to marital violence: a comparison between England the USA' by S. Maidment, and 'Inter-spousal rape: the need for law reform' by J. L. McFadyen. Parts Three and Four deal with violence against children; Part Five, special aspects of family violence, includes some papers on incest.

492. Harding, S. Family reform movements: Recent feminism and its opposition. *Feminist Studies*, Vol. 7, No. 1, 1981, p. 57–75.

The author postulates two competing ideologies of the family in the United States since the Second World War, one stressing ideas of equality, individualism and reason, the other ideas of hierarchy, 'wholism' and morality, and each generating a strategy for forming and maintaining a family. Feminist family reforms can be seen as based on the egalitarian principle, and the attacks of their opponents are rooted in the hierarchical ideology of the family, where the family defines a woman's identity and status. The article discusses these competing family strategies, describes some of the social trends affecting family organization and examines the ideas and reforms of feminism and oppostion to it in the context of family strategies. The author concludes that both feminism and opposition to it are family reform movements, mobilizations of women with conflicting interests in families, who defend, promote and adapt their strategies in relation to each other and to economic, demographic and socio-cultural trends. In the author's view the feminist movement in the United States is currently suspended, most of its organizational energies absorbed in defending basic goals and gains in the face of concerted opposition, but given its social bases and the range of unresolved issues to be dealt with, the movement will remobilize in more favourable political conditions. This analysis does not permit the elimination of one of the competing strategies, or one becoming subsumed in the other. Both will continue in opposition to each other, with an uneasy truce if large numbers of women are not primarily committed to one or the other, but most women combine some ideas from both. None of the outcomes envisaged from this interaction helps those who seek to look beyond the family to new ways or organizing social networks, personal identity, intimacy, sexuality and reproduction.

493. Giraldo, Z. I. *Public policy and the family: wives and mothers in the labour force*. Lexington, Lexington Books, 1980, 218 p.

The major focus of the book is on patterns of family life, seen from the perspective of the family life-cycle, and the pressures which have changed the family in recent history – public policy is a secondary consideration. In the first part of the book, the author describes the family structure of the American population, the changes it has undergone, and variations in the family life cycle on the basis of changes in the social, economic and political climate. Labour force participation of wives and mothers, and the resulting impact on the family is discussed, and the author points out that the growing conflict between the demands of the home and the demands of employment may become the major factor dominating public policy towards the family in the future. Part II looks at the inequities in the tax system, and the dual income family; Part III discusses the Equal Rights Amendment, and the fears of those who oppose it regarding the destruction of the family. States which have legislation approximating to the ERA are looked at in terms of judgements made in the courts on family related issues. The author concludes that the implementation of the ERA in these states has a supportive and flexible impact on families. Part IV looks in more detail at the impact of employment and the dual job, dual career family on children and mothers, concluding that women seem to be able to continue to raise children successfully whilst working outside the home. The final chapter is a survey of families in Mecklenburg County, North Carolina, looking at the problems raised in the above chapters in terms of a specific workforce.

494. Malos, E. *The policies of housework*. London, Allison and Busby, 1980.

A selection of papers drawn from writers in the United Kingdom, Canada and the United States which provides a summation of the debate instigated from within the women's movement in the late 1960s and 1970s on housework. It deals with examples from the 'Wages for Housework' campaign, and the Marxist based discussions of the role and function of domestic labour in a capitalist formation. The book provides some useful source material and a historical background to the debate. A brief and briefly annotated bibliography is included.

495. Nilson, L. B. The social standing of a married woman. *Social Problems* (Evanston), Vol. 23, No. 5, 1976, p. 581–592.

The author questions the traditional way of designating a married woman's social status by her husband's occupational attainment, and suggests that both husband and wives' occupational attainment should be taken into account. In a random sample from Milwaukee, men and women as a whole tended to subscribe to a status enhancing rather than competing model of female attainment. The author argues then, that people take into account the occupational attainments of both husbands and wives in an additive way when assessing the wife's social standing. See also 'The social standing of a housewife', *Journal of Marriage and the family*, No. 3, Fall, 1978, p. 541–548. Here, the author suggests that the role of housewife has only recently been conceived of as an occupation. This study, based on a survey of 479 Milwaukee area adults, assigns it an average prestige score of 70, comparable to a newspaper reporter, radio announcer, tenant farmer or insurance agent.

496. Rubin, L. B. *Worlds of pain: Life in the working class family*. New York, Basic Books, 1976, 268 p.

Based on an intensive study of 50 white working class families and 25 professional middle class families, this book is concerned with class differences in subjective and objective experiences which lead to differences between middle and working class families in attitudes and behaviour. A wealth of detailed information and interview material is used to demonstrate that 'the economic realities of working class life and the constraints they impose on living are the common ingredients from which a world of shared understanding arises, from which a consciousness and a culture grows that is distinctly working class' (p. 210).

IV. Education

497. Fishel, A. and Pottker, J. *National politics and sex discrimination in education*. Lexington, Lexington Books, 1977, 159 p.

The authors review four case studies, which involved the legislative, executive and judicial branches of the federal government in order to indicate the nature of the politics involved in challenging the existence of sex discrimination in education. The instances were (1) The *Cohen* v. *Chesterfield County Maternity Leave* case, where a woman challenged the requirement that a pregnant teacher must leave teaching in the fourth, fifth or sixth month of pregnancy; (2) the US Office of Education Task Force on Women's Education (this chapter is written by H. Knox and M. A. Millsop) whose recommendations have made little headway; (3) the Enactment of the Women's Educational Equity Act, embedded ultimately in a wider educational measure and underfunded; and (4) Title IX, a federal law banning sex discrimination in education, seven years of struggle. When members of both House and Senate realized the impact which the implementation of this law (passed in 1972) would have on educational policies and practices, it came under constant assault, with attempts to change the law and undermine its impact.

498. Fitzpatrick, B. *Women's inferior education: An economic analysis*. New York, Praeger Publications, 1976, 189 p.

The author outlines the situation in tax-supported post secondary education in the United States where women are a minority. She points out that this is not because their qualifications for entry are lower, girls consistently perform better than boys in secondary education, despite myths to the contrary (p. 5). Various explanations for this state of affairs are considered, and although lack of aspiration might play a part in some women's educational career pattern, this is not considered an adequate explanation. The author looks at discriminatory admissions policies in a range of institutions. This is followed by a state by state analysis of opportunities in post-secondary education for women, and a considera-tion of the economic motives for discrimination. Finally, there are some recommendations, which could lead to more equal educational oppor-tunities for women and men.

499. *Harvard Educational Review*. Women and education – Part I, Vol. 49, No. 4, 1979, and Part II, Vol. 50, No. 1, 1980.

Two special issues of the HER on women and education. Articles include, in Part I: F. Howe, 'The first decade of women's studies'; M. Westkott, 'Feminist criticism of the social sciences'; M. R. Walsh, 'The rediscovery of the need for a feminist medical education'; J. D. Finn, L. Dulberg, and J. Reis 'Sex differences in educational attainment'; A. K. Shulman, 'Overcoming silences: Teaching writing for women'; K. Boulware-Miller, 'Recent studies of Black women'. In Part II: K. Lyman and J. J. Speizer, 'Advancing in school administration'; M. Sadker and D. Sadker, 'Sexism in teacher education texts'; G. Sassen, 'Success anxiety in women'; S. Tobias and C. S. Weissbrod, 'Anxiety and mathematics: An update'; and M. B. Zinn, 'Women in Mexican American families'.

500. Holahan, C. K. Stress experienced by women doctoral students, need for support, and occupational sex typing: An interaction view. *Sex Roles*, Vol. 5, No. 4, 1979, p. 425–436.

This study was concerned with emotional stress experienced by women doctoral students as a function of type of department and personal need for support. The subjects were women registered as doctoral students at a large state university in 1975, of whom 86 were from departments in which there was a female minority, 177 from departments with relatively equal proportions of men and women, and 114 from departments with a majority of women. Stress from time pressure, marital pressures, and overall stress were all found to be interactive functions of need for support and type of department. The women in the minority female department showed the strongest relationship between need for support and each of the three stress variables. The author discusses the implications of these findings for women in graduate school.

501. Houseknecht, S. K. and Spanier, G. B., Marital disruption and higher education among women in the US. *Sociological Quarterly*, Vol. 21, No. 3, 1980, p. 375–390.

The general inverse relationship between marital disruption (separation and divorce) and educational status, commonly assumed by family sociologists, is demonstrated for both men and women using 1970 US Census data. Highly educated females (five or more years of college) have a dramatically higher disruption rate than women with only four years of college. Three factors increase the likelihood of marriage breakdown for this highly educated group – being non-white, employed and earning a high income. Four possible explanations for the relation between marital disruption and education are suggested: (1) insecure identities on the part of the males and a sense of status loss on the part of the females; (2) female economic independence; (3) female career commitment; and (4) non-shared social support systems.

502. Rosen, B. C. and Aneshensel, C. S. Sex differences in the educational-occupational expectation process. *Social Forces*, Vol. 57, No. 1, 1978, p. 164–186.

A path analysis of status expectations focusing on how sex influences the educational and occupational expectations of a large sample of American adolescents. Exogenous background variables have greater total effect for females, whilst intervening social-psychological and achievement variables have less. In academic achievement females have lower expectations than males and the distribution of occupational choices parallel the current sex segregation of the occupational sector.

503. Wasserman, E., Lewin, A. Y. and Bleiweis, L. H. (eds). *Women in Academia: evolving policies toward equal opportunities*. New York, Praeger, 1975, 169 p.

A collection of papers which aim to reveal the present status of equal opportunity legislation, document the history of discrimination, and discuss the implications and implementation of non-discriminatory policies for academic institutions. Includes a discussion of cases of affirmative action.

504. Wirtenberg, T. J., Nakamura, C. Y. Education: Barrier or boon to changing occupational roles of women? *Journal of Social Issues* (Ann Arbor), Vol. 32, No. 3, 1976, p. 165–180.

Traditional educational institutions have contributed to occupational stratification by sex, but they can play a part in integrating the occupational world. Research into young women's occupational aspirations is reviewed in this paper, and three major sex-biased educational practices discussed: these are textbooks and instructional materials, differential curricular for males and females, and vocational counselling and testing. Recent legislation is evaluated for usefulness in modifying sex bias.

V. Demographic features

505. Ryan, M. P. Reproduction in American history. *Journal of Interdisciplinary history* (Cambridge, Mass) Vol. 10, No. 2, 1979, p. 319–332.

A review article discussing three books: J. Barrett Litoff, *American midwives 1860 to the present*, Westport, Conn, Greenwood Press, 1978,

197 p; J. C. Mohr, *Abortion in America: the origins and evolution of national policy*, New York, Oxford University Press, 1978, 328 p.; J. Reed, *From Private vice to public virtue: The birth control movement and American society since 1830*, New York, Basic Books, 1978, 447 p. The author concludes that these three books offer a base and incentive for exploring the integral historical problem of the analytical connections between the social relations of reproduction (the private, domestic and women's activities) and the public social male sphere.

VI. Other

506. Brodsky, A. M. A decade of feminist influence on psychotherapy, *Psychology of Women Quarterly*, Vol. 4, No. 3, 1980, p. 331.

In the last decade, feminism has had an impact on the theories, treatment techniques, and assessment instruments of psychotherapy. Changes in attitudes toward women as therapists and as clients have reflected the general advances of the women's movement, and women clients are more likely to seek women therapists and to receive treatments specifically developed for crises affecting women, such as rape, pregnancy and domestic violence. There are difficulties in designing empirical studies to demonstrate bias in psychotherapy, and there is resistance amongst some women to women's movement attempts to bring about change. The author detects encouraging changes, when comparing the writing on women and psychotherapy in recent professional journals with examples from the 1960s.

507. Butler, M. and Paisley, W. *Women and the mass media: Sourcebook for research and action*. New York, Human Sciences Press, 1980, 432 p.

Reviewing a vast range of studies of the media, the work is intended as a basic sourcebook and is divided into five parts. Part 1, antecedents, looks at women's rights in America, at sexism in language and image and at the growth of the American mass media. Part 2, sexism in media content, discusses how media content is studied, and the content of television commercials and programmes, magazines and newspapers, books and films. Part 3, institutional sexism in the media, considers both how institutional media are studied, and the findings of such studies with respect to employment, decisions affecting portrayal, and training. Part 4 covers sexism and media audiences, methodology and content of studies on media audiences and the impact of the media on them. Part 5 indicates directions for future research and action, discussing legal, economic and social action to combat sexism in the media.

508. Diamond, I. *Sex roles in the State House*. New Haven and London, Yale University Press, 1977, 214 p.

Two perspectives are taken in this study of the role of women in American politics. The first involves a broad examination of the contours of sex differences in state legislatures. The basic hypothesis developed is that sex differentiation decreases as competition for political office increases, and the author cites the example of certain New

England states where there is greater participation of women than in other states. The different career patterns of men and women are examined and seen to be more similar when competition is intense. The second part of the book is a more intensive analysis of sex roles and interpersonal relationships, drawing on interviews with female legislators. The author considers the advantages and disadvantages of being a woman in a male domain and identifies four types of roles taken by these women (1) housewife-benchwarmer; (2) traditional civic worker; (3) women's rights advocate; and (4) passive women's right advocate, each with distinctive patterns of legislative life. The author concludes that the political consequences of women being in the legislature are dependent on the prevalence of these different types rather than the actual number of women, but a more general conclusion is that women will not win political equality without a fundamental restructuring of institutions in the larger society.

509. Ditkoff, G. S. Stereotypes of adolescents towards the working woman. *Adolescence*, No. 14, 1979, p. 277–282.

The primary hypothesis in this study, that contemporary adolescents would show less agreement with stereotypical statements about women's role and women workers than adolescents in 1973 was confirmed. Despite the fact that the attitudes of female adolescents were less traditional than those of male adolescents, there was a greater degree of change over the past five years for males. Adolescents are becoming less stereotyped in their views, but many stereotypes still exist. The author points out that twelve of twenty occupations were classified as primarily male or female by at least 50 per cent of the male and female adolescents in the 1978 sample. Socio-economic status influenced these attitudes, with adolescents from high income backgrounds being most liberal, from low socio-economic backgrounds being least liberal, and the middle levels intermediate.

510. Juran, S. A measure of stereotyping in fear of success cues. *Sex Roles*, Vol. 5, No. 3, 1979, p. 287–297.

Prior studies suggest that sex role stereotypes influence responses to Horner's fear of success cue. This study investigates stereotypes about both sex roles and achievement settings. One hundred and sixty college males and females wrote stories to different cues, then rated the masculinity/femininity of their characters. Both 'John' and 'Anne' were rated more masculine as medical students than in a neutral setting. Anne was rated more feminine than John in the neutral setting but equally masculine as a medical student. Anne's success was not regarded as maladaptive, but competent. As a result of these findings the author argues that Horner's cue reflects stereotypes, and that a more ambiguous cue might assess motives more effectively.

511. Kahn, S. E. and Schroeder, A. S. Counsellor bias in occupational choice for female students. *Canadian Counsellor*, Vol. 14, No. 3, p. 156–159, 1980.

School counsellors in British Columbia were asked to select three appropriate occupations for each subject in case studies. When the case study described a female, the counsellors chose occupations that paid less and were more closely supervised.

512. Levine, A. and Crumrine, J. Women and the fear of success: A problem in replication. *American Journal of Sociology*, Vol. 80, No. 4, 1975, p. 964–973.

An attempt to replicate and expand on M. Horner's findings, which led to a widely disseminated conclusion that women have a motivation to avoid success. Seven hundred male and female students were asked to write stories on the basis of randomly assigned cues concerning the success of a male or female medical student. Content analysis showed that the majority of stories contained fear of success imagery, but that there were no significant differences in the percentages of men and women respondents who included such imagery in their stories. The authors suggest that their findings underline the need for careful examination and replication before tentative concepts in controversial areas become conventional wisdom.

513. Lewis, D. K. A response to inequality: Black women, racism and sexism. *Signs*, Vol. 3, No. 2, 1977, p. 339–361.

The paper attempts to explain the initial rejection and then more favourable reaction to the women's movement on the part of black women in the United States. A model of inequality is developed. Detailed information on the status of black women is provided and the author argues that the structural changes in the relationship between blacks and whites resulting from the black liberation movement, heightened black women's perception of sexism, since they experience deep seated sexism as they begin to increase their participation in the public sphere. This is particularly true for middle class black women.

514. Mackinnon, C. E. *Sexual harassment of working women*. New Haven, Yale University Press, 1979.

Defining sexual harassment as 'the unwanted imposition of sexual requirements in the context of a relationship of unequal power' (p. 1), the author looks at women's work, at the experience of sexual harassment and at specific sexual harassment cases. She considers the legal context and sexual harassment as sex discrimination on two bases – an inequality argument, and a differences argument. The book provides a skilful analysis of the legal questions posed in using the law to support women who challenge practices of sexual harassment. By putting the problem in the context of women's inferior labour market position, providing a description of the nature and extent of sexual harassment, and indicating that it grows from and reinforces traditional roles of men and women in the society, the author makes a convincing case for the fact that sexual harassment does constitute unlawful discrimination within the meaning of the Equal Protection Clause. The author adds a new dimension to the Equal Protection Clause, by arguing that the focus in equal protection law should not be on differences or their arbitrariness, but on the basic issue of inequality in sex discrimination – 'the only question for litigation is whether the policy or practice in question integrally contributes to the maintenance of an underclass or a deprived position because of gender status'.

515. Mason, K. O. Czajka, J. and Arber, S. Change in US women's sex role attitudes, 1964–1974. *American Sociological Review*, Vol. 41, No. 4, 1976, p. 573–596.

The authors used data from five sample surveys taken between 1964 and 1974 to investigate changes in American women's sex role attitudes. They found that there had been considerable movement towards more egalitarian definitions of women's roles and that this change was reflected in women at all socio-economic levels. The analysis suggests that women's attitudes about their rights in the labour market are also becoming more strongly related to their attitudes about their roles in the home, and that higher educational attainment and more recent employment are associated with less traditional outlooks.

516. Sachs, A. and Wilson, J. H. *Sexism and the law: A study of male beliefs and legal bias in Britain and the United States.* Oxford, Martin Robertson, 1978, 257 p.

A study which documents the existence of sexism in the law and in the legal profession in the United Kingdom and the United States. The authors define sexism as 'the tendency to think about and behave towards people mainly on the basis of their gender, to generalize about individuals and groups on the basis of their biology rather than to recognize their actual interests and capacities' (p. ix). In the British part of the study, the authors aim to expose by detailed descriptions of specific cases involving women's rights both 'the myth of judicial neutrality, and the myth of male protectiveness'. They argue that the positions upheld by judges and the legal profession reflected the stereotyped attitudes towards women, which existed in the broader society, but a crucial assumption is that these judicial pronouncements about women masked specific and discoverable material interests that judges as upper class males shared generally with members of their own class and gender. They drew attention to the fact that despite differences in the two systems of law – the British system, enshrining the supremacy of parliament, with judges seeing themselves as acting as impartial interpreters of particular words in particular statutes; the American constitution guaranteeing individual rights and judges seeing themselves as guardians of the constitution, who should apply in as just a fashion as possible the wide words of the amendments to particular problems – a perusal of cases shows that the judges in the two countries arrived almost invariably at the same conclusions at almost precisely the same times, irrespective of the constitutional route they took. For example, they upheld and justified the exclusion of women from the franchise until the second decade of the 20th century. The history and practices of exclusion of women from the legal profession in both countries is also detailed, as are changing judicial patterns of family law in both countries.

517. Serbin, L. A., Connor, J. M. and Iler, I. Sex stereotyped and non-stereotyped introductions of new toys in the preschool classroom: an observational study of teacher behavior and its effects. *Psychology of Women Quarterly*, Vol. 4, No. 2, 1979, p. 261–265.

In a first study the behaviour of teachers in introducing sex typed and non-sex typed toys in the classroom was observed in nine pre-school classes. Results indicated that teachers called on more boys to demonstrate a 'masculine' toy than girls. No significant differences were found in the mean number of boys and girls called on to demonstrate 'neutral' or 'feminine' toys, but teachers were more variable in demonstrating the sex typed feminine toys than the non-stereotyped toy. In a second study, two sets of toys, each including five dolls and five trucks were introduced using stereotyped and non-stereotyped introductions to two classes of three and four-year-old children. No significant sex differences in toy choices were found following the non-stereotyped introductions. Following the stereotyped introductions, the children's toy choices were consistent with sex-role stereotypes. The results are consistent with laboratory studies which suggest that bias in the introduction of toys by adults may contribute to the sex typing of specific activities.

518. *Signs*, Vol. 1, No. 1, Autumn, 1975. The new scholarship: Review essays in the social sciences. p. 119–192.

Five review essays looking at recent research on women in the social sciences, focusing on the development of a new perspective on women. One on anthropology by C. B. Stack, M. D. Caulfield, V. Estes, S. Landes, K. Larson, P. Johnson, J. Rake, and J. Shirek, is particularly thorough and rich in references, but all provide good coverage of the areas concerned. M. Brown Parlee deals with psychology; J. R. Chapman provides briefer coverage of economics; K. Boals reviews political science and a final overview is made by S. S. Angrist.

519. Smith, M. E. The Portuguese female immigrant: The 'marginal man'. *International Migration Review*, Vol. 14, No. 1, 1980, p. 77–92.

The author analyses the role of Portuguese women in the migration decision of typical male dominated families and their importance in the departure from Portugal and the acculturation process in the United States. The intention is to redress the imbalance in previous migration literature, which neglects the role of women in these processes.

520. Stimpson, C. R. and Person, E. S. (eds). *Women: Sex and sexuality*. Chicago, University of Chicago Press, 1980, p. 345.

A selection of papers previously published in *Signs – Journal of Women in Culture and Society*, Vols. 5, No. 4 and 6 No. 1, Summer and Autumn 1980. A wide range of methodologies, frames of reference and values are brought together to deal with the complex issue of female sexuality. Amongst the papers, A. K. Shulman talks about the sexual bases of the radical feminism of the late 1960s and early 1970s, E. S. Person discusses psychoanalytic perspectives and connections between sexuality and identity, and A. Rich considers compulsory heterosexuality and lesbian existence. Other papers cover reproduction and a woman's right to choose, menstruation, pornography and prostitution. A series of review essays on, for example biological influences on human sex and gender, and social and behavioural constructions of female sexuality, are included.

521. Sutherland, S. L. The unambitious female: Women's low professional aspirations. *Signs*, Vol. 3, No. 4, Summer 1978, p. 774–794.

A study of a representative sample of 1,000 Canadian university students, which looks at (1) the pattern of prejudice against women by both women and men; (2) the sense of anxiety which characterizes the female members of the sample; (3) the low level of aspiration of women in the sample compared with men; and (4) other aspects of female marginality, including political participation. The author identified insecurity, anxiety and low self-esteem as factors explaining women's modest aspirations, and, by using a measure of values and value systems developed by Rokeach, indicates that the value structures demonstrated by the males in the sample facilitate ambition, self sufficiency and accomplishment in work, whereas those of women 'seem self-harmfully idealistic and dependent upon other people for their *raison d'être*'. (p. 791). The author also discusses the fact that families provide less material support for their daughters, and that family childhood experiences seem to mark women more deeply than men.

522. Tresemer, D. W. *Fear of success.* New York, Plenum Press, 1977.

An overview of research on fear of success (FOS) generated originally by a study by M. S. Horner ('Sex differences in achievement motivation and performance in competitive and non-competitive situations', Doctoral dissertation, University of Michigan 1968) see also Entries 510 and 512. Tresemer takes the main questions raised in the study of FOS and accumulating and reworking the results in a large number of studies, concludes: (1) Women do not show more FOS than men; (2) men do not respond to a cue with an achieving female with more FOS than females; (3) for both genders there has been a very erratic and weak trend to a slight decrease in FOS imagery over the past decade; (4) almost none of the expected associated factors are consistently correlated positively or negatively – gender role identification, anxiety, age; (5) the relationship between FOS imagery and performance in different situations (e.g. female achievement behaviour in competition with men) is not clearly established. The author also points to technical difficulties with the conceptualization and execution of FOS studies, but does not want to abandon FOS as a distinctive psychological construct. He considers that the original anthropological and psychoanalytic approaches to the study of the concept were rich and interesting unlike the barren conventional social psychological/personality methods reviewed here, and wants to suggest an approach synthesizing the best in each of these perspectives.

523. Tuchman, G., Kaplan Daniels, A., Benet, J. (eds). *Hearth and home: Images of women in the mass media.* New York, Oxford University Press, 1978, p. 333.

'The volume hopes to delineate a national social problem – the mass media's treatment of women' (p. 5). In essays, reporting new research, the social scientists whose work appears in this collection are looking into the trivialization and symbolic annihilation of women by the media. In Part 1, television, articles include 'Dominant or dominated? Women on prime time television' by J. Lemon and 'Where are the women in public broadcasting?' by M. S. Cantor. Part 2 on women's magazines includes 'Imagery and ideology: The cover photographs of traditional women's magazines' by M. Ferguson, and 'Magazine heroines: Is MS just another member of the family group' by E. B. Phillips. Part 3 looks at newspapers and their women's pages, including 'The women's page as a window on the ruling class' by G. William Domhoff. Part 4 deals with televisions effect on children and youth, and asks 'Will media treatment of women improve?' J. Benet. This section includes 'The image of women in television: An annotated bibliography' by H. Franzwa. Sectional introductions link the separate chapters to the major theses of the study and a concluding chapter looks as the policy implications of the material in the book.

524. Weitz, S. *Sex roles: Biological, psychological and social foundations*, New York, Oxford University Press, 1977, 283 pp.

The author emphasizes an interdisciplinary approach, the fact that no one input (biological, psychological or social) can give the whole answer to sex role differentiation, and that male and female roles must be seen as part of a sex role system. She reviews a wide range of material covering biological and psychological explanations, social aspects including the family, domestic and occupational roles, and symbolism – sexual pollution and menstruation, taboo, witchcraft, language and the arts. Sex role change through space and time is considered with reference to material on the USSR and Eastern Europe, Asia, Israel and Sweden, and the history of American feminism.

525. Wine, J. D., Moses, B. and Smye, M. D. Female superiority in sex difference competence comparisons: A review of the literature. In: Stark-Adamic, C. (ed.). *Sex roles: origins, influences and implications for women.* Montreal, Eden Press Women's Publications, 1981.

The literature comparing female and male competences is reviewed, including sex differences in intellectual abilities and achievements. Females equal or surpass males in all intellectual tasks, when performance is required. The under-representation in advanced occupational and educational pursuits is a direct reflection of societal opportunity and reward structures. The literature comparing female and male social competences is reviewed in detail, and the authors conclude that females surpass males in (1) being more attentive to social stimuli, (2) being more accurate decoders of social stimuli, (3) being more effective encoders of social messages, (4) being more responsive to variations in social input, (5) having language and speech patterns which indicate greater complexity and interpersonal sensitivity, and (6) showing pro-social patterns as opposed to antisocial patterns of social behaviour. The volume includes another paper by the same authors 'Assertiveness:

sex differences in relationships between self-report and behavioural measures'.

4. WESTERN EUROPE

I. General

BIBLIOGRAPHIES

526. *Die Frau in den Arbeitsbeziehungen.* Issued for an international symposium on Women in Industrial Relations, Vienna 1978, sponsored by the International Institute for Labour Studies and the Austrian Federal Ministry for Social Affairs.

An annotated bibliography of 100 recent (to 1978) books and studies on Austrian women in the working process, and related subjects (health, education, political participation). Separate editions in English and German are available.

527. Frank, M. Feminist publications in West Germany today. *New German Critique*, No. 13, 1978, p. 181–194.

A bibliographical essay on feminist resources in the Federal Republic of Germany, including background information on the history of various publications, and focusing on periodicals, publishing houses and special issues. This is followed on pages 197–229 by a bibliography with extensive annotations under the headings general works on feminist topics, matriarchy, patriarchy, sexism, socialist feminism, liberal reformism, women and work and violence against women.

528. Høyrup, E. *Women and mathematics, science and engineering.* A partially annotated bibliography with emphasis on mathematics and reference to related topics. Roskilde University, Skriftserie fra Roskilde Universite s bibliotek, 4, 1978.

Briefly annotated bibliography of references in this field from the United States, the United Kingdom, Denmark, Sweden, Federal Republic of Germany, and France. Headings are: Women in mathematics, publications dealing with the topic, women mathematicians in history, spatial visualization, women at university, women and problem solving, sex differences in thinking and cognition, creativity, achievement.

529. Ministere des Affaires Economique. *De Vrouw in de Samenleving* (The feminine condition). A selective bibliography compiled by H. Verbeeck under the direction of A. Philips. Brussels, Ministry of Economic Affairs, Bibliotheque Centrale, 1975.

A two volume bibliography of materials in twenty major Belgian libraries to the end of 1974, with 1,212 citations, fully bilingual in French and Dutch. Entries are predominently from the Netherlands, France, Federal Republic of Germany, United Kingdom. The headings are economics; social situation; legal situation, historical and ethnographic approaches, psychology and sexuality, maternity, family planning and abortion, politics, the mass media, the arts, the church and religion, delinquency and prostitution, sports, military service.

530. Scheer, L. (ed.) *Women and industrial relations: An annotated bibliography of contemporary Austrian publications.* Vienna, Federal Ministry of Science and Research, 1978, 87 p.

An extensively annotated bibliography of German language publications on industrial relations under the headings: legal framework, public life, education and training, health, employment, working conditions, trade unions, social security, and social situation. English and German editions are available. This contains abstracts of sections of *Report on the Status of Women*, published by the Federal Chancellery of Austria in 1975. The latter publication formed the basis for a short report (30 p.) *The Status of Women in Austria*, published by the Austrian Federal Ministry of Social Affairs, 1976, in English, which also includes material from their own research projects.

531. Weitz, M. C. An annotated bibliography of recent studies on French women. *Contemporary French Civilization*, Vol. 3, No. 3, Spring 1979, p. 443–467.

A bibliography in English of recent work on French women, excluding literary studies and works. Listed under the headings bibliographies, general works, documents, recent titles, reviews and research aids, the material is chiefly concentrated on work in the 1970s and all but 'recent titles' are annotated.

OTHER

532. Abadan-Unat, N. (ed.). (With the assistance of D. Kandiyoti and M. Kiray) *Women in Turkish Society.* Leiden, Brill, 1982. (In English.)

This book is a collection of papers, which were presented at a seminar on Women in Turkish Society held in Istanbul in 1978, plus some additional material. The aim was to provide data, which could help to identify major problems relating to women in order to clarify policy formulation and implementation, and the areas covered in the collection are legal rights, labour force participation, education, health status, fertility, familial roles and political participation. Papers include: 'Women professionals in Turkey' by A. Oncu, which suggests that the incursion of women into the professions of medicine and the law, which has occurred, can be seen as a case of class consolidation – middle class women have gained entry rather than peasant or working class men; 'Women and social change' by N. Abadan-Unat provides a historical overview of legal and political changes and an analysis of contemporary socio-economic factors affecting women. Demographic features are dealt with in papers by L. Erder and C. Kagitcibasi. Two papers look at women and politics – O. Tokgoz discusses 'Effects of television on the politicization of women', and S. Tekeli, 'Women in Turkish politics'. Family structure is the subject of a paper by S. Timur, and within family relationships between mothers and daughters of D. Kandiyoti's 'Dimensions of psycho-social change in women: an intergenerational comparison'. G.

Kazgan looks at labour force participation, occupational distribution, educational attainment and the socio-economic status of women in the Turkish economy. Other papers deal with education, religion, migration, health, nutrition, women in small towns, and women-orientated policy in relation to economic planning. Two other volumes have appeared, as products from this seminar, published in English by the Turkish Social Science Association, Ankara in 1978: (1) M. Aren, *Women in Turkish Society: A bibliography*, and D. Kandiyoti, *Women in Turkish Society*, a report of the seminar, which includes resumes of the presented papers and discussions. See also D. Kandiyoti, *Major Issues on the status of women in Turkey: Approaches and priorities*, Ankara, Turkish Social Science Association, 1980, which is a report of a second seminar held in 1980, and designed to provide clear-cut policy recommendations and priorities for action on women in Turkey.

533. Bugnion, P. Swiss women and decision making. *Labor and Society*, Vol. 1, No. 2, April 1976, p. 53–68.

The author assesses the situation of Swiss women with reference to the definition of equality established during International Women's Year. She concludes that progress is being made but that equality of rights does not yet exist. Equality of opportunity is denied because of the effect of education and tradition, and equality of responsibilities is far from being achieved by Swiss women.

534. Commission on the Status of Women. An official department attached to the Portuguese Prime Minister's Office.

The Commission was officially set up in November 1977, although it has been functioning since 1974. Research is conducted into the status of women in the areas of (1) legislative studies and comparative law, family law and labour law, and policy proposals are made to the relevant government departments as a result; (2) sociological and psychological studies on stereotypes and conditioning of the role of men and women in society. The Commission publishes a quarterly bulletin (since 1975) with studies on the status of women, and a monthly bibliographic bulletin, which has entries under the headings: women's role in society, feminism and emancipation, women and work, equal access, opportunities and pay, maternity rights, education of women, family and law, sexuality, abortion and family planning.

535. Fraire, M. (Series co-ordinator). *Lessico politico della donna* (Political lexicon of women) Milano, Gulliver Edizioni, 1978, and following.

A series of six books entitled (1) *Women and the law*; (2) *Women and medicine*; (3) *Theories of feminism*; (4) *Sociology of the family*; (5) *The emancipation of women*; (6) *Cinema, literature and the visual arts*. Each contains chapters by specialists on the relevant topic. Number one includes a bibliography covering the general areas dealt with in the six books, and individual chapters also include useful bibliographies.

536. Held, T. and Levy, R. *Femme, famille et societe – enquete sociologique sur la situation en Suisse*. Vevey, Editions Delta S. A., 1975, 405 p.

(Collection Sociologie en Suisse.) (Originally published as *Die Stellung der Frau in Familie und Gesellschaft*. Frauenfeld and Stuttgart, Huber, 1974.)

A report of the first large scale sociological study on women, the family and society, undertaken by the Swiss National Commission for Unesco. Using statistical data and the results of an interview enquiry of a representative group of couples and single women in Switzerland, the authors analyse both the objective and subjective situation of women in the areas of work, income, education, family life and participation in other fields of social activity. At the objective level, emphasis is laid on the intra and extra familial participation of women; at the subjective level, on women's views of the segregation of sex roles and domination of women by men, and on women's consciousness of discrimination. The authors conclude that a change in the position of women requires a fundamental change in society.

537. Kandolin, I and Uusitalo, H. *Scandinavian Men and women: A welfare comparison*. University of Helsinki, Research Group for Comparative Sociology, Research Reports No. 28, 1980, p. 70.

The authors compare the welfare of men and women in each of the Scandinavian countries in terms of health, education, labour force participation, occupation, income, social mobility, friendship, recreation, political and social activity and subjective wellbeing. The authors conclude that women's welfare is lower than men's on all indicators used (with the exception of mortality) although there are some variations between countries, and women's subjective welfare seems similar to men's. Finland has slightly less inequality than the other countries, and Norway has the greatest inequality between the sexes.

538. Modern Greek Studies Association. *Women and men in Greece: A society in transition*. A symposium held at the University of Pennsylvania, November 1980. Mimeo of abstracts. (Address: Box 337, Harvard Square Branch, Cambridge, Mass 02238.)

A wide range of papers were included. Perhaps of particular interest in this context, indicating the range of studies on women are: J. S. Cavounidis, 'Women's work in Greece: a mode of production approach'; M. H. Clark, 'The changing sexual division of labour in rural Greece'; M. Dimen, 'Women and the state in Kriovrisi'; S. Engberg, 'Women's liberation movements in Greece'; R. Manidaki, 'Greek women's employment in the changing economic and social environment'; S. Nicolaidou, 'Participation of modern Greek women in ritual and religious life in the Greek orthodox church: A sociological approach'; L. Nikolaou-Smokovitis, 'Women managers in Greek banking organizations'; E. Pepelasis, 'Women in education and sciences'; A. Scourby 'College students of Greek descent: gender roles and family transactions'; E. Skouteri-Didaskalou, 'The production of dowry and domestic labour in modern Greece: A historical approach'; S. Buck Sutton, 'Home and work: Dilemmas and choices for married female migrants in Athens'; and V. Tsouderou 'Women in Political life'.

539. Moussourou, L. *Contemporary Greek women: Basic data*. Athens, Enimerosi 1, 1976, 125 p. (Series on Contemporary Greek Society No. 1). (Greek.)

The study is based on national statistics with the aim both of disseminating the information available more widely, and indicating inadequacies in these data. It covers education, with comparative data for males and females, women's position in the labour force, the family, migration, and the material conditions in which housewives live.

540. National Committee on Equality between Men and Women. *Step by Step*. Stockholm, Liberförlag, 1979, 197 p.

A document drawn up by the National Committee as a National Plan of Action for Equality. The report supplies facts about women and men in Sweden in all aspects of life, summarizes what has happened in the efforts to promote and achieve equality in the past five years and points to problems and obstacles for continued progress. Practical measures are suggested for the future. Topics covered are: education and training, working life, family policy and family law, housing and community planning, health and social problems, representation, and the moulding of public opinion.

541. National Council of Women. *The role of women's organizations in Norway*. Oslo, National Council of Women, 1980.

A report to the World Conference of the United Nations Decade for Women, Copenhagen 1980, produced by the Equal Status Council of Norway. It describes the diversity of women's organizations in Norway, the relationships between them, and their relation to public authorities, finally assessing their role in society. The report states that although the government machinery possesses the expertise and capacity to assist the public policy of promoting equal status between men and women, to which the Norwegian government is committed, it cannot replace or reduce the importance of organizations working to improve the position of women. These organizations serve to develop new ideas and goals and produce a general perspective on long term efforts to achieve the aim of equal status between men and women, to develop consciousness of women in particular, but also society in general, and to put pressure on the authorities in connection with the crucial concerns of women.

542. MacCurtain, M. and O'Corrain, D. (eds). *Women in Irish society: The historical dimension*. Dublin, Arlen House, The Women's Press, 1978, 125 p.

Arising from a series of radio lectures for International Women's Year, the aim of this collection was to give an historical dimension to the part played by women in Irish society, and to analyse and comment on some of the more important issues and challenges, which have concerned Irish women this century. Amongst the topics covered are 'Women, work and trade unionism', by M. E. Daly, 'Women and the family', by P. Redlich, 'Women in Irish national and local politics, 1927–77', by M. Manning, and 'Women and work in Ireland', by E. McCarthy.

543. Michel, A. (ed.). *Femmes, Sexisme et Sociétés*. (Women, sexism and society). Paris, Presses Universitaires de France, 1977, 208 p. (French).

A collection of papers on the status of women in society, divided into three sections: (1) The social sciences and sexual stratification, with papers critical of existing approaches to women in the social sciences, suggesting new methods of analysis and new paradigms for the study of human groups. There are papers by C. Delphy on women in stratification studies, N. C. Mathieu on biological paternity and social maternity (see Entry 370), J. Lipman-Blumen on interdiciplinary research on sex roles, and F. Kretz on new models of inter-individual relations in intimate groups. (2) Production and reproduction of sex roles in different societies. This has papers by E. Boulding on the relation between geographical mobility and the status of women; A. Steinman on twenty years of research into sex roles in different societies, M. J. Chombart de Lauwe on mass media images and the socialization of children, and M. Lorée on images of women in advertising. (3) Innovations by women in systems of sexual stratification and new perspectives, with papers by M. Lockwood Carden on the new feminist movement in the United States, K. E. Walker on social recognition of women's domestic labour, H. Yvert-Jalu on divorce in the Soviet Union, and E. Milner on alternative models for sex roles in society. The editor has organized and integrated the papers, and each section is preceded by an introduction, which provides an overall statement of the problem and perspectives, and relates the chapters in the section to the overall theme and to each other.

544. *Papers Revista de Sociologia: Mujer y sociedad*. (Women and society). Barcelona, Ediciones Peninsula (For the Autonomous University of Barcelona) 1978. (Spanish.)

A series of papers on the position of women in Spanish society, dealing with sexual ecology, sex discrimination at school, women in Spanish universities, feminism, the press and society in Spain, images of women in publicity in Spanish magazines, the unmarried mother and society, the condition of women in Spain after the war, and women as a social class – some historical antecedents. A short bibliography is included.

545. Rasanen, L. Beframjandet av kvinnans ställning i Finland. (Improvement of the position of women in Finland.) *Nordisk Forum*, No. 12, 1976, p. 60–63.

A comparison of the situation of women in each of the Scandinavian countries with respect to an improvement in women's position.

546. Russo, G. C. *Status sociale della donna* (The social status of women). Rome, De Luca Editore, 1978, 736 p.

The findings of a survey of 6,000 people, this study looks at career conflict between husband and wife, the woman manager and her career, men and the problem of women, the 'priesthood' of women in their families and society, the condition of housewife, women and work outside the home, participation in public life, religion, and psychological implications of the feminine condition.

547. Sandberg, E. *Equality is the goal*. A Swedish report for International Women's Year. Advisory Council to the Prime Minister on Equality between Men and Women, 1975. (In English.)

The object of the report is to present the results and experiences of work being done in Sweden towards equality between women and men. The historical background is briefly sketched, then data on changes and developments in women's position are discussed, covering the following areas: employment, women's economic position, education, health, housing and the environment, the family and the law, children and women's influence in the community. Comparative data derives from two surveys of living conditions in Sweden, the first dating from 1967–68 and the second from 1974. Although up to 1975, there had been considerable advance, the author reports that much remains to be done, and draws attention to factors, which militate against rapid movement toward the goal of equality between women and men.

548. Shaffer, H. G. *Women in the two Germanies: A comparative study of a socialist and a non-socialist society*. Oxford, Pergamon Press, 1980.

The study is interdisciplinary in nature, with an emphasis on economics and the status of women under the law, in education, in the labour force, in government, and in their social position in the family.

549. Sudau, C. Women in the GDR. *New German Critique*, No. 13, 1978, p. 69–81.

An empirical analysis of the status of women in the German Democratic Republic, considering the official ideology of equality between the sexes with the actual situation, in comparison with the situation in the Federal Republic of Germany. In the GDR, housework and childcare continue to be a female responsibility, although childcare facilities are more easily available, but shopping is more difficult. Other points noted are that women are under-represented in the political elite, there are salary differentials between men and women, the birth rate is declining, and the divorce rate is rising.

550. Weitz, M. C. The status of women in France today. *Contemporary French Civilisation*, Vol. III, No. 1, Fall 1978, p. 29–45.

The author considers that French women have attained almost as much in the last three or four years as they have in the preceding centuries. Here she reviews what has been achieved in terms of opportunities for women, the steps which led to these gains, gives an historical assessment of the process, some indication of what remains to be done, and examines French women's movements.

II. Women's work and labour force participation

551. Auer, P., Bauer, C., Fornlitter, L., Kreisky, E. *Frauen im öffentlichen Dienst – öffentliche Dienste für Frauen*. (Women in Public Service – Public Services for women.) Untersuchungsreihe zur situation der Frau

in Wien. Erstellt im Auftrag des Magistrats der Stadt Wien. Vienna, 1977, 282 p.

A report prepared for the Vienna City Council, which includes a history of women in the city civil service and details the increasing trend to feminization (as is the case internationally). Female participation in the city civil service in Vienna increased annually by 2 per cent and reached 45 per cent in 1975. Women are discriminated against in terms of promotion, since the higher in the hierarchy the job, the fewer the women in that category. They are also discriminated against in attaining tenured or permanent positions. In 1973, 36 per cent of women in the civil service in Vienna had such positions, as opposed to 71 per cent of men. In the federal service, only 26 per cent of women had permanent status in 1975.

552. Avdi-Kalkani, I. *The Greek women in professional occupations*. Athens, Papazisis, 1978, 159 p.

In three parts, this study discusses: in Part one, the history of professional and working women, since the formation of the Greek state in 1832, divided into periods on the basis of key events in Greek history. In Part two, the position of the Greek working woman today, impediments to equality of the sexes in work, patriarchal ideology in the service of state policy, and positive results from equal participation of women in production are considered. Part three – measures which could be taken to achieve equality – discusses constitutional changes, changes in time patterns of work, including flexible hours, part-time work, and accommodation of work time to domestic requirements, and a change in women's consciousness.

553. Baudoin Report on Discrimination and Disparity in women's work. Issue 15 of 'Pour une politique du Travail'. Paris, Ministry of Labour, 1980.

A report by a group of French civil servants on discrimination and disparity in women's work. There are three sections. Part 1 is a summary of the legal features of the situation in France today, in relation to men's and women's work; Part 2 is a review of experience in other countries and an inventory of measures, recommended by a range of institutions and individuals canvassed by the researchers, for eliminating the observed inequalities; Part 3 suggests measures which could be taken by the government.

554. Buchberger, C. V. *Die Frau in der Gewerkschaft*. (Women in the Trade Unions.) Zur Situation der Gewerkschaftsfunctionarinnen in Oberösterreich. Diplomarbeit, Linz 1976. 117 p.

This Ph.D. thesis describes Austrian trade union policy with respect to women between 1945 and 1975. The Federation of Austrian Trade Unions (ÖGB) established a Women's Department in 1945. At first, this was a central department for women's affairs, but later women's organizations were set up in individual unions and in provincial executive committees. A women's trade union congress has been held every four years, and sends its recommendations to the general congress of the Federation. This study analyses the role of the Women's Department in recent legislation relating to rent reform, pension changes, the lengthening of maternity leave, improvement of the assistance to children and families, and the reform of the Family Law. It also includes the results from a questionnaire survey of 166 women trade union officials, which asked about their personal situation in the family, on the job, and in public life, and their attitude towards women's emancipation and the trade unions.

555. Dorrer-Fischer, R., Kropf, K., List, E. Analyse der Situation der berufstätigen Frau in Wien mit besonderer Betonung der Arbeitsmarktsituation. (An analysis of the status of employed women in Vienna, with special reference to the labour market.) Untersuchungsreihe zur Situation der Frau in Wien. Erstellt im Auftrag des Magistrats der Stadt Wien. Vienna, 1977, 353 p.

According to the census of 1971, 62 per cent of all Viennese women between 15 and 60 years of age are gainfully employed. The employment rate of women in Vienna has always been high: at the beginning of the century, at least a third of each age group in the female population of working age was economically active. This study, done for the Vienna City Council, presents comprehensive material on the open and hidden discrimination against women in the labour market, in the trade unions, and in vocational training. Unemployment among women is lower in Vienna than in Austria as a whole, because the higher unemployment rate in manufacturing is compensated for by a lower rate in the services.

556. Eckman, E. Women and work: *Law, reality and the women's movement in Italy*. Paper presented at the International Political Science Association Study Group, Round Table Conference, University of Essex 1979.

The paper looks at the 1977 law passed by the Italian government for 'equal treatment for men and women in labour matters' and at criticisms of the law made by the left and feminists. The reality of women's lives in the labour force is described, in agriculture, industry, sales and service, housework and the 'black' economy.

557. Kanellopoulos, C. N. *Male-Female pay differentials in Greece*. Athens, Centre of Planning and Economic Research, 1981. (*mimeo* in English.)

The author estimates earnings functions for separate samples of male and female employees working in industrial and commercial firms in Athens. If discrimination is defined as unequal pay for equal productive characteristics, discrimination exists against Greek women – the paper shows that the pay advantages enjoyed by men cannot be explained solely by superior qualifications. Three main factors place Greek female employees at a disadvantage – shorter seniority within the firm, shorter previous experience, and an unfavourable occupational distribution.

558. Kyle, G. *Gästarbeterska i manssamhället*. Studier om industriarbetande kvinnors villkor i Sverige, Stockholm, Liber Förlag, 1979, 368 p. (In Swedish with English summary p. 265.)

A study undertaken within a project on 'Women in industrial society, with special emphasis on the labour movement and women's issues' at the University of Gothenburg. The emphasis here is on (1) Analysis of reasons why formal equality was not followed by real equality between the sexes. Men still hold practically all positions of power and influence in Sweden. (2) Analysis of attitudes and proceedings of the labour movement concerning issues of equality. Here, both the Swedish Social-democratic Party, in power from 1932–76, and the Federation of Trade Unions are considered. The author looks at the world of work; professional training 1870–1970 – where the educational system, attitudes of decision makers, and women in professional training are considered; childcare policy; and women or immigrants 1945–70. In this last section, she asks have women and immigrants been matched against each other as labour force; what arguments are used for and against the two categories; what were the consequences for childcare? A study of three enterprises is undertaken. As one of her conclusions, the author considers that 'legislation is not enough to realize true equality' (p. 275). Measures, which may disturb the labour market and the interests of both employers and unions, must be taken.

559. Liljeström, R. with Mellström, G. F. and Svensson, G. L. *Roles in Transition*. Stockholm, Liber Förlag, 1978, 257 p.

This is a report of an investigation of 50 working class families, carried out for the 'Advisory Council on Equality between Men and Women'. This Council was set up in 1972, and superseded in 1976 by the National Committee on Equality between Men and Women. The study took place in three municipalities, where a pilot scheme to encourage women to enter 'male' jobs in industry had taken place. The families studied had had some contact with this scheme and also had children. The study is based on extensive interviews with family members, and officials in the companies which took part in the scheme, and quotations from these interviews are used to illustrate the respondents' feelings about their experience. The investigation looks at women and men in the workplace, parents and responsibility for children, leisure, interest in society and politics, the family-work combination, and a three-generational perspective on life and work, with the respondents comparing themselves to their parents, and their children's situation.

560. Notes et Etudes Documentairs. *Les Femmes dans la fonction publique.* La documentation Francaise, nos. 4056–4057, Paris, 1974.

Discusses the feminization of public functionaries – one woman in five is an employee of the state compared with one man in ten. In the first part of the study, the author traces the history of this growing involvement and the current situation, with statistical data, and a description of the characteristics of female compared with male public functionaries. The latter mainly concern family situation, level of responsibility and distribution by ministry. The author also considers the reasons for the lower level of responsibility of female compared with male public servants. In a second part, particular legal measures which could be taken to benefit female public servants and facilitate a conciliation between their professional and family obligations are considered. A third part looks at reactions provoked by the growth in the number of women as public servants, and the broad outline of trade union responses.

561. Peikert, I. Frauen auf dem Arbeitsmarkt. (Women in the labour market.) *Leviathan*, Vol. 4, No. 4, 1976, p. 494–516.

One of the largest problem groups on the labour market are female workers. The article summarizes quantitative evidence from the Federal Republic of Germany, with respect to the job characteristics of female workers. Indicators such as qualifications, stability of employment, working conditions, prestige, career mobility, wages and concentration of female employment in certain segments of the occupational structure reveal a consistent pattern of discrimination. The prevailing interpretation, and the background assumptions of state policies, is that such discrimination can be explained by personal attributes, attitudes and behaviour, the acceptance of traditional roles, limited participation in vocational training, lack of motivation to achieve professional status, and so on. The author argues that this interpretation severely distorts the evidence. An alternative explanatory model is developed which – using in part the assumption of dual labour market theory – starts out with managerial strategies. The argument is that these managerial strategies systematically structure the working process and recruitment policies, in order to exploit the conditions of female workers, for example limited commuting capacity, dependence on part-time work, discontinuous labour force participation, and low level of unionization. These managerial strategies then condition working attitudes, such as interest in advancement and motivation, producing 'traditionalistic' attitudes, which are in fact not traditional, but constantly reproduced by the dynamics of managerial strategies for the utilization of female working power. The final section of the article discusses relevant aspects of labour market policies of the state.

562. Voutyra, S. *The Greek woman in salaried work.* Athens, Papazisis, 1981, 147 p.

The author discusses the policy of the ILO on working women; contemporary developments on working women internationally; EEC policy on equality of pay and the Greek law – Greece was required to come into line with EEC directives on equal pay by 1979, but practice falls short, as in other countries, of the letter of the law; as does the actual situation of working women, compared with men, in different sectors of the economy. The author then discusses his own views on the working woman and reviews research which has been done on the topic.

563. *Zeitschrift fur Demokratisierung der Arbeitswelt.* No. 6, 1977, 40 p. Frauen, was wollen sie? (Women, what do they want?).

This issue of the Austrian *Journal for the Democratization of the Working Environment* contains a number of articles discussing women's employment problems. They include: (1) The results of surveys made of the image of women as presented in Austrian schoolbooks, excerpts from the gender specific teaching plans in secondary schools are also quoted. (2) A paper by Dorrer-Fischer points out that, although half of all Austrian married women are employed, they are still paid less and fired first on the grounds that they are 'secondary workers' and that their main role is homemaking. She presents evidence of open wage discrimination in the collective agreements in many branches of unions, and hidden discrimination, resulting from occupational segregation. Average earnings for female blue collar and office workers fell as a proportion of male earnings in the period 1967 to 1976. (3) Maier and Rieser give statistics on women in academic posts at the Technical University of Vienna, where there are no female professors or assistant professors, and only 17 women lecturers on a staff of 467.

III. Family and household

564. Badinter, E. *L'Amour en plus.* Paris, Slammarion, 1980. English translation: *The myth of motherhood*, London, Souvenir Press, 1981.

Using a range of historical material on France to illustrate and provide evidence for her position, Badinter argues that maternal love is not rooted in nature, but is rather an historical product. It appeared in France at the end of the 18th century under the influence of Rousseau. The general point made by the book is that women have not always conformed to the stereotypical idea of demonstrated maternal instinct, and the existence of the ideology of motherhood has been harmful in creating feelings of guilt and inadequacy in many women. The author considers that maternal attitudes are changing at the present time, now that fathers are taking a greater part in raising children.

565. Balbo, L. *Stato di famiglia: Bisogni privato collettivo.* (State of the family: private and collective needs.) Milano, Etas Libri, 1976, 159 p.

An analysis of the extent to which the family defines needs and the state relies on the family both for this definition of needs, and for meeting such needs. See also *Inchiesta*, 46–47, 1980, for a series of articles on the theme of the welfare state with a contribution by Balbo.

566. Den Bandt, M-L. *Sex role socialization and voluntary childlessness in the Netherlands.* Paper presented to the XVIIth International Seminar of the Committee on Family Research (International Sociological Association), Helsinki, Finland, 1979.

There has been a rapid escalation in the number of childless marriages in Holland. The author reviews demographic, empirical and sociological research on childlessness and discusses her work in progress with the National Programme for Demographic Research on this topic. While a decision not to have children runs counter to the socialization practices and traditionally high birth rates of the Dutch population, it is now projected that up to 20 per cent of marriages contracted in or after 1980 will remain childless. Public opinion on the question is undergoing rapid change, but the childless are still stereotyped negatively.

567. Du Boulay, J. *Portrait of a Greek mountain village.* Oxford monographs on Social Anthropology, Oxford, Clarendon Press, 1974, Chapter VI 'Men and women – marriage', p. 121–141.

The author argues that the family and home (house) is not just a unit drawn together for economic and social reasons in a Greek village, but is part of a way of thinking in which the individual draws her/his validity from the group and her/his role and position in the kinship group both past and present. The author outlines material and symbolic practices, which delineate the nature and experiences of males and females in this social setting. For example, with respect to sensuality and sexuality, men are by nature considered to be intelligent, sensual only in the susceptibility to women, but women are weak and sensual in their very nature – so it is the responsibility of the woman if a man desires her. A woman needs the protection of a man (husband, father, brother) to validate her life. This puts widows into a difficult situation in village life. A man has a certain degree of freedom, so long as he fulfils his duty of protecting and providing for his family. A woman, on the other hand, is never free from the responsibility to control and subdue her inner nature, and must stay in the home, a loyal, hardworking, obedient, diligent wife and mother. Any fall from this standard is a reflection on her entire character.

568. Fodor, R. Day care policy in France and its consequence for women: A study of the Metropolitan Paris area. *International Journal of Urban and Regional Research*, Vol. 2, No. 3, 1978, p. 463–481.

The paper investigates (1) The apparent choices available, how public daycare services are created, their costs and availability in the Metropolitan Paris area, and their effects on women continuing to work after childbirth. (2) The relationship between policy and the expression of class opposition through different levels of state that create policy – the Caisse National des Allocations Familiales (CNAF), which represents labour and management; municipalities and department councils, which represent opposing political parties, and the roles of other interests, e.g. unions, parents associations, feminist groups. Existing literature and statistical data are reviewed and a survey was carried out to interview key informants who were state or municipal policy makers, recognized authorities on the subject and interest groups. Conclusions were that day care policy reinforces social inequality on three levels: between women and men in access to the workplace; between less skilled and more skilled labour power; and between peripheral and central metropolitan residents.

569. Gronseth, E. Worksharing: A Norwegian example. In: Rapoport, R. and Rapoport, R. N. *Working Couples*, London, Routledge and Kegan Paul, 1978, p. 108–121.

A report of an experiment and study on worksharing undertaken by the Norwegian Family Council, a group of researchers and some volunteer worksharing couples from 1971 to 1975. Sixteen worksharing families, seven families who wanted to adopt the pattern but found no employment possibilities, and five ordinary families were located and recruited to the project over a three and a half year period. A worksharing pattern refers to families in which the couple genuinely share work responsibilities both in the home and in the occupational world. This can mean a couple sharing the same job, or each having separate part-time jobs in the same or different organizations. The essential elements are part-time work and equal sharing of all domestic work. For the total 23 new middle class worksharing couples in the study it appeared in general that practical and personal problems and motives were the driving force, with sex equality rationales and ideology coming essentially as a consequence of these other concerns. A general conclusion from the detailed results of the study was 'that for families with small children with an average working man's income or higher, where both parents have above average education, where the wife has a firm and personal occupational commitment, where both are committed to the welfare of each other and their children, and are strongly motivated for a worksharing pattern, the adoption of this pattern generally results in the expected positive changes' (p. 119).

570. Grasso, L. *Madre amore donna: per un analisi del rapporto madre figlia.* (Mother love and woman: towards an analysis of the relation between mothers and daughters.) Guaraldi, Florence, 1977.

Through a historical and anthropological investigation, plus direct interviews with women, the author shows how the relationship between mother and daughter is one of the most painful foci of the relationship between one woman and another.

571. Heintz, P., Held, T. and Levy, R. Family structure and society. *Journal of Marriage and the Family*, Vol. 37, No. 4, 1975, p. 861–870.

This article presents a theoretical approach, linking aspects of traditional family structure with the positions of its members in the social structure. Basic elements of this approach are the comparison of structurally defined life horizons for husband and wife, the value-producing capacity of the roles they assume, and the social and structural conditions for the fulfilment of these roles. These conditions are defined in terms of class and degree of development of the society. For the main types of combinations of such conditions, the interests of husband and wife and ensuing conflicts ('structural dissent') are deduced and their effects on the traditional family structure are discussed and illustrated by data from a study on the status of women in Switzerland.

572. Melsted, L. Swedish family policy. *Current Sweden*, No. 225, June 1979.

The article describes the positions of the various political parties in Sweden on family policy issues in the Autumn of 1979, prior to the election. The issues discussed are public childcare provision, parental insurance, child allowances, leave of absence and the six-hour working day. In general, the social democrats and liberals are close to each other on these issues, the centre and conservative parties argue in ways that bring them to similar conclusions on some points, and the communists advocate the same developments as the social democrats, but argue more forcibly for rapid improvements.

573. Szinovacz, M. E. *The situation of women in Austria, economic and family issues.* Vienna, Austrian Federal Ministry of Social Affairs, Women's Division, 1979.

An assessment of the main issues affecting the living conditions of Austrian women based on the micro census of September 1977, and covering trends in employment, household activities and childcare in the period 1969–77. On household activities, the author argues that both employed and non-employed mothers help to perpetuate traditional role expectations regarding the division of labour in the home by requiring different participation of sons and daughters in household tasks.

IV. Education

574. *Committee on sex roles and education of Danish Ministry of Education. Konsroller og uddannelse*. (Sex roles and education.) No. 1. Copenhagen, Undervisnings-ministeriat, 1978, 200 p.

An extensive report on sex roles in the Danish educational system prepared by a working committee chaired by L. Vohn of the Ministry and including members from all sectors of the educational system in Denmark. The educational system is studied for its contribution to sex roles in the wider society, with respect especially to employment and vocational training. One finding was that social class (defined on five levels) affected the school leaving ages of boys and girls differentially; social class location was important for boys only in the lowest class, whilst it affected the choices of girls throughout the class structure. Considerable statistical information and documentation is provided in this report, sections of which are reproduced in English, and available from: Undervisnings-ministeriat, Frederiksholms Kanal 21, Copenhagen K, Denmark.

575. *Nuovo Donnawomanfemme*. La scuola in mano alla donna o la donna in mano alla scualo? (School in the hands of women – women in the grip of school?) A debate published in this journal, No. 2 March 1977, p. 5–19.

Themes covered in this discussion include: the difficulties and conflicts facing women instructors and teachers who refuse to regard their work as an extension of the maternal role; part-time work; problems in transmitting a culture which women have had no part in forming; women's difficulties in educational institutions; and an economic and sociological analysis of the massive influx of women into the teaching profession.

576. Shafer, S. M. The socialization of girls in the secondary schools of England and the two Germanies. *International Review of Education*, Vol. XXII, No. 1, 1976, p. 5–23.

The author argues that the socialization of girls in England and in the Federal Republic of Germany and the German Democratic Republic in secondary schools points to the role conflicts which eventually face women in these countries. In the United Kingdom and the Federal Republic of Germany, girls theoretically have the same options as boys;

in practice they have less science and vocational education. In the German Democratic Republic girls are made aware that they can expect to work whilst married, and like boys are expected to prepare for an occupation. In all three countries, males predominate in the decision-making roles in government, industry and schools. The article is based on a research study conducted in the United Kingdom, Federal Republic of Germany and German Democratic Republic in 1972–73.

V. Other

577. Blom, I. Women's history: No longer a neglected field of study? *Research in Norway*, 1976, p. 4–10.

The article discusses various definitions of women's history, traces earlier contributions in this field by Norwegian scholars, and gives a picture of the problems and promises of contemporary research.

578. Boddendijk, F. R., Klein, M. and Nolte, E. *Mijnheer de Voorzitter . . .* (Mr. Chairman . . .), Mededelingen No. 8. Amsterdam, Urige Universiteit, 1980, 192 p.

A factual and theoretical account of women's participation (or not) in the political arena between 1945 and 1979. In Dutch.

579. Brunt-de Wit, E. Vrouwen op het platteland. (Women's liberation in the country), *Sociologische Gids*, July/August 1975, p. 264–279.

Countrywomen are a relatively neglected category in the women's liberation movement in the Netherlands and in the popular and sociological publications that deal with women's emancipation. This paper presents some research data about the formal aims and everyday activities of countrywomen's voluntary associations. The formal goals stress the importance of an orientation towards societal processes, whilst the local activities contradictorily seem to be designed to focus countrywomen on their role as housewives and mothers. The main function of these associations seems to have been the introduction of bourgeois urban patterns of life into the country, and in this they have succeeded so well that countrywomen lag behind urban women more than ever, since the growing women's liberation movement encourages city women not to confine themselves to housekeeping and motherhood. In the process the countrywomen's associations have reduced themselves to political nonentities and it will be difficult to find a way to connect them and their members to the political aims of women's liberation. See also in the same issue of the journal an article by H. d'Ancona, 'Vrouwenemancipatie: een onderzoeksterrein'. ('Women's emancipation and research') (p. 254–263). This article discusses research on women taking place in the Netherlands, identifying three types: (1) based on census data and focusing on women's participation in society compared with that of men; (2) focusing on women's consciousness of their position; (3) based on the idea that emancipation can only occur in a 'feminized' society.

580. Falkenberg, S., Rahm, T. and Waern, Y. Sex role concepts in eight and

twelve year olds. *Scandinavian Journal of Psychology*, Vol. 18, No. 1, 1977, p. 31–37.

Using Piaget's cognitive developmental theory and the role theory of Sarbin as points of departure, children's perception of sex roles were investigated. It was suggested that sex role perception could be described on two levels. The first involves a sex role enactment based on superficial understanding, and the second involved a sex role taking, based on a deeper level of understanding. A standardized interview of 20 narratives, 10 covering the first level and describing the objectively observable behaviour, and 10 at the second level, describing supposedly constant personality characteristics of a typical boy or girl, were presented to the children in the study. These 8 and 12 year olds listened to each story and were then asked whether a typical boy, girl, or both would have behaved in this way or expressed the personality quality. The results suggest that both 8 and 12 year old children understand the superficial and the deep aspects of sex roles. The younger children accept the sex role differences, whereas the older children are starting to question them. There was also evidence of a developmental difference in experiencing sex roles between boys and girls. The 8 year old girls in the study most strongly recognized the sex role differences and were therefore the most rigid in their sex role conceptions. The 12 year old girls were the most liberal group in their approach to sex roles. The boys fell in between, with small developmental differences.

581. Falteri, P. Mass media, donna e pressione culturale. *Nuova Donna-womanfemme*, No. 2, 1977, p. 71–79.

The crisis in the study of mass communication becomes particularly evident when one makes an examination of the functions and cumulative effects of the mass media, with respect to the socialization of women and their role in the transmission of culture. The author argues that the principal contradiction in the communicative process is found in the private use of messages which have a public destination. This contradiction is accentuated for the mass of women, who are relegated to the private domain.

582. Faugeror, C., Poggi, D. Les femmes, les infractions, la justice pénale. (Women, lawbreaking, and penal justice.) *Revue de L'Institut de Sociologie*, Editions de l'Universite de Bruxelles, Nos. 3–4, 1975, p. 367–385.

The article presents the results of research on perceptions of the gravity of criminal behaviour and of criminal justice. The study is based on a representative sample (1,800 individuals) of the French-speaking population. Women have a specific image of criminal justice and penal norms, they are more attached than men to the social order and traditional values. However, a contradictory finding, which the authors consider deserves further investigation, was that women were also associated with movements for change. The differences between men and women diminish progressively as the level of education increases. At a high level of education, women criticized the system of justice and social organization to a greater extent than men. The more education women have, the less they resist change.

583. Grasso, L. *Compagno padrone*. (Comrade boss.) Florence, Guaraldi, 1976, 308 p.

A documented analysis of interpersonal relations in workers's families of the traditional and extra left family.

584. Guerin, C. De la bénévole a l'elue locale. *Les Cahiers de L'Animation*, No. 10, 1975, p. 17–37.

The author examines female participation in political life in general, in reaction to statistics in an article in *Le Monde* in April 1975 indicating stagnation in such participation. The author found, on the contrary, that in local government and local councils, women seemed to be very much present. A series of interviews, carried out in the Paris area, indicated that the role played by women in local life and voluntary associations often provided a springboard for election to local government.

585. Haavind, H. Forskning om kvinner – en situasjonsrapport fra Norge. (Research on women – the present Norwegian situation.) *Nordisk Forum*, No. 12, 1976, p. 10–18.

A detailed discussion of current conflicting trends in women's research, including a short bibliography.

586. Haavio-Manila, E. Development of sex differences in economic activity and mental health in Scandinavia. *Acta Sociologica*, Vol. 22, No. 1, 1979.

In this study, sex differences in first admissions to mental hospitals in Finland, Norway and Sweden are examined, against the background of changes in the economic activity of men and women in 1939–76. There is some evidence in this historical data of support for the hypothesis that meaningful economic activity has a beneficial effect on the mental health of women. Men seem more vulnerable to crisis situations, such as war and rapid structural change in society. There are low hospital residency rates for men in areas of economic development when both sexes share the role of economic provider. This paid work of women does not seem to threaten the mental health of men.

587. Keyes, J. G. *Women in Finland: Coping with success*. Paper given at the annual meeting of the Canadian Sociology and Anthropology Association, May/June 1978.

The paper examines equality of the sexes as seen by twenty-four Finnish women, in the light of Scandinavia's reputation for egalitarianism. On the basis of this interview study, the author suggests that three points are brought into focus: (1) While Finland's reputation as a pioneer in women's equality, and its statistics on women's achievements are true, they do not measure encumbrances which women still feel in terms of childcare, the more or less subtle downgrading in employment, and their shunting into traditional fields in education. The women see the irony of the objective appearance of women's progress, when they do not feel that their situation is yet one of real equality. (2) Despite Finland's advanced position in egalitarianism, men are still far better situated for jobs, leadership, status, salary, and for positions in the church and the government. (3) When it comes to the problems of the working mother, such as inadequate day care, the priority of the husband's career, and household chores, the problems of Finnish women resemble those of women in all western industrial societies.

588. Marks, E. and de Courtivron, I. (eds). *New French Feminisms: An anthology*. Amherst, Ma, The University of Massachusetts Press, 1980, 270 p.

A collection of over 50 selections from French feminist writings of the past decade, covering the entire spectrum of positions, from militant to moderate, political to poetic, and including both well known and unknown authors. Much of the work, influenced by the intellectual tradition in France, is speculative and theoretical, as opposed to the empirical tradition in Anglo-Saxon feminist literature. Most texts have not appeared in English before.

589. Micela, R. Inconscio materno e teoria della personalita. Nota critica a Lacan. (The mother's unconscious and the theory of personality; critical note on Lacan.) *Nuova Donnawomanfemme*, No. 6/7, 1978, p. 176–89.

The author suggests that the appearance of new social subjects in the political struggle and at the level of consciousness, necessitates the formulation of a theory of the personality free from the ideological conceptions, which have arisen from past historical and scientific conditions. This new theory of the personality is based on a new theory of the unconscious, which critically examines the position of the mother. Thus the mother/child relationship should be analysed in the light of needs which are historically determined or culturally induced. The author criticizes both the Freudian theory of the libido, which is centred on the biological conception of impulses, and the theories of Lacan which developed out of Melanie Klein's theory of objects. Although Lacan overcomes Freudian biologism, and ties the Oedipus complex to the reality of social relations, he still maintains an extremely idealistic and anti-historical approach to family relationships, and reduces the mother's symbolic function simply to phallic representation. In this way, he gives sanction to women's social inferiority.

590. Moeller Gambaroff, M. Emanzipation macht Angst. (Emancipation creates fears.) *Kursbuch*, No. 47, March 1977, p. 1–25.

The author analyses the experience of women representative of a specific privileged group: they had a satisfactory profession, were economically independent, and relieved from housework. The main contention is that the women's movement has generated fears, anxieties and insecurities in women. This situation is seen as arising from the failure of the organized women's movement to create an autonomous identity for women. It is also related to the anti-male orientation of many organized women's groups, which is seen by the author as based on the mother/child relationship 'the individual overcoming of matriarchy precedes the collective overcoming of patriarchy'. The author is dealing with psychological aspects of women's emancipation, and does not deny the reality of women's social oppression. On the contrary, she argues that patriarchy is generated through capitalism, which can only be stabilized through the perpetual antagonism of the sexes.

591. Mossuz-Lavau, J. and Sineau, M. Sex, social environment and left wing attitudes. *International Journal of Sociology*, Vol. 8, No. 3, 1978.

The paper examines the behaviour of French women in the political domain, as compared with French men, indicating that, for the 30 years since women have had the vote, they have been less interested in politics, vote less frequently and were less likely to vote for candiates of the left than men. From the results of a questionnaire survey of adolescents and young adults, the authors examine the relationship between sex and political attitudes, paying particular attention to the social environment, and considering the occupation of the subjects and the occupation of their father or mother. They conclude that attainment of a certain cultural level, rather than employment in a particular occupation, explains the political behaviour of women.

592. Papariga, A. *For the liberation of women*, Athens, Contemporary Times, 1981, 239 p.

From a perspective of a progressive democratic feminist movement, the author considers the prospects for the liberation of women in Greece. Covering both historical and contemporary material on the position of Greek women at work, in the home and in the broader social context, she brings out the problems facing such a feminist movement, and suggests that the solutions lie in a more radical reform of the society. Some comparative data on socialist and capitalist countries – Cuba, Poland, USSR, Czechoslovakia, South Africa, the United Kingdom and the United States, France, Federal Republic of Germany, Denmark and Japan are included.

593. Repetto, M. The development of women's liberation in Italy after World War II. *The Structure of Knowledge: A feminist perspective*, Proceedings of the Great Lakes Colleges Association Fourth Annual Women's Studies Conference, 1977.

The 1947 Italian constitution acknowledged women's rights to equality, but during the Second World War and the Fascist period, little progress was made to this end. Four traditions affecting Italian society are outlined, Catholicism, rural traditions, the lay tradition of liberal thought and Marxist traditions. The author describes women's role during the Resistance, the beginnings of the women's movement in Italy, and outlines the gradual progression of feminist activities. There have been impressive legislative gains, but any social change in this area requires a change in the relationship between men and women.

594. Riksbankens Jubileumsfond. (A foundation of the State Bank of Sweden.) *Kvinnorslivi det Svenska samhallet* and *Aktuell kvinnoforskning*. Stockholm, Riksbankens Jubileumsfond, 1981.

A two volume presentation of research on women in Sweden. These are reports of a series of studies on women. Some of the work included is: Women and politics; Women and household work; Equality between the sexes, within the labour market; Econometric studies of the structure and function of the labour market; An idea-historical investigation of the ideology of the new women's movement; Unmarried women and Swedish social change; Mass market literature for girls and boys, a comparative linguistic analysis; Women and the development of the welfare state; and Feminism as an ideology, a structural analysis.

595. Schlaeger, H. The West German Women's Movement. *New German Critique*, No. 13, Winter 1978, p. 59–68.

A short analysis of the Women's Movement in Federal Republic of Germany. The author concludes: 'The women's movement, in so far as it consists of so-called autonomous groups, is not a force to be reckoned with. However, there is a force to be reckoned with, even in the Federal Republic: the women who would probably be shocked if they were called "feminists". Originally spurred to action by issues raised by the women's movement, they have begun to defend themselves in factories, unions, the churches, even at times in the political parties, and – what is even worse! – in the family. They have no correct line – neither leftist nor feminist – and sometimes they have no theory at all except for the conviction that things cannot continue as they are. But I believe that they can hardly be manipulated from any side. German women have moved beyond the women's movement – and the movement has not noticed yet.' (p. 67–68).

596. Schone, F., van der Steen, J. and Vijhuizen, J. Het man-Vrouwbeeld in de leerboekjes van een lagere school. *Sociologische Gids*, July/August 1975, p. 280–296. (Man and Woman in the textbooks of a primary school.)

Textbooks in use at a primary school were analysed, to reveal the image of the roles of men and women that they offer. Men are depicted much more than women in these books and they give a strongly conventional image of the activities and behaviour of men and women. Men and women have different roles: women live only in the family and care for husband and children; men, on the other hand, have an occupation and know how to take action in the world outside the family. Children in the school were given a questionnaire to complete to discover their images of the roles of men and women. There was little difference between the images the books present and the image of the roles of men and women which the children had.

597. Støren, T. and Wetlesen, T. S. (eds). *Kvinnekunnskap: En artikkelsamling om kvinners situasjon i mannssamfunnet*. Oslo, Gyldendal Norsk

Forlag, 1976, 239 p. (Knowledge about women: A collection of articles on women's situation in a male society.)

A collection of articles from differing viewpoints – sociological, historical, economic, psychological and legalistic-political – which came primarily from a conference at the University of Oslo, on women, research, and liberation. Papers include: Women's political activity; Motherhood – voluntary and with responsibility; Culture and the conception of women – a discussion of religious conceptions of women; Ideology and concepts of women – women as defective men in the work of Aristotle, Thomas Aquinas and Freud; On the oppression of women, by men, and the techniques of dominance; Women in paid and unpaid work; Sexuality, what it is and what it means in a woman's life; Sex and power in different cultures, a social anthropological comparison of myths and facts of women's place in hunting societies, small agricultural societies, class societies, and the international market economy; The family and marriage law: Legal equality – a reality or a cover-up? and Nervousness and anxiety – an answer to women's situation in life?

Journals

Two resources, which provide considerable information on work on the status of women and details of publications and journals are:

1. ISIS International Bulletin No. 16, 1980: *The Feminist Press in Western Europe*. Other topics covered in this quarterly bulletin have been migration, liberation movements, battered women, health. (Case Postale 301, 1227 Geneva, Switzerland.)

2. *Resources for Feminist Research*, formerly Canadian Newsletter of Research on Women/Recherches sur la Femme – Bulletin d'Information Canadien. Department of Sociology, Ontario Institute for studies in Education, 252 Bloor St. West, Ontario, Canada. An interdisciplinary, international periodical on women and sex roles, published three times a year, giving annotated listings of research work in progress and publications both in Canada, and internationally, special issues of periodicals, feminist publications and bibliographies. Also produced by the same group are *Women: A bibliography of Special Periodicals Issues*, Volumes I and II, special publications of the Journal Nos. 3 and 4, August 1976, covering the period 1960–1975, edited by M. Eichler, J. Marecki, and J. Newton, and No. 4, 1978, an updating edited by J. Newton, both covering a wide range of periodicals, which have devoted special issues to women.

A very brief and partial list of journals follows:

Aspects of Education, Vol. 19, June 1977 'The education of women.'

E.V.A. (Emancipatories Vrouwen Vormingswerk Adviesgroep: Emancipatory women educational advisory group). A journal of 5 or 6 issues a year containing information on government activities concerning women's emancipation in Holland.

Historisk Tidskrift (Sweden) No. 3, 1980 is an issue about women in production and reproduction.

Inchiesta (Italy) No. 18, April/June 1975, special issue on women.

Kvinnovetenskaplig Tidskrift (Sweden). Interdisciplinary women's studies journal, aimed at developing theory and providing a forum for debate and information on women's research. Quarterly.

Management International Review, Vol. 17, No. 1, 1977, has a series of articles on women.

Memoria (Turin, Italy). A new academic feminist journal (1981), the focus is on history and psychoanalysis.

m/f Nos. 5 and 6 (1980). Special edition on the politics of sexuality, with articles on pornography, rape, psychoanalysis and social relations, the universality of the Oedipus conflict, and motherhood. This journal focuses on theorizing the production of women's subordinate position in the social formation in relation to and within a theory of class, with an emphasis on psychoanalytic conceptualizations on the construction of the sexed subject in society.

NAVF Sekretariat for Kvinneforskning (Norwegian Research Council for Science and the Humanities, Centre for Research on Women, Munthesgatan 29, Oslo 2, Norway). Co-ordinates, initiates and publishes research results on women's issues. Publishes a newsletter five times a year, a summary report available in English.

New German Critique, No. 13 Winter 1978. Special feminist issue. Some items from this issue are included in the bibliography.

Noi Donne (Italy) Weekly magazine of the Union of Italian Women, a traditional left-wing women's organization. The contents have been influenced by the resurgence of the women's movement.

Population Trends. A quarterly journal produced by the Office of Population Censuses and Surveys, UK. Contains articles and statistics on demographic developments, medical and epidemiological studies, census reports, vital registration and social surveys. Frequent articles on areas of relevance to the status of women.

Review of Radical Political Economics. Four special issues on women: Vol. 7, 1975 (now unobtainable); Vol. 8, No. 1, 1976; Vol. 9, No. 3, 1977; Vol. 12, No. 2, 1980. (USA.) Another is in preparation.

Scandinavian Journal of History, No. 1, 1980, the theme is Women's struggle for power. (Almqvist Wiksell, Box 62, 10120 Stockholm, Sweden.

Science and Society (USA) Vol. 42, No. 3, Fall 1978, 'Women and contemporary capitalism: Some theoretical questions'.

Sweden Women's History Collections, Göteborg University library, Box 5096, S-40922, Göteborg, Sweden. An excellent women's history collection, including manuscripts and press cuttings. There is regular indexing of books, periodicals and articles on women in Sweden and internationally. They publish a monograph series, and a quarterly bibliography of recent literature with subject headings in English and Swedish.

Vindicacion Feminista (Barcelona, Spain). A feminist magazine which ceased to publish regularly in 1978 for financial reasons, but publishes irregular special issues on particular themes, such as sexuality and divorce.

Women's Studies International Quarterly. (Pergamon Press, Oxford.) A multidisciplinary journal for the rapid publication of research communications and review articles in women's studies.

Indexes

Country Index*

* References are to Entry numbers.

Subject Index*

* References are to Entry numbers.

Author Index*

* References are to Entry numbers.

Notes

NOTES

NOTES

NOTES

NOTES

NOTES

NOTES

NOTES